S0-BIF-666

謹呈

Kazuo And Philhian

Miyohei Shinohara

PATTERNS OF JAPANESE ECONOMIC DEVELOPMENT

A Publication of the Economic Growth Center, Yale University,
and the Council on East Asian Studies, Yale University

PATTERNS OF
JAPANESE ECONOMIC DEVELOPMENT
A QUANTITATIVE APPRAISAL

Edited by

KAZUSHI OHKAWA

and

MIYOHEI SHINOHARA

with

LARRY MEISSNER

New Haven and London, Yale University Press, 1979

Toyo Keizai Shimposha has granted permission
to reprint data from the LTES series.

Publication of this book has been possible because
of major financial assistance from the Japan
Foundation, the Sumitomo Fund of the
Council on East Asian Studies
at Yale University, the International
Development Center of Japan, and the Economic
Growth Center at Yale University.

Copyright © 1979 by Yale University.
All rights reserved. This book may not be
reproduced, in whole or in part, in any form
(beyond that copying permitted by Sections 107
and 108 of the U.S. Copyright Law and except by
reviewers for the public press), without written
permission from the publishers.

Designed by Sally Harris
and set in Monophoto Times Roman type
by Asco Trade Typesetting Ltd., Hong Kong.
Printed in the United States of America by
The Murray Printing Co., Westford, Massachusetts.

Published in Great Britain, Europe, Africa, and
Asia (except Japan) by Yale University Press,
Ltd., London. Distributed in Australia and
New Zealand by Book & Film Services, Artarmon,
N.S.W., Australia; and in Japan by Harper & Row,
Publishers, Tokyo Office.

Library of Congress Cataloging in Publication Data

Main entry under title:

Patterns of Japanese economic development.

(A publication of the Economic Growth Center, Yale University, and the Council
on East Asian Studies, Yale University)
  Includes bibliographies and index.
  1. Japan—Economic conditions—Addresses, essays, lectures. 2. Economic
development—Case studies—Addresses, essays, lectures. I. Okawa, Kazushi,
1908–   II. Shinohara, Miyohei, 1919–   III. Meissner, Larry.   IV. Series:
Yale University. Economic Growth Center. Publications.
HC462.P37   330.9′52′04   78–23317

ISBN 0-300-02183-6

Contents

*Each of the other chapters is followed by its references.

PART 3: PRODUCT ALLOCATION

PART 4: FACTOR SHARES, PRICES, AND POPULATION

Foreword

This volume is one in a series of studies supported by the Economic Growth Center, an activity of the Yale Department of Economics since 1961. The Center is a research organization with worldwide activities and interests. Its purpose is to analyze, both theoretically and empirically, the process of economic growth in the developing nations and the economic relations between the developing and the economically advanced countries. The research program emphasizes the search for regularities in the process of growth and changes in economic structure by means of intercountry and intertemporal studies. Current projects include research on technology choice and transfer, income distribution, employment and unemployment, household behavior and demographic processes, agricultural research and productivity, and international economic relations, including monetary and trade policies, as well as a number of individual country studies. The Center research staff hold professorial appointments, mainly in the Department of Economics, and accordingly have teaching as well as research responsibilities.

The Center administers, jointly with the Department of Economics, the Yale master's degree training program in International and Foreign Economic Administration for economists in foreign central banks, finance ministries, and development agencies. It presents a regular series of seminar and workshop meetings and includes among its publications both book-length studies and journal reprints by staff members, the latter circulated as Center Papers.

Hugh Patrick, Director

Preface

In connection with the ongoing LTES project, two international conferences have been held on the economic growth of Japan, in 1966 and in 1972, sponsored by JERC (Japan Economic Research Center). At the 1972 meeting the publication committee recommended preparation of a single volume summary of the statistical estimates and suggested Kazushi Ohkawa and Miyohei Shinohara be coeditors.[1] This volume is the result.

A special study group was formed at Tokei Kenkyukai (Institute of Statistical Research) to prepare what was tentatively titled RSE (the Revised Summary Edition of LTES). First drafts were presented at a workshop held in Tokyo in December 1974. From outside the group, Simon Kuznets, Tsunehiko Watanabe, Yuichi Shionoya, and Yasukichi Yasuba kindly participated, giving valuable comments.

Since then, over three years have been spent incorporating the comments received at this workshop as well as the discussion held among ourselves into final drafts. During this time Larry Meissner was invited to Tokyo twice to assist us, and rather extensive revisions have been made in response to his painstaking efforts. During the course of the work the number of project participants increased to some 25. While only half are named as authors of specific chapters—generally those who led the original research for the LTES volume covered by a chapter—this has been very much a team effort.

What has come to be called the Hitotsubashi group, though it has included some from other universities, has spent almost 25 years on this project. During that long period many have come and gone, each

1. Committee members (in alphabetical order) were Dale Jorgenson, Lawrence R. Klein, Simon Kuznets (chairman), Kazushi Ohkawa, Saburo Okita, Gustav Ranis, Henry Rosovsky, Tsunehiko Watanabe, and Yasukichi Yasuba.

making a contribution. To all of them, we are grateful, for without their efforts this volume would not have been possible.

Toyo Keizai Shimposha has generously permitted publication of most of the data in this volume before implementing its own plan to publish a summary version in Japanese. Funding for publication has come from the Sumitomo Fund gift to Yale University, whose Council on East Asian Studies and Economic Growth Center also assisted, and from the Japan Foundation under a special grant. The Japan Foundation and Asia Foundation provided travel grants.

Tokei Kenkyukai served as the office for carrying out much of this project. Kokusai Kaihatsu Senta (IDCJ, the International Development Center of Japan) funded and hosted the 1974 workshop, and assisted a great deal in preparing the entire draft, including travel grants and office space.

As individual scholars, Simon Kuznets, as chairman of the publication committee, continuously cooperated with us, as did Gustav Ranis and Hugh Patrick as successive directors of the Economic Growth Center at Yale. Nobukiyo Takamatsu spent many hours checking the data and sources to assure the most recent of our estimates have been used and to identify the differences among authors. Tamiko Sakatani at IDCJ and Louise Danishevsky at the Economic Growth Center diligently deciphered our (and Larry Meissner's) handwritings and editing notations on the manuscript as it metamorphosed into final typed form. To all of them we express our sincere thanks.

Editors' Note

Japanese personal names are written in the western order of given plus family name. Japanese government agencies are always cited by their Japanese names to facilitate finding the sources in library card catalogs, although in the text common English abbreviations are sometimes used (see below). English titles are given in the bibliographies only where the work can be used by those not reading Japanese. Information contained in figures and tables is included in the index. Appendix tables are in the same topical sequence as the text. In part 1 the references for all three chapters follow chapter 3; in parts 2–4 each chapter is followed by its references.

ABBREVIATIONS

Agencies
  EPA   Economic Planning Agency (Keizai Kikakucho)
  ESB   Economic Stabilization Board (Keizai Antei Honbu)
  MITI Ministry of International Trade and Industry (Tsusho Sangyosho)

Published works
  ARNIS *Annual Report of National Income Statistics*
  GRJE   *Growth Rate of the Japanese Economy Since 1878*
  LTES   *Estimates of Long-Term Economic Statistics of Japan*
  SIL   *Choki Keizai Tokei no Seibi Kaizen ni Kansuru Kenkyu*

Introduction

Japanese economic development has attracted students of growth theory, economic historians, and countless others fascinated by the country's successes (and failures). The process is studied as a model, or at least an object lesson for the developing countries, it is analyzed and compared to the other developed countries for insights into how modern economies are structured and operate, and of course it is studied by those interested in Japan for its own sake. This book is designed to help all these groups in their work on Japanese development.

Statistics on Japan are abundant—so much so they can be a source of confusion, as studies sometimes present just bits and pieces of data from diverse sources in the course of exposition and analysis. In the 1950s a project was begun to provide a set of data as complete and accurate as possible. The result is the *Estimates of Long-Term Economic Statistics of Japan since 1868*, commonly referred to as LTES, a projected 14 volumes published by Toyo Keizai Shimposha starting in 1965. As of early 1979, ten volumes had appeared. The tables in LTES have English headings, notes, and a summary of the estimating procedures.

While the detailed LTES data are thus available to non-Japanese, to make the series more accessible it was decided to publish this book to do the following:

1. Present the most important series in a national income accounting framework in one volume (while all the LTES volumes are not yet published, the research for them is substantially finished).

2. Introduce important new work not covered by LTES (Minami and Ono's discussion in ch. 11 on factor incomes).

3. Provide data from forthcoming LTES volumes (Yamamoto

and Yamazawa's trade data in ch. 7, which includes important revisions in price indexes, and Umemura's population and labor force series in ch. 14).

4. Include revisions and extensions of already published LTES series.

5. Discuss the patterns and the data to help understand some of the whys.

6. Describe data sources and methods so a user can relate material to his own analytic work or comparisons with other countries or refer back to more detailed data.

7. Provide references to analytic and descriptive studies of the data and patterns.

This is, in short, a reference book, a handy guide not just to the LTES series but to Japanese economic studies in general. While about half tables, the text provides a summary of the patterns in the data and describes some of the analysis done on Japanese economic development.

PART 1: OVERALL PATTERNS

1

Aggregate Growth and Product Allocation

Kazushi Ohkawa

Study of the quantitative aspects of development is a relatively new field of economics. Although there are many pre-World War II works on national income and expenditure, most are not systematic and reliable enough to clarify the quantitative aspects of modern economic growth. Not until the beginning of the 1950s were more or less systematic studies undertaken in the developed countries, under the leadership of Simon Kuznets.

In 1951 Yamada published his pioneering work on Japan and one of our preliminary studies (published as Tsuru and Ohkawa 1953) was presented to the International Conference on Income and Wealth. GRJE was published in 1957 as an interim report. The most important prewar work was done by Hijikata (1933; other early studies by both Japanese and foreigners are discussed in GRJE, pp. 35–47).

The significance of national income estimates in analysis has greatly expanded in recent times, aided by government compilation of official statistics, international standardization, and progress in evaluation techniques. In Japan official estimates were made during the occupation, but during the 1950s use of national income statistics for grasping the macro-pattern of the economy was very limited. One reason was strong reservation about their reliability, but more important might have been a simple lack of any scholarly intention of using them for analytical purposes, and thus a lack of interest in improving long-term series extended to prewar years. Such an intention was a driving force in our group's studies.

By the beginning of the 1960s progress in constructing a conceptual framework, reconciling and integrating various estimates, as well as improving reliability through continued research, had created a set of statistics usable in analytic studies. Most of these have been published in LTES. I believe the entire revised series can be used to formulate national product and expenditure, even though several parts need further exploration, as is discussed in chapter 3. Linked with the official postwar series, the data are more or less satisfactory for broad continuous observation and for illuminating the pattern of Japanese economic growth since 1885, if carefully used and interpreted.

Estimates prior to 1885 are of course desirable, but due to the limited availability of relevant statistical records, we refrain from making them. Especially for services and other intangibles, estimation faces great difficulties, and much more time and effort are needed to overcome them. Available evidence shows the years 1868–85 are the transition period, characterized by institutional innovations. Real modern economic growth started later (see Ohkawa and Rosovsky 1965), and our estimates cover its entire period.

SOME CONCEPTUAL PROBLEMS AND THE QUANTITATIVE HISTORICAL PATTERN

Although simplicity is preferred, national income accounts have become more and more elaborate even for developing countries. Such complexity has the disadvantage of requiring too much data, given the limited availability of basic statistical materials. Similar problems exist with estimates for the early years for developed countries, because reliable sources are limited and there is no way to create new data by design.

For estimating prewar national product and expenditure, the so-called conventional concepts and premises have been adopted. They are similar to those used in the government's postwar official estimates. I share the view the concepts behind and the procedures for estimating national income accounts can be plural. This volume presents one possible estimate but other kinds of series can be constructed. As an example, there can be different frameworks for short-term and long-term settings. The conventional framework is designed primarily for short-term purposes; when applied to long-term analysis, it may be biased in scope, netness, and valuation. This may be especially true in Japan's case because growth and structural change have been so rapid by international standards. Nonetheless, no special devices have been used. The rationale of adopting the conventional framework is its historical and international comparability.

The essentials of statistical procedure depend on the proposed use, and since our aim is to clarify the quantitative aspects of modern economic growth, two points seem especially important: the meaning of quantification in long-term measurement, and the significance of what we call the historical pattern.

The Meaning of Quantification

Measuring a macroindicator of economic *activity* is one of the essentials. For this we use GNE (gross national expenditure) and its equivalent, GNP (gross national product). The use of GNP is reasonable and useful for our purpose because of its comprehensiveness, consistency, and netness. In view of a recent tendency to distrust GNP, I must stress our emphasis is on the level of activity, rather than the level of welfare.

An inseparable aspect of this problem is the composition of GNP and changes in it over time. Nonetheless, this problem has drawn less attention than it deserves. Two circumstances may explain why. First, increasing use of GNP by political and administrative authorities in the postwar years has become an international phenomenon. Developed countries stress GNP growth rates, and developing countries use it to set objectives for their economic plans. Second, the historical experience of modern economic growth in western developed countries has revealed no striking differences in compositional changes. Thus they are more similar to one another than to, say, Asian countries, including Japan.

A more technical problem is the relativity of measuring the quantitative features of modern economic growth. I will not repeat the discussion of problems dealt with elsewhere, such as scope (particularly the nonmarket portion of the traditional economy) and netness (see GRJE). Possible estimation errors are covered in chapter 3. Here I mention only my basic view on this controversial problem.

Quantitative measurement based on market prices of goods and services can and should be accepted despite some misgivings if only because we have no alternatives. The important point is to make appropriate reservations in interpreting the results. In particular, one must recognize quantification depends on the price system used. Different price systems give different results, this is inherently unavoidable. A technical discussion of the index number problem is beyond the scope of this chapter, but I reject the classical view, which assumes the existence of a true value between the plural measures resulting from utility-maximizing behavior for different preference scales (a system of indifference curves). This was a controversial issue during the early postwar years, and I refer those interested to my theoretical study (Ohkawa 1953).

In long-term measurements, price relativity is especially serious because of structural evolution and major changes in the price system. For example, in aggregate observations a general international phenomenon is that the prices of consumption goods, of services, and of investment goods usually change differently. Since investment goods prices have a tendency toward relative decline in latecomer countries such as Japan, their proportion in earlier years is smaller when later period valuations are used. Use of constant price and real-term volumes is necessary, however, so care in interpreting them is imperative.

The Historical Pattern

In applying our conceptual framework of social accounts, we call a long-lasting, regular movement in aggregate or composite series a historical pattern. Such patterns provide the traditional fields of empirical analysis with two interrelated aids. First, by serving as a basis or starting point, they enable us to understand how the facts are related, and this permits quantitative analysis to proceed more efficiently. Patterns are easier to find if what they look like is known, though of course care must be taken not to ignore unexpected patterns or to force the data to fit. Second, historical patterns make it possible to pose significant new questions. Indeed, I believe most of the major problems to be analyzed empirically and/or theoretically can be formulated from empirical findings of historical patterns. A most remarkable example is Kuznets' finding of a secular pattern in the savings ratio in the United States. This finding posed new problems with respect to personal behavior in consumption and savings, and engendered considerable controversy.

Studies such as this require the use of certain simple statistical procedures, such as averages, trends, and growth rates. It is something of an art to decide which procedure is best suited to both the original data and the historical reality of the phenomena at issue. However, the procedure should be as neutral as possible to avoid injecting one's own biases. In other words, we emphasize the importance of the historical laboratory.

AGGREGATE OBSERVATION: NATIONAL PRODUCT AND PRIVATE
CONSUMPTION

The aggregate results of our estimates are examined in this section. GNE (gross national expenditure) and PC (personal consumption) are taken up, in both current and constant prices, and their long-term changes are measured by average compound rates of growth. GNE is a measure of a nation's overall economic activity; PC is a measure of the national level of living and thus pertains directly to peoples's welfare. Using a GNE and PC approach instead of referring to net national product or the like is not meant to imply PC is the best measure of welfare. Preference between current and future consumption (savings) is an important problem but is not discussed here.

GNE is used in most of this chapter as our series for it is probably more accurately estimated than GNP. In the overall picture the differences in the two concepts do not matter to the analysis. For more detailed study the distinction is important, but most of our GNP component estimates are sufficiently good for such use. Changes in the composition of both national product and expenditure are discussed later.

International Comparison of Initial Conditions

Japan's initial level has often been considered very low: 1874–79 GNP per capita has been estimated at $74 using 1965 US dollars and exchange rates, while western initial levels are in the range of $200 to $300 (data from Kuznets 1971). These values were obtained by taking the 1965 GNP level in each country's own prices, converting to dollars, and discounting back at each country's GNP growth rate.

When working back from 1969, the 1887 Japanese level is $172 (LTES 1:16). This is still an understatement because, compared to western countries, Japan has had a greater gap between prices at the foreign exchange level and domestic prices. Use of purchasing power parity narrows the difference: for example, the ratio of purchasing power parity to exchange rate valuation for 1970 is 1.63 (US weights) and 1.31 (Japan weights) (Kravis 1975, p. 176). Use of the 1970 ratios for 1887 gives $251 (Fisher formula). The actual 19th century ratios for Japan were probably higher, making Japan's initial per capita GNP even closer to that of other developed countries. Still, we do not hesitate to say Japan was initially a relatively backward country economically. Allowing for reduction of the 1887 figure of $172 for

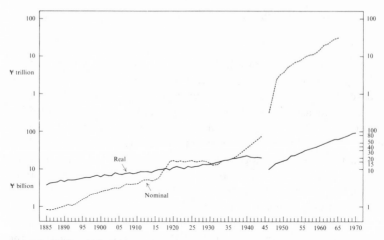

Fig. 1.1. GNE, 1885–1969

Source: Appendix tables A7 and A8 (current prices), and A9 and A10 (real terms).
Notes: A similar table appears in LTES 1 (p. 12, fig. 1-1). However, real GNE has been revised because of changes in the export and import price indexes.

   Both pre- and postwar real term series are given in 1934–36 prices, using tentative price indexes linking pre- and postwar years. Incidentally, real terms instead of constant prices are used because the deflated series are not necessarily valued at constant prices due to the price index formula used (see ch. 3). The dotted lines are the unrevised estimates by the EPA, tentatively used here but in need of revision to be consistent with prewar and the subsequent postwar series.

years closer to the actual start of modern economic growth, Japan's initial per capita GNP level was certainly lower than those of western nations, although probably not as much as has been generally believed.

GNE

   Annual values of GNE for the entire period 1885–1969 in both current and real prices are shown in figure 1.1. The contrast between real and current prices is striking—over half of prewar nominal growth was due to inflation.

   The dislocation caused by World War II is enormous; economic activity fell to the level of 30 years earlier. Pending more reliable estimates, a good approximation of GNP in real terms was 10,874 million yen in 1946, below the 10,929 level of 1918. Real GNE of 20,360 million yen in 1952 is close to the 19,949 million we estimate for 1937. The hyperinflation immediately after the war was unprecedented. Such an enormous rise in prices makes it hard to use con-

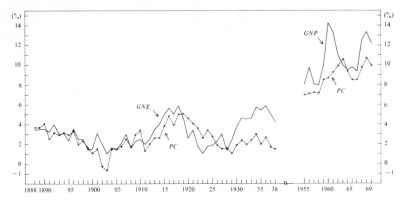

Fig. 1.2. GNE and Personal Consumption, 1885–1969, in Real Terms: Growth Rates

Source: Appendix tables A9 and A10.

Notes: A similar table appears in LTES 1 (p. 15, fig. 1-2). However, real GNE has been revised as explained in fig. 1.1. Also see fig. 1.1 for an explanation of real term series.

Based on smoothed series of moving averages (prewar, seven years except five years for the beginning and end of the period; postwar, five years except three years for the beginning and end of the period). The smoothing eliminates business cycle effects and other short-term variation as well as possible statistical estimation errors in the annual series. Unless otherwise specified, the same procedure is adopted for all the time series used.

Table 1.1 GNE and Price Increases

Current prices	Constant 1934–36 prices	Price level			Current prices	Constant 1965 prices	Price level
806	3,890	20.7	1885[a]	1952[b]	6,259	10,506	59.6
36,851	23,178	159.0	1940[a]	1970[b]	70,982	56,363	125.9
7.2	3.3	3.8	Annual growth[c]		14.4	9.8	4.2
4,572	593	771	Increase[d]		1,134	536	211

[a] Million yen; data from LTES 1:178 and 1:213, with revision.
[b] Billion yen; data from LTES 1:179 and 1:214.
[c] Bridge calculation, annual compound rate in percent.
[d] 1940 level as a percentage of 1885 level; 1970 as a percentage of 1952.

ventional price indexes, but our tentative measure suggests the price level in 1952 was 300 times the 1934–36 base.

Long swings and secular trend pattern

Figure 1.2 shows an overall picture, using our estimates plus some other preliminary data, of the historical performance of real GNE

Table 1.2. Long-Term Pattern of Aggregate Growth Rates, Constant Price Series: Average Annual Growth Rates
(In percent)

Period (length in years)	GNE	Total Population	Per capita GNE	Personal consumption		
				Total	Per capita[a]	Difference from per capita GNE[b]
A. Long-swing phases						
(U) 1887–97 (10)	3.21	0.96	2.25	3.15	2.19	−0.06
(D) 1897–1904 (7)	1.83	1.16	0.67	1.02	−0.14	−0.81
(U) 1904–19 (15)	3.30	1.19	2.11	2.99	1.80	−0.31
(D) 1919–30 (11)	2.40	1.51	0.89	2.60	1.09	0.20
(U) 1930–38 (8)	4.88	1.28	3.60	2.23	0.95	−2.65
(D) 1938–53 (15)	0.58	1.36	−0.78	0.89	−0.47	0.31
(U) 1953–69 (16)	9.56	1.03	8.53	8.63	7.60	−0.93
B. Trough-to-trough and peak-to-peak						
(T) 1887–1904 (17)	2.64	1.04	1.60	2.27	1.23	−0.37
(P) 1897–1919 (22)	2.72	1.18	1.54	2.37	1.09	−0.54
(T) 1904–30 (26)	2.92	1.32	1.60	2.83	1.51	−0.09
(P) 1919–38 (19)	3.44	1.35	2.09	2.44	1.09	−1.00
(T) 1930–53 (23)	2.08	1.29	0.79	1.36	0.07	−0.72
(P) 1938–69 (31)	5.21	1.06	4.16	4.51	3.45	−0.71
C. Secular trends						
1887–30 (43)	2.81	1.21	1.60	2.61	1.40	−0.20
1904–38 (34)	3.26	1.25	2.01	2.69	1.44	−0.57
1887–1938 (51)	3.13	1.22	1.91	2.55	1.33	−0.58
1887–1969 (82)	3.92	1.21	2.71	3.29	2.08	−0.63
1904–69 (65)	4.19	1.17	3.02	3.55	2.38	−0.64

Table 1.2 (continued)

Sources: REVISION of LTES 1:16 (table 1-1) and 1:20 (table 1-3). The revision is the result of changes in the prewar import and export price indexes, and thus in the GNE price index. This table is calculated from data in appendix tables A3 and A4 (GNE and PC) and table A53 (population).

Notes: Annual growth rates are calculated as a percentage increase from the preceding year, then a period average growth rate is taken as the simple average of the individual years' growth rates, except 1938–53 is a simple bridge between the two years because of the lack of consistent data. Turning points are based on GNP: 1887, 1953, and 1969 are tentative.

The series are smoothed as explained in fig. 1.2.

U = upswing; D = downswing; P = peak; T = trough.

[a] Personal consumption's growth rate minus that of total population.

[b] Per capita personal consumption's growth rate minus that of per capita GNE.

and PC in terms of growth rates measured in smoothed series. The long-term performance is summarized in tables 1.1 and 1.2.

In my view, modern economic growth started in Japan with the end of the Matsukata deflation (1881–85); the years 1868–85 were a transition period for which no reliable macrodata are available. During the initial upswing, which includes the years of the Sino-Japanese War (1894–95), annual average growth rates were 3 to 4%. Around 1897, the year the gold standard was adopted, it appears to peak. The growth rate then dropped rather sharply, forming the first downswing, and until the Russo-Japanese War (1904–05) the growth rate exceeded 2% only in 1901. Any satisfactory analysis of the Meiji period must deal with this distinct growth swing.

The next upswing is at the time of World War I, with 1912–19 forming the core. This is followed by a sharp downswing that lasted into the worldwide depression of the 1930s. Japan faced a most difficult time politically and socially, as well as economically during the second downswing. The third upswing dates from the beginning of the 1930s but was ended by World War II. Thus two cycles and a third upswing occurred during the prewar period.

Abnormally high rates of growth during the years immediately after World War II undoubtedly resulted from the recovery and rehabilitation, but from the mid 1950s what we consider normal postwar growth can be observed. One is tempted to emphasize discontinuities between the two periods divided by World War II because of the widespread social, political, and economic changes brought on by defeat. However, we contend the postwar growth pattern can be better understood in terms of historical continuity and that it forms the fourth upswing of Japan's modern economic growth. Comparing prewar (1887–1938) and entire–modern (1887–1969) growth rates in table 1.2, panel C, helps place postwar growth in better perspective. The postwar growth rates in figure 1.2 show a period of relatively slower growth around 1961–65, which may be similar to a dip in the 1910s, and it is ignored here to get a broad picture. Rosovsky and I have tentatively treated this interval as a downswing in terms of private fixed investment, (1973, 2 and 9).

Even in the early stages of our work, the existence of long swings in Japan's growth since the mid 19th century has been suggested, and as our estimates have become more reliable this has been confirmed. Early discussions of long swings in Japan in English are Shinohara (1962) and Fujino (1968). It is not easy, however, to identify precise dates for the peaks and troughs of long swings, and without doing so it is impossible to identify the secular trend pattern, which concerns us much more, beyond intuitive impressions. The present aim, however, is not to develop an elaborate discussion of the technical problems of swing periodization. The periodization given elsewhere is in terms of private gross fixed investment, but the periodization based on GNP used in table 1.2 shows only minor differences of one or two years in peaks and troughs (see table 1.9).

In table 1.2, panel A, swing regularity is perfect for the entire period and thus confirms the existence of long swings. Period average growth rates tend to increase in each successive upswing phase (U); in downswing phases (D) they increase from lines 2 to 4, but decrease from lines 4 to 6. An extraordinarily small rate of growth for 1938–53 (line 6) was of course due to war dislocation, which is considered an ad hoc decelerating factor. Panel B shows the average growth rate increases in each peak-to-peak period whereas in trough-to-trough periods it is mixed—an increase for the first, but a decrease for the second, again reflecting war dislocation. As noted in chapter 3, the data for linking prewar and postwar periods, 1938–53 in this case, are less reliable. We believe the 1953 GNP level had barely recovered the highest prewar level, that of 1938. Japan's swing pattern displays trend acceleration, a long-term historical pattern of growth rates characterized by progressive increase. Such a pattern has not been found in western countries (see Kuznets 1971, especially pp. 37–43). Ohkawa and Rosovsky (1973) is the principal study of trend accleration. Tests for a trend pattern of growth rates can of course be done by other methods, and the period average approach cannot claim to be the best or sole one. (For other methods, including using somewhat different datings, see LTES 1:17, table 1–2; and Ohkawa and Rosovsky 1973, p. 28, table 2.2.) Both are consistent with what is given here.

Since the early 1970s Japan's high growth rate has dropped sharply. I think the Japanese economy is turning from trend acceleration to trend deceleration. This requires further study.

Per Capita GNE

Growth rate swings of per capita GNE, shown in table 1.2, panel A, column 3, are essentially the same as those of GNE, being largely unaffected by the population growth pattern. There is no trend acceleration between the first two upswings because of the rising rate of population increase, and the abrupt increase in population due to postwar repatriation contributes to the negative value of the 1938–53 downswing. However, acceleration is clearly recognizable for per capita GNE for successive peak-to-peak rates, as shown in panel B.

Secular growth rates shown in panel C may appear far more moderate than usually expected for Japan's experience. For example, per capita GNE increased at an average of 2.8% for the entire period 1887–1969, less than one-third the postwar rate. Further, the prewar average rate was less than 2%. Despite the operation of growth-accelerating factors, the depressed 1920s and war-afflicted 1940s did much to pull down the average growth rate of per capita GNE.

International Comparison

Several years ago Kuznets observed:

Even after downward revision of the Japanese growth rates derived from the original series published in 1957 [in GRJE], the rates—for both total and per capita product—are at the upper end of the range for developed countries. Only the aggregate product growth rate of the United States and the per capita product growth rate of Sweden approach those of Japan. . . . If further revisions of the long-term series for Japan still leave the rate of growth of the total and per capita product at the upper end of the range among the developed countries—and it is difficult to assume otherwise—the question is as to the major factors that would explain this high growth record. (1968, pp. 385–87)

Our further revisions meet Kuznets' expectation that Japan's growth rate for both total and per capita product is at the upper end of the range. A comparison of Japan with Kuznets' recent measurement of western experiences is in table 1.3. For product per capita, Japan and Sweden are the highest; for total product, only the United States is close to Japan.

Increases in the Consumption Level

Per capita personal consumption expenditure in real terms is defined as the consumption level. This section is intended to establish its historical pattern and clarify its characteristics, particularly in light of the moderate per capita GNE growth described earlier.

Table 1.3 International Comparison of Total Product and Population Growth

		Duration of period	Total product	Population	Product per capita
		(Years)	(Percent per decade)		
Japan	(A) 1885–89 to 1968–70	82	48.3	16.3	32.0
	(B) 1874–79 to 1963–67	88.5	48.3	12.1	32.3
United	(A) 1859 to 1963–67	105	39.2	18.7	17.3
States	(B) 1834–43 to 1963–67	125.5	42.4	21.2	17.5
Sweden	1861–69 to 1963–67	100	37.4	6.6	28.9

Sources: Kuznets (1971, pp. 11–14). Japan (A) is my own measurement based on the revised series in this volume. It is a direct bridge calculation made to be comparable with Kuznets' data.

Notes: The scope of total product, base year of pricing, and other factors are not necessarily the same among countries but this does not cause any trouble for our present purpose.

For other developed countries in Europe growth rates range as follows (percent per decade):

Total product	20.5 (France)	to 32.5 (Denmark)
Population	3.0 (France)	to 13.4 (Netherlands)
Product per capita	12.4 (U.K.)	to 22.9 (Italy)

Personal consumption includes only household consumption. Given the importance of expense accounts and company-provided benefits such as housing and commuting passes, private consumption (business and community, as well as household) may be a better welfare measure, but data are limited. My basic views on the problems of concept and measurement appear in Ohkawa (1953) and will not be discussed here unless necessary. Chapter 8 deals with components of consumption and presents additional data.

PC (personal consumption expenditure) appears to be similar to GNE for long swings, but PC and GNE are dissimilar in the shape and trends of the swings (fig. 1.2; growth rates, table 1.2). During the first upswing no remarkable difference appears, but in the first downswing PC grows at a lower rate, particularly toward the turn of the century. In both the second upswing and downswing a distinct time lag in PC change shows up. A most distinct difference appears between PC and GNE in the third upswing: an even sharper lag in PC increase. Although reliable information is not available for the 1940s, undoubtedly the lag performance of PC has continued during the postwar upswing. Table 1.2 does not suggest a secular trend of increase in the

PC growth rate for any prewar period. This important dissimilarity between PC and GNE must have emerged during the 1930s, when PC had an extraordinarily slow growth rate (panel A, line 5).

The rate of population increase had greater importance to PC than to GNE, as shown by column 6 in table 1.2. The same is true for aggregate PC and GNE. The figures in panel A, column 5, show not only rather moderate growth rates of per capita PC, but also negative values for 1897–1904 (line 2) and 1938–53 (line 6). The negative figure for 1938–53 implies consumption in 1953 was still below the 1938 level. Although measurement is less reliable for this particular period, this lower figure is believable and can be explained by war dislocation.

The negative figure for the late Meiji era demands special attention even though it is minor. As noted previously, different methods may give somewhat different rates of growth, and a decrease in per capita PC during the period 1897–1904 cannot be taken as absolute, although at the least it strongly suggests severe stagnation in per capita PC must have occurred in the first downswing. The original annual growth rates based on the smoothed series of PC contain negative figures for four years of this particular period, including those of the Russo-Japanese War. If a longer downswing phase, say 1897 to 1911, is used, the average growth rate of per capita PC is 0.6%, still very low but not negative. This is an important problem to study in the initial phase of Japan's modern economic growth.

Not only does PC tend to increase behind GNE (col. 4), but also their related movements display a swingwise regularity, with negative figures for downswings except in 1897–1904 (panel A, line 2). Upswing phases of PC growth tended always to accompany an increase of GNE with certain time lags, the most severe lag being in the 1930s; the pattern also appears in the postwar upswing phase. On the other hand, the dislocation caused by the war makes it more difficult to find a common downswing pattern. However, panel B suggests a regular pattern including both upswings and downswings: the growth rate of per capita PC is smaller than that of per capita GNE whether using trough-to-trough or peak-to-peak intervals.

Secular growth rates shown in panel C confirm a moderate and distinctly smaller increase of consumption level than per capita GNE. The average prewar rate of 1.3 to 1.4% is unexpectedly moderate compared to per capita GNE growth. PC increased an average of 62% of the GNE increase in the prewar period and 74% in the postwar period. This feature of per capita consumption growth rates is more

Table 1.4. Personal Consumption per Capita: Annual Percentage Increase in Real
    Terms

1.4	Germany (1851–60 to 1911–13)
1.3	Canada (1870–1930)
1.5	Canada (1926–30 to 1946–50)
0.5	Italy (1861–70 to 1931–40)
0.9	Norway (1865–1930)
1.5	Norway (1900–50)
0.8	United Kingdom (1880–89 to 1930–39)
0.4	United Kingdom (1900–09 to 1945–54)

Source: Kuznets (1962, appendix table 6).

distinct in international comparison. Despite high-ranking per capita
product growth, the increase in prewar per capita consumption is
definitely smaller than Sweden's 2.3% and the United States' 2.1%,
the two comparable countries in terms of product growth rates. Japan's
1.3% growth rate ranks with those of western developed countries
having much lower product growth rates (table 1.4).

PRODUCT ALLOCATION PATTERN: EXPENDITURE COMPOSITION

The distinct difference between the GNE and personal consumption
growth pattern found in the preceding section suggests the significance
of compositional changes in Japan's growth. In this section I discuss
only the overall pattern, leaving examination of changes within components to other chapters (foreign trade, ch. 7; consumption, ch. 8;
capital formation, ch. 9; and government, ch. 10).

Compositional Changes in Gross National Expenditure

A simple indication of changes in GNE composition is given in
table 1.5. The decline in the share of PC (personal consumption) is
impressive—starting from some 80%, by international historical
standards a generally expected level for the initial years of modern
economic growth, it dropped as low as 50% in the late 1960s. The
lowest prewar figure was 57% in 1938. Such low levels are unique to
Japan. I believe prewar government spending helped to depress PC,
particularly in the first and third downswings as well as during the war
years.

Unlike western developed countries, Japan does not exhibit any
overall pattern of ongoing increases in the proportion of GC (govern-

Table 1.5 Percentage Composition of GNE in Current Prices

	PC	GC[c]	I_m	I^d	X	M	X − M	D
1887[a] (T)	79.6	7.3	2.3	11.1	7.2	−7.5	−0.3	2.7
1897 (P)	78.0	7.4	5.0	12.6	9.7	−12.7	−3.0	6.0
1904 (T)	75.0	12.4	4.9	10.0	14.0	−16.3	−2.3	11.0
1911 (T′)	76.0	8.1	6.2	11.3	15.1	−16.7	−1.6	5.2
1919 (P)	70.0	6.2	5.6	14.5	21.2	−17.5	3.7	5.4
1930 (T)	73.0	11.1	10.4	5.7	18.2	−18.4	−0.2	4.4
1938[a] (P)	61.7	11.6	12.6	14.8	21.4	−22.1	−0.7	13.7
1953 (T)	65.9	11.2		21.9	3.3	−2.3	1.0	2.5
1969[b] (P)	54.3	8.6		36.0	11.7	−10.5	1.0	2.1

Source: A smoothed series (as described in fig. 1.2) calculated from annual data in
appendix tables A1, A2. Annual compositional data are found in LTES 1:239 (table 33).
Notes: A table similar to this appears in LTES 1:27 (table 2-1), but since it appeared
the EPA has revised the postwar data, thereby superseding its 1953 and 1969 entries.
Abbreviations:
PC = personal consumption
GC = government consumption
I_m = military investment
I = investment (excluding military except as noted in some other tables)
X = exports
M = imports
D = defense (current and military investment).
[a] Five-year average.
[b] Three-year average.
[c] Military investment is not included in government consumption in the prewar period
but is included for 1953 and 1969. However, it was sufficiently small to make the postwar
series comparable.
[d] Inventory change has been deducted from postwar GNE and investment to make the
figures comparable to the prewar ones. Inventory change was 2.9% of 1953 GNE (with
inventory changes included) and 4.2% in 1969.

ment current expenditure). Instead GC is quite volatile, in part because
the Sino-Japanese War (1894–95), Russo-Japanese War (1904–05),
and the Pacific War (1938–45, including the conflict in China) involved
tremendous amounts of spending. Even excluding military and ad hoc
factors such as the Kanto earthquake (1923), no increasing share is
seen. Sometimes it is asserted military expansionism characterizes
Japan's prewar growth pattern. However, table 1.5 shows while a
policy of low military spending in the 1920s does correspond to a
downswing, and while the 1930s upswing was concurrent with high
spending levels, military expenditure's share of GNE fell sharply
during the second upswing (1904–19). The evidence is at best am-
biguous, and it is my view no long-term trends or swings can be related
to the level of military spending.

Japan's trade situation has often been described as chronic deficit, since this was the usual situation from the time of initial growth until the mid 1960s. The notable exception is World War I. Since the overall balance of payments primarily reflects changes in the trade balance (see ch. 7), growth has consistently faced a foreign payments restraint. This means the prewar upswings, except the second at the time of World War I, need particular explanation. The principal ameliorating factor in the first upswing was the de facto devaluation of silver, which lasted until the gold standard was adopted in 1897. The third upswing was supported by yen devaluation.

The revised export and import series in chapter 7 are for Japan Proper; trade with overseas territories (Korea and Taiwan) is classified as foreign trade, as in LTES 1 and LTES 14.

Both export and import proportions had a secular trend of increase during the entire prewar period irrespective of peak and trough years. As industrialization proceeded, import requirements, particularly raw materials and fuels, increased because of the domestic paucity of such resources. This expansion of imports has been broadly matched by expanded exports as far as the long-term trend is concerned. Trade appears to have little association with long swings.

The postwar proportion of both exports and imports is slightly over 10%, much smaller than the prewar and present levels of most western developed countries. The postwar trade proportion has become much smaller than the domestic investment proportion, whereas during the prewar period the difference between the two was slight. External factors, including the loss of colonies, may be one reason for this. Basically, however, a relative decrease in Japan's import requirements through domestic substitution is the major cause, helped by relatively low prices of raw materials.

The initial low level of investment as a proportion of GNE deserves mention. Until 1911 it never exceeded 13% (18% including military). Thereafter it began to increase (see Yasuba 1974). The investment proportion of most contemporary developing countries has increased more sharply during their initial phases than it did in Japan. Japan's 1960s investment proportion (35% in 1969 for gross fixed domestic investment) is the highest level ever attained in a market economy. I am inclined to interpret this as a long-lasting trend rather than as a peculiarity of postwar growth.

Changes in the overall composition of GNE reflect changes in relative prices (discussed in ch. 12) and different growth rates of real terms series for the various components (table 1.6). Panel A confirms

Table 1.6. Average Annual Growth Rates of GNE Components, in 1934–36 Prices
(In percent)

Period (length in years)		I[a,b]	PC	GC[a]	X	M	GNE
A. Long-swing phases							
1 (U)	1887–1897 (10)	6.03	3.15	5.22	7.11	12.43	3.21
2 (D)	1897–1904 (7)	1.49	1.02	10.38	8.07	6.72	1.83
3 (U)	1904–19 (15)	7.03	2.99	−0.14	7.42	5.23	3.30
4 (D)	1919–30 (11)	1.23	2.60	5.73	4.97	5.64	2.40
5 (U)	1930–38 (8)	10.95	2.23	5.98	8.05	5.34	4.88
6 (D)	1938–53 (15)	0.03	0.89	−3.84	−5.11	−4.73	0.58
7 (U)	1953–69 (16)	15.06	7.90	4.55	13.60	14.73	9.56
B. Trough to trough and peak to peak							
(T)	1887–1904 (17)	4.16	2.27	7.34	7.53	10.08	2.64
(P)	1897–1919 (22)	5.27	2.37	3.21	7.63	5.70	2.72
(T)	1904–30 (26)	4.57	2.83	2.34	6.38	5.40	2.92
(P)	1919–38 (19)	5.32	2.45	5.83	6.27	5.27	3.44
(T)	1930–53 (23)	3.83	1.36	−0.42	−0.53	−1.23	2.08
(P)	1938–69 (31)	7.79	4.51	0.49	4.55	5.31	5.21
C. Secular trends							
	1887–1930 (43)	4.41	2.61	4.32	6.83	7.25	2.81
	1904–38 (34)	6.07	2.69	3.20	6.78	5.21	3.26
	1887–1938 (51)	5.44	2.55	4.58	7.02	6.86	3.13
	1887–1969 (82)	6.33	3.25	3.03	6.09	6.27	3.92

Source: Calculated from data in appendix tables A3 and A4.
Notes: Calculated as explained in table 1.2 from a series smoothed as explained in fig. 1.2.
A similar table appears in LTES 1:28 (table 2-2), computed from LTES 1:244 (table
38) and 1:240 (table 35); however, the revision in export and import price indexes
obsoletes the export, import, surplus on current account, and GNE data in the three
tables.
[a] Military investment is counted as investment and thus is excluded from government
consumption.
[b] No allowance is made for inventory changes.

the long swings for I (domestic investment). Note domestic investment
growth rates are much more volatile than GNE rates, and a trend of
successive increases through swings is much more distinct and stronger
for I than for GNE. Foreign trade seems to show regular movement
in long swings except in the early periods, but this is somewhat blurred,
particularly for imports. External factors, such as the limited possibility of increasing imports during World War I (line 2) and increasingly
strong barriers against imports during the 1930s (line 5), help explain
this.

A comparison between investment and exports reveals an interesting

(In percent)

Period (length in years)	Weighted growth rates[a]						Relative shares of growth rates[c,d]				
	I	PC	GC	X	M	Total[b]	I	PC	GC	X	M
A. Long-swing phases											
1 (U) 1887–97 (10)	0.58	2.66	0.40	0.26	−0.66	3.24	17.9	82.1	12.3	8.0	−20.4
2 (D) 1897–1904 (7)	0.16	0.85	1.08	0.49	−0.69	1.89	8.5	45.0	57.1	25.9	−36.5
3 (U) 1904–19 (15)	1.06	2.37	−0.01	0.75	−0.71	3.45	30.7	68.7	−0.3	21.7	−20.6
4 (D) 1919–30 (11)	0.22	2.14	0.54	0.60	−1.22	2.28	9.6	93.9	23.7	26.3	−53.5
5 (U) 1930–38 (8)	1.99	1.59	0.78	1.71	−1.26	4.80	41.5	33.1	16.3	35.6	−26.3
6 (D) 1938–53 (15)	0.75	0.44	−1.07	−0.47	0.56	−0.21	357.1	209.5	−509.5	−223.8	−266.7
7 (U) 1953–69 (16)	4.42	4.75	0.48	1.26	−1.39	9.53	46.4	49.8	5.0	13.2	−14.6
B. Trough-to-trough and peak-to-peak											
(T) 1887–1904 (17)	0.47	1.92	0.63	0.32	−0.82	2.52	18.7	76.2	25.0	12.7	−32.5
(P) 1897–1919 (22)	0.75	1.87	0.37	0.61	−0.73	2.87	26.1	65.1	12.9	21.3	−25.4
(T) 1904–30 (26)	0.81	2.14	0.19	0.83	−0.79	3.18	25.5	67.3	6.0	26.1	−24.8
(P) 1919–38 (19)	0.93	1.96	0.61	0.91	−1.17	3.23	28.8	60.7	18.9	28.2	−36.2
(T) 1930–53 (23)	0.89	0.61	−0.14	−0.10	0.25	1.51	58.9	40.4	−9.3	−6.6	16.6
(P) 1938–69 (31)	1.50	2.89	0.08	0.36	−0.35	4.48	33.5	64.5	1.8	8.0	−7.8
C. Secular trends											
1887–1930 (43)	0.64	2.07	0.46	0.57	−0.92	2.82	22.7	73.4	16.3	20.2	−32.6
1904–38 (34)	0.92	2.14	0.30	0.62	−0.70	3.28	28.0	65.2	9.1	18.9	−21.3
1887–1938 (51)	0.82	2.01	0.42	0.75	−0.94	3.06	26.8	65.7	13.7	24.5	−30.7
1887–1969 (82)	1.10	2.60	0.31	0.88	−1.39	3.50	31.4	74.3	8.9	25.1	−39.7

Source: Calculated from appendix tables A3 and A4.

Notes: See table 1.5 for abbreviations.

Calculated as explained in table 1.2 from a series smoothed as explained in fig. 1.2.

A similar table appears in LTES 1:30 (table 2-3), computed from LTES 1:213–14 (tables 18 and 18A); however, revision of the export and import price indexes obsoletes these and GNE data in the three tables, as well as all of table 2-3's relative share data.

[a]The weights are the percentage share of each component in real terms at the midyear of each period.

[b]The total growth rate differs slightly from the GNE growth rate due to structural changes.

[c]Relative shares are each component's weighted growth rate as percentages of the aggregate growth rate. Because of rounding not all rows add to 100.

[d]Relative shares on line 6 are distorted by the negative growth rates of GC and X caused by war dislocation.

relation: during upswings both moved together, while during down-swings exports grew much faster than domestic investment except for the war-affected 1930s. This may explain why export swings are blurred. In early years exports grew faster than investment, as shown in panels B and C, which suggests exports played a greater role during the initial growth phase (see discussion in chs. 5 and 7).

An export-drive thesis has often been asserted in discussing short downswings of Japanese business cycles, as well as growth in longer intervals such as the 1920s and early 30s. Sometimes such marketing efforts have been put forward as a general explanation of Japan's export expansion, but I believe this is inadequate as a single cause.

No obvious regularity is seen for GC (government current expenditure), although a stabilizing function similar to exports appears on close examination of the data. GC also appears to have a sort of regular pattern: from 1887 to 1930 (through the first three periods in panel B), a declining trend is seen. This suggests the government also played a greater role in the initial growth phase.

In panel B, trend acceleration in the investment growth rate appears in peak-to-peak periods. The same is true for trough-to-trough periods until 1930–53. A quite similar pattern appears for GNE. A trend of successive decline is found for the export growth rate, both peak-to-peak and trough-to-trough, though again interrupted by 1930–53. For imports, the rates differ little for successive peak-to-peak periods, while trough-to-trough periods exhibit a pattern similar to exports.

Tables 1.7 and 1.8 further demonstrate the patterns just described, and indicate some additional ones. Weighted growth rates of individual components are useful for showing what each component contributed (in an accounting sense) to forming both long swings and long-term trends. The figures, together with their relative shares shown in table 1.8, are almost self-explanatory and reconfirm the previous discussion. However, a few observations may be worthwhile.

Table 1.7, panel B, shows the relative contribution of personal consumption has tended to decrease whereas investment tends to increase. Thus, from having by far the largest relative contribution in the initial phase, in the 1930s personal consumption's contribution dropped below that of investment. Export's relative contribution tended to increase during the prewar period, even exceeding investment's contribution in the interwar years. Since then, however, it has decreased sharply. Imports have a different pattern than exports in the early periods, but by the postwar period changes in the two were similar. Government consumption made its largest contribution in 1887–1904,

Table 1.8. Changes in Weighted Growth Rates of GNE, in 1934–36 Prices
(In percent)

Period[a]	I	PC	GC	X	M	Total
A. Successive long-swing phases						
2 − 1	−0.42	−1.81	0.68	0.23	−0.03	−1.35
3 − 2	0.90	1.52	−1.09	0.26	−0.02	1.56
4 − 3	−0.84	−0.23	0.55	−0.15	−0.51	−1.17
5 − 4	1.77	−0.55	0.24	1.11	−0.04	2.52
6 − 5	−1.24	−1.15	−1.85	−2.18	1.82	−5.01
7 − 6	3.64	4.31	1.55	1.73	−1.95	9.74
B. Successive upswing phases						
3 − 1	0.48	−0.29	−0.41	0.49	−0.05	0.21
5 − 3	0.93	−0.78	0.79	0.96	−0.55	1.35
7 − 5	2.43	3.16	−0.30	−0.45	−0.13	4.73
C. Successive downswing phases						
4 − 2	0.06	1.29	−0.54	0.11	−0.53	0.39
6 − 4	0.53	−1.70	−1.61	−1.07	1.78	−2.49

Source: Calculated from table 1.7.
Note: This table is simply the difference obtained by subtracting each line in table 1.7 from the line above it. Some lines do not add because of rounding differences.
[a] See table 1.7 for the years in each period.

when it was second after personal consumption. The importance of the public sector in product allocation is confirmed for the initial growth phase.

The initial growth phase, the mechanism of which basically differs from that of the subsequent growth phases, is described in Ohkawa and Rosovsky (1973, pp. 12–18; 1965, pp. 53–66). The principal difference is that in later phases the modern private sector, particularly its capital formation, becomes the dominant driving force, while in the earlier period the traditional sector was most important and the modern sector's development depended on it. Since revised series are given, this demarcation requires further testing. Table 1.8, panel A (changes in the weighted growth rates in successive long-swing phases) indicates only I (investment) has had a systematic relationship with the total, both have the same sign pattern. Panel B clearly shows trend acceleration for investment and the total in upswing phases.

Gross Domestic Capital Formation

One of the most important findings in the preceding discussion is the strategic role played by investment. Figure 1.3 shows gross domestic fixed capital formation in terms of annual rates based on smoothed

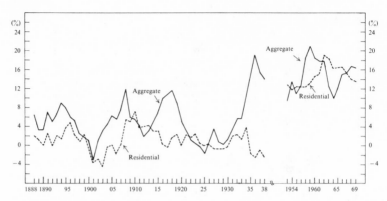

Fig. 1.3. Annual Growth Rates of Gross Domestic Fixed-Capital Formation in 1934–36 Prices, 1888–1969

Source: Reproduced from LTES 1:32 (fig. 2-3). Underlying data in LTES 1:218–22 (tables 21 and 21A).
Note: Moving averages (prewar, seven-year; postwar, five-year) centered on year plotted.

Table 1.9. Peaks and Troughs in GNE and Investment

	T[a]	P[b]	T	P	T	P	T	P	T	P	T	P
GNE	—	1897	1904	—	—	1919	1930	1938	1953	—	—	—
I[c]	—	1894	1901	1908	1912	1918	1925	1936	1945	1959	1964	—
Ip[d]	1887	1894	1901	1908	1912	1918	1932	1938	1953	1959	1964	1969

[a] Trough.
[b] Peak.
[c] Total investment, excluding military.
[d] Private investment.

series. It has already been noted that for both peaks and troughs, investment demarcation precedes GNE demarcation (table 1.9). For all prewar peaks and the first trough, the lead is one to three years. Further, this also shows the duration of up- and downswings appears to be shorter for investment than for GNE, since in both the second and third GNE upswings, investment makes two swings. Actually, GNE falters in each of the two upswings, but for broad observation other factors make it preferable to treat these stumbles as part of single phases. These two characteristics, particularly the first, appear to support the view that domestic capital formation has been the driving force in Japan's growth mechanism. Chapter 9 discusses capital formation data. Here I look at some of the patterns in those data.

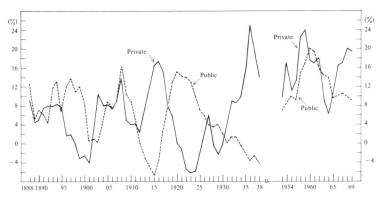

Fig. 1.4. Annual Growth Rates of Gross Domestic Fixed-Capital Formation: Private and Public Sectors, in 1934–36 Prices, 1888–1969

Source: Reproduced from LTES 1:33 (fig. 2-4). See fig. 1.3 for underlying data source and note.

Private versus Public

Annual growth rates are shown in figure 1.4 for both private and public investment, excluding residential construction and military investment. Peaks and troughs of Ip (private investment) almost coincide with those of I (aggregate investment); deviation, if any, is by one or two years (table 1.9). During the initial growth phase, government investment often surpassed the level of private investment even when military investment is excluded, and in general played a much greater role than private investment.

The swing pattern of aggregate investment can be assumed to have been formulated by private investment. However, around 1912 (the demarcating year in fig. 1.4) private and public investment cycles change from moving in phase to being almost 180° out of phase for the remainder of the prewar period. The out-of-phase swings may be thought of as a leader–follower relationship: complementary investment requirements resulting from private investment are fulfilled by the public sector with varying time lags depending on the historical situation. On the other hand, emphasis can be put on public construction specifically undertaken during the long downswing of the 1920s and early 30s. These two interpretations may not be mutually exclusive. In long-term perspective, however, the complementary relation seems to represent a general characteristic of Japan's investment allocation performance.

The postwar period again displays more or less in-phase behavior until around 1965, though with some time lag in public investment. Through the rest of the 1960s, public investment grew at a flat 10%, while the private rate surged. The remarkable leveling off of the growth rate of public investment during the latter part of the 1960s deserves particular attention. One reason for it was a more or less deliberate government decision to decrease its share of investment so as not to compete too much with the private sector. This was possible even though public investment maintained a large growth rate in absolute terms. In 1971, a year of little increase in private investment, public investment leaped 25%, so fiscal policy may produce a countercyclical pattern like that of the interwar period.

Residential Construction

As noted in chapter 9, estimation of residential construction is relatively less reliable due to data limitations. With this reservation, the following pattern broadly emerges from figure 1.3. The growth rate of residential construction has continuously been much lower than that of aggregate investment. No distinct upswings are seen. A peak occurred during the early years, but for later years none is found. In general, residential construction played only a small role in the prewar capital formation pattern. World War II damage resulted in a tremendous shortage of residences, and this became even more serious because of the abrupt population increase caused by repatriation. Nevertheless, no distinct catch-up process appears in figure 1.3 until the beginning of the 1960s. Clearly investment allocation was biased toward production at the expense of current welfare—the same historical pattern previously identified with respect to personal consumption.

Compositional Changes

Long-term compositional changes in gross domestic fixed-capital formation in real terms are given in table 1.10. Peak and trough years have been selected in principle on the basis of investment swings, but with special treatment of the 1930s. The years 1925–32, covering the great depression, are separately demarcated, and the 1936 peak is accordingly shifted to 1938. This device gives periods of approximately uniform length.

There are no clear-cut phases of allocation between agriculture (including forestry and fisheries) and nonagriculture (everything else). Agriculture had a consistently low investment growth rate (chs. 4 and

Table 1.10. Percentage Composition of Gross Domestic Fixed-Capital Formation
(Prewar in real terms, postwar in current prices)

	A[a]		B[b]				
	Private	Public	Livestock and Perennial Plants	Producers' durables	Nonresidential construction	Residential construction	Military investment[c]
1887 (T)	78.6	21.4	19.3	17.7	22.8	40.2	3.9
1894 (P)	76.6	23.4	16.0	26.2	26.5	30.9	7.9
1901 (T)	64.0	36.0	13.7	22.7	34.9	28.7	12.1
1908 (P)	66.6	33.3	9.5	32.4	39.7	18.4	10.5
1912 (T)	64.6	35.4	7.5	34.7	39.7	18.1	10.2
1918 (P)	79.8	20.2	4.8	52.9	28.7	13.6	11.5
1925 (T)	59.9	40.1	4.5	35.6	46.9	13.0	14.0
1932 (T')	58.8	41.2	3.9	39.0	45.8	11.3	13.5
1938 (P)	79.1	20.9	2.5	59.5	31.4	6.6	31.2
				Nonresidential Investment[b]			
1953 (T)	63.8	36.2		81.6		18.4	—
1959 (P)	69.6	30.4		83.3		16.7	—
1964 (T)	66.3	33.7		82.3		17.7	—
1969 (P)	72.8	27.2		82.3		17.7	—

Source: Reprinted from LTES 1:35 (table 2–4) except military investment is treated differently (see n. d).

Notes: Averages center on the years shown (seven-year [prewar] and five-year [postwar] with the exceptions of a five-year average for 1887 and a three-year for 1969).

[a] Excludes residential construction and military investment.

[b] For postwar years the official government estimates do not decompose nonresidential investment as we have done for prewar years; military excluded.

[c] Military investment data are not available for the postwar period. The figures given are a percentage of military plus nonmilitary gross domestic fixed-capital formation. (In LTES 1:35 military investment is taken as a percentage of nonmilitary.)

Table 1.11. Decomposition of the Growth Rate of Gross Domestic Fixed-Capital Formation
(In percent)

Period (length in years)	Weighted growth rates[a]				Relative shares[c]		
	Private	Public	Residential	Total[b]	Private	Public	Residential
1 (U) 1887–94 (7)	3.51	1.29	0.46	5.26	66.7	24.5	8.8
2 (D) 1894–1901 (7)	0.47	1.91	0.56	3.21	23.1	59.5	7.4
3 (U) 1901–08 (7)	4.30	1.84	−0.14	6.00	71.7	30.7	−2.4
4 (D) 1908–12 (4)	2.02	1.74	0.94	4.70	43.0	37.0	21.0
5 (U) 1912–18 (6)	7.62	0.23	0.31	8.16	93.4	2.8	3.8
6 (D) 1918–25 (7)	−1.32	3.24	0.15	2.07	−63.8	156.5	7.3
7 (D') 1925–32 (7)	1.29	1.10	0.04	2.43	53.1	45.3	1.6
8 (U) 1932–38 (6)	9.72	−0.55	−0.06	9.11	106.7	−6.0	−0.7
9 (U) 1953–59 (6)	8.98	3.11	2.13	14.22	63.2	21.9	−14.9
10 (D) 1959–64 (5)	7.79	4.58	2.82	15.19	51.3	30.2	17.5
11 (U) 1964–69 (5)	9.83	2.54	2.63	15.00	65.5	16.9	17.6

Source: Reprinted from LTES 1:36 (table 2-5). Underlying data from LTES 1:223–24 (tables 22 and 22A).
Note: Annual growth rates are period averages calculated from smoothed series; military excluded.
[a]Weights are the average of the components' percentage share in the beginning and end year of each period.
[b]The total is the sum of the weighted growth rate of each component. This is not necessarily equal to the growth rate of aggregate capital formation, military excluded, because of structural changes.
[c]The relative shares are each component's weighted growth rate as a percentage of the total rate.

9). A vigorous trend of increase in producers' durable equipment (of course with swings) compared to a small increase in nonresidential construction is seen for the entire prewar period. The percentage of military investment increased in the prewar period. By the 1920s it even surpassed residential construction, and with the war in China it reached an extraordinary level by the end of the 1930s.

Table 1.11 is intended to confirm what I have said about individual components, using a calculation procedure similar to table 1.7. Except for the 1925–32 period (line 7), which is treated as a special case, and 1908–12 (line 4), private investment alternates regularly between bigger and smaller growth rates in intervals of five to seven years. Successive upswings exhibit a secular trend of growth rate acceleration, except between the ones on either side of World War II (lines 8 and 9). Both public and residential investment are less regular. The sum of the relative shares of these two, however, shows a more regular performance, decreasing in upswings and increasing in downswings. This reflects the lower volatility of the two components and also suggests they played a stabilizing function by making total investment swings narrower than those in private investment alone.

A perfect conformance between the output and investment growth rates has not been found, but it can be said surges of private investment in modern industries formulate the core of upswing phases of aggregate output growth rates. Our periodization is generally longer for output and shorter for investment. Some inconsistencies may appear to exist between the two, but actually this is not the case. Downswing phases are shorter in Japan than in other countries, except during the 1920s, which is associated with a prolonged investment downswing (table 1.8, panel A, line 6).

The performance of investment upswings is reminiscent of what Gerschenkron (1962) has called a big spurt—a concept derived from European experience. Japan's investment spurt, however, is not a one-shot phenomenon, as it is in Gerschenkron's discussion, but instead has been repeated several times, each time increasing in strength. Rosovsky and I have designated three spurts of private capital formation: 1912–18, 1932–38, and 1953–59, with 1964–69 another possibility (table 1.9, line Ip); the 1887–94 and 1901–08 upswings in the table are considered part of the initial growth phase rather than spurts in modern private investment. Trend acceleration, the major characteristic of Japan's historical pattern of growth, cannot be interpreted without clarifying the mechanism of repeated investment spurts (see

Table 1.12. National Savings

(Percentage of GNP; net savings is a percentage of NNP)

	National savings			Capital depreciation allowances	Net private savings[d] (Series A)	Net private savings[d] (Series B)	Net public savings	Savings–Investment Balance in the public sector[e]	Gross domestic savings	Net increase in foreign claims
	Gross[a]	Gross[b]	Net[c]							
1887	12.6	13.2	2.8	10.0	-0.7	9.4	3.4	1.7	12.7	0.1
1894	16.5	16.5	8.3	9.0	8.6	15.4	-0.8	-2.8	14.3	2.2
1901	13.1	14.7	4.8	8.7	3.4	12.0	0.9	-2.4	13.0	0.1
1908	15.7	17.5	6.0	8.7	2.6	12.1	2.8	-1.1	16.5	0.8
1912	14.4	15.8	6.2	9.0	0.4	11.2	5.6	0.9	16.2	1.8
1918	24.7	26.1	16.3	9.8	10.5	15.6	3.3	0.2	20.0	4.7
1925	13.8	15.0	3.7	10.3	-1.6	11.1	5.1	-0.7	16.2	2.3
1932	13.7	15.5	4.6	9.7	5.0	14.6	-0.8	-6.2	13.6	0.1
1938	18.0	22.6	8.2	10.2	15.0	29.2	-6.9	-10.4	22.0	4.0
1954	25.8		18.7	8.7	19.9*		4.9	-2.2	25.6	0.2
1959	33.4		25.9	10.1	26.6*		6.8	-0.5	33.8	0.4
1964	35.0		26.0	12.3	29.4*		6.7	-2.8	34.8	0.2
1969	39.7		30.5	13.3	19.4*		7.0	1.5	38.7	1.0

Source: Reprinted from LTES 1:42 (table 2-8). Underlying data from LTES 1:190–91 (tables 6 and 6A).

Note: Five-year averages of annual ratios centered on the years shown. Based on current price series.

[a] Source of military investment not treated as savings.

[b] Source of military investment treated as savings.

[c] Net savings as a percentage of NNP.

[d] See the explanation in the main text. Figures marked with an asterisk include statistical discrepancies.

[e] Savings minus investment as a percentage of GNP. Military investment is excluded from investment.

Ohkawa and Rosovsky 1973, especially chs. 2 and 8, for further discussion).

Savings

A central place for investment in resource allocation naturally leads to the importance of savings—the nation's behavior in financing investment. Savings are especially important since most of Japan's investment has been financed domestically except for special periods, particularly the beginning of the 20th century, when foreign capital borrowing was relatively sizable (see ch. 7). With respect to the current account, apart from a few years such as those of World War I, changes in net foreign claims were generally minor. Short-term differences between domestic and national savings are not our subject. For these reasons, the historical pattern of the domestic investment proportion of GNE described earlier approximates that of the savings ratio estimated by ex post accounting (see table 1.6). What has been said about the investment ratio (I/GNE) therefore essentially can be applied to the savings ratio (S/GNE, S = savings) both for swings and secular trend. The concern here is to confirm the savings ratio's aggregate pattern, clarify its compositional changes (table 1.12), and examine the savings–investment flow between the private and public sectors.

The savings estimates have been derived indirectly, using investment data. When statistical discrepancies between GNP and GNE are significant, a possible margin of error is involved in the savings data thus estimated. For a number of years this is a problem for our estimates. Together with excluding explicit estimates of inventory changes for prewar years, this means care must be exercised in using the present data, as is discussed in chapter 3.

A regularity of swings and trend is clearly confirmed for the gross national savings ratio (table 1.12, col. 1). Particularly impressive is a secular trend of increase from a moderate ratio of 12% in the initial years toward a high of 40% in the late 1960s. Japan's recent extremely high savings ratio is definitely the historical consequence of the sustained operation of several factors, instead of being merely a phenomenon peculiar to postwar growth. The gross domestic savings ratio (col. 9) demonstrates this a bit more distinctly because it separates the exceptionally sizable effects of changes in foreign claims in 1918 and 1938. This is, I believe, important and calls for deeper analysis. It is one of the notable characteristics of the Japanese experience and is a sharp contrast to Kuznets' finding of a long-term constancy in the savings ratio of the United States. For some results of earlier analyses of Japan's case, see Ohkawa (1970) and Odaka (1975).

The pattern appears blurred for net savings (col. 3). The very nature of swings and trend acceleration in the growth rate leads one to expect a milder pattern because capital depreciation allowances usually tend to strengthen these patterns. Beyond this, no definite answer is possible at this stage of analysis. Depreciation is computed using the straight-line method over assumed useful lives. Since actual capital consumption varies with utilization for most items, there is an underestimation in upswings and an overestimation in downswings. Moreover, given the size of the traditional sectors for the earlier years, overestimation probably increases as the series is extended back in time, since actual lives most likely exceeded the assumed ones. In any case, it is legitimate to interpret the historical pattern in terms of gross instead of net savings.

The contributions made by three sectors—government, private corporate, and personal (household)—will now be considered. Each sector's decision making differs in terms of institutions and behavior. The data in columns 5–7 are not satisfactory enough to analyze this fully, but they do permit us to arrive at a broad judgment. The aggregate savings pattern is mainly the result of the savings behavior of the private sector.

To deal with the problems of estimation errors and methodological shortcomings, I list two kinds of net private savings ratio. Series A (col. 5) is our original series, computed in conjunction with the other components. However, the negative values in 1887 and 1925 seem unlikely, and this, with our uneasiness over the depreciation series, leads us to compute series B (col. 6). Series B is based on the hopeful assumption capital depreciation allowances and net changes in foreign claims can be allocated solely to the private sector without causing too much distortion. Here again we rely much more on gross rather than net series. It is easy to see the gross figures endorse our view more clearly, regarding both swings and trend.

A breakdown into corporate and household sectors is not shown because the data for corporate savings are less reliable for early years. It is reasonable to expect, however, that the ratio of private corporate savings to GNP must have increased with modernization of the economy. A tentative estimate, derived from smoothed averages, shows that the ratio, 2.0% in 1908, rose to 9.5% in 1937 and to 12.3% in 1966. Therefore, both corporate and household sectors clearly contributed to forming the secular trend of increase in the aggregate savings ratio.

The household sector is a mixed one in Japan, as it is elsewhere. This sector is significant, however, because of the relative importance of unincorporated firms (in both the farm and nonfarm sectors) especially in the early years. Much more effort is needed to provide basic data to clarify the phenomena relevant to this point, such as the debated issue of a flow of private savings from agriculture to the modern sector.

Government savings are estimated conventionally as a balance of current revenue over expenditure. As expected from the previous discussion and the succession of wars, the ratio of government expenditure to GNE is erratic (for the revenue side, see ch. 10). A stable positive ratio of a fairly large magnitude for postwar years draws particular attention in this respect. The savings–investment balance, in terms of its share of GNE in table 1.12, column 8, shows postwar government saving is close to public investment. Among the developed countries, this situation is unique to Japan and is related to the unbalanced allocation of investment between the public and private sectors previously discussed for the postwar period.

The prewar ratio is comparable because military investment is excluded from public investment. It appears to show a pattern of investment greater than savings, with only a few exceptions. In view of a smaller national savings ratio for the prewar period, particularly for early years, this unbalanced ratio must have had greater significance to the mechanisms of growth including, but not limited to, inflationary pressures. A sectoral flow of savings from the private to the public sector may have been the dominant pattern, although more research is needed to confirm this.

References follow chapter 3.

2

Production Structure

Kazushi Ohkawa

Change in sectoral composition is inherent in modern economic growth. The industrial sector is the most dynamic sector during most of the process, and much of the change in other sectors is induced by their interaction with industrialization. The growth of banks and other institutions providing services to manufacturing and the movement of labor out of agriculture are two examples.

This chapter discusses the evolution of the production structure in terms of GDP and NDP, and a conventional broad classification. In this discussion agriculture includes forestry and fisheries. Industry consists of three subsectors. Two are manufacturing (including mining) and construction and facilitating industries (transportation, communications, and public utilities). The third sector, services, covers trade, banking, insurance, real estate, and personal and public services.

The three main sectors are each covered in more detail in separate chapters (agriculture in ch. 4; manufacturing, ch. 5; and services, ch. 6). Here the emphasis is on intersectoral comparisons, with an overview of the tremendous evolution in output composition. The ratios of a sector's output and labor to those of other sectors are used to supplement the orthodox approach of looking just at a sector's share of the aggregate series.

Japan's modern economic growth started from a typically traditional production structure. The fast rate of growth since the mid 19th century suggests the Japanese experience will provide insights into significant problems of economic development, and these are also taken up here.

Table 2.1. Sectoral Shares of NDP in Current Prices
(Percent of NDP)

		Ma	F	C	N	S	A
1887*	(T)	13.6	2.6	3.8	20.0	37.5	42.5
1897	(P)	15.8	3.1	4.5	23.4	35.1	41.5
1904	(T)	17.4	4.5	3.9	25.8	36.4	37.8
(1911)		20.3	6.4	4.4	31.1	33.4	35.5
1919	(P)	26.2	7.9	4.2	38.3	31.8	29.9
1930	(T)	25.8	11.7	5.8	43.3	36.7	20.0
1938*	(P)	35.3	8.2	8.2	51.7	30.0	18.5
1953	(T)	26.3	8.9	4.5	39.7	38.3	22.0
1969	(P)	30.5	7.9	7.5	45.9	45.4	8.7

Source: LTES 1:46 (table 3-1), underlying annual data in appendix tables A11 and A12 (= LTES 1:202–03, tables 9 and 9A).

Notes: Based on moving averages of annually calculated percentages, seven-year (five-year for years marked with asterisks) for prewar, three-year for postwar, centered on the years shown.

In current market prices for prewar and in current factor cost for postwar years.

Abbreviations:

T = trough	C = construction
P = peak	N = industry (subsectors M + F + C)
U = upswing	S = services
D = downswing	A = agriculture
Ma = manufacturing and mining	M = imports
F = facilitating industries	X = exports.

SECTORAL OUTPUT: SHARES AND GROWTH RATES

Changes in output composition are shown in table 2.1 using the same long-swing periodization as table 1–2, with 1911 inserted because of the stutter in the 1904–19 upswing. For the transition years 1868–85 statistical data are limited. It is, however, reasonably safe to take the 1887 figures as the initial conditions. These show Japanese industrial production structure was very close to the 1950s situation in other Asian nations, and distinctly different from the initial conditions of western nations.

The pattern of a shift from agriculture to industry, with services keeping a fairly stable share, is as expected from international experience. Japan's share changes are the fastest among developed countries. The shift shown in table 2.2 was a steady one, despite long-swings, with just a few exceptions. The principal one is the disruption caused by World War II. The others are manufacturing's drop in the 1919–30 downswing, and declines in facilitating industries and services

Table 2.2. Changes in Sectoral Shares of NDP in Current Prices
(in percentage of NDP at current prices)

Period (duration)		Ma	F	C	N	S	A
(U)	1887–97 (10)	2.2	0.5	0.7	3.4	−2.4	−1.0
(D)	1897–1904 (7)	1.6	1.4	−0.6	2.4	1.3	−3.7
(U′)	(1904–11) (7)	2.9	1.9	0.5	5.3	3.0	−2.3
(U′)	(1911–19) (8)	5.9	1.5	−0.2	7.2	−1.6	−5.6
(U)	1904–19 (15)	8.8	3.4	0.3	12.5	−4.6	−7.9
(D)	1919–30 (11)	−0.4	3.8	1.6	5.0	4.9	−9.9
(U)	1930–38 (8)	9.5	−3.5	2.4	8.4	−6.7	−1.5
(D)	1938–53 (15)	−0.9	0.7	−3.4	−11.7	8.3	3.5
(U)	1953–69 (16)	4.2	−1.0	3.0	6.2	7.0	−13.3

Note: This table is simply the difference obtained by subtracting each line in table 2.1 from the line above it.

Some columns do not add because of rounding.

For abbreviations see table 2.1.

Table 2.3. Price Indexes in 1938
(1887 = 100 for each sector)

Agriculture	Manufacturing	Services
737	415	717

Source: Author's calculation from data in table 2.13.

in the 1930s, attributable in large part to rapid expansion of war industries.

Compositional changes in sectoral output in current prices are a combined result of changes in the relative prices of sectoral output and divergent growth patterns of sectoral output measured at constant prices. Commodity price indexes are discussed in more detail in chapter 12. An overview of price changes is given in table 2.3, which shows that in earlier years the constant price share is much higher for agriculture, somewhat higher for services, and lower for industry. However, the broad secular pattern described above is not altered.

The conventional industrial classification is not entirely satisfactory for elucidating certain types of changes in the economy's structure since both traditional and modern production organization are found in each sector. In manufacturing and the facilitating industries the organizational shift must have been rapid, while in construction and services it was slower, and there was almost no shift in agriculture.

Table 2.4. Factory Production, in Constant Prices

	Output of manufacturing	Factory production	Ratio
1890	1,311	413	31.5
1900	2,086	972	46.6
1909	2,742	1,268	46.2
1914	3,533	1,859	52.6
1925	7,043	4,594	65.2
1937	17,320	12,854	74.2
1953	6,078	5,602	92.2
1965	30,321	29,371	96.9

Source: Ohkawa and Rosovsky 1973, p. 81 (table 4-4). The original data for output, are from LTES 10:144–47 (table 10, series A). For factory production the data are from *Kogyo Tokeihyo* (Tsusansho) for the years since 1909; for earlier years, our estimates in GRJE, pp. 79–80.

Notes: Million yen for prewar (1934–36 prices); billion yen for postwar (1960 prices).

A factory is an industrial establishment with more than five workers. Output is gross of intermediate goods. Data in terms of added value or net product are not available for the early years.

Table 2.5. Output Share of Noncorporate Enterprises in 1963
(Net of capital depreciation, 1960 prices)

(In percent) Agriculture	Construction	Facilitating industries	Mining	Manufacturing
96.6	32.7	6.1	8.7	19.7

Services	Commerce	Finance	Aggregate
50.2	46.1	6.8	34.5

Source: Ohkawa and Rosovsky 1973, p. 260.

All this is expected, but it is difficult to quantify comprehensively. Tables 2.4 and 2.5 each illustrate an aspect of this pattern. Before 1909 no official data are available for factory production, but our estimates suggest the major part of manufacturing output was non-factory production, mostly handicrafts. (A factory is defined as an industrial establishment with more than 5 workers.) In 1914 factory production, mostly by small and medium size firms (those with fewer than 500 employes), reached about half of manufacturing output.

Swing periodization in terms of GNE growth rates is used below as a first approximation for examining the relation between aggregate and sectoral growth rates for both swings and trends. Sectoral growth

Table 2.6. Sectoral Growth Rates of GDP in Real Terms
(Average annual growth rates in percent)

A. Swing periods (duration)	A	Ma	F	C	S	GDP
(U) 1887*–97	1.42	5.92	9.00	5.80	3.76	3.20
(D) 1897–1904	1.62	4.95	8.94	2.89	1.48	2.19
(U) 1904–19	1.81	6.80	9.31	3.47	3.28	3.74
1904–11	1.67	6.43	10.01	5.60	1.16	2.65
1911–19	1.94	7.13	8.70	1.61	5.14	4.67
(D) 1919–30	0.56	4.58	7.26	6.45	0.66	2.43
(U) 1930–38*	1.30	8.88	9.47	3.05	3.54	4.86
(U) 1955–64	3.68	17.12	13.71	16.47	10.49	12.28
B. Full-swing periods						
(T-T)[a] 1887–1904 (17)	1.50	5.52	7.80	4.60	2.82	2.87
(P-P)[b] 1897–1919 (22)	1.75	6.21	9.19	3.28	2.71	3.25
(T-T) 1904–30 (26)	1.28	5.86	8.44	4.71	2.17	3.20
(P-P) 1919–38 (19)	0.87	6.39	5.49	7.72	1.87	3.45
C. Secular trends						
1887–1930 (43)	1.37	5.73	8.19	4.68	2.43	3.03
1904–38 (34)	1.29	6.57	7.17	5.84	2.49	3.58
1887–38 (51)	1.36	6.22	7.38	5.43	2.60	3.32

Sources: Reprinted from LTES 1:49 (table 3-2). Underlying data in appendix table A13 (LTES 1:227, table 25). The smoothed series data are in LTES 1:243 (table 37) and annual changes in LTES 1:247 (table 40).

Notes: Based on the moving average (seven-year for prewar, (five-year for dates marked with asterisk, three-year for postwar) of real-term series (prewar in 1934–36 prices and postwar in 1960 prices). Period rates are averages of the annual growth rates. Official national income statistics do not give sectoral deflators and our own estimates are used. Pre-and postwar linked deflators are not used because they do not seem reliable enough.

For abbreviations see table 2.1.

[a] Trough to trough.

[b] Peak to peak.

Table 2.7. Manufacturing Peaks and Troughs

Trough	Peak	Trough	Peak	Trough	Peak
1887	1895	1902	1916	1922	1938
[	15 years	] [	20 years	]	

rates are given in table 2.6. Long swings similar to those of GNE are clearly seen for services. Swings are less consistent for manufacturing, facilitating industries, and construction, and they are shorter than for GNE, especially before World War I. Peaks and troughs for manufacturing are in table 2.7. Swings are not found for agriculture. As to secular trends, no distinct trend acceleration appears for any sectors.

Table 2.8. Sectoral Decomposition of Weighted Growth Rates of GDP in Real Terms
(Average annual growth rates in percent)

Period (duration)	A	Ma	F	C	N	S	Total[a]
1 U 1887*–97 (10)	0.54	0.53	0.18	0.16	0.87	1.78	3.19
2 D 1897–1904 (7)	0.55	0.51	0.30	0.09	0.90	0.70	2.15
3 U 1904–19 (15)	0.53	1.00	0.60	0.11	1.71	1.47	3.71
4 1904–11 (7)	0.54	0.85	0.53	0.20	1.58	0.51	2.63
5 1911–30 (8)	0.55	1.23	0.66	0.06	1.95	2.18	4.68
6 D 1919–30 (11)	0.13	0.97	0.83	0.26	2.06	0.26	2.45
7 U 1930–38* (8)	0.24	2.47	1.26	0.17	3.90	1.20	5.34
8 U 1955–64 (9)	0.51	5.57	1.39	0.79	7.75	4.03	12.29

Source: Reprinted from LTES 1:50 (table 3-3). Underlying data are the same as in table 2.6.
Notes: See notes to table 2.6. The weights are an average of each sector's proportion of output at the beginning and end years of a period.
   For abbreviations see table 2.1.
[a] The totals differ from GDP in table 2.6 because of the effects of structural changes.

Table 2.9. Changes in Growth Rate of GDP by Sector
(In percent)

Period	A	Ma	F	C	N	S	Total
2 − 1	0.01	− 0.02	0.12	− 0.07	0.03	− 1.08	− 1.04
3 − 2	− 0.02	0.49	0.30	0.02	0.81	0.77	1.56
4 − 2	− 0.01	0.34	0.23	0.11	0.68	− 0.19	0.48
5 − 4	0.01	0.38	0.13	− 0.14	0.37	1.67	2.05
6 − 3	− 0.40	− 0.03	0.23	0.15	0.35	− 1.21	− 1.26
6 − 5	− 0.42	− 0.26	0.17	0.20	0.11	− 1.92	− 2.23
7 − 6	0.11	1.50	0.43	− 0.09	1.84	0.94	2.89

Note: This table is simply the difference between lines in table 2.8.

Table 2.10. Weighted Growth Rates of Sectoral Output: Measured Peak to Peak and
Trough to Trough
(In percent)

	Agriculture	Industry	Service	Total
1887–1904 (troughs)	0.55	0.88	1.34	2.77
1897–1919 (peaks)	0.52	1.45	1.25	3.22
1904–1930 (troughs)	0.34	1.86	0.96	3.16
1919–1938 (peaks)	0.17	2.83	0.66	3.66

Source: LTES 1:51.

This may be contrary to expectation, particularly for manufacturing and the facilitating industries. Manufacturing does appear to accelerate between successive prewar upswings, but this is not so spectacular compared to the postwar jump.

Weighted sectoral growth rates are given in tables 2.8–2.10. Agriculture's contribution was small but steady until the 1920s, when it dropped. Industry's contribution showed a secular trend of sustained increase throughout swings. In contrast, service's contribution makes rather regular swings. Industry's performance is thus of particular significance to the trend acceleration, while agriculture and services have no positive effects. Changes in industrial structure in terms of output shares are thus confirmed as important in forming the trend performance of aggregate growth.

OUTPUT PER WORKER, RELATIVE PRICES, AND
PRODUCTIVITY DIFFERENTIALS

Secular changes in sectoral shares of labor are noteworthy, and some of them will be discussed comparing services and industry. In chapter 4 labor in agriculture is treated in relation to output, and there is a related discussion in chapter 6. This section focuses on output per worker in terms of sectoral comparison, which is used as a simple, rough indicator of partial labor productivity without making adjustments for changes in labor days or hours, composition, or quality.

Only the three main sectors are covered because of lack of more detailed labor data for the years before 1905. These broad sectors are heterogeneous and their mix of production organization has changed over time, so the results are approximations. Certain discrepancies in coverage between output and labor estimates are usually unavoidable, in addition to errors in estimating output and labor themselves. No attempt will be made to explain in detail the wide differentials shown in table 2.11, since my concern is to examine the relative changes in

Table 2.11 Sectoral NDP per Gainfully Occupied Person, 1887
(In yen)

	Agriculture	Industry	Service
Current prices	18.7	47.2	93.3
1934–36 prices	99.0	143.8	582.2

Source: Author's calculations.
Note: Five-year averages centered on 1887.

Table 2.12. Ratios of Output per Worker by Sector

	A/N			S/N			(A + S)/N		
	Current prices	Constant prices	Index[a]	Current prices	Constant prices	Index[a]	Current prices	Constant prices	Index[a]
1885–89	41.7	68.3	100.0	174.8	371.4	100.0	65.0	121.1	100.0
1894–99	43.2	55.0	128.7	141.5	311.6	96.5	63.3	107.2	110.0
1901–07	35.7	44.3	132.0	121.0	222.9	115.3	54.6	83.7	121.5
1908–14	34.0	37.6	148.1	103.0	166.4	131.5	50.3	68.0	137.8
1915–22	32.0	32.5	161.3	87.9	161.4	115.7	47.6	68.4	129.7
1927–33	24.8	27.4	148.3	92.2	99.3	197.3	46.8	50.9	171.3
1936–40	23.6	20.8	185.9	63.4	77.0	174.9	37.6	40.2	170.0
1947–55[b]	30.0	22.6	217.4	76.2	80.9	200.1	37.1	40.1	172.4
1955–60	28.9	22.5	210.4	77.6	70.5	233.8	52.1	45.3	214.3
1960–65	28.7	19.1	246.1	87.1	45.7	404.9	60.0	33.5	333.7

Sources: Reproduced from LTES 1:56 (table 3-5). Underlying data: Output is NDP, in current prices from appendix tables A11 and A12 (LTES 1:202–03, tables 9 and 9A), in constant prices from LTES 1:226 (table 24); prewar gainfully occupied population is from appendix table A53; postwar labor force employed is from the *Rodoryoku Chosa* (Sorifu).

Notes: For abbreviations see table 2.1.

Output price indexes are tentatively linked between pre- and postwar years by use of GNP deflator as a substitute for NDP deflator. Price indexes for A and N are from wholesale prices compiled by the Bank of Japan. Price indexes for S are thus derived as residuals.

[a] The ratio of each period's current price ratio to constant price ratio expressed as an index, with the 1885–89 ratio = 100. For example, col. 1 divided by col. 2 for each period, divided by the 1885–89 ratio of col. 1 to col. 2.

[b] The figures for 1947–55 are tentative, being simple averages of the five-year average centered on each period boundary.

subsequent years. These are given in table 2.12. The index column is intended to show the effects of changes in the relative prices (or terms of trade) between the two sectors, taking the initial values given. There are significant changes in the secular pattern. Relative productivities of sectors have often been discussed without distinguishing between real and value productivities. Failure to do so is misleading when the terms of trade change.

Let us consider the relationship between the patterns found for the real and for the current price series. In general a higher rate of productivity increase in the modern sectors, in this case represented by industry, leads to lower prices relative to the traditional sectors if the markets work more or less competitively.

In Japan's case, there seem to be three phases. First, until around the beginning of the 20th century, the pace of both the growing productivity gap and relative price changes were relatively moderate. The second phase covers the rest of the prewar period and perhaps extends to around 1960. The productivity gap widened, but corresponding changes in relative prices were too weak to offset this. The third phase may be too short to characterize, but the terms of trade seem to have turned in favor of low-productivity sectors with the effect of increasing their per capita income to a certain extent. The basic change in the demand–supply situation of labor is probably a major factor responsible for such a difference between the second and third phases.

Table 2.13 illustrates the overall performance of relative prices. In view of the price behavior of annual smoothed series, years of peaks and troughs are selected with the addition of 1911 and trough-to-

Table 2.13. Relative Inflation Rates

	A	Ma	S	PC	I	X	M	GNE deflator index
1887–1904	107.7	83.8	94.6	98.1	86.9	88.6	67.3	225.1
1897–1919	92.1	81.8	93.2	98.1	68.2	77.5	74.6	359.7
1904–30	80.3	69.5	123.0	99.5	72.8	58.0	61.4	242.4
1919–38	103.4	83.7	129.9	103.8	100.5	60.3	83.1	114.7
1887–1938	111.3	62.7	108.3	100.5	70.0	44.5	46.4	662.1

Source: REVISION of LTES 1:59 (table 3-6). Revision is in X and M, and thus in the GNE deflator. Underlying data are in appendix tables A30 for X and M, and A50 for all others.
Notes: For abbreviations see table 2.1.
  Noda discusses these data in ch. 12.

trough and peak-to-peak periods are used to show the trends. Distinct patterns are discernible. At the production stage, output prices of services and agriculture rise faster than the general price level while manufacturing prices rise more slowly. A corresponding contrast is seen for personal consumption compared to investment at the final demand stage. For international trade, prices generally increased at a slower rate, especially for exports (see further discussion in ch. 7).

The findings seem to have a number of significant implications. What we are concerned with here might be called spread effects of differential price rises at the primary production stage on other aspects of the inflationary growth of the economy. These effects can be described as follows. A sustained faster productivity increase in the modern sector, here represented by manufacturing, leads to ever-declining relative prices of modern goods. Together with the effects of import prices, this decline makes it possible to keep the relative prices of investment goods relatively low, though they are offset to a certain extent by a rise of relative output prices in the construction sector, as usually occurs internationally. Further, by way of industrial specialization supported by cheap labor, export prices rise least.

The fastest price rises are in services and agriculture, and these contribute to keeping consumer's goods and services prices relatively high. Slower productivity increases in these two traditional sectors, previously confirmed, are basically responsible for this price differential, although wage behavior mitigates it to a certain extent.

Spread effects cannot be ignored even for the traditional sectors. This is illustrated by the spectacular example of chemical fertilizers, which are produced by the manufacturing sector and used as a major modern input in agriculture. The fast decline in the relative prices of these intermediate goods was responsible for inducing technological progress in the traditional sectors (see Hayami and Ruttan 1971). Even with such effects, the net result was a relative price rise in agriculture and especially in services because it had the least spread effect. Postwar price performance is merely a strengthened process of these long-lasting forces with new effects from wage behavior in the low-productivity sectors.

Using the familiar GNE periodization, table 2.14 shows average annual rates of productivity growth for the aggregate and major sectors. The principal points in panel B are a sustained high rate of around 4% for industry, a declining trend for services, and a turning point from a trend of acceleration to deceleration for agriculture.

Table 2.14. Average Annual Rates of Increase in Productivity by Sector
(In percent)

	Simple Growth Rates				Weighted Growth Rates[a]				Productivity gain from sectoral shift
	A	N	S	NDP	A	N	S	Total	
A. Long-swing phases									
U 1887–97	1.47	3.42	2.04	2.56	0.56	0.46	0.99	2.01	0.55
D 1897–1904	1.52	4.05	−0.67	1.60	0.52	0.70	−0.32	0.90	0.70
U 1904–19	2.86	4.69	1.21	3.01	0.85	1.11	0.56	2.52	0.49
1904–11	2.91	6.14	−0.81	1.93	0.95	1.34	−0.37	1.92	0.01
1911–19	2.81	3.42	2.95	3.96	0.81	0.92	1.30	3.04	0.92
D 1919–30	0.64	3.44	−1.18	1.44	0.14	1.30	−0.47	0.97	0.47
U 1930–38	1.62	5.53	1.54	3.94	0.30	2.51	0.55	3.36	0.58
U 1955–64	4.40	8.92	6.93	9.02	0.58	4.31	2.67	7.76	1.26
B. Full-swing periods									
1887–1904[b]	1.49	3.68	0.92	2.16	0.53	0.57	0.45	1.55	0.61
1897–1919[c]	2.43	4.49	0.60	2.56	0.78	0.92	0.28	1.98	0.58
1904–30[b]	1.91	4.16	−0.19	2.35	0.49	1.28	−0.08	1.85	0.50
1919–38[c]	1.05	4.32	−0.03	2.49	0.21	1.80	−0.01	2.02	0.47

Source: Reproduced from LTES 1:54 (table 3–4).

Notes: Period average rates are based on annual growth rates calculated from smoothed series of both output in constant prices and labor employed. Growth rates of output per worker are simply derived by deducting the latter from the former.

[a] The weights are the averages of the share of output (smoothed values) at the beginning and the end years of each period.

[b] Trough to trough.

[c] Peak to peak.

Productivity differentials among sectors are not only large but have grown larger over time. This growth is simply an alternative expression of what we found previously with the simple ratio approach. The phenomenon itself appeared in our earlier estimates for agriculture and manufacturing and has been called differential structure to emphasize the growing gap of productivities between the modern and traditional sectors (Ohkawa and Rosovsky 1968). The revised agriculture and manufacturing series and the addition of services firmly establish this.

The trend to increased productivity appears stronger than swings during the initial phase of modern economic growth, again suggesting the initial phase had a growth mechanism different from that of subsequent periods. The rate of productivity increase in agriculture is treated in detail in chapter 4. Its initial acceleration may be reduced if there was a trend of increased working-days per worker, a highly possible phenomenon. Even so this achievement deserves particular attention. Accelerated growth took place not only in the modern sectors but also in the traditional sectors. This has been called concurrent growth (Ohkawa 1972, part III).

Aggregate productivity growth has two components: productivity proper and structural effects; increased sectoral productivity as well as labor's shift from low- to high-productivity sectors contributes to this growth. The former is measured by weighted growth rates in table 2.14 and the latter is roughly given by subtracting the sum of weighted sectoral growth rates from the NDP rate, as is shown in the table's last column. The relative magnitude of the shift term is significant in Japan's case and has been examined in detail elsewhere (Ohkawa 1977). Here attention is on the sectoral term. Panel A provides further confirmation of our conclusions on swings in terms of sectorals relative to the total. The contribution of services to aggregate swings is decisive, which suggests demand variation plays an important role in forming the swings. In panel B industry's trend acceleration is distinctly discernible in contrast to a deceleration of services.

Adjustments for changes in the quality and quantity of the labor force do not alter these conclusions with respect to the secular trend of divergence in the sectoral ratios of product per worker. Adjustments do result in less divergence (larger values of the ratio of agricultural to industrial labor and smaller values of the services to industry ratio) because industry is less affected than the others. But the question is whether the adjustments alter the pattern of greater equality through time. I suggest they do not.

Table 2.15. Ratio of Agriculture to Industrial Output Adjusted for Labor Force Composition

Census date	Period	Unadjusted	Adjusted for		Unadjusted	Adjusted for	
			Female workers	Family workers		Female workers	Family workers
		(In current prices)			(In constant prices)		
1920	1915–22	32.0	56.9	—	32.5	57.8	—
1930	1927–33	24.8	44.1	—	27.4	48.7	—
1940	1936–40	23.6	47.7	—	20.8	42.1	—
1950	1937–55	30.0	58.9	46.5	22.6	44.4	35.0
[a]	1955–60	28.9	58.9	45.4	22.5	45.9	35.3
[b]	1960–65	28.7	59.4	51.1	19.1	35.4	42.0

Source: Author's calculations.
Note: See explanation in text.
[a] Average of 1955 and 1960 censuses.
[b] Average of 1960 and 1965 censuses.

Adjustments require somewhat arbitrary assumptions, yet they are worthwhile for checking the point at issue. I illustrate this view with extreme examples for the different sectoral proportions of female workers. An assumption is to exclude female workers in agriculture while making no adjustment for industry. The resulting ratios are shown in table 2.15, columns 2 and 5, with the unadjusted figures shown for comparison. The period-to-period change is almost the same as before with a slight exception in case of current price series. I am not asserting female workers had no job opportunities in the nonagricultural sector. This exclusion is intended to illustrate that even such an extreme assumption does not alter our conclusion. One may contend this is not really the extreme case; all family workers should be excluded (table 2.15, cols. 3 and 6). Only for 1960–65 does this suggest a different pattern, and this relates to the turning point with respect to the demand–supply situation of labor around this period. For the ratio of service to industrial labor, such an adjustment produces almost no change.

SECULAR CHANGES IN THE PRODUCTION STRUCTURE

International comparisons of secular changes in the production structure are not as simple as comparisons of expenditures. Kuznets' systematic and laborious work (1971) provides relevant data for other countries. Although these data are somewhat limited for our specific purpose, I believe using them in comparison with ours permits us to draw broad conclusions.

Table 2.16 lists relevant items for all countries having sufficient data available from the initial period of their modern economic growth. A few countries composed largely of European settlers are excluded because their development is not comparable to that of established societies. Average annual rates of change are calculated, though the initial sectoral ratio of each country varies considerably. The secular trend of decline found for Japan also appears for most of the western industrial countries with respect to both the ratio of agricultural to industrial output (A/N) and the ratio of services to industrial output (S/N). This is particularly clear for the constant price series. Again as in Japan, S/N declines faster than A/N in western countries, suggesting the ratio of agriculture to services output has a generally rising trend.

Table 2.16. Output per Worker, Ratios by Sector and Secular Changes in Developed Countries

		Ratio to industrial output		Average annual rate of change[a]	
		Agriculture	Services		
		(A/N)	(S/N)	(A/N)	(S/N)
A. In constant price volumes					
Germany[a]	1850–59	1.22	3.10	−0.95	−1.58
	1935–38	0.52	0.73		
Sweden[c]	1861–70	0.56	1.60	−0.36	−0.57
	1963–67	0.39	0.89		
Italy[d]	1861–70	1.13	3.79	−0.76	−1.34
	1963–67	0.53	0.99		
United States	1839[e]	0.46	0.67	−1.01	−1.21
	1899[e]	0.25	0.47		
	1899[f]	0.67	0.98	−0.91	−1.24
	1929[f]	0.51	0.69		
Japan[g]	1885–89	0.68	3.71	−1.67	−2.74
	1960–65	0.19	0.46		
B. In current price volumes					
Great Britain	1801–11	1.84	2.03	−0.47	−0.26
	1907	1.15	1.56		
	1907	1.10	1.46	−0.27	−0.77
	1963–67	0.93	0.96		
Sweden	1861–70	0.51	1.14	−0.13	−0.24
	1963–67	0.45	0.86		
Italy	1861–70	1.09	2.33	−0.63	0.75
	1881–1900	0.96	2.72	−0.79	−1.20
	1963–67	0.51	1.04		
United States	1839	0.42	0.46	−0.31	0.39
	1899	0.34	0.81	0.86	−0.21
	1929	0.44	0.76	0.46	−0.40
	1963–65	0.52	0.66		
Japan	1885–89	0.42	1.75	−0.49	−0.91
	1960–65	0.92	0.87		

Source: Kuznets 1971, pp. 290–92 (table 45); Japan is from table 2-12. Kuznets gives the ratios as "sectoral product per worker relative to adjusted country-wide product per worker," and the ratio A/N is converted from this. S/N is cited directly from his table.

Notes: Output is mostly GDP, specifically excluding the output of financial sectors such as banking, insurance, and real estate and the income from dwellings. For Japan, NDP, imputed income for dwellings excluded, is used.

The ratios of sectoral labor productivities are taken in the same terms as for Japan. Some difference exists between these data and Japan's case with respect to the concept and coverage; however, the effects are felt to be minor and can essentially be ignored in order to derive broad conclusions.

Table 2.16 (continued)

[a]The average annual rate of change is calculated as follows. Let y_a and y_i stand, respectively, for the output per worker of sectors A and N. A compound rate of change G from year 0 to year t (n years) is given by

$$Yat = (1 + Gy_a)^n \cdot Yao,$$
$$Yit = (1 + Gy_i)^n \cdot Yio.$$

Therefore we have

$$\frac{Yat}{Yit} \bigg/ \frac{Yao}{Yio} = \left(\frac{1 + Gy_a}{1 + Gy_i}\right)$$

In the table, Gy_a/Gy_i is calculated, taking 100 as the initial ratio.
[b]1913 prices. [c]1959 prices. [d]1963 prices.
[e]1859 prices. [f]1929 prices. [g]1934–36 prices.

Despite all these common experiences, Japan is unique in its speed of change in constant prices. This is less true in current prices, so changes in the relative price structure must have been particularly important in Japan's case. This is derived from bridging two points in time. Unfortunately, available data for the interim are limited. Kuznets' data, given in tables 2.16 and 2.17, however, are informative. In several countries the ratios increase in recent years, though the precise dates of a shift in the secular trend cannot be determined. In another group of countries, however, a declining trend still appears, especially for lower income countries, though we should be cautious in interpreting this pattern.

Table 2.17's cross-section pattern is not consistent with the secular trends mentioned above. However, since the initial ratio of A/N tends to be higher in developed countries, a tendency for A/N to increase might appear in cross-section observations.

Japan is perhaps a model of differential structure in the sense its rapidly growing gap in sectoral productivities has been sustained without a turning point. This is relevant to contemporary lower income countries, with some qualification, with respect to the different behaviors of the ratios. S/N in constant prices tends to decline for all cases whereas A/N in constant prices has a mixed timepath. To clarify this, the ratio of agricultural to nonagricultural output (A/(N + S)) is relevant. Its reciprocal (N + S)/A is a weighted average of N/A and S/A (the sectoral shares of labor are the weights). A tendency of secular decrease in S/A is universal and tends to cancel out a rising trend in N/A, with the net effect the rate of change in A/(N + S) is relatively moderate, particularly when the two weights are about equal. If A/(N + S) is adopted, even Japan's secular trend of a growing pro-

Table 2.17. Recent Changes in Output per Worker, Ratios by Sector

A. Time series for developed countries

	Constant prices			Current prices	
	A/N	S/N		A/N	S/N
Belgium (1963 prices)			Great Britain		
1910	0.47	2.21	1907	1.10	1.46
1963–67	1.05	1.12	1963–67	0.93	0.96
Germany, Federal Republic					
(1954 prices)			Netherlands		
1950	0.28	0.95	1950	0.67	0.80
1963–67	0.41	0.69	1965	0.76	0.92
Denmark (1955 prices)			Denmark		
1950–51	0.69	0.74	1950–51	0.73	0.74
1963–67	0.78	0.68	1963–67	0.55	0.75
Norway (1963 prices)			Norway		
1950	0.54	0.96	1950	0.48	0.78
1963–67	0.35	0.78	1963–67	0.37	0.82

B. Cross sections of postwar years for group of countries

			A/N	S/N	A/(N + S)
I	($127)	1950	0.36	1.08	0.35
		1960	0.35	0.92	0.37
II	($169)	1950	0.45	1.18	0.41
		1960	0.43	1.00	0.42
III	($299)	1950	0.52	1.43	0.43
		1960	0.44	1.11	0.41
IV	($651)	1950	0.51	0.90	0.54
		1960	0.65	0.81	0.70
V	($1,018)	1950	0.58	0.79	0.54
		1960	0.85	0.67	0.66

Source: Panel A is from Kuznets 1971, pp. 290–92 (table 45). The procedure is the same as for table 2.16. Panel B is from Kuznets 1971, p. 298 (table 46). The procedure is the same as in table 2.16. A/(N + S) is converted from (N + S)/A in the original table.
Notes: For abbreviations see table 2.16.

Notes for panel A are the same as for table 2.16.

In panel B the groups are arrayed in increasing order of 1950 GDP per capita in 1958 U.S. dollars and the sectoral shares in product are in constant prices.

Table 2.18. Ratio of Agricultural to Nonagricultural Output (A/N + S), Constant Price Series

1885–95	1908–14	1927–33	1936–40	1955–60	1960–65
0.92	0.28	0.28	0.24	0.27	0.26

Source: Calculated from the same data used for table 2.12.

ductivity gap shows a break (table 2.18). So unlike Kuznets' case, this term is not appropriate for our purpose unless qualified.

One may suppose the degree of differential structure is associated with the rate of aggregate growth, since Japan ranks first in this regard as well as in growth rates of product per worker. However, table 2.16 shows a fairly wide range in the average annual rates of change in A/N and S/N, and it appears impossible to find any clear association between these and the differences in aggregate growth rates. For example, Sweden is the only western country whose growth rate per capita income can compare to Japan, but its average rate of change in sectoral ratio of productivities is rather low. The supposed association implicitly assumes the productivity growth rate in the modern sector is high compared to that in the traditional sector and is accompanied by a fairly fast increase in the labor force employed there. However, Sweden is a counterexample.

To be conclusive in this respect, requires the laborious task of comparing the rates of sectoral productivity growth internationally. But even without it, a broad picture can be drawn. Japan's rate of productivity growth in industry as represented by manufacturing appears to be among the fastest, and that of agriculture (excluding forestry and fishing) appears to rank at least above the average of other advanced nations. Less informative is services, but I am inclined to say at least the prewar growth rate of output per worker in this sector might be less than the average of developed countries. A high rate of productivity growth in the modern sectors is certainly relevant to forming the differential structure, but at the same time the traditional sectors, particularly agriculture, can also be growing fairly rapidly by international standards.

Using sectoral shares of gainfully occupied population as an indicator shows Japan was economically backward compared to western nations. In Japan the share of labor in agriculture in 1870–80 was 65–77%, close to the developing countries' share today. It is impossible to find western nations with such a high range in the initial years of their modern economic growth. A share slightly over 60% is found only for Scandinavian countries. Japan's lack of natural resources is not only in minerals but also in arable land. The extremely unfavorable man–land ratio at the time of the Meiji Restoration (1868) was one of Japan's principal initial conditions, and little could be done to expand the cultivated area even with new technology (see ch. 4). This is again similar to the situation now facing most of the developing populous countries in Asia.

Table 2.19. Capital Per Worker in 1934–36 Prices

	Agriculture	Industry	Service
1905			
in yen	205	791	489
Index[a]	26	100	62
1936			
in yen	533	3219	882
Index[a]	17	100	27
Increase[b]	260	407	180

Source: Calculated from capital data in appendix table A42 and work force data in appendix table A54.
[a] Agriculture and service as a percentage of industry.
[b] 1936 as a percentage of 1905 level.

Thus labor and land are the factors most relevant to forming Japan's pattern of differential structure because they continued to restrain the rate of output growth per occupied person in the traditional sectors. Yet agricultural productivity increased somewhat. Apart from the initial growth phase, previously discussed, the sectoral labor and capital allocation took a dualistic growth pattern. The modern technology borrowed from abroad required larger amounts of capital per worker than traditional technology. Further, the capital–labor proportion of modern technology is relatively rigid, whereas that of traditional technology is somewhat flexible. These characteristics imply a close connection between the growth rate of capital stock and the growth rate of labor productivity in dualistic growth. The pace of transferring labor from the traditional to the modern sector is constrained by the rate of capital accumulation, and additional capital applied to transferring a worker to the modern sector results in a marked increase in productivity. By contrast, workers who cannot be absorbed into modern sectors for lack of capital can be and are absorbed into the traditional sectors at lower levels of product per worker.

Some insight is given by our revised estimates of capital stock, summarized in table 2.19. Comparing the three major sectors, the rate at which labor productivity increased corresponds broadly to the rate at which capital per worker increased. Distribution of capital and labor within the service sector needs to be clarified, particularly because modern activities had an expanding share. However, these data do suggest capital stock increases in the traditional sectors were substantial.

Table 2.20. Compound Annual Growth Rates of the Labor Force in Services and Agriculture

(In percent)

Upswings	1887–96	1904–11	1911–21	1933–38
	0.25	0.26	−0.27	0.24
Downswings	1896–1904	1921–33		
	0.54	0.70		

Source: Computed from appendix table A54.

The performance of labor employed seems to reveal what we call residual employment in the traditional sectors. A comparison of labor growth between industry and services shows an inverse pattern of changes. During upswings the industrial labor force grew faster whereas in downswings services grows faster, with the possible exception of 1931–37. Agriculture also exhibits the same inverse movement with industry. This is confirmed using a slightly different periodization in table 2.20.

The residual employment is basically of a structural nature, forming an overoccupied situation in the traditional sectors. This concept pertains to an ongoing situation where the marginal product of labor gainfully occupied in a sector is lower than that of the modern sectors. Of course the differentials in average labor productivity can exist competitively to the extent differing output elasticities of labor among sectors cancel, equalizing marginal productivities. For Japan we have scattered evidence of a sustained and even growing inequality of marginal productivities and hence overoccupied employment in the traditional sectors, (Ohkawa 1972), and we believe this is the core of the differential structure. This pattern may be particularly relevant to the contemporary developing countries, a point also suggested by Kuznets (1971, p. 302).

CAPITAL–OUTPUT RATIO

The historical pattern of the capital–output ratio in its incremental term ($I/\Delta GNP$) tells us about the quantitative relationship between the output growth rate and the investment proportion since $I/\Delta GNP = (I/GNP)(GNP/\Delta GNP)$. As for the secular performance of the ratio in western developed countries, research by Kuznets (1956–64) and others suggests no common pattern. This may be due to the com-

Table 2.21. Incremental Capital–Output Ratios for Swing Periods

Upswings	1887–97	1904–19	1930–38	1953–69
I/ΔGNE	2.87	3.83	4.59	2.62

Downswings	1897–1904	1919–30	1938–53	
I/ΔGNE	5.40	6.77	(46.9)	

Notes: Military is INCLUDED in investment. I/ΔGNE is computed from (I/GNE)/ (ΔGNE/GNE), with I and GNE both measured in real terms. I/GNE is the average over the period, and ΔGNE/GNE is the average of annual rates in the period. The extraordinarily large 1938–53 ratio suggests a limit to this sort of approach, at least in the face of major dislocations such as war.

plexity of factors involved in determining the magnitude of this simple term. On the other hand, Japan's incremental capital–output ratio seems to show a secular pattern. Some authors believe Japan's high growth rate can be explained by its lower capital–output ratio compared to the western experience, and this may in fact be a factor. Point-in-time international comparisons of the ratio cannot be precise in part because of differences in price structures. The same problem applies to long-term observations, which are further complicated since the ratio depends in large part on how a country utilizes available capacity, technology, and resources.

Trend acceleration of the output growth rate took place with an ever-increasing investment proportion; that is, ΔGNP/GNP and I/GNP, and hence I and GNP have parallel trends, suggesting no sizable change in the capital–output ratio is expected for the broad historical pattern. In fact, an unchanged capital–output ratio was suggested in our earlier estimates (Ohkawa 1972). Table 2.21 shows the aggregate incremental capital–output ratio for the up- and downswing phases demarcated in table 1.2. The measured ratio differs greatly over the period, which may be surprising because these are averages based on smoothed series which eliminate short-term fluctuations. Between up and down phases, however, a broad regular difference is seen, with smaller ratios (2.6 to 4.6) for ups and larger ratios (5.4 to 6.8) for downs.

As for secular patterns, the ratio tends to increase through the three prewar upswings. This is also true for both downswings. In the postwar upswing the ratio decreases even below the initial ratio for 1887–97. Taken together, these observations suggest a secular trend of increase during the prewar period and of decrease in the postwar years. A trend of increase in the capital–output ratio from the initial phase to some certain stage of development has been asserted by several authors, for example, Bicanic (1962).

Meaningful sectoral decomposition requires measurement of the capital–output ratio by sector. Because of data limitations, a comprehensive approach is not possible for the entire period under review. A preliminary formulation is an agriculture–nonagriculture division. Even in this simple treatment a consistent coverage of output and investment cannot be expected. Nevertheless, it sheds light on some significant points. Table 2.22 lists all the data in terms of the investment periodization by now familiar to us. An extremely small ratio for the nonagricultural sector (panel B, col. 4) in the early years may not be reliable. What we primarily want to clarify here is the pattern of changes over time.

Long swings are seen for the nonagricultural sector, with a trend of increase for the first three periods, whereas agriculture shows no such swings. To that extent, nonagriculture is primarily responsible for the aggregate pattern previously found. Much more significant are the long-term trends in panel B. Nonagriculture displays a distinct tendency to increase in every prewar period except the last, whether measured trough to trough or peak to peak. On the other hand, the ratio in agriculture seems more irregular. However, the sequence of the average values in each successive upswing and downswing at least shows no tendency toward change in the earlier years, in sharp contrast with a tendency of distinct increase in the subsequent years. Data discontinuity prevents presenting postwar ratios, but a larger ratio in agriculture has been confirmed in Ohkawa and Rosovsky (1973, pp. 95–117).

The different historical pattern found between agriculture and nonagriculture is important, as the weighted ratios in table 2.22, panel B, show. The initial growth phase is characterized by relatively high weights for agriculture in both investment and the capital–output ratio. This is relevant to the large proportion of self-investment in traditional agriculture, that is, the input of self-employed labor and the growth of plants and livestock. It is important to distinguish between self-investment and investment involving money outlays, particularly when discussing sectoral flow possibilities for savings–investment. Subsequently, a declining weight for agriculture meant

Table 2.22. Incremental Capital–Output Ratios in Agriculture and Nonagriculture for Prewar Swing Periods

A. Swings

Period (length in years)	Agriculture			Nonagriculture		
	Output growth rate[b]	Investment proportion[c]	Capital–output ratio[d]	Output growth rate[b]	Investment proportion[c]	Capital–output ratio[d]
1. (U) 1887–94 (7)	1.23	7.57	6.15	4.68	2.76	0.59
2. (D) 1894–1901 (7)	2.73	7.42	2.72	2.46	3.58	1.46
3. (U) 1901–08 (7)	1.10	7.52	6.84	2.38	4.70	1.97
4. (D) 1908–12 (4)	1.99	7.79	3.91	2.36	6.76	2.87
5. (U) 1912–18 (6)	2.27	7.39	3.23	5.48	9.94	1.81
6. (D) 1918–25 (9)	0.00	8.02	∞[e]	3.31	10.16	3.07
7. (D') 1925–32 (9)	0.94	9.17	9.76	3.71	7.42	2.00
8. (U) 1932–38 (6)	1.72	8.63	5.60	5.03	10.95	2.17

B. Trough to Trough (T-T) and Peak to Peak (P-P)

	Simple capital–output ratio		Weighted capital–output ratio[f]		
	Agriculture	Nonagriculture	Agriculture	Nonagriculture	Total[g]
(T-T) 1887–1901 (14)	4.44	1.03	1.08	0.83	1.91
(P-P) 1894–1908 (14)	4.78	1.72	1.39	1.31	2.70
(T-T) 1901–12 (11)	5.77	2.30	1.25	1.80	3.05
(P-P) 1908–18 (10)	3.50	2.23	0.63	1.82	2.45
(T-T) 1912–25 (13)	8.00*	2.49	0.71	2.31	3.01
(P-T') 1918–32 (14)	15.33*	2.54	0.59	2.47	3.06
(P-P) 1925–38 (13)	7.84	2.08	0.49	1.79	2.28

Table 2.22 (continued)

Source: A REVISION of LTES 1:40 (table 2.7). The revisions are in the nonagriculture entries in panel A, and thus in the weighted ratios in panel B. Output data are from appendix table A 12 (LTES 1:227, table 25); investment data are from appendix table A42.

[a] Agriculture includes forestry and fishery.

[b] Output is real GDP excluding imputed rent for residential buildings. Figures are averages of annual values except for the periods marked with asterisks, which are simple bridge calculations between the beginning and end years.

[c] Investment is gross. Figures are averages of the proportion in the beginning and end years of each period.

[d] Calculated as the investment proportion divided by the output growth rate using smoothed series.

[e] The ratio for agriculture approaches infinity since the output growth rate is near zero.

[f] The weighted capital–output ratio is calculated as follows (subscript a denotes agriculture, n, denotes nonagriculture). The relation between the aggregate and sectoral capital–output ratio is defined as

$$\frac{I_a}{\Delta Y_a} \cdot \frac{\Delta Y_a}{\Delta Y} + \frac{I_n}{\Delta Y_n} \cdot \frac{\Delta Y_n}{\Delta Y} = \frac{I}{\Delta Y}$$

The weight is then calculated from

$$\frac{\Delta Y_a}{\Delta Y} = \frac{\Delta Y_a}{Y_a} \Big/ \frac{\Delta Y}{Y} \cdot \frac{Y_a}{Y}$$

[g] Actually, corresponds approximately to the ratio for private nonresidential investment rather than the aggregate capital–output ratio.

the sector's rising capital–output ratio had little influence on the aggregate ratio. Instead the sustained rise in the nonagricultural ratio became the major contributor to increasing the aggregate ratio.

It is beyond the scope of this volume to explain the factors that shaped such a historical pattern of capital–output ratios. The following are, however, my suggestions. In agriculture, increased use of biological and chemical technology helped keep the capital–output ratio almost unchanged during the initial growth phase, despite a significant investment proportion (larger than has been suggested by some authors). A rise in the ratio for the interwar years was basically due to a slowdown of this type of technological progress (see ch. 4).

The rising trend in the nonagricultural ratio may be due to a combination of three factors. (1) Modernization itself increases the capital–output ratio, as the ratio is generally higher for modern, compared to traditional, production organization even in the same industry. (2) As has often been suggested, economic modernization requires increasing investment in infrastructure and the facilitating sectors, which involves especially high capital–output ratios. (3) For an economically backward country, technology borrowed from abroad is essential for economic modernization. Time and experience are needed to establish these technologies and adapt them to the domestic situation, a process that differs from one industry to another. During this transition, an industry's capital–output ratio is higher than when full efficiency has been realized. In Japan's case, the second factor is vividly illustrated by comparing manufacturing (including mining) and the facilitating industries (transportation, communication, and public utilities) in terms of the sectoral distribution of output and capital in the private nonagricultural sector. (For further discussion see Ohkawa and Rosovsky 1973: appendix note (first factor), ch. 4 (second factor), and ch. 8 (third factor).)

References follow chapter 3.

3

Data and Methods

Kazushi Ohkawa and Miyohei Shinohara

Japan is a country with rich data sources even for the early years of development. This may be in part the result of efforts taken by the Meiji leaders of economic growth, as symbolized by a voluminous survey, *Kogyo Iken*, published by the government in 1884. These efforts probably relate to an established tradition of government and merchant record keeping. The available data, however, are mostly production oriented and are rather poor for income and expenditure patterns. This is why our earlier estimates used the output–production approach. In the revised edition of his book (1956) Yamada lists series estimated from three aspects—production, income, and expenditures—for years since 1918. The discrepancies are enormous.

The LTES project has been an effort to make consistent estimates of product and expenditure, but no overall attempt has been made with respect to the income approach because much more data exploration and estimation are needed. This shortcoming is not unique to Japan. Feinstein (1972) used a three-aspect (output, income, and expenditure) approach in estimating the United Kingdom's long-term economic statistics, and the differences between the expenditure and income approaches are large, especially for the early years.

In this chapter data and estimating procedures used in chapters 1 and 2 are discussed. Each of the other chapters has a similar section, so the emphasis is on modifications made in the process of integrating the component series into GNE and GNP. Subsequent sections deal with overall reliability of the current price series by examining the discrepancies between output, income, and expenditure estimates and with the problems of deflating. Linking the prewar LTES estimates with the official postwar ones is also discussed. A final section is an

overview of attempts to construct historical series of economic activity
and how these attempts relate to contemporary developing countries.

LTES volume 1 integrates the data in other LTES volumes into an
estimate of national income and expenditure, and also provides some
related data. However, estimates for some items are still entirely
lacking (e.g., nonhousehold consumption) or are partly so (estimates
of value added by manufacturing and service output, and regional
differences in consumer prices are example). All such problems in
the process of integration are being dealt with on Ohkawa's responsibility with the help of Nobukiyo Takamatsu.

Establishing consistency among component series has required
further revision for two reasons. Each LTES volume has been written
on its authors' own responsibility, although within a general framework
set at the start of the project. The framework was flexible; no rigid,
predetermined ideas or formulas were imposed on any members of
the project. A few disadvantages have appeared as a result. There are
discrepancies among some of the related estimates (for example,
between capital formation and capital stock); and there have been
differing views on how to interpret the original data (for example,
producers' durables in the nonagricultural sector and some items of
personal consumption). Second, a longer than expected period has
been required to complete the project, and simultaneous estimation
of all items has been impossible. Emergence of newly discovered data
and/or development of better estimating procedures has sometimes
created discrepancies between estimates in early volumes and later
ones (such as changes caused by revision of export and import prices).

Revisions caused by better estimating procedures have been worked
out without difficulties, whereas integration work due to new data
has required intensive discussions. More agreement has been achieved
in this volume, but discrepancies among related estimates remain
because differing views of data interpretation have not been completely
eliminated. In such cases, Ohkawa has selected one of the series to
compute national income in chapters 1 and 2 and in LTES 1.

Postwar official national income statistics have been revised comprehensively twice, and minor changes have been made occasionally.
For the years 1945–50/51, the reliability of data for this period is
questionable, and as yet no revision has been carried out. LTES

estimates end at 1940. For the years 1941–44 estimates of the Keizei Antei Honbu are available, but again reliability is a problem, at least compared to our series. The tumult caused by the war and its aftermath makes revision of the estimates for these years extremely hard. No one has attempted an estimate for 1945. However, without presenting data for the 1940s, we cannot really link our series and the postwar official series. Thus our link is tentative, as discussed later in this chapter.

NATIONAL PRODUCT AND EXPENDITURE

Framework and Sources

Chapters 1 and 2 primarily present estimates first published in LTES 1, and more detail is found in the English Summary of Estimating Procedures (LTES 1 : 159–73). The overall framework and the revisions since LTES 1 was published in 1975 are discussed here.

Table 3.1 shows the components for each of the three approaches to looking at a country's aggregate economic activity. For the income approach we have estimated national income, indirect taxes, and current subsidies. For the expenditure and output approaches the names of the members of our research group most responsible for each item are listed followed by the LTES volume containing the detailed data and the chapter in this volume discussing and summarizing those data.

Historical data on national income have generally been derived from expenditure and output data using income product ratio data by industry, but direct income estimates have been made for the service sector. The statistical discrepancies among the three approaches should be checked. For our series, however, this is not comprehensively possible because of the lack of independence among the estimates, so only income/output versus expenditure will be discussed. Our series is the first permitting this kind of reliability check. Compared to our preliminary estimates of national product in GRJE the present series have made great progress. The GRJE data are almost entirely output approach, and a partial check against the limited available income and expenditure-approach data shows discrepancies are sizable and fluctuate widely from year to year. For the estimates here, statistical discrepancies appear to be within an acceptable range when adequate qualifications are made. This is discussed further later in

Table 3.1. Components of Different Approaches to Measuring Economic Activity

Income approach

National income (NNP (net national product) at factor cost)
    + Indirect taxes
    − Current subsidies
= NNP at market prices
    + Depreciation (provision for consumption of fixed capital)
    + Statistical discrepancies
= GNP at market prices
(the first three items have been estimated)

Expenditure approach

Private consumption (Shinohara: LTES 6; ch. 8)
    + Government consumption (Emi: LTES 7; ch. 10)
    + Gross domestic fixed-capital formation (Emi: LTES 4; and Ishiwata: LTES 3;
        ch. 9)
    + Increase in stocks (not estimated)
    + Exports of goods and services and factor income received from abroad (Yamamoto:
        LTES 14; ch. 7, with Yamazawa)
    + Imports of goods and services and factor income paid abroad (Yamamoto: LTES
        14; ch. 7, with Yamazawa)
= GNE

Output approach

Agriculture (including forestry and fishery) (Agriculture: Yamada and Hayami;
        Forestry: Kumazaki; LTES 9; ch. 4)
    + Manufacturing (including mining) (Shinohara: LTES 10; ch. 5)
    + Facilitating industries (transportation, communication, public utilities) (railroads
        and electric utilities: Minami: LTES 12; incorporated by Ohkawa in LTES 1;
        ch. 2)
    + Construction (SIL 2; ch. 2)
    + Services (wholesale and retail trade, banking, insurance, real estate, and public
        administration) (SIL 3; incorporated by Ohkawa in LTES 1; ch. 2)
= NNP at market prices

Notes: The individual responsible for the data collection, the LTES volume containing
the detailed data and Japanese discussion of them, and the chapter in this book are given
in parentheses. Also see LTES 1:165–67.

the chapter. There are other partial checks. Estimates of factor shares
by Minami and Ono (ch. 11) use an income approach for the nonagriculture sector for 1906–40. The discrepancies between the output
and income approaches are acceptable except for the industrial sector
in the 1920s.

One major gap in our estimates under the expenditure approach is

Table 3.2. Inventories as a Percentage of GNE

Period	Percentage	Period	Percentage
1886–97	3.96	1898–1903	2.12
1913–19	4.13	1904–12	1.31
1931–39	5.67	1920–30	0.11
1955–61	4.70	1962–65	2.72

Source: Inventory data from Fujino and Akiyama 1973; GNE data from appendix tables A1 (prewar) and A2 (postwar).

the absence of data on increase in stocks. Our examination of the scattered data suggested we would not be able to arrive at an acceptable series. Immediately after we finished LTES volume 1, Fujino and Akiyama published their own research on this problem. Table 3.2 shows their estimates of inventory changes as a percentage of our GNE estimates using the GNE swing periodization discussed in chapter 1. The ratio seems reasonable for both up and down swings, and we believe this is the best series there is at present. However, we do not include the Fujino–Akiyama series in our GNE estimate for two reasons. Although their figures seem consistent with ours over each swing phase, on an annual basis this is not necessarily so and further examination is needed to identify the reason for this. In addition, the series used here for private consumption and fixed-capital formation include some inventory changes. At present we are not able to eliminate possible duplication. Use of moving averages— usually seven-year for the prewar period, based on the average length of the Juglar cycle (Fujino 1965)—should eliminate most inventory fluctuation.

Modification of LTES Series

In preparing the national income estimates for LTES 1 and this book, a number of modifications were made to component series originally published in other LTES volumes.

Consumption

The largest change was for private consumption expenditure. Shinohara's current price series appears to be increasingly over-estimated as we go back to earlier years, mainly because the adjustments for regional price differences are too conservative. However, there are no systematic data to measure regional variations directly over time. Using postwar data for regional price differences between urban and rural districts and an index of urbanization in terms of population distribution, indirect estimates were made of prewar differences. All consumption items were then divided into two groups. The first, group A, is major food and fuel products from the agricultural sector, for which both farm (nationwide average) and Tokyo retail prices are available for the entire prewar period. All other items except house rent belong to group B.

For group A the price level of items bought by nonfarm households located between rural districts and big cities such as Tokyo was constructed using the weighted average of the rural and big-city price indexes. Farm prices are weighted by a ratio of producers' self-consumption to the total amount of production of each good, and Tokyo retail prices are weighted by an urbanization index (a ratio of the population of the six largest cities to total population). For group B the long-term trend of narrowing regional price differences is tentatively assumed to be similar in both the pre- and postwar periods. Using postwar government regional price data for personal consumption, the annual rate of change in the ratio of nationwide to Tokyo prices is calculated in terms of its elasticity with respect to an urbanization index (in this case, expressed by the ratio of farm population to total population). For 1950–67 it is 0.1489, which implies regional price differences decreased about 0.15% for each 1% decrease in the farm population ratio. Figures obtained by a direct application of this coefficient have been compared to other scattered data and to the price difference performance of group A. Although the 0.15 value for elasticity appears good for most of the Meiji period, we believe it should be reduced by half, to 0.075, for 1906–40. Imputed house rent is also reestimated to correct for possible underestimation in LTES 6 (see LTES 4:125).

Shinohara's original estimate is of private rather than personal consumption, including the expenditures of private nonprofit institutions as well as so-called business consumption. Although the latter is excluded from postwar official estimates of private consumption, we believe it is better to include it in view of the real circumstances of Japanese society. Lack of data makes it extremely difficult to separate expenditures for business consumption from those of total consumption. In our view business and community consumption must have been fairly large as we go back to earlier years. This is a question to be further explored.

The consumption components in chapter 8 add to more than total consumption as given in chapter 1 (and LTES 1) because only aggregate consumption was recomputed. Although price variations among regions adjusted for in the aggregate series were different for individual items, the series in chapter 8 nonetheless reflect the composition and patterns of consumption.

Gross Domestic Capital Formation

A combination of three approaches has been used to estimate gross domestic capital formation: by sector (private versus government), by industry, and by type (producers' durable equipment and construction). Because of limited data, estimates by both use and production are combined.

For the private agricultural sector, an indirect estimate based on capital stock data is used. This material is from LTES 3 adjusted for an increase in the expected lives of buildings and structures and agricultural implements. In addition, small agricultural implements are excluded, because they are defined as current expenditures, and nonresidential buildings and structures have been reestimated in association with the capital stock used for direct farm production (such as livestock, perennial plants, and machinery) using postwar cross-section data (Norinsho 1955).

Producers' durable equipment in private nonagricultural industries for 1905–40 is taken from Ishiwata's estimates in LTES 3. This differs from the capital formation estimates by Emi in LTES 4. The discrepancy between the two comes essentially from their different views on interpreting the limited available data. Emi estimated total producers' durable equipment and investment (both military and nonmilitary) by the commodity-flow method and then deducted his calculation for government investment to obtain the private sector as a residual. His estimate for the government sector uses the government accounts and is thus an expenditure approach. Ishiwata, on the other hand, estimated total nonmilitary producers' durable equipment for the nonprimary sector without a breakdown between private and government. Emi's estimate for nonmilitary government investment is subtracted from the capital formation series implied by Ishiwata's capital stock series to give the private nonagricultural sector investment series used here and in LTES 1.

The modifications made in the other components of GNE and NNP are included in the notes and sources for the tables presenting these series in the appendix.

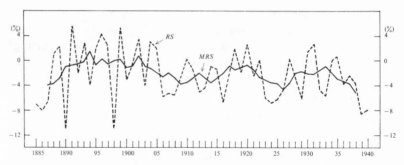

Fig. 3.1. Statistical Discrepancies

Source: Reproduced from LTES 1:72 (fig. 4-1).
RS: annual figures of (GNE − GNP)/GNE
MRS: smoothed series (seven-year moving averages)

Overall Qualification of Current Price Series

The difference between GNE and GNP, called SD (statistical discrepancies), is used in this section to test the series. Appendix table A9 gives the annual figures for SD, and figure 3.1 charts the ratio of SD to GNE.

The smooth series in figure 3.1 is important for the major purpose of identifying historical patterns. Except at the end of the 1930s it ranges between +2 and −4%, implying a systematic bias of GNE being less than GNP. From the mid 1890s until 1905 the ratio of SD to GNP is relatively close to zero. From 1905 on, the size of its negative value increases, suggesting different systematic causes between the two periods. The average SD ratio is −1.3% before 1905 and −2.8% after 1905. One source of these systematic discrepancies is of course the lack of estimates of inventory changes. Another source is duplication of interest income estimates. Rather than making arbitrary adjustments of one kind or another we have outlined our interpretation of the causes in the hope that it will serve as a useful suggestion to users.

Inventory changes explain about 1.7 percentage points of SD before 1905 and 1.4 percentage points after 1905. This is based on taking a flat half of the Fujino–Akiyama estimates of inventory changes on the assumptions the smoothed average of SD has eliminated annual fluctuations and half the inventories are already included in our estimate of the growth of domestic capital formation, as discussed earlier. Interest duplication is perhaps one percentage point of SD on average, though larger in earlier years, judging from reliable data provided by official estimates for the years since 1953.

With these possible adjustments the ratio of SD to GNE fluctuates between -2 and $+2\%$ for the period since 1905, but for years before then, discrepancies are still quite large. These figures are more guesses than rigorous modifications. We feel our series from around 1905 probably have no systematic bias beyond these. In the Meiji period the data sources are more limited and less reliable, and this contributes to greater discrepancies.

Why is GNE greater than GNP? A definite answer is impossible, but the following are relevant. When the commodity-flow method was applied, a constant margin was used for estimating both consumption and investment expenditures. The margin in the broadest sense pertains to the total cost of distributing goods, from the primary production stage (farm, factory) to the final demand stage. Despite our adjustments, regional price differentials may still be underestimated for consumption goods and services. In the absence of estimates of self-produced income generated by self-supplied fixed investment of farm households, agricultural income is underestimated. Indirect estimates of service sector income are another source of differences. All these topics are discussed more completely in LTES 1 (pp. 171–73).

The smoothed series of the SD ratio shows three broad swings: 1887–1909, 1908–26, and 1926–38. The first one and a half swings, that is until around 1920, can be broadly associated with the long swings discussed in chapters 1 and 2; however, throughout the entire period and especially after 1920 the relatively large minus ratio can be explained by ad hoc factors. Two of the technical assumptions made in our estimates are relevant to this pattern: the constant margin ratio already mentioned caused GNE to be greater than GNP in upswings and the reverse to be true in downswings; and our provisions for the consumption of fixed capital are estimated by a direct calculation under assumptions on service lives that differ somewhat from those implied in certain available business accounting records. As discussed in the section on savings in chapter 1, actual depreciation tends to be larger during upswings and smaller during downswings, while our estimates are straight line. This helps explain the strange performances of private net savings tentatively estimated. During the long downswing of the 1920s net savings appears quite small and even has negative values.

Turning to the annual fluctuation of the SD ratio, there are quite a few years SD is over 4% and in seven years it is over 10%. The adjustment suggested for the smooth series would still leave these years with fairly large discrepancies. The effect of crop fluctuations in the very early period is probably quite important here, as consumption undoubtedly fluctuated much less than actual production and our consumption estimates are based on a constant ratio of output. In the case of rice, the elasticity of its consumption with respect to crop fluctuations has been estimated as 0.4–0.5 (Ohkawa 1945, ch. 4). This helps explain all the early years except 1885 and 1887. Other ad hoc factors include, for 1923–25, possible defects in the original data due to the Kanto earthquake, and for 1939–40, the extraordinary military expenditures (ringunhi) as discussed in chapter 10.

All these comments are intended to indicate the degree of reliability in these estimates. However, an acceptable range of statistical discrepancies cannot necessarily be considered a genuine check of reliability when the same original data sources are used for both output and expenditure estimates, as has been unavoidable in some of our series. Users are therefore cautioned to heed the description of data and methods in the individual chapters. When users pay careful attention to the qualifications, these series are reliable enough for describing broad historical patterns.

Deflating

There are both conceptual and technical problems in estimating any series in real terms for such a long period of time. Among the problems remaining in our series because of data limitations are weakness of the producers' durable price indexes, use of cost estimates in construction (profits are not included), substitution of the private consumer price index for government expenditure other than personnel, and indirect procedures used in the service sector as discussed in chapter 6. Important new work by Yamamoto and Yamazawa on the export and import price indexes appears in chapter 7. This is a revision from LTES 1, and of course it has caused adjustment in a number of aggregate indexes. As is discussed more fully in chapter 12, the various price indexes are not uniform in their method of calculation.

COMPARISON WITH PREVIOUS ESTIMATES

Insofar as there are differences between series in this book and those in the LTES volumes, as well as in monographs written by members of our research group, the data used in this book take precedence. Many of the series have been significantly revised since our preliminary work was published in GRJE in 1957. This evolution is discussed by Yasuba (1973, p. 165), although some of the series have been further revised since then.

OUTLINE OF DIFFERENCES WITH OTHER ESTIMATES OF NATIONAL PRODUCT DATA

Miyohei Shinohara and Nobukiyo Takamatsu

Several basic secondary sources have differences in data on national product and its components. This section is an attempt to dispel any confusion readers may have in using the various studies of long-term changes in the Japanese economy. The studies are LTES 1 on national income, LTES 3 on capital stock, SIL (an in-house study of the data and methods used in the LTES project), Ohkawa and Rosovsky 1973 (here abbreviated OR), and this volume (abbreviated PJED).

PJED and LTES 1

Both GNP and GNE are identical in current prices, but the price deflators for exports and imports have been revised since LTES 1 appeared; GNE in constant prices is different. While this changes many of the series (as noted in PJED's tables), LTES 1 is still very much usable as a source of more detailed data than given in PJED for many series, particularly the unrevised current price ones.

LTES 1 and OR

GNE, in current prices in LTES 1, is less than that in OR except for 1940. There are two reasons for this. The balance of payments differs because payments of services and transfers to Taiwan for the colonial period 1911–40 are included in "payments to the rest of the world" in LTES (1:197, col. 8) but not in OR (p. 299, col. 11). In LTES 1 an adjustment was made for regional differences in housing and land rent, but this was not done in OR.

For NDP in current prices, LTES 1 is a bit higher before 1920 and lower after 1921. Net factor income from abroad differs since 1911, due to revisions of Korea's data conducted by Yuzo Yamamoto for LTES 14. Yamamoto has also made some revisions to other current account components and these are included in PJED and LTES 1 and 14. The agriculture component of NDP is a little higher in LTES since revised capital stock data are used, changing the amounts of depreciation and current input in agriculture and forestry somewhat from those in LTES 9 and OR. Manufacturing and mining is a little higher in LTES. In mining OR utilized a single net value-added ratio, but LTES applies net value-added ratios broken down into four categories: metal ore, coal, petroleum, and others. The construction and facilitating industries (including electricity) category is identical in both. Some double counting of interest in OR and several other studies was removed from LTES. The double counting was for the value added by the commodity-producing sector; interest payments were included, so interest received in the service sector from other industries should be excluded, but in fact this was not always possible. For government saving, LTES 1 takes government revenue minus government current expenditures, while OR simply summed the savings of central and local governments, thus including some inter-governmental overlapping.

OR and SIL

For GNE in current prices, SIL is larger than OR in every year. OR take into consideration the revised regional price differentials in estimating personal consumption expenditures, while SIL does not. In OR small agricultural implements are included as current inputs, whereas in SIL they are included as investment, and nonresidential buildings and structures have been reestimated in OR. Government consumption is by fiscal year in SIL, by calendar year in OR. Exports and imports in OR are based on Yamamoto's new estimates, but in SIL they are based on earlier worksheets done in 1961 and 1962 under the supervision of Ohkawa and Akasaka. For NDP by industry, OR compute depreciation from their capital stock estimate, but SIL uses ratios from GRJE. By industry, NDP in agriculture as well as in the construction and facilitating industries is the same. In manufacturing and mining NDP is identical before 1937, but for 1938–40 SIL figures are a bit higher. In services OR is higher than SIL.

Deflators

The fundamental difference in price deflators among the studies is the revision of exports and imports data to classify trade with Korea and Taiwan as foreign during the colonial period. This somewhat changes the overall GNE deflator.

Population and Labor Force

OR p. 310 (table 15) *Should not be used* as there are serious errors due to mistakes in laying out the table.

For the labor force, Minami (1973, pp. 312–13) used Umemura's worksheet but made different adjustments. Briefly, Umemura divides the total labor force into primary and nonprimary industries using the assumption the ratio between the relative industrial compositions of labor force (A) and the relative industrial composition of the number of deaths (B) is constant over time. Minami's amended estimate assumes the absolute difference of A and B is constant over time, at least for the 1906–40 period (Minami 1973, pp. 93–98). Umemura's estimates are given in appendix tables A53 and A54 and he discusses them in chapter 14.

Capital Stock

The main difference between LTES 3 and SIL is that LTES 3 adjusts for commercial buildings also used as residences. Small agricultural implements are excluded, and agricultural residential buildings and structures are reestimated in PJED, LTES 1, and OR, but not in LTES 3 and SIL. The commercial building series was further revised for LTES 1 after LTES 3 appeared.

Personal Disposable Income

Odaka's study of personal consumption and disposable income in 1934–36 prices (1975, p. 576, table 5) is the most recent careful study of the subject. Odaka defines Yd (personal disposable income) as

$$Yd = GDP + A - D - T + Tr - Gy - Sc$$

where A = net income from abroad, D = depreciation, T = tax, Tr = transfer payments, Gy = net income from government enterprise, and Sc = corporate retained income.

In LTES 1 personal disposable income is

$$Yd = GNP - D - \text{government revenue} + Tr + \text{government subsidies} - Sc$$

Since GDP + A = GNP, and if T + Gy = government revenue −
subsidies, both formulas are almost identical. However, the worksheet
on GNP Odaka used was revised before appearing in LTES 1, so the
two personal disposable incomes series are not identical. Moreover,
Odaka's table gives per capita personal disposable income only in
1934–36 prices, while LTES uses current prices. The change in data
does not alter the importance of Odaka's contribution.

LINKING THE PREWAR AND POSTWAR SERIES

Miyohei Shinohara

Most LTES series end with 1940 while reliable postwar ones, primarily official government-collected data, do not begin until the 1950s.
In the 1940s statistics are scanty, with price and value data strongly
influenced by hyperinflation. Even a direct link, omitting the war and
reconstruction period, is often difficult because of changes in estimating procedures, concepts, and classifications. This is especially true of
real-term series. Controlled prices during the war and its aftermath
led to black markets. Thus even when there are continuous estimates
of physical volumes, the value in current prices is hard to establish.
While there are estimates of black market prices, they are primarily
limited to consumer goods. The mix of black and controlled market
transactions is not known.

The *Kogyo Tokeihyo* was not compiled for 1943 and 1944, so there
are no systematic continuous data for the manufacturing sector. On
the other hand, the LTES project has prepared a continuous output
series in constant prices for the agriculture sector. Bombing devasted
the capital stock. After the war, damage was estimated by the ESB
(Keizai Antei Honbu), but these semiofficial series were tentative and
may not be reliable. When real capital stock is estimated by the perpetual inventory method, finding effective deflators is also a problem.

Ohkawa's global integration of GNE components in chapters 1 and
2 uses ESB data to provide continuous series when our own estimates
are lacking, although he refrains from drawing any conclusions from
the data. This is a procedure common to most of the other chapters
and to the LTES project in general.

When underlying concepts change or data are classified in different
ways, detailed comparative analysis is difficult. For instance, prewar

household consumption is broken down into nine categories: food, clothing, fuel and personal care, transportation, communication, social expenses, and education, recreation, and others; but there is no postwar counterpart until 1957. Postwar private consumption is separated into expenditures by households and by private nonprofit institutions. However, prewar estimates of consumption include institutions since the commodity-flow and retail-valuation methods are used for most series. Further, prewar consumption is domestic while the postwar official private consumption series is national in that it includes consumption by residents abroad. Prewar, most business consumption (expenditures for entertainment, employes' welfare, and so on), is included, while in postwar consumption data, mostly estimated by family budget surveys, it is excluded. Business consumption in 1965 and 1970 amounted to about 8% of the official estimate of personal consumption expenditures. In comparing the postwar with the prewar consumption, one should keep these differences in mind.

Emi's estimate of prewar fixed-capital formation is classified as government or private, and each is broken down into construction (building and structures) and equipment. However, postwar official statistics (ARNIS) classify total government fixed-capital formation only by type of purchaser (central or local government, general or special accounts, or government enterprises and public corporations). Thus there are no estimates dividing construction and equipment into private or government fixed-capital formation.

Private residential building in the agricultural sector was not estimated in LTES 4, although Ohkawa and others provided estimates in LTES 1. If private residential building in both the nonfarm and farm sector thus estimated is deducted from private construction and equipment (in a narrow sense), then the prewar series can be linked to the postwar category *minkan setsubi toshi* (private construction plus equipment, exclusive of private residential investment). Prewar capital formation data do not include construction in mining, nor is inventory investment covered. Lack of an explicit inventory investment series can be defended to some extent because commodity flows to final consumers and investors are mostly unadjusted, so inventory investment is partially included.

Another difficulty is that capital formation was not estimated for 1941–50 with the same procedures as those for 1874–1940 and 1951 onward. It was estimated by utilizing financial statistics (annual increases of loans for equipment and plant and for inventory changes), which may have a strong upward bias due to hyperinflation, particularly for inventory investment.

In LTES 9, on agriculture and forestry, Umemura and others prepared basic quantum data by each commodity item for 1874–1963 in order to construct a continual constant price series for 1941–63 as well as for 1874–1940; but because of black markets, the current price series is not estimated for 1941–49. There are actually four constant price series owing to the 1874–76, 1904–06, 1934–36 and 1954–56 weightings used in LTES 9.

For manufacturing, during the period 1874–1940 the constant price output series was in principle derived by summing output in 1934–36 prices by commodity or by industry. Output for 1951–70 is mostly based on the *Kogyo Tokeihyo*, and this is linked with the prewar data after converting it to 1934–36 real terms. As a statistical procedure, the current price output series for 1951–70 were first deflated by manufacturing subgroups, using the Bank of Japan's wholesale price indexes classified by industry, 1965 = 100. These real-term volumes in the postwar base were then converted to those with the prewar base. Thus this is not necessarily a constant price series. Moreover, the Bank of Japan's postwar wholesale price index is a linking of several Laspeyres price indexes based successively on the weights of January 1948, 1952, 1960, 1965, and 1970.

In LTES 8, and chapter 12, the 1934–36 prices of consumer's goods, investment goods, agricultural and manufacturing products are linked with the postwar prices in 1955 by Fisher's formula. However, the linking of postwar price indexes at several dates poses a serious index number problem compared to indexes of a simpler formula, and it involves more than just the Laspeyres–Paasche difference. Nevertheless, at the present stage of our estimation, we cannot avoid this methodological procedure.

A HISTORICAL FRAMEWORK FOR APPRAISING THE RELIABILITY OF ESTIMATES

Kazushi Ohkawa

Our project's experience of successive revisions of estimates, and the progress made in applying new methods, developing data sources, and identifying future problems can be generalized into a conceptual framework. This framework is in part my response to requests for evaluations of the reliability of our estimates. Such requests are often based, though not always consciously, on a desire for perfectionism. Today there are elaborate systems of social accounts whose application in advanced countries is minimizing errors and omissions in actual estimates. People acquainted with these systems are likely to use them as standards for earlier estimates. This tacitly assumes the modern accounting system can be applied to quantifying the development process irrespective of historical phases. I disagree with such a notion, preferring relativism, which identifies an overall relationship between the ways of applying the social accounting framework and various phases of economic development. I believe this is an important perspective on the reliability question and is more meaningful than merely guessing a range of percentage errors.

Stages of Accounting

Accounting for the economy involves three essentials: (1) three dimensions of economic activity (output, expenditure, and income distribution), (2) behavior agents (the three decision-making units, that is: households, enterprises, and governments), and (3) markets (which involve pricing, factors, and output levels; the rest of the world is ignored). The concern here is how modern economic growth changes the relationships among these essentials.

The development process involves structural changes in each of the activities and compositional changes with respect to production agents; the shifts from agriculture to industry and from households to corporate enterprises are obvious examples. The changes broadly correspond to the formation of a national market both in outputs and factors—the move from consumption of self-produced to purchased goods being part of the process. Thus the estimation method applicable to production, expenditure, and income distribution relates to historical change in the agents and markets.

The output approach (usually, the estimation of gross domestic product at factor cost by industrial origin) can in principle be applied regardless of development level and irrespective of agents. The expenditure approach (usually, estimates of expenditure on gross domestic product at market prices) is also applicable to any development level and structure, so there is again no conceptual difficulty to having continuous expenditure estimates. The output and expenditure approaches differ in that the output approach looks at the supply side, while the expenditure approach is concerned with the demand side. For both, a major data difficulty is with household self-consumption and self-production. Using the accounting convention of treating self-consumed (nonmarketed) goods as household production and evaluating it at producer prices, and using a variety of strategies to net out intermediate goods at least partially eliminates the problem. As the composition of final demand shifts over time to modern agents, the proportion of self-supplied consumption and investment becomes smaller. While governments are perhaps the best record keepers, households (including noncorporate business activity) are the worst, especially for their consumption. For this reason the output approach is easier to use.

The income approach (distribution of income among agents) is extremely difficult, if not impossible, to apply until there are well developed factor markets, which generally means until a substantial portion of activity is conducted by corporate enterprises. Factor inputs in precorporate periods are often imputed in a manner analogous to market-price evaluation of self-consumption. However, the sum of the market-price evaluation of each factor tends to exceed total income produced.

This discussion may be summarized by distinguishing three stages of accounting. In the first, just the output approach is possible, then the expenditure approach can be added, and finally all three. Initial, partial use of expenditure data is considered an intermediate stage between the first two.

Evaluating the statistical reliability of the source data is beyond the scope of this section. National income estimates often depend on given data rather than on data designed for this specific purpose. Until the introduction of modern census and sampling techniques, series are likely to be less reliable, and the exact range of errors cannot be determined. There are a number of strategic points, virtually universally common to each stage. Our intention is to interpret Japan's experience in relation to the problems of other nations, particularly contemporary developing countries.

The estimates become more reliable as cross checks become more possible. No cross checks are possible for stage 1; a cross check is possible in stage 2 between production and expenditure; and in stage 3 the cross check between income and expenditure is usually done.

Table 3.3. Stages of Data Reliability for Asian Countries

Stage (recent possible revisions are not counted)

1   (Output data only, no check)
    India[a], Pakistan[a]
1a (Also some expenditure data, so partial check)
    Burma[a], Sri Lanka, Philippines, Thailand, Japan (before 1905 and series in GRJE)
2   (Both output and expenditure data, so one cross check)
    South Korea, Taiwan, Malaysia, Japan (LTES data 1905–40)
3   (Output, expenditure, and income data, multiple cross checks)
    Japan (postwar)

[a] Base year or benchmark constant price series; see text.

If desired a triple check can be made. Statistical discrepancies are the conventional indicator of these checks. In terms of the ratio to GNP, Japan's postwar official estimates range within 4% on an annual basis, and are much closer for most years. In comparison, our revised estimates of the prewar period since around 1905 are less reliable, being stage 2 data. For the period before 1905 the estimates can be classified as between stages 1 and 2; as such they are in general even less reliable. Reliability of the data of other nations can be broadly evaluated by the stage to which they belong, as table 3.3 shows.

Problems of Stage 1: Reliability of the Output Approach

Estimates of intermediate inputs, as illustrated by Japan's various goods-producing sectors, are not very reliable, particularly for the early phase of development. One indirect technique used is estimation of specific components by using a fixed income–ratio. Rough aggregate estimates of sectoral purchase of individual items are also necessary. Lower reliability, however, stems more from two major causes: nonmarketed production and the treatment of the service sector. In the former, there may be a tendency to underestimate the product, as well as biases of valuation from using wholesale prices instead of farm prices at the primary production stage. The service sector situation is much more relevant to the problem of our estimates. I believe reliability is especially low for this sector, and this is probably unavoidable. Separate presentation of a goods-producing sector and a service sector may be useful. Separating the nonmonetary sector (items not entering a market or otherwise not involving fairly explicit prices) from the monetary sector is sometimes tried because non-

monetary estimates are less reliable (for example, Kenya). I cannot
support this device, however, because the two sectors divided cannot
be defined clearly, as industrial sectors can.

Problems of Stage 2: Consistency between Output and Expenditure Estimates

Stage 1 problems remain, particularly for the service sector, although
estimates generally become more reliable in the production approach
because of improvements in the available original source data. On the
other hand, a partial approach is sometimes used at the beginning of
estimating expenditures on national product: investment, government,
and foreign trade are estimated, and personal consumption is taken
as a residual. As Japan's experience suggests, direct estimates of consumption depend firstly on family budget data and secondly on the
commodity-flow method, supplemented by expenditure data. Sampling
biases in family budget data make them relatively less reliable, but
commodity flow also presents problems in estimating margins and
appropriate prices, including wide regional differences. When use of
family budget data for a benchmark is possible, commodity-flow
reliability can be increased. When these techniques are unavailable,
personal consumption estimates tend to rely on production data supplemented by export and import statistics. To the extent the same
data are used by the two approaches, a consistency check between
output and expenditure becomes less meaningful. In theory the total
of distribution margins between primary production and final demand
should be equal to the income produced by the services sector, but
there are inevitably differences. Possible discrepancies between the
two approaches cannot be specified in a reliable way, as Japan's case
suggests, and I believe this is one of the biggest sources of aggregate
statistical discrepancies in stage 2.

Problems of Deriving Constant Price Volumes

Estimates of constant price volumes are indispensible to understanding development performance, but for both aggregate and component
series they are less reliable than current price volumes at stages 1 and
2, even apart from such factors as the problems caused by war-induced
dislocation in Japan and Germany's hyperinflation in the 1920s. Actually, some of the countries in stage 1 do not officially estimate
constant price series and others officially recognize their weakness

even at stage 2. Countries in stage 1 often use direct evaluation by base-year prices to extrapolate benchmark values by production indexes. For the goods-producing sector, especially agriculture, extrapolated benchmark values may be better than inadequate price indexes for deflating the current price volume. (For a comparison between direct valuation and the use of index numbers for agriculture see LTES 9.) Again the most difficult problem is undoubtedly the service sector, and often indirect methods such as the use of representative goods are resorted to. The influence this has on aggregate series should be considered carefully.

According to our classification for stage 2, deflating practices are ideally expected at both primary production and final demand stages. Actually, however, only a limited number of countries do this. Indeed, even Japan's official postwar estimates lack constant price products. Of course, complete constant price volumes at the primary production stage (output approach) can be estimated, but a relatively large gap, which pertains primarily to the service sector, arises between them and the final demand (expenditure) series. To avoid this a residual approach is often used. Taking actual national practices into account, I am inclined to say providing fairly reliable deflated expenditure series is a major landmark in the estimates of national accounts. This seems possible only in the later part of stage 2 or in stage 3.

Concluding Remarks

My discussion so far has been sketchy; yet it may aid in interpreting the methods of estimating the quantitative aspect of economic development in relative terms. It also implies our estimating experience for Japan is highly relevant to developing nations. Our own evaluation that our Japanese series are less reliable in earlier phases of development is to be expected and thus may be acceptable.

This does not mean, however, that there is no technical possibility of improving the quality of estimates at any stage. Revision is always worthwhile, in particular at earlier stages. My stage classification implies the existence of conceptual limitations in applying certain types of accounting approaches, but within these limits it is still possible to increase reliability. Past experience is a good example; the long process of improvement from GRJE to the present series eventually made it possible to evaluate reliability in terms of statistical discrepancies, although subject to the conditions previously mentioned. Future efforts to improve reliability may make it possible to reduce the statistical discrepancies of the initial phase of development (before 1905) in order to move the period into stage 2.

The situation of contemporary developing countries in stage 1 differs from that of Japan's early development phase in that they may take advantage of accumulated technical knowledge of national accounts, surveys, and other sources to shift to stage 2 earlier in the development process.

REFERENCES FOR PART 1

Bicanic, Rudolf. 1962. "The Threshold of Economic Growth." *Kyklos* 15:7–28.

Feinstein, C. H. 1972. *National Income, Expenditure and Output of the United Kingdom*, 1855–1965. Cambridge University Press.

Fujino, Shozaburo. 1965. *Nihon no keiki Junkan*. Keiso Shobo.

———. 1968. "Construction Cycles and Their Monetary-Financial Characteristics." In *Economic Growth: The Japanese Experience Since the Meiji Era*, edited by Lawrence J. Klein and Kazushi Ohkawa. Richard D. Irwin.

———, and Ryoko Akiyama. 1973. *Zaiko to Zaiko Toshi, 1880–1940*. Hitotsubashi Daigaku, Keizai Kenkyujo.

Gerschenkron, Alexander. 1962. *Economic Backwardness in Historical Perspective*. Harvard University Press.

GRJE [*The Growth Rate of the Japanese Economy Since 1878*]. Kazushi Ohkawa in association with Miyohei Shinohara, Mataji Umemura, Masakichi Ito, and Tsutomu Noda. 1957. Kinokuniya.

Hayami, Yujiro, and Vernon W. Ruttan. 1971. *Agricultural Development: An International Perspective*. Johns Hopkins University Press.

Hijikata, Seibi. 1933. *Kokumin Shotoku no Kosei*. Nihon Hyoronsha.

Inukai, Ichiro, and Arlon Tussing. "Kogyo Iken: Japan's Ten-Year Plan, 1884." *Economic Development and Cultural Change* 16 (1967 Oct.):51–71.

Keizai Shingicho. 1954. *Nihon Keizai to Kokumin Shotoku* (The English version is *National Income and National Economic Accounts of Japan, 1930–50*). Gakuyo Shobo.

Keizai Shingikai, NNW Kaihatsu Iinkai. 1973. *NNW Kaihatsu Iinkai Hokoku*.

Kravis, Irving B., et al. 1975. *A System of International Comparisons of Gross Product and Purchasing Power*. Published for the World Bank by Johns Hopkins University Press.

Kuznets, Simon. 1962. "Quantitative Aspects of the Economic Growth of Nations: VII, The Share and Structure of Consumption." *Economic Development and Cultural Change* 10 (1962 Jan.).

———. 1966. *Modern Economic Growth: Rate, Structure and Spread*. Yale University Press.

———. 1968. "Notes on Japan's Economic Growth." In *Economic Growth: The Japanese Experience Since the Meiji Era*, edited by Lawrence Klein and Kazushi Ohkawa. Richard D. Irwin.

————. 1971. *Economic Growth of Nations: Total Output and Production Structure.* Harvard University Press.

LTES [*Estimates of Long-Term Economic Statistics of Japan*]. Series edited by Kazushi Ohkawa, Miyohei Shinohara, and Mataji Umemura. 14 v. 1965– Toyo Keizai Shimposha.

1. National Income. 1974. Kazushi Ohkawa, Nobukiyo Takamatsu, and Yuzo Yamamoto.
2. Population and Labor Force. Forthcoming. Mataji Umemura et al.
3. Capital Stock. 1966. Kazushi Ohkawa, Shigeru Ishiwata, Saburo Yamada, and Hiromitsu Ishi.
4. Capital Formation. 1971. Koichi Emi.
5. Savings and Currency. Forthcoming. Koichi Emi and Masakichi Ito.
6. Personal Consumption Expenditure. 1967. Miyohei Shinohara.
7. Government Expenditure. 1966. Koichi Emi and Yuichi Shionoya.
8. Prices. 1967. Kazushi Ohkawa, Tsutomu Noda, Nobukiyo Takamatsu, Saburo Yamada, Minoro Kumazaki, Yuichi Shionoya, and Ryoshin Minami.
9. Agriculture and Forestry. 1966. Mataji Umemura, Saburo Yamada, Yujiro Hayami, Nobukiyo Takamatsu, and Minoru Kumizaki.
10. Mining and Manufacturing. 1972. Miyohei Shinohara.
11. Textile Industry. Forthcoming. Shiro Fujino and Akira Ono.
12. Railroads and Electric Utilities. 1965. Ryoshin Minami.
13. Regional Economic Statistics. Forthcoming. Mataji Umemura, et al.
14. Foreign Trade and Balance of Payments. Forthcoming. Ippei Yamazawa and Yuzo Yamamoto.

Minami, Ryoshin. 1973. *The Turning Point in Economic Development.* Kinokuniya.

Norinsho. 1955. *Koka Keizai Chosa.*

Odaka, Konosuke. 1975. "Kojin Shohi" and (with Shigeru Ishiwata) "Juyo Hendo to Susei Kasoku." In *Kindai Nihon no Keizai Hatten*, edited by Kazushi Ohkawa and Ryoshin Minami. Toyo Keizai Shimposha.

Ohkawa, Kazushi. 1945. *Shokuryo Keizai no Riron to Keisoku.* Nihon Hyronsha.

————. 1953. *Seikatsu Suijun no Sokutei.* Iwanami-shoten.

————. 1967. "Seicho Kyokumen to Susei Kasoku." *Keizai Kenkyu* 18 (1967 Jan.)

————. 1970. "Chochikuritsu no Choki Hendo: Kojin Chochiku o Chushin to Suru Dai-Ichiji Sekkin." *Keizai Kenkyu* 21 (1970 May).

————. 1972. *Differential Structure and Agriculture.* Kinokuniya.

————. 1977. "Measures of Effects of Structural Changes on Productivity Growth." In *Econometric Studies of the Economy of Japan*, edited by Richard F. Kosobud and Ryoshin Minami. University of Illinois Press.

Ohkawa, Kazushi, and Henry Rosovsky. 1965. "A Century of Japanese Economic Growth." In *The State and Economic Enterprise in Japan*, edited by William W. Lockwood. Princeton University Press.

————. 1968. "Postwar Japanese Growth in Historical Perspective." *In Economic Growth: The Japanese Experience Since the Meiji Era*, edited by Lawrence Klein and Kazushi Ohkawa. Richard D. Irwin.

————. 1973. *Japanese Economic Growth: Trend Acceleration in the Twentieth Century*. Stanford University Press.

Shinohara, Miyohei. 1962. *Growth and Cycles in the Japanese Economy*. Kinokuniya.

————. 1973. "Kuznets and Juglar Cycles during the Industrialization of 1874–1940 by Growth Cycle Approach." In *Economic Growth: The Japanese Experience Since the Meiji Era*, v. 1, edited by Kazushi Ohkawa and Yujiro Hayami. Japan Economic Research Center, Center Paper No. 19.

SIL [*Choki Keizai Tokei no Sebi Kaizen ni Kansuru Kenkyu*]. Keizai Kikakucho. 3 v. 1967–69.

Sorifu Tokeikyoku. *Rodoryoku Chosa* (Labor Force Survey) (Annual).

Tsuru, Shigeto, and Kazushi Ohkawa. 1953. "Long-Term Changes in the National Income of Japan Since 1878." In *Income and Wealth*, ser. 3 (Proceedings of the Royamont Conference), edited by Milton Gilbert. Bowes and Bowes.

Tsusansho (Tsusho Sangyosho). *Kogyo Tokeihyo* (*Census of Manufactures*) (Annual).

Yamada, Yuzo. 1951, revised 1956. *Nihon Kokumin Shotoku Suikei Shiryo*. Toyo Keizai Shimposha.

Yasuba, Yasukichi. 1973. "General Comments on the Summary of Statistical Estimates' Findings." In *Economic Growth*, edited by Kazushi Ohkawa and Yujiro Hayami. Japan Economic Research Center.

————. 1974. Review of Ohkawa and Rosovsky. In *Developing Economies* 12 (1974 Mar.).

PART 2: PRODUCTION AND TRADE

4

Agriculture

Saburo Yamada and Yujiro Hayami

Trends in Output

Growth rates for total production, total output, and gross value added in agriculture are shown in table 4.1.[1] The major trends are the same for all three series. From 1880 to 1965 agricultural output grew at the annual compound rate of about 1.6%. Three major phases are distinct: relatively fast growth up to the late 1910s, relative stagnation in the interwar period, and a spurt in the post-World War II period. There is some evidence the growth rate accelerated at the beginning of this century.

The relatively rapid growth in the initial phase and the acceleration during the period from the Russo-Japanese War (1905) to World War I are broadly parallel with nonagricultural growth. This parallelism breaks down in the 1920s and 30s. While the nonagricultural sector continued to expand, agriculture began to stagnate. Growth rates in this period declined to half those of the previous period in terms of total production, total output, and gross value added. Although there is some indication agricultural production resumed rapid growth in the mid 1930s, increasing shortages of labor and other inputs due to military involvements in China and the Pacific War caused a sharp decline in agricultural production.

After the devastation of the war, agriculture recovered rapidly,

---

1. The original, more detailed version of this chapter is Yamada and Hayami 1973. Definitions of output concepts are given in the section on data and methods. Also see Hayami 1975.

Table 4.1. Agriculture: Annual Growth Rates of Total Production, Output, and Gross
Value Added, in 1934–36 Prices
(In percent)

Period	Total production	Total output	Gross value added
1880–1900	1.5	1.6	1.8
(1880–95)	(1.2)	(1.4)	(1.3)
1900–20	1.8	2.0	1.9
(1905–20)	(1.9)	(2.0)	(1.9)
1920–35	0.9	0.9	0.8
1935–45	−1.8	−1.9	−2.1
1945–55	3.3	3.2	3.0
1955–65	3.4	3.6	3.2
Prewar period:			
1880–1935	1.5	1.6	1.6
Postwar period:			
1945–65	3.3	3.4	3.0
Whole period:			
1880–1965	1.5	1.6	1.5

Source: Appendix table A17.
Note: Compound growth rates between five-year averages of the data centered on the
years shown.

regaining the prewar level by the end of the Korean War. The postwar
spurt in agricultural growth was not simply a recovery phenomenon.
Even after the recovery phase, total production, total output, and
gross value added in agriculture continued to grow at annual rates
higher than 3%, although there is a sign of deceleration since 1960.
From these observations, we have adopted the six-phase periodization
in table 4.1.

Extremely different growth patterns are found in production by
commodities, corresponding to differences in the rates of changes in
technology and demand (table 4.2). As a result, both the real and the
current price series composition have changed greatly (appendix tables
A16 and A17).

Production of rice grew relatively slowly compared to other products.
However, because it is by far the most important commodity, changes
in the growth rate of rice production have been the major determinant
of the pattern for total agricultural production.

Rapid growth in sericulture (the production of silk cocoons) until
the 1920s and its sharp contraction due to the depression and competition from artificial fibers contribute to the formation of a distinct
kink in the growth rate from the 1900–20 period to the 1920–35

Table 4.2. Agriculture: Annual Growth Rates of Production by Major Commodity
Groups in 1934–36 Prices

(In percent)

	Crops			Sericulture	Livestock
Period	Rice	Others	Total		
1880–1900	0.9	2.1	1.3	3.9	6.8
1900–20	1.7	1.4	1.6	4.7	3.8
1920–35	0.4	0.7	0.5	1.7	5.7
1935–45	−0.4	−1.6	−0.8	−10.3	−7.6
1945–55	1.4	4.5	2.5	−0.5	16.3
1955–65	2.2	1.9	2.1	−0.3	11.0
Prewar period:					
1880–1935	1.1	1.5	1.2	3.6	5.4
Postwar period:					
1945–65	1.8	3.2	2.4	−0.4	13.6
Whole period:					
1880–1965	1.1	1.5	1.2	0.9	5.6

Source: Appendix table A17.
Notes: Compound growth rates between five-year averages of the data centered on
the years shown.

Hayami (1975) has a similar table (table 2-3, p. 20) except there labor is in male
equivalents (here it is the simple sum of male and female workers), and land is in paddy
field equivalent (here no quality adjustment is made). This applies to a number of
other tables in this chapter: 4.3 (table 2-9, p. 30), 4.4 (table 2-8, p. 30), 4.6 (figure 2-8,
p. 29), and 4.7 (table 2-8, p. 30).

period. During World War II sericulture was reduced to such a low
level that production changes no longer affect the aggregate growth
rate.

Livestock raising started from a negligible level, and despite its
rapid growth, its share did not rise to a significant level before World
War II. However, because of its dramatic postwar increase, exceeding
10% per year, livestock has become a critical component in the growth
rate of aggregate agricultural output.

Trends in Inputs and Productivity

Input growth rates are given in tables 4.3 and 4.4. Four major
categories are analyzed in this study: labor, land, fixed capital stock,
and nonfarm current inputs. An index of total input is also calculated.
These input categories, as well as total productivity, are defined in
the section on data and methods later in this chapter. Inputs of the

Table 4.3. Agriculture: Annual Growth Rates of Inputs

(In percent)

Period	Total input	Labor			Land			Fixed capital		Current inputs	
		Male	Female	Total	Paddy field	Upland field	Total	Machinery and implements	Total	Fertilizer	Total
1880–1900	0.4	0.1	0.1	0.1	0.2	0.8	0.5	0.7	0.9	1.6	1.8
1900–20	0.5	−0.5	−0.7	−0.6	0.4	1.1	0.7	2.0	1.3	7.7	4.7
1920–35	0.5	−0.1	−0.1	−0.1	0.3	−0.1	0.1	1.8	0.9	3.4	3.2
1935–45	−0.9	−1.7	2.0	0.1	−0.3	−0.6	−0.4	−0.2	−1.4	−4.9	−6.6
1945–55	3.4	1.5	0.3	0.9	0.3	0.1	0.2	3.0	2.0	13.4	15.0
1955–65	1.0	−3.5	−2.5	−3.0	0.3	−0.2	0.1	11.5	7.8	3.7	8.5
Prewar period:											
1880–1935	0.4	−0.2	−0.2	−0.2	0.3	0.7	0.5	1.5	1.0	4.3	3.2
Postwar period:											
1945–65	2.3	−1.0	−1.1	−1.1	0.3	−0.1	0.1	7.2	4.9	8.4	11.7
Whole period:											
1880–1965	0.7	−0.6	−0.2	−0.4	0.2	0.3	0.3	2.6	1.6	4.1	3.9

Sources: Appendix table A18.
Notes: Compound growth rates between five-year averages of the data centered on the years shown. See notes to table 4.2.

Table 4.4. Agriculture: Output, Input, and Productivity Growth Rates and Contributions to Output Growth

(In percent)

Period	Annual compound rates of growth			Relative contributions to output growth by	
	Total output	Total input	Total productivity	Input	Productivity
1880–1900	1.6	0.4	1.2	25	75
(1880–95)	(1.4)	(0.3)	(1.1)	(21)	(79)
1900–20	2.0	0.5	1.5	25	75
(1905–20)	(2.0)	(0.5)	(1.5)	(25)	(75)
1920–35	0.9	0.5	0.4	56	44
1935–45	−1.9	−0.9	−1.0	47	53
1945–55	3.2	3.4	−0.2	106	−6
1955–65	3.6	1.0	2.6	28	72
Prewar period: 1800–1935	1.6	0.4	1.2	25	75
Postwar period: 1945–65	3.4	2.3	1.1	68	32
Whole period: 1880–1965	1.6	0.7	0.9	44	56

Source: Table 4.6.
Notes: Annual compound growth rates between five-year averages of the data centered on the years shown.
See notes to table 4.2.

two primary factors, labor and land, changed relatively slowly. Labor declined by 15% during the prewar period and by 25% between 1955 and 1965. Land increased by only 30% in the whole period, 1880–1965.

According to Masahiko Shintani's estimates (in Hayami 1975, pp. 23–25) the trend in flow-labor input in work days before World War I represents a sharp contrast to the trend in the number of workers, although they tended to move more or less parallel after 1920. From 1880 to 1920 workdays rose 30% while the number of farm workers decreased 10% so work days per worker increased 45% from about 110 days per year to 160. This seems to reflect increased labor utilization due to double-cropping paddy fields and expansion of sericulture as a sideline to staple cereals for small-scale family farms. To a large extent changes in labor and land have canceled each other in total input growth. Capital grew relatively slowly in the prewar years, but has risen at a rapid pace in the postwar period. Growth of current nonfarm inputs, particularly fertilizers, has been much faster than other inputs.

Despite sharp differences in the rate of increase in real input, factor shares have changed relatively little, as shown in table 4.5. This stability seems to reflect a rational response of producers, substituting toward factors with relatively declining prices. The shares of labor and fixed capital stayed fairly stable, while the share of current inputs increased, and that of land decreased. However, there are indications that during the 1960s capital began to gain share from labor.

Rapid price increases for farmland in the prewar period suggest land was the factor limiting production, whereas the postwar acceleration of the farm wage implies labor has become more scarce in recent years. The rapid decline in fertilizer prices relative to land has been a strong inducement for heavier applications of fertilizer. Likewise, it is clear the decline in the price of machinery relative to wages has stimulated substitution of machinery for labor.

Table 4.5. Agriculture: Factor Shares in the Total Cost of Production, Five-Year Averages

(In percent)[a]

	Labor wage		Land rent			
	Male	Female	Paddy field	Upland field	Capital interest	Current inputs
1885[b]	35.9	16.9	20.5	8.3	10.9	7.6
1890	32.8	17.4	23.0	7.7	10.6	8.5
1895	33.2	18.3	22.8	8.2	9.7	7.8
1900	32.8	19.3	22.8	8.2	9.5	7.5
1905	32.4	18.5	23.4	7.3	9.9	8.6
1910	33.0	17.6	22.6	7.6	9.8	9.3
1915	31.9	17.1	22.5	7.2	10.3	11.0
1920	30.7	18.4	23.5	6.1	10.2	11.1
1925	32.4	20.5	20.7	5.5	10.0	10.9
1930	33.1	21.5	17.4	6.0	10.5	11.6
1935	29.4	18.6	22.2	5.4	11.1	13.3
1940	24.5	22.6	22.1	5.1	11.6	14.1
1945[c]	30.4	25.1	14.4	4.1	11.2	14.8
1950	36.4	27.7	6.6	3.0	10.8	15.6
1955	30.8	24.7	14.4	6.0	10.3	13.8
1960	25.8	22.6	18.2	7.4	11.2	14.8
1965	25.3	23.3	14.0	6.3	13.8	17.2
1970[d]	25.5	22.4	14.2	5.7	15.2	17.0

Source: Yamada and Hayami 1973.
[a] Five-year averages centered on years shown.
[b] 1885–89 averages.
[c] Averages of 1940 and 1950
[d] 1968–71 averages.

Total input for the whole period rose at an annual rate of 0.7%, while total output rose at 1.6%. This implies less than half the growth in total output is explained by growth of inputs; the other half is explained by the increase in productivity (production efficiency). With a rate of 0.9% per year, total productivity more than doubled.

There are large variations among periods in the growth rate of total productivity as well as its relative contribution to the output growth rate. The increase in the rate of output growth from the 1880–1900 period to the 1900–20 period is associated with both a rise in the input growth rate and an acceleration of productivity growth, but the latter is the dominant factor. The interwar stagnation in the output growth rate is explained solely by the deceleration in productivity growth. While output growth during the postwar recovery (through around 1955) is largely explained by increases in inputs, the postrecovery period is dominated by the rise in productivity. This implies the sharp decline in agricultural production during the war was caused primarily by shortages of inputs.

Table 4.6. Agriculture: Indexes of Five-Year Averages of Output, Input, and Productivities

	Total output	Total input	Productivities			Land–labor ratio
			Total	Labor	Land	
1880	100.0	100.0	100.0	100.0	100.0	100.0
1885	110.6	101.3	109.2	110.5	108.6	101.8
1890	119.7	102.8	116.4	119.3	115.1	103.7
1895	122.5	105.4	116.2	121.8	115.2	105.7
1900	138.6	108.2	128.1	136.4	126.5	107.8
1905	152.1	111.5	136.4	148.8	134.7	110.5
1910	170.4	117.8	144.7	167.4	143.4	116.7
1915	193.3	119.9	161.2	196.8	157.0	125.4
1920	205.5	119.3	172.3	228.8	162.6	140.7
1925	208.2	121.6	171.2	239.9	166.6	144.0
1930	223.4	127.3	175.5	249.3	176.3	141.4
1935	236.3	128.7	183.6	267.3	183.3	145.8
1940	236.2	127.0	186.0	275.0	183.7	149.7
1945	195.9	116.2	168.6	219.1	159.5	137.4
1950	220.9	147.3	150.0	216.8	178.1	121.7
1955	268.0	165.5	161.9	275.4	211.4	130.3
1960	334.0	170.5	195.9	388.4	260.5	149.1
1965	382.0	183.1	208.6	528.0	300.8	175.5

Source: Appendix tables A17 and A18.
Note: Five-year averages centered on years shown.

While the total productivity index is a measure of change in production efficiency, the index of labor productivity (output per worker) is a more appropriate measure of economic progress defined as the increase in the returns to labor. As an expository device it is useful to assume output per worker equals arable land area per worker multiplied by output per hectare of arable land. Table 4.6 compares the trends in the indexes of output per worker, output per hectare, and land area per worker, together with the index of total productivity. The major element in explaining the increase in labor productivity has been the increase in land productivity, although the improvement in land area per worker has also been significant. For the whole period the relative contribution of increased land productivity has been more than 60% of the increase in labor productivity (table 4.7).

Indexes of land productivity and total productivity have shown similar trends and similar growth rates, particularly for the period before World War II. This suggests technical progress or improved

Table 4.7. Agriculture: Labor and Land Productivities, Land–Labor Ratios, and Relative Contributions to Labor Productivity Growth
(In percent)

	Annual compound rate of growth in			Relative contributions to labor productivity growth of	
Period	Output per worker	Output per hectare	Land area per worker	Land productivity	Land–labor ratio
1880–1900	1.5	1.1	0.4	73	27
(1880–95)	(1.4)	(1.0)	(0.4)	(71)	(29)
1900–20	2.6	1.3	1.3	50	50
(1905–20)	(2.8)	(1.2)	(1.6)	(43)	(54)
1920–35	1.0	0.8	0.2	80	20
1935–45	−2.0	−1.5	−0.5	75	25
1945–55	2.3	3.0	−0.7	130	−30
1955–65	6.6	3.5	3.1	53	47
Prewar period:					
1880–1935	1.8	1.1	0.7	61	39
Postwar period:					
1945–65	4.5	3.3	1.2	73	27
Whole period:					
1880–1965	2.0	1.3	0.7	65	35

Sources: Appendix tables A17 and A18.
Notes: Growth rates between five-year averages of the data centered on years shown. See note to table 4.2.

efficiency in agricultural production in Japan has been primarily land saving (increasing output per unit of land area). Because land has been a relatively scarce factor from the beginning of Japan's modern economic growth, the efforts of farmers as well as agricultural scientists have been concentrated on increasing land productivity.

Seed improvement and the rapid increase in fertilizer use and other current inputs have been the primary substitutes for land. For the development of such biological-chemical (BC) technology in Japan, however, the relatively high level of land infrastructure in the initial stage and its later improvement were important prerequisites. Initial progress in BC technology in the early Meiji period, primarily based on the initiatives of innovative farmers and landlords exploiting indigenous potential, was facilitated by a relatively well-developed irrigation system, covering 1.8 million hectares, about 40% of total cultivated land area and more than 60% of lowland paddy. Although there had been active movements for land infrastructure improvements among the older, more experienced farmers (*gono* class) during early Meiji, the area improved was so small it did not significantly affect the trend in total improved area until the end of the 19th century.

However, as better rice varieties were diffused and fertilizer input levels raised, land infrastructure became a major bottleneck in production. The growing imbalance increased returns to investment in land infrastructure, which induced public investment as well as an institutional innovation, the Arable Land Replotment Law, designed to facilitate organization of farmers in the construction of land infrastructure. Improvements in irrigation and drainage systems induced development of more fertilizer-responsive, higher-yielding varieties. Such varieties were effective in counteracting the rising costs of irrigation and drainage construction, thereby maintaining investment incentives. Without the induced development of technology, the contribution of land infrastructure improvement to agricultural growth would have been very small. Since the late 1950s, however, this basic motivation has been changing drastically as labor has become scarce because of migration to the nonfarm sector.

Contributions of the growth in the land–labor ratio were relatively large in the 1900–20 and 1955–65 periods, during which increases in output and productivities were rapid. The improvement in the land–labor ratio in the 1900–20 period may be overestimated because at that time large areas of less productive land (mainly upland field in Hokkaido and Tohoku) were brought into cultivation. The ratio

Table 4.8. Agriculture: Output, Labor and Land Productivities, and Land–Man Ratios for Selected Developed Countries, 1880–1960
(Annual growth rates in percent)

	Output (1960 = 100)		Output per male worker (WU)			Output per hectare (WU)			Land–man ratio (ha/man)		
	Index for 1880	Annual growth rate	1880	1960	Annual growth rate	1880	1960	Annual growth rate	1880	1960	Annual growth rate
Japan	28	1.6	2.4	10.7	1.9	2.7	7.5	1.3	0.9	1.4	0.6
Denmark	24	1.8	10.5	47.4	1.9	1.2	4.6	1.7	8.8	10.3	0.2
France	43	1.1	7.9	35.9	1.9	1.1	2.5	1.1	7.2	14.4	0.9
United Kingdom	54	0.8	15.7	44.0	1.3	1.1	1.9	0.7	14.3	23.2	0.6
United States	29	1.6	14.6	99.5	2.4	0.5	0.8	0.6	25.4	109.5	1.8

Source: Hayami and Ruttan 1971.
Note: WU stands for wheat units.

Table 4.9. Agriculture: Output, Labor and Land Productivities, and Land–Man Ratios for Selected Asian Developing Countries
(Annual growth rates in percent)

	Output (1965 = 100)			Output per male worker (WU)			Output per hectare (WU)			Land–man ratio (ha/man)		
	Initial year	Index for initial year	Annual growth rate	Initial year	1965	Annual growth rate	Initial year	1965	Annual growth rate	Initial year	1965	Annual growth rate
Taiwan	1913	22	2.9	2.8	9.7	2.4	3.6	12.5	2.4	0.8	0.8	0.0
Korea (South)	1920	37	2.2	2.6	4.3	1.1	2.4	6.0	2.1	1.1	0.7	−0.9
Philippines	1950	56	4.0	3.4	4.0	1.1	1.8	2.2	1.3	1.9	1.8	−0.3

Sources: Ban 1973, Crisostomo and Barker 1973, and Lee and Chen 1973.
Note: WU stands for wheat units.

dropped sharply after World War II because of repatriation and movement from war-torn cities. In the 1950s and 60s renewed economic growth led to a dramatic increase in the ratio as the industry and service sectors drew people out of agriculture.

Comparisons with Developed Countries

For the 1880–1960 period, table 4.8 shows that the growth rates of agricultural output and productivities in Japan do not stand out. But unique aspects of Japanese agriculture exist in the levels of productivities and factor endowments. Labor productivity is much lower than in other developed countries, while land productivity is much higher. This relates to differences in resource endowments, that is, to the land–man ratio. The ratio was only 0.9 hectare of agricultural land per male farm worker in 1880 and 1.4 hectares in 1960 for Japan, but as high as 7 to 110 hectares for the others. The Japanese experience is in particularly sharp contrast to that of the United States, where labor productivity increased primarily because of improvements in the land–man ratio rather than increases in land productivity.

Comparisons with Developing Countries in Asia

Given the resource endowment conditions, it is more relevant to compare Japan to Asia, as is done in table 4.9, than to developed countries. The agricultural growth path of Taiwan, for instance, has been very similar to the Japanese. However, the Japanese experience is unique within the Asian perspective as well. While Japan's agricultural growth was accompanied by gradual improvements in the land–man ratio, Taiwan's was realized despite a constant ratio. Agricultural growth in Korea and the Philippines was accompanied by deteriorating land–man ratios. Different growth rates for population and for employment in the nonagricultural sector among these countries account for most of the differences.

Output

Unless otherwise noted, data are from LTES 9. Total output is defined as total production in agriculture minus agricultural intermediate products. Total production is the simple aggregate of all individual agricultural products, covering 101 commodities or commodity groups, sold outside agriculture or consumed by farm households. Subaggregates are rice, other field crops, sericulture, and livestock. Intermediate products include agricultural products used as inputs for agricultural production such as seed and feed (feed processed in the nonfarm sector or imported from abroad is not included).

Subtracting nonfarm current inputs from total output yields gross value added in agriculture (equivalent to gross domestic product in the ordinary terms of national income accounting). Nonfarm current inputs are the current inputs supplied to agriculture from the nonfarm sector, such as fertilizers.

The individual products are aggregated by 1934–36 average constant prices. Although this might involve serious bias, typical of quantity indexes of the Laspeyres type, a comparison of total output growth rates with other output series using different aggregation procedures (table 4.10) indicates no significant effect on the conclusions on agricultural output growth rates.

Table 4.10. Agriculture: Comparison of Annual Compound Growth Rates in Total Output using Different Index Formula
(In percent)

	1880–1900	1900–20	1920–35	1945–55	1955–65
Laspeyres Index					
1934–36 price weights	1.6	2.0	0.9	3.2	3.6
1954–56 price weights	1.7	2.0	0.8	3.4	3.5
Linked[a]	1.8	2.2	0.9	3.4	3.6
Paasche Index, deflated by					
Weights for 1934–36	2.0	2.3	1.0	c	3.7
Weights for 1954–56	1.8	2.0	0.9	c	3.9
Linked price index[b]	1.7	2.1	1.0	c	3.9

Source: Reprinted from Hayami 1975 (p. 18, table 2-2), computed from data in LTES 9:148–65 adjusted by the authors.
Note: Growth rates between five-year averages of the data centered on the years shown.
[a] Four quantity indexes of price weights for 1874–76, 1904–06, 1934–36, and 1954–56 are linked in a chain by multiplying consecutively their average ratios at 1896–98, 1918–20, and 1944–46.
[b] Four price indexes of quantity weights for 1874–76, 1904–1906, 1934–36, and 1954–56 are linked in a chain by multiplying consecutively their average ratios at 1896–98, 1918–20, and 1936.
[c] Not available.

It is now well known that the series of agricultural output in GRJE, primarily based on official statistics (Noshomusho, various issues), underestimate earlier periods and thus overestimate the growth rate. In the LTES estimation we corrected the insufficient coverage and also tried various methods to correct the underreporting of rice yield and area in the official statistics. The basic procedure was to estimate outputs of agricultural products in 1874, 1899–1901, 1909–11, and 1920, using statistical yearbooks of prefectural governments and other sources and interpolating among these benchmark years when necessary.

After publication of LTES 9 we found an important original source on rice production (Chiso Kaisei 1951 and 1955). This bulletin reports in detail the results of a survey of land areas and crop yields conducted by the Land Tax Revision Bureau between 1875 and 1881. The survey is considered the most accurate available for the period, since it cost the central government about one year's revenue. We have adopted the survey's rice yield data as the benchmark for the estimation of rice yields and areas by interpolation by prefectures. This increased our estimate of rice production for the 1870s more than 5% compared to the figures in LTES 9. The LTES agricultural production series have been extended for the period since 1963 using government indexes (Norinsho 1971/72, pp. 330–33).

Inputs

Four major categories of agricultural input are considered: labor, land, fixed-capital stock, and nonfarm current inputs.

Labor is measured in terms of the number of gainful workers, male and female compiled separately. We have not attempted to estimate labor service flow in terms of work days or work hours. Shintani (1974) has compiled a series for work days, but data limitations necessitate making a number of somewhat arbitrary assumptions. His estimates count only labor applied directly to production of crops and livestock products, excluding overhead labor for such farm activities as transportation, marketing, construction and maintenance of irrigation facilities, and cutting wild grass for feed and fertilizers. For these reasons we do not utilize his results.

Prewar data for labor were estimated by deducting forestry workers from the Umemura estimates of the number of gainful workers in agriculture and forestry (LTES 2 and ch. 14). The deduction for forestry workers was based on the ratio in the various population censuses (interpolated for intercensus years). Postwar data since 1964 are those from the *Labor Force Survey* (Sorifu) connected with the data in LTES 9.

Land is measured in terms of arable land area; paddy field area and upland field area are compiled separately. No adjustment is made for changes in the quality of arable land. Masakatsu Akino has estimated investment in land improvement and constructed a land quality index, but somewhat arbitrary assumptions are needed to utilize the available data. (His estimates, still incomplete, are included in Hayami 1975, p. 235.) The official statistics of arable land area are subject to under-reporting for the early period, and are also subject to discontinuities due to changes in definition and the method of survey. Underreporting and statistical discontinuities were corrected in LTES 9 by interpolation and extrapolation by prefectures, connected to the series through the sample remeasurement survey conducted by the Ministry of Agriculture and Forestry starting in 1956.

Fixed capital is gross of depreciation and includes livestock and perennial plants, machinery and all other implements, and farm buildings excluding residences. Aggregations are made in 1934–36 constant prices. The data are from LTES 3, except farm buildings were reestimated by Ohkawa and Takamatsu for the national income estimates in LTES 1. These series are joined to the official series prepared by Norinsho (1971) for the period since 1963, based on the average ratio for 1960–63.

Nonfarm current inputs are the current inputs in agriculture supplied by the nonfarm sector. They include fertilizers, agricultural chemicals, feed processed by domestic industry (such as fish meal and oilseed cake) and imported from abroad, and other miscellaneous items including fuel and electricity. Aggregations are made in 1934–36 constant prices. The series in LTES 9 for 1878 to 1963 are connected with the series obtained by deflating the current input values in Norinsho (1971) for the period since 1963.

Total Input and Total Productivity

Indexes of labor, land, fixed capital, and nonfarm current inputs are aggregated into a single index of total input by using the factor share weights in table 4.5 and the chain-link index formula:

$$I_t = I_{t-1} \sum_i w_{i,t-1} \frac{q_{it}}{q_{i,t-1}} \quad (t = 1, 2, 3, \dots)$$

where

$$I_t = \text{total input index for year t}$$
$$q_{it} = \text{quantity index of input i in year t}$$
$$w_{it} = \text{applicable factor share of input i}$$

The successive annual aggregates are thus linked to form a single index by multiplying in a chain, the weights being revised every fifth year.

Factor shares for input aggregation are the costs of individual factor inputs in agricultural production divided by total factor cost in current prices. The cost of labor was estimated by multiplying the number of gainful workers in agriculture by the wage rate of annual contract farm workers. This wage rate is adopted because data for daily wages of farm labor are usually for the planting and harvest seasons and are thus too high to be used as an annual average of the wage rate for our purpose.

The cost of land for the prewar period was estimated by multiplying the area of arable land by the average annual rent. Postwar, the land reform laws have kept rent at a level much lower than its marginal productivity. To estimate the functional share of land, fictitious rent was assumed as 8% of arable land value. (Various institutional interest rates have prevailed for difficult loan arrangements in Japan. In most cases the range has been from 6 to 10%.)

The cost of capital stock should include depreciation and interest on the net stock of capital, but because of data limitations and the arbitrariness involved, depreciation has not been estimated. Instead, the cost of the services of capital is taken as interest on the gross capital stock at 8%. The cost of nonfarm current inputs was estimated as the value paid by farmers for the items of current inputs supplied from the nonfarm sector, as previously explained.

REMAINING PROBLEMS

The major deficiencies in our data of agricultural output are that they include only final products—products sold to the nonfarm sector or consumed by farm households—and capital formation using resources within the agricultural sector is not counted in output. Capital formation should cover changes in the inventories of livestock and perennial plants such as mulberry and fruit trees, construction of equipment and buildings by farm labor, and land improvement by farm labor including construction of local irrigation and drainage facilities by communal work. The last category is not included in capital stock estimates.

It appears reasonable to hypothesize that capital formation using farm resources, especially farm labor, was more important in the earlier period. If such capital formation is included, the initial levels of agricultural output may have been higher and thus the growth rate significantly lower. This problem is related to deficiencies in the measurement of inputs. The major source of such capital formation is farm labor, which in turn affects the utilization of labor. For example, improvements in irrigation and drainage promote multiple cropping, which increases work days and hours per farm worker. Measurement of labor in terms of the number of workers is unsatisfactory, especially when we attempt to estimate capital formation by farm labor. Shintani (in Hayami 1975) has estimated work days, but only for direct production, so his series does not help estimate capital formation.

Land improvement through the construction of irrigation, drainage, and other facilities, by both farm and nonfarm resources, implies either an addition to the stock of fixed capital or an increase in the stock of land measured in efficiency units. It is likely that at least part of the growth in the unexplained residual called total productivity can be explained by investment in land improvement. Estimation of such investment is critical for identifying the sources of agricultural growth. Akino's work (in Hayami 1975, p. 235) helps clarify this aspect, but further assessment of the data is necessary.

The sum of factor cost components estimated individually at market prices is often more than the value of output estimated from production data. The discrepancies increase the further back one goes. They are most likely due to overestimation of wage earnings, but further research is needed to clarify the issue.

COMPARISON WITH PREVIOUS ESTIMATES

The pioneering GRJE estimates, based primarily on official statistics, implied an extremely rapid rate of agricultural growth for the early Meiji period, approaching 3% per year for the two decades before 1900. Such rates were questioned by Nakamura (1966). He argues land tax evasion practices such as concealing arable land and underreporting crop yields meant the official data grossly underestimated early Meiji output. Although underestimation decreased over time, it did not completely disappear before 1920. Nakamura attempted to correct undermeasurement of land area by extrapolating the trend for 1890–1910 back to 1873. This procedure seems largely acceptable.

Two points of major controversy, however, have been Nakamura's claim average rice yield in 1873–77 was already 1.6 koku per tan (29 hectoliters per hectare), about 40% higher than the official yield, and his adjustment for underreporting of rice yield by linearly connecting this value with the official average yield of 1918–22. These points lead to a dramatically lower growth rate of aggregate agricultural production compared to GRJE estimates for the period before 1920. For 1880–1900, the Nakamura rate of 0.9% per year is only one-third GRJE's 2.8%.

Nakayama (1966) recognized the unreliability of official statistics but on the basis of rice consumption data rejected the Nakamura hypothesis of 1.6 koku per tan. In Nakayama's opinion the primary defect in the GRJE series was underestimation due to incomplete coverage of agricultural products before 1920. His correction of the incomplete coverage based on constant ratios in later years resulted in a moderate revision of GRJE estimates.

In LTES 9 we attempted to correct possible underestimation of both land area and yields before 1890 by prefectures, based primarily on trends after 1890, while also correcting incomplete coverage of crops. Our basic hypothesis was that not only area underestimation but also yield underestimation was largely corrected in the official statistics after the completion of the 1885–89 cadastral survey (Chio Chosa). These revisions produced an estimate of agricultural growth rate just in the middle of the GRJE and Nakamura estimates. In terms of critical review of original data and consistency with other economic variables, we consider our estimates more plausible than either GRJE or Nakamura's (Hayami 1968; Hayami and Yamada 1969; and Yamada and Hayami 1973, appendix C).

Further revision of rice yield data in this study, as previously explained, has resulted in minor changes from the LTES 9 estimates. A major difference between the LTES and present estimates is that in the latter, acceleration in the growth rate can be observed at the beginning of this century, whereas in LTES little change occurred from the 1880–1900 to the 1900–20 period. The acceleration seems more plausible, since propagation of improved rice varieties became nationwide in this period; the area planted in improved varieties jumped from 4% of total area planted to rice in 1895 to 14% in 1900 and 30% in 1905.

Yuize (1966) also provides a long-term estimate of agricultural output. Trying to link the output series before World War II to the official index of agricultural production published in Norinsho *Tokei-hyo* since 1955, Yuize constructed a total output index for 1909–65 using the same definition and the same index formula as the official index. The growth rates calculated from the Yuize index are 1.8% for the period 1908–12 to 1918–22, and 1.3% for 1908–12 to 1958–62, very close to our 1.9 and 1.4%, respectively. This consistency implies there is not much problem linking our total output index with the official index of agricultural output.

REFERENCES

Ban, Sung Hwan. 1973. "Growth Rates of Korean Agriculture, 1918–1968."
      In *Agricultural Growth in Japan, Taiwan, Korea and the Philippines*, edited
      by Yujiro Hayami, Vernon W. Ruttan, and Herman Southworth. University
      of Hawaii Press, forthcoming.
Chiso Kaisei Jimukyoku. *Fuken Chiso Kaisei Kiyo.* 1951. Original publication
      data unknown, reprints published in 1951 (v. 1) and 1955 (v. 2 and 3).
Crisostomo, Cristina, and Randolph Barker. 1973. "Growth Rates of Philip-
      pine Agriculture, 1948–1971." In *Agricultural Growth in Japan, Taiwan,
      Korea and the Philippines*, edited by Yujiro Hayami, Vernon W. Ruttan, and
      Herman Southworth. University of Hawaii Press, forthcoming.
Hayami, Yujiro. 1968. "On the Japanese Experience of Agricultural Growth."
      Rural Economic Problems 4 (1968 May).
—— with the assistance of Akino Masakatsu, Shintani Masahiko, and
      Yamada Saburo. 1975. *A Century of Agricultural Growth in Japan: Its
      Relevance to Asian Development.* University of Tokyo Press and University
      of Minnesota Press.
——, and Vernon W. Ruttan. 1971. *Agricultural Development: An Inter-
      national Perspective.* Johns Hopkins University Press.
——, and Saburo Yamada. 1969. "Agricultural Productivity at the Be-
      ginning of Industrialization." In *Agriculture and Economic Growth: Japan's
      Experience*, edited by Kazushi Ohkawa, Bruce F. Johnston and Hirofumi
      Kaneda. University of Tokyo Press.
Lee, T. H., and Y. E. Chen. 1973. "Growth Rates of Taiwan's Agriculture,
      1911–70." In *Agricultural Growth in Japan, Taiwan, Korea and the Philip-
      pines*, edited by Yujiro Hayami, Vernon W. Ruttan, and Herman South-
      worth. University of Hawaii Press, forthcoming.
LTES [*Estimates of Long-Term Economic Statistics of Japan*]. Series edited
      by Kazushi Ohkawa, Miyohei Shinohara, and Mataji Umemura, 14v. 1965–.
      Toyo Keizai Shimposha.
9. Agriculture and Forestry. 1966. Mataji Umemura, Saburo Yamada,
      Yujiro Hayami, Nobukiyo Takamatsu, and Minoru Kumazaki.

Nakamura, James I. 1966. *Agricultural Production and the Economic Development of Japan, 1873–1922.* Princeton University Press.

Nakayama, Seiki. 1966. "Shokuryo Jukyu no Choki Seicho Bunseki." *Nogyo Sogo Kenkyu* 20 (1966 Oct.).

Norinsho. *Norinsho Tokeihyo* (Annual published 1924–43, 1946–).

———. 1971. *Nogyo oyobi Noka no Shakai Kanjo, Showa 44 Nendo.*

Noshomusho. *Noshomusho Tokeihyo* (Statistical yearbooks published 1883–1923).

Sorifu Tokeikyoku. *Rodoryoku Chosa. (Labor Force Survey)* (Annual).

Shintani, Masahiko. 1974. "Nogyo Bumon niokeru Tokarodo Nissu no Suikei." *Keizai Kenkyu* 25 (1974 Jul.).

Yamada, Saburo, and Yujiro Hayami. 1973. "Growth Rates of Japanese Agriculture, 1880–1970." In *Agricultural Growth in Japan, Taiwan, Korea and the Philippines,* edited by Yujiro Hayami, Vernon W. Ruttan, and Herman Southworth. University of Hawaii Press, forthcoming.

Yuize, Yasuhiko. "Nogyo Seisan Shisu no Suikei." *Hitotsubashi Ronso* 56 (1966 Nov.).

5

Manufacturing

Miyohei Shinohara

Long-term changes in the level and structure of manufacturing output are analyzed in this chapter. One concern is to link output estimates gross of intermediate goods for 1874 to 1940 given in LTES 10 with government-compiled data for 1952–70. Secular trends, long swings, Juglar cycles, structural changes, and relative price changes in manufacturing as a whole and in subsectors are also discussed. The use of gross estimates (rather than net) does not affect the analysis here, but in the comprehensive framework of national income the gross figures must be made net in the value added sense. Since 1955 the ratio of gross to net output has been approximately stable. However, for 1929–40 and 1950–55 the ratio does seem to vary some, and before 1929 the derivation of net output in chapter 2 is of a preliminary nature.

MANUFACTURING GROWTH

Table 5.1 summarizes, in overlapping decades, distribution of production in current prices for 1874–1970, omitting the abnormal period of World War II and its aftermath.[1] Table 5.2 is the constant price output series based on 1934–36 prices, with levels of production for 1941–51 interpolated using MITI's indexes of production. While food products in constant prices show a radical decrease over the century, from 58.5 to 12.3%, their increase in relative price moderates the decline to being from 36.2 to 13.0% in current prices. Prewar industrial

---

1. Overlapping decade averages have been used to eliminate the effects of shorter cycles while looking for long-term patterns. Seven-year moving averages were adopted for many series after determining that was the average length of the prewar Juglar cycle (Fujino 1965).

Table 5.1. Manufacturing: Sectoral Composition of Output in Current Prices, 1874–1940 and 1952–70
(In percent)

Period	Food products	Textiles	Lumber and wood products	Chemicals	Stone, clay, and glass products	Iron and steel	Nonferrous metals	Machinery	Printing and publishing	Others
1874–83	36.2	26.5	5.2	18.1	2.3	0.78	2.5	2.6	0.29	5.8
1877–86	37.0	27.8	4.9	16.6	2.0	0.66	2.6	2.4	0.34	5.7
1882–91	36.8	33.1	3.6	13.5	1.8	0.62	2.6	2.2	0.37	5.5
1887–96	32.0	41.0	2.8	12.1	1.8	0.58	2.1	2.1	0.34	5.1
1892–1901	33.3	40.2	3.4	10.9	1.8	0.54	1.9	2.8	0.46	4.8
1897–06	35.3	35.0	3.7	11.3	1.9	0.86	2.1	4.4	0.73	4.7
1902–11	35.2	32.6	3.3	11.6	2.3	1.4	1.9	6.0	1.0	4.7
1907–16	30.9	33.0	2.6	11.4	2.4	3.0	2.8	8.5	1.3	4.2
1912–21	22.9	34.8	2.4	10.7	2.6	5.0	3.4	13.5	1.3	3.5
1917–26	23.8	36.5	2.7	10.3	2.9	4.7	2.7	11.4	1.7	3.4
1922–31	25.5	35.7	3.1	11.0	3.0	4.8	2.3	8.9	2.4	3.4
1927–36	21.0	31.8	3.0	13.2	2.7	7.7	2.7	12.0	2.6	3.3
1931–40	15.2	24.3	3.3	15.4	2.4	12.1	3.1	18.7	2.1	3.5
1952–61	16.3	14.1	4.6	17.6	3.4	13.2	4.5	21.3	2.8	2.2
1957–66	14.5	11.2	4.8	17.0	3.5	13.1	4.5	25.6	2.9	2.9
1961–70	13.0	9.2	4.8	16.2	3.5	13.3	4.7	28.9	3.0	3.3

Source: Appendix tables A19 and A20.

Table 5.2. Manufacturing Output in 1934–36 Prices, 1874–1970: Sectoral Composition
(In percent)

Period	Food products	Textiles	Lumber and wood products	Chemicals	Stone, clay, and glass products	Iron and steel	Nonferrous metals	Machinery	Printing and publishing	Others
1874–83	58.5	10.8	6.3	11.0	1.9	0.37	1.1	1.4	0.25	8.6
1877–86	56.6	12.5	5.9	11.0	1.5	0.38	1.3	1.5	0.31	9.0
1882–91	53.4	18.0	4.7	9.5	1.3	0.40	1.4	1.4	0.45	9.4
1887–96	48.6	24.6	3.7	8.7	1.5	0.37	1.3	1.5	0.54	9.2
1892–1901	47.3	26.5	3.7	8.6	1.5	0.53	1.1	2.2	0.79	7.9
1897–1906	45.9	25.1	4.1	9.2	1.6	0.54	1.1	3.7	1.3	7.4
1902–11	42.1	25.2	3.7	9.7	2.1	1.0	1.6	5.6	1.8	7.3
1907–16	37.2	27.3	3.0	9.6	2.2	1.7	2.6	7.7	2.3	6.4
1912–21	31.6	27.6	2.5	9.2	2.1	2.4	4.4	12.5	2.7	5.0
1917–26	30.6	28.3	2.4	9.2	2.4	3.6	4.4	12.3	2.9	4.0
1922–31	28.2	29.8	2.6	10.7	2.7	5.4	3.7	10.5	3.1	3.4
1927–36	20.9	30.3	2.8	13.2	2.6	8.2	3.3	12.5	2.7	3.4
1932–41	15.3	24.9	2.8	15.9	2.6	10.6	3.3	19.2	2.3	3.1
1937–46	13.7	16.5	2.8	15.9	2.4	12.2	4.0	27.7	2.1	2.7
1942–51	17.0	11.0	3.4	14.7	3.0	11.8	5.1	27.9	3.4	2.7
1947–56	20.0	14.3	3.4	18.8	3.9	9.9	4.4	18.3	4.1	2.8
1952–61	16.6	13.2	2.6	19.7	3.9	10.2	4.2	23.5	2.8	3.3
1957–66	14.3	10.8	2.2	19.9	3.7	10.3	4.0	28.2	2.2	4.4
1961–70	12.3	8.6	1.8	19.9	3.6	10.5	3.8	32.8	1.8	4.9

Source: Appendix tables A21 and A22.

Table 5.3. Manufacturing Subsectors, 1874–1940 and 1952–70: Relative Price Index
(Manufacturing as a whole, 1934–36 = 100)

Period	Food products	Textiles	Lumber and wood products	Chemicals	Stone, clay, and glass products	Iron and steel	Nonferrous metals	Machinery	Printing and publishing	Others
1874–83	62.3	248.6	81.5	167.0	124.9	232.3	236.4	217.2	116.4	68.5
1877–86	65.6	224.6	82.6	151.7	131.7	176.5	210.4	165.5	111.0	64.6
1882–91	69.4	194.4	76.8	141.6	134.1	155.9	184.5	151.5	92.0	59.6
1887–96	66.8	167.5	75.0	141.5	122.9	157.0	161.0	143.9	64.7	56.2
1892–1901	69.1	154.4	85.9	129.7	115.8	152.2	169.6	126.3	57.7	60.6
1897–1906	77.0	140.5	91.4	122.2	118.4	155.9	180.6	117.7	54.4	63.7
1902–11	83.6	130.4	89.5	120.0	112.6	142.6	136.6	107.8	55.1	64.6
1907–16	84.5	121.6	88.2	119.3	110.8	150.8	98.7	105.5	54.7	66.9
1912–21	76.8	122.9	94.3	117.5	119.4	198.1	83.2	104.5	51.5	72.0
1917–26	77.2	128.3	114.4	112.0	122.7	157.7	60.7	91.5	56.8	88.4
1922–31	90.2	119.9	119.8	105.3	112.4	92.2	62.6	85.3	79.4	99.9
1927–36	100.2	105.7	107.0	101.4	104.2	93.0	80.3	93.7	97.3	99.3
1931–40	99.2	96.6	113.6	98.3	97.2	108.7	90.1	100.7	93.2	105.1
1952–61	97.7	109.9	168.8	90.2	86.7	127.9	110.0	89.5	98.5	66.7
1957–66	101.3	103.2	211.7	86.4	92.6	129.3	110.0	91.7	127.9	65.7
1961–70	105.8	106.4	253.6	82.0	98.6	126.3	120.3	88.9	160.8	67.5

Source: Table 5.1 divided by table 5.2.

growth was strongly textile oriented, although this trend was reversed in the postwar period. A very marked relative price decline prevailed in textiles in the prewar period.

Changes in industrial structure and relative prices often happen together. In the short run an increase in an industry's share may increase its relative price, due to demand-shift effects. This happened particularly during the war for the iron and steel and machinery industries. However, over the longer period, with some exceptions, industries with increasing output share in constant prices may reduce relative prices because unit costs are lowered through economies of scale and technological progress. These generally become export industries due to their comparative advantage in unit costs. Such a relation can probably be found in many industries in advanced economies. On the other hand, modern industries introduced into developing countries have not always displayed this negative correlation, nor have they developed as export industries. Thus relative price decline associated with relative output expansion by some industries may be an important keystone for development through foreign trade.

There is another possible cause for declining relative prices in association with rising output share. Technology may lower input prices or increase productivity of capital or labor, permitting an industry to expand by replacing similar products that cannot compete at the lower

Table 5.4. Manufacturing Subsector Output in 1934–36 Prices: Growth Rates
(Percent per annum)

1874–1940	1874–1900	1900–40	1935–70	1955–70	
5.2	4.7	6.1	8.0	16.2	Total manufacturing Subsector:
3.0	3.5	3.0	6.4	11.1	Food products
6.6	10.5	6.4	3.5	10.4	Textiles
3.6	1.6	5.0	6.1	10.8	Lumber and wood products
5.6	3.2	7.6	8.9	15.7	Chemicals
6.1	3.3	7.4	8.8	15.2	Stone, clay, and glass products
12.0	4.9	15.7	8.1	16.5	Iron and steel
7.7	5.1	9.2	8.7	15.3	Nonferrous metals
10.6	8.4	10.2	10.5	23.7	Machinery
10.0	12.1	7.6	6.2	9.6	Printing and publishing
3.0	4.2	3.2	9.1	21.0	Others

Source: Appendix tables A21 and A22.
Notes: Prewar growth rates (cols. 1, 2, and 3) are computed by fitting exponential curves to annual data.
   The compound growth rate between end years is used for 1935–70 and 1955–70.

prices or by defining totally new products. Changes in relative prices of major manufacturing subsectors are given in table 5.3.

Trend rates of growth in manufacturing in constant prices are given in table 5.4, and overlapping decade rates in table 5.5. Computing 1935–70 growth rates eliminates most postwar rehabilitation factors. Trend acceleration is observable in each successive period for chemicals; stone, clay, and glass; and others (such items as lacquerware, toys, umbrellas) (table 5.4, cols. 2–4). On the other hand, neither machinery nor iron and steel had much growth acceleration. However, my research suggests naval construction and other military procurement accounted for over one-third of iron and steel output in the mid-1930s, and when the influence of this demand is removed, some upward drift in postwar rates is discernible. This is indicative of how large the two industries had become in the 1930s before the extensive destruction of facilities and loss of markets brought on by the war. Decelerating industries were textiles and printing and publishing.

When the 1900–40 trend is extrapolated to the present, the actual postwar trend of manufacturing output as a whole surpassed the prewar trend around 1964–65. The prewar peak was reached about 1955. Textiles fall considerably short of their prewar trend, reflecting the retreat of the industry as a major exporter. Stone, clay, and glass exceeded their prewar trend around 1960. Lumber and wood products have a curvilinear trend on a semilog graph for the prewar period, but if the 1900–40 trend on a scale ratio is extended into the postwar years, the postwar trend crosses it around 1965.

As already noted, iron and steel is of particular interest. While the output growth rate since the war may be a bit higher than before and during the war, the postwar trend in 1970 was still below an extrapolation of the prewar trend. In machinery, major peaks appeared during World War I and the military buildup of the 1930s. Omitting these and just extrapolating the 1905–15 and 1923–34 trend, the postwar trend crosses it around 1960.

The initial prewar trend in chemicals may reflect a tendency for growth of such traditional items as salt, animal fats, and vegetable oils, with the emergence of modern chemicals coming late in the period. For whatever reason, the rate begins to accelerate about 1925. The resulting curvature makes it hard to determine an overall prewar trend. If the post-1925 trend is extrapolated to represent the modern chemical industry, output in the early 1970s was still below the prewar trend.

In general, the fastest growing postwar areas have been those in-

Table 5.5. Manufacturing Subsector Output in 1934–36 Prices, 1874–1970: Growth Rates
(Percent per annum)

Period		Food products	Textiles	Lumber and wood products	Chemicals	Stone, clay, and glass products	Iron and steel	Non-ferrous metals	Machinery	Printing and publishing	Others	Total
1874–83	to 1877–86	1.7	8.0	0.5	2.8	-3.3	4.3	7.9	7.2	10.4	4.5	2.8
1877–86	to 1882–91	3.1	12.1	-0.1	1.4	1.3	5.0	7.2	2.8	12.2	5.2	4.3
1882–91	to 1887–96	4.2	13.1	1.1	4.2	8.9	4.8	4.7	7.5	10.1	5.7	6.2
1887–96	to 1892–1901	4.3	6.5	5.1	4.6	5.2	3.8	0.8	13.0	13.3	1.9	5.0
1892–1901	to 1897–06	1.7	1.3	4.2	3.9	3.6	11.2	2.8	13.5	13.4	1.0	2.4
1897–06	to 1902–11	1.4	3.2	1.3	4.2	8.1	17.2	10.3	12.4	10.0	2.9	2.7
1902–11	to 1907–16	3.3	7.7	1.8	5.8	7.4	17.6	17.2	12.9	11.6	3.1	5.9
1907–16	to 1912–21	4.3	7.9	3.7	6.7	6.8	15.3	19.8	18.6	10.5	2.6	7.7
1912–21	to 1917–26	4.8	6.1	4.4	5.5	8.6	14.5	5.6	5.1	7.4	0.8	5.5
1917–26	to 1922–31	2.8	5.7	6.5	7.8	6.4	13.5	0.8	1.4	5.5	1.6	4.6
1922–31	to 1927–36	0.8	7.3	8.8	11.6	6.6	15.9	4.8	10.8	4.4	6.5	6.9
1927–36	to 1932–41	1.4	3.8	7.4	10.9	7.6	13.7	7.5	17.5	4.1	6.4	8.4
1932–41	to 1937–46	-3.4	-9.8	-1.1	-1.1	-2.1	1.8	3.3	6.4	-3.0	-4.5	-1.1
1937–46	to 1942–51	-4.7	-16.1	-4.3	-10.3	-4.7	-9.4	-3.0	-8.6	1.5	-8.8	-8.8
1942–51	to 1947–56	11.2	13.5	7.4	13.0	13.7	3.9	4.1	-1.1	11.9	8.3	7.6
1947–56	to 1952–61	12.3	15.1	11.3	18.1	16.9	17.7	16.2	22.9	8.3	20.8	17.6
1952–61	to 1957–66	11.8	11.3	11.4	16.1	14.6	16.1	14.7	20.3	10.3	22.6	16.4
1957–66	to 1961–70	10.8	9.4	11.1	15.9	14.9	16.3	14.4	20.2	10.2	19.1	15.8

Source: Appendix tables A21 and A22.

Table 5.6. Manufacturing Shipments in Current Prices in 1955 and 1970
(In billions of yen)

1955	1970	Index[a]	Category
1,096	4,390	401	Textiles
86	957	1,113	Apparel
274	2,232	815	Lumber and wood products
65	1,009	1,552	Furniture and fixtures
651	6,565	1,008	Iron and steel
283	3,055	1,080	Nonferrous metals
312	6,803	2,180	Machinery
251	7,331	2,921	Electrical machinery
371	7,276	1,961	Transportation equipment
56	892	1,593	Instruments and related items
133	2,465	1,853	Miscellaneous products

Source: Kogyo Tokeihyo, 1955 and 1972 editions.
[a] 1970 output as a percentage of 1955 level.

volving increasing fabrication. As examples, between 1955 and 1970 apparel grew almost three times as fast as textiles, and furniture grew almost twice as fast as lumber and wood products (table 5.6). This increased fabrication was aided by technological advances (see Shinohara 1970, pp. 214–19, for further discussion).

LONG SWINGS

Table 5.7 gives a broad overview of long swings, particularly the duration and amplitude of growth cycles in subsectors of the industry, and suggests the extent of the negative impact of World War II on various industries. In manufacturing as a whole, the peaks suggest growth cycles of 20 to 25 years' duration before World War II. There are some differences depending on whether a seven- or ten-year (figure in parentheses) moving average is adopted. This again shows construction-related industries have different swing patterns.

Before the war, the up- and downswings in manufacturing as a whole closely followed the movement of textiles and others, although until the depression, textiles usually had higher growth rates than total manufacturing. There was a lag of about five years in the long swing of food products compared to manufacturing. However, when we use a smoothing procedure such as seven-year moving averages, a different result emerges, as is described later.

Long swings in construction have a different pattern than those in

Table 5.7. Manufacturing Long Swings

(In terms of 1934–36 price series)

Trough	Peak	Trough	Peak	Trough	Peak	Trough	Peak	Category
1882 (1882)	1888 (1891)	1902 (1900)			1915 (1914)	1922 (1924)	1936 (1934)	Manufacturing industry
1884 (1881)	1889 (1891)	1902 (1901–02)			1919 (1917)	1929 (1928)	1936 (1934)	Food products
1883 (1885)	1889 (1890)	1901 (1900)			1913 (1914)	1921 (1924–05)	1934 (1930)	Textiles
1881 (1883)	1896 (1895)			1908 (1906)			1924 (1930)	Lumber and wood products[a]
1881 (1885)	1894 (1896)	1905 (1906)			1914–15 (1913)	1919 (1921)	1935 (1933)	Chemicals
1882 (1880)	1889 (1890)	1900 (1900)	1909 (1907)	1914 (1916)	1924 (1921)	1929 (1927)	1936 (1934)	Stone, clay, and glass products[b]
1881 (1883)	1886 (1885)	1894 (1895)	1906 (1907)		1916 (1914)	1923 (1924)	1936 (1934)	Iron and steel[c]
					1914 (1914)	1921 (1924)	1936 (1934)	Nonferrous metals[c]
1885 (1886)	1897 (1896)	1911 (1910)			1914 (1914)	1921 (1924)	1936 (1935)	Machinery[c]
								Printing and publishing[d]
1880 (1880)	1887 (1888)	1896 (1899)			1916 (1914)	1919 (1924)	1934 (1935)	Others

Source: Author's calculations.

Notes: Seven-year moving averages (figures in parentheses are for ten-year moving averages).

[a] The long upswing in the growth rate was continuous after 1908.

[b] A movement not seen in other industries arose, particularly after 1900.

[c] Based on LTES 10's series B. See notes to table A19.

[d] No long swing can be seen in printing and publishing.

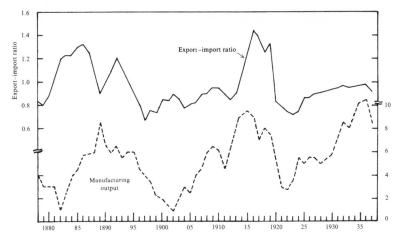

Fig. 5.1. Export–Import Ratio and the Long Swing in Manufacturing

Notes: The solid line is a three-year moving average of the export–import ratio. The dashed line is a seven-year moving average of the annual growth rates of manufacturing output.

manufacturing. During the depression of the 1920s and 30s, growth in construction-related industries such as lumber and wood, and stone, clay, and glass, as well as iron and steel did not slow as much as, say, the machinery industry. Construction activity largely reflected domestic factors, while manufacturing as a whole seems to have been closely related to export activity in the textile and others subsectors. In the downswing of the 1920s, government spending on construction projects such as rural roads increased significantly. The 1923 Kanto earthquake also increased the construction level. The 1947–56 to 1952–61 peak may well involve strong rehabilitation factors, a reaction to the deep drop in the immediate postwar years. Actually, the post-recovery peak comes much later, probably in the early 1970s before worldwide economic malaise and the oil embargo of 1973 brought on Japan's first real-term output decline.

To ascribe dates to peaks and troughs in manufacturing long swings, figure 5.1 adopts seven-year moving averages to smooth the effects of shorter business cycles based on Fujino's (1965) finding prewar Juglar cycles averaged seven years. The figure shows there were very marked growth cycles, with 20 years between troughs (1882, 1902, and 1922). However, from the first peak (1889) to the second (1915) is 26 years, and from the second to third (1936) is 21 years. When a ten-year

moving average is applied (to correspond with the length of the postwar
business cycle), the cycle durations are 19 and 24 years between troughs,
23 and 20 years between peaks. For the postwar period figure 5.1
illustrates both ten and seven-year moving averages. Using the seven-
year average still leaves a Juglar swing (from a trough in 1955 to
another in 1965). The ten-year average smooths it considerably, but
reveals a trough in 1962 which is difficult to understand.

Prewar long swings in manufacturing activity remarkably parallel
the export–import ratio, as indicated in figure 5.1. The export–import
ratio seems to lead some in the pre-1900 period. It has been suggested
the two series also be analyzed in relation to the monetary framework
(Abramovitz 1973, pp. 253–65). This has yet to be done, but it is
clear that understanding Japan's long swings requires more than mere
emphasis on construction cycles caused by demographic factors such
as population and labor-force growth and migration. Balance of
payments, exports and imports, and other aspects of an open economy
also display a significant impact. From the figure one may infer growth
was export-led. My own tentative view is that growth was a virtuous
circle propelled by feedback between investment spurts and export
promotion.

JUGLAR CYCLES

In the pre-World War II period there are not only long swings
(Kuznets cycle) but also Juglar cycles. For years since 1874 these
appear by comparing three-year moving average (A) to seven- (or ten-)
year moving average (B or B') series, using the ratios $(1 + A)/(1 + B)$ or
$(1 + A)/(1 + B')$ (see the graph in LTES 10:31–32). Movements of
these ratios in both current and constant prices were checked, and the
current price series was adopted here simply because it more distinctly
reflects the cycles. Table 5.8 shows comparable peaks and troughs
in various industries.

In constant prices the degree of concomitance of Juglars is much
less among industries, and in some subsectors there is little regularity.
Measured in money terms, the series reflects the influence of excess
demand (or supply) insofar as it is transmitted into price fluctuations.
In medium-length periods (seven to ten years) this is important back-
ground to the stock adjustment process of fixed assets. Further, since
Fujino (1965) has computed Juglar cycles using the diffusion index
and bank debit data, there is a check on the money-term series.

Table 5.8. Juglar Cycle by the Growth Cycle Approach

	Food products	Textiles	Lumber and wood products	Chemicals	Stone, clay, and glass products	Iron and steel	Nonferrous metals	Machinery	Printing and publishing	Manufacturing industry
Trough	1883–84	1883	1883	1882	1883–84	1883	1885	1883–84	1886	1883
Peak	1888	1888	1887	1886	1887	1887	1889	1888	1890	1888
Trough	1891	1891	1891	1892	1890	1891	1890	1891	1893	1891
Peak	1897	1898	1896	1896	1900	1895	1899	1899	1896	1898–99
Trough	1903	1901	1902	1901	1903	1899	1902	1902	1903	1901–03
Peak	1906	1906	1907	1905–06	1906	1904	1906	1904–06	1905–06	1906
Trough	1909	1908	1909–10	1909	1909	1907	1908	1908	1908	1909
Peak	1912	1910–11	1912	1912	1911	1911	1910–11	1911	1911	1911
Trough	1914–15	1914	1915	1914–15	1914	1913	1913	1914	1913	1914
Peak	1918	1918	1918	1917	1917	1916	1916	1917	1919	1917
Trough	1921–22	1921	1921	1921	1921	1920	1919–20	1920	1922	1921
Peak	1927–28	1928	1927	1928	1928	1924	1928	1927–28	1924	1928
Trough	1930	1930	1930–31	1930	1931	1930	1930	1930	1929	1930
Peak	1933	1933	1933	1933	1933	1933	1932	1934		1933
Trough	1936	1935	1935	1935	1936	1935	1935	1936		1935

Source: Author's calculations.

Note: Dates determined by turning points in the ratios $(1 + A)/(1 + B)$ and $(1 + A)/(1 + B')$ as explained in the text. When the ratios yield different dates, both are given.

Table 5.9. Juglar Cycle Duration

	Estimation by growth cycle approach			Fujino's chronologies[a]	
	Juglar cycle in manufacturing	Duration from peak to peak	Duration from trough to trough	By bank debits[b]	By diffusion index
Peak	1880			1881 l.h.	1880 Nov.
Trough	1883			1883 l.h.	1883 Sep.
Peak	1888	8		1889 l.h.	1890 Jul.
Trough	1891		8	1891 f.h.	1891 Oct.
Peak	1898–99	10–11		1896 l.h.	1897 Nov.
Trough	1901–03		10–12	1901 l.h.	1901 Jun.
Peak	1906	7–8		1906 l.h.	1907 May
Trough	1909		6–8	1908 f.h.	1909 Jan.
Peak	1911	5		1913 l.h.	1913 Sep.
Trough	1914		5	1914 l.h.	1914 Dec.
Peak	1917	6		1920 f.h.	1920 Apr.
Trough	1921		7	1921 f.h.	1921 Apr.
Peak	1928	11		1928 l.h.	1929 Mar.
Trough	1930		9	1930 f.h.	1930 Nov.
Peak	1933	5		1939 l.h.	1939 Dec.
Trough	1935		5		
	Average	7.6	7.4		

Sources: The growth cycle approach is the author's; Fujino's chronologies are from Fujino 1965, pp. 19 and 35.
[a] There are also a trough in the last half of 1898 and a peak in the first half of 1900 for Fujino's bank debit approach; in terms of his diffusion index these are 1898 Nov. (trough) and 1899 Dec. (peak).
[b] f.h. = first half, l.h. = last half of year.

Food products and textiles were as much as 60% of output in the early industrialization period and about 40% even in the 1930s, so their waves closely reflect the Juglar in manufacturing as a whole. The amplitudes of swings in iron and steel, nonferrous metals, and machinery are larger than those in other industries, manifesting higher sensitivities to the Juglar cycle. Despite their small shares in total manufacturing output, they generally displayed movements concomitant with those in manufacturing as a whole, although there are some leads or lags.

Table 5.9 shows how my Juglar cycle chronology compares with Fujino's. There is a surprising conformity despite the extensive differences in estimating procedures and statistical sources. Both Fujino's and my estimates almost coincided for troughs, but the dates of peaks

Table 5.10. Manufacturing Export–Import Ratio and Juglar Cycles

Export–import ratio		Juglar cycles in manufacturing
3-year moving average	3-year divided by 7-year moving average	
Negative correspondence		
1879 (T)	1879 (T)	1880 (P)
	1882 (P)	1883 (T)
	1885 (T)	
1886 (P)	1887 (P)	
1889 (T)	1889 (T)	1888 (P)
1892 (P)	1892 (P)	1891 (T)
1897 (T)	1897 (T)	1898–99 (P)
1902 (P)	1902 (P)	1902 (T)
1904 (T)	1904 (T)	1906 (P)
1910 (P)	1910 (P)	1909 (T)
1912 (T)		1911 (P)
Positive correspondence		
	1913 (T)	1914 (T)
1916 (P)	1916 (P)	1917 (P)
1923 (T)	1920 (T)	1921 (T)
	1926 (P)	1928 (P)
	1932 (T)	1930 (T)
1934–35 (P)	1933 (P)	1933 (P)
	1937 (T)	1935 (T)

Source: Author's calculation.
Note: P = peak; T = trough.

are somewhat different. The peak and trough in World War II may not be correct, as the current-price data stop with 1940. If the war period is included, the Juglar cycle peak in current prices may be 1939 as Fujino computed, rather than 1933. However, the three-year moving average of growth rates in constant prices peaked in 1934 and then had a declining tendency. The other principal difference with Fujino is an extra swing, with an 1898 trough and 1900 peak, which does not appear in my analysis.

The export–import ratio series, almost parallel to long swings, are inversely related to Juglar cycles for the period before 1911–12, with peaks in the export–import ratio coming with Juglar troughs and conversely (table 5.10). After 1913–14 there is no discernible relationship. Perhaps an inverse Juglar association prevailed because imports vary even more compared to exports during the Juglar cycle than during long swings. The output boom–import surplus correspondence is primarily a short-run phenomenon, but it may still appear in the medium-term cycle. The massive export expansion brought on by World War I and the devaluation of the 1930s seem to have swamped the relationship, however (see the related discussion in ch. 7)

DATA AND METHODS

For 1874–1940 the statistical data on gross output are from LTES 10 while the 1952–70 data are from the *Census of Manufactures* (*Kogyo Tokeihyo*) with the addition of output by government corporations. The 1941–51 period is one of hyperinflation and black markets, so the series in the census are something of a guess. In LTES (10:35–38), MITI's production index is tentatively used to link the pre- and postwar periods, and also for the 1952–70 period. However, in this chapter MITI's production index is used only for interpolating between 1940 and 1952 levels.

There are some differences between MITI's production index (a real-term series based on data in *Seisan Dotai Chosa*) and the *Census* (adjusted to include government corporations and then deflated by the Bank of Japan's wholesale price indexes for the appropriate manufacturing subsector). The divergence is significant after around 1960, especially in some sectors. More work is needed to reconcile the two series. One source of possible systematic underestimation in the MITI indexes is exclusion of some of the new products continually emerging during the rapid postwar growth. This is less of a problem with the deflated *Census* series and thus one reason they are used in this chapter.

OTHER ESTIMATES

One of the first to make industrial production estimates was the Nagoya College of Commerce. The first version of their index, covering 1893–1931, appeared in 1933 and a revised series for 1868–1936 came out in 1938. Detailed descriptions of the underlying data and estimating procedures have been lost. Research shows such serious defects the series cannot be used, and thus work based on it (such as Hilgert 1945) must be used with care, if at all (see discussions in Shinohara 1961, p. 74, and 1962, pp. 86–87; Shionoya 1966).

Reliable indexes of industrial production have been compiled by Yasuba (1966, 1971) and by Shionoya (1966). The Yasuba index appeared in 1966, but was revised in 1971. Covering 1905–35, Yasuba aimed at directly computing an index of the physical volume of production, based on the volumes of production of individual commodities (64 in the original index, 91 in the later version). He took particular care with the machinery industry, since other indexes are weak in this area for the prewar period. Although much effort has been made to collect the scattered data on various kinds of machinery and equipment, such data are inadequate for constructing long-term historical series in each category of the industry.

Shionoya's index measures not only volume of production, but also current and real-term values of output for 1874–1940. He first estimated the value of production, and after estimating the real-term series, derived a volume index. The real-term series are deflated values, using deflators by industry from LTES 8. Shionoya's methodology permits coverage of the increasing diversification of industrial products, but he has been criticized for using the 1938 Nagoya indexes by industry for interpolations (Yasuba 1966). Also, one of Shionoya's sources, the *Fuken Tokeihyo*, often omits some prefectures. In the Shinohara index I have tried to adjust for this underestimation, which exists in Shionoya's results for 1889–91 and 1901–03. Also for the Shinohara index, a long-term production series of major commodity items was compiled and utilized (instead of using the Nagoya index) for the interpolations among benchmark years before World War I.

Despite differences and shortcomings specific to each, the Yasuba, Shionoya, Shinohara, and official indexes are fairly close and display a similar pattern for total output, although there are problems remaining in estimating output in some subsectors, especially machinery and lumber and wood products.

INTERNATIONAL COMPARISON

Japan's rate of industrial production growth for the 1881–1912 period appears similar to the long-term rates of several other advanced countries, but in part this is an estimation problem. An extremely comprehensive census of production was made in 1874 in Japan (*Zenfuken Bussanhyo*), and the reported output is considerably higher than the level expected from extrapolating back the data in later statistical yearbooks (primarily the *Kojo Tokeihyo*). For example, in textiles the census levels are more than twice the extrapolated figures. Some of the *Zenfuken* data therefore may involve a little overestima-

Table 5.11. International Comparison of Prewar Industrial Growth Rates

1881–1937		1881–1912		1912–37		
Index	Annual growth rates	Index	Annual growth rates	Index	Annual growth rates	
817	3.7	402	4.6	203	2.9	United States
240	1.6	166	1.7	144	1.5	United Kingdom
538	3.1	330	3.9	163	2.0	Italy
518	2.9	369	4.2	140	1.4	Germany
1,295[a]	4.6	455[b]	4.7	285[c]	4.5	U.S.S.R.
1,929	5.4	374	4.3	517	6.8	Japan

Sources: United States: Frickey 1947 and Fabricant 1940; United Kingdom: Hoffman 1940; Italy: Gerschenkron 1962 and OEEC 1955; Germany: Wagenfuhr 1933 and OEEC 1955; U.S.S.R.: Nutter 1962; Japan: author's calculations.
Notes: Annual growth rates are compound percentage rates between the end years.
The indexes are the last year's output levels as a percentage of the first year's.
[a] 1880–1937.
[b] 1880–1913.
[c] 1913–37.

tion, but if data as complete as the *Zenfuken* were available for other countries their initial levels would probably be higher, and thus their growth rates lower, than those given in table 5.11.

The growth rates of other advanced countries slowed in the 1912–37 period, while Japan's rate accelerated. Even if the other countries' rates for 1881–1912 were lowered as I have suggested, this deceleration would most likely still appear.

REFERENCES

Abramovitz, Moses. 1973. "Comments on Shinohara's Paper." In *Economic Growth*, edited by Kazushi Ohkawa and Yujiro Hayami. Japan Economic Research Center.
Baba, Masao, and Masahiro Tatemoto. 1968. "Foreign Trade and Economic Growth in Japan, 1858–1937." In *Economic Growth*, edited by Lawrence Klein and Kazushi Ohkawa. Richard D. Irwin.
Fabricant, Solomon. 1940. *The Output of Manufacturing Industries, 1899–1937*.
Frickey, Edwin. 1937. *Production in the United States, 1860–1910*.
Fujino, Shozaburo. 1965. *Nihon no Keiki Junkan*. Keiso Shobo.
Fuken Tokeihyo. (Published irregularly between 1899 and 1923 by Kakufuken).
Gerschenkron, Alexander. 1962. *Economic Backwardness in Historical Perspective*. Harvard University Press.
Hoffman, Walther. 1940. *Wachstum and Wachstumformen*.

Kojo Tokeihyo (*Factory Statistics*). Published in 1909, 1914, and then annually 1919–23 by Noshomusho and annually 1924–38 by Shokosho.

Kogyo Tokeihyo (*Census of Manufactures*). Published annually by Tsusho Sangyosho (MITI) and its predecesor, Shokosho, 1939, except for 1943–45.

LTES [*Estimates of Long-Term Economic Statistics of Japan*]. Series edited by Kazushi Ohkawa, Miyohei Shinohara, and Mataji Umemura. 14 v. 1965–. Toyo Keizai Shimposha.
    8. Prices. 1967. Kazushi Ohkawa et al.
    10. Mining and Manufacturing. 1972. Miyohei Shinohara.

MITI. See Tsusho Sangyosho.

Nutter, G. Warren. 1962. *The Growth of Industrial Production in the Soviet Union.*

OECD (Organization for Economic Cooperation and Development). 1973. *Industrial Production 1955–71.*

OEEC (Organization for European Economic Cooperation). 1955. *Industrial Statistics, 1950–55.*

Shinohara, Miyohei. 1961. *Nihon Keizai no Seicho to Junkan.* Sobunsha. (An English-language book with the same title, *Growth and Cycles in the Japanese Economy.* (1962, Kinokuniya), is somewhat different in contents.)

———. 1970. *Structural Changes in Japanese Economic Development.* Kinokuniya.

Shionoya, Yuichi. 1966. "Nihon no Kogyo Seisan Shisu, 1874–1940." In *Sangyo Kozo*, edited by Miyohei Shinohara. Chikumashobo.

Tsusho Sangyosho. *Seisan Dotai Chosa.*

Wagenfuhr, Rolf. 1933. "Die Industrie und Wirtschaft." *Viertel-jahrshefte zur Konjunktur forschung.* 31.

Yasuba, Yasukichi. 1966. "Industrial Production Index, 1905–35." In *Keizai Seicho no Riron to Keisoku*, edited by Kenichi Inada and Tadao Uchida. Iwanami.

———. 1971. "A Revised Index of Industrial Production for Japan, 1905–20." *Osaka Economic Papers* (1971 Mar.).

Zenfuken Bussanhyo. 1874. Reprinted 1959 by Meiji Bunken Shiryo Kanko Kai as v. 1 of *Meiji Zenki Shogyo Hattatsu Shishiryo.*

6

Services

Kazushi Ohkawa and Nobukiyo Takamatsu

By the conventional classification used here, services is a diverse, almost residual, subsector of that is often called the tertiary sector. Three categories are covered in this chapter: trade (wholesale and retail), finance (banking, insurance, and real estate), and personal services (professionals and servants). Together the first two are called commerce–services B (= subsector II in LTES 1). Two items generally considered services that are not discussed here are home ownership (for housing's relation to other areas, see chs. 8 and 9), and public administration (ch. 10). Aspects of services' total output and relation to other major sectors are included in an overall discussion of national product in chapter 2. This chapter deals with structural change, productivity, and the data themselves.

Services is one of the most difficult areas in which to gather information. The output is intangible or at best short lived, and the largest input is labor, followed by the buildings containing the activity. Moreover, historically most of those rendering services have been small, noncorporate enterprises and individuals (such as servants) who had no reason, even after taxation was instituted, to keep records, let alone turn them into some central compiler. Insofar as there are tax records, we combed them thoroughly in preparing estimates for GRJE, and since then we have continually broadened our sources. Income (our measure of output) received by each of the three categories cannot be estimated from the available material, and there are other limitations in data continuity and reliability for both input and output. Nonetheless, the series are reliable enough to indicate the broad historical pattern of output, input, and their relation to the aggregate.

Table 6.1. Services: Distribution of Income Earners by Status, 1885–1940
(In percent; total number in thousands of income earners)

Proprietors

	Total number	Corporations	Individuals			Unpaid family workers	Employes
			Tax-paying	Nontax-paying	Total		
1885	2,121	a	17.3	34.6	51.9	39.3	8.8
1895	2,347	a	17.3	34.6	51.9	39.2	8.9
1905	2,517	0.2	17.2	34.4	51.9	37.6	10.4
1915	3,132	0.4	17.2	34.3	51.9	34.4	13.7
1925	3,785	0.7	17.1	34.2	51.9	31.2	16.9
1930	4,154	0.9	14.3	37.7	52.9	30.1	17.1
1935	4,533	1.3	13.8	31.7	46.7	25.0	28.3
1940	4,956	1.0	17.6	22.1	40.6	20.6	38.7

Source: LTES 1:131 (which gives the underlying data annually for 1885 to 1940).
Note: There was a minimum income level before any tax liability was incurred.
[a] Less than 0.075%.

STRUCTURAL CHANGES

Considerable structural change of two kinds has occurred within the sector in terms of both the relative importance of the components and the labor force. Finance has become a major element as modern banking and insurance expanded to serve the growing economy, although this is difficult to show explicitly. The role of banking in development is discussed by Patrick (1967; also see Fuji Ginko 1967, Yamamura 1972, and Feldman 1976).

There has been a shift in the labor force away from small-scale proprietorships (often with only family workers and providing traditional services) in all three categories, a trend related to the emergence of banks, and later, the growth of department stores and trading companies. No comprehensive data by these subsectors are available for proving the historical pattern of such a trend. Table 6.1, derived from the income-estimating procedure outlined in the data and methods section at the end of this chapter, and table 6.2, although only for four years, provide the closest statistical evidence available. The large number of employes in 1940 in tables 6.1 and 6.2 is somewhat misleading, since except in financial institutions most worked in

Table 6.2. Services: Number of Business Taxpayers and Employes for Selected Years, 1897–1926

(Thousands)

	Financing		Commerce		Other services	Total
	Modern	Traditional	Trade	Others		
A. Number						
1897 Taxpayers	0.62	29.36	288.12	54.10	22.95	395.90
1897 Employes	12.57	39.09	623.70	74.07	112.73	864.28
1906 Taxpayers	2.27	47.88	316.39	19.05	20.51	407.01
1906 Employes	37.85	58.25	635.13	39.54	104.29	878.89
1915 Taxpayers (C)	2.15	2.10	4.44	1.28	0.17	10.38
1915 Taxpayers (N)	0.06	35.56	232.46	13.44	12.87	294.90
1915 Employes (C)	54.29	10.82	35.90	10.31	2.89	116.58
1915 Employes (N)	0.73	41.80	478.88	30.96	75.20	629.60
1926 Taxpayers (C)	1.79	2.18	16.82	2.30	0.43	23.90
1926 Taxpayers (N)	0.02	60.21	774.45	33.11	24.83	893.28
1926 Employes (C)	115.91	13.45	138.51	19.81	8.47	303.00
1926 Employes (N)	1.09	63.62	1,271.40	54.29	121.28	1,513.08
B. Average number of employes per taxpayer in part A						
1897	20.28	1.33	2.16	1.37	4.91	2.18
1906	16.63	1.22	2.01	2.08	5.09	2.16
1915 (C)	25.20	5.16	8.08	8.05	17.08	11.24
1915 (N)	12.72	1.18	2.06	2.30	5.84	2.13
1926 (C)	64.90	6.16	8.24	8.60	19.52	12.86
1926 (N)	54.55	1.06	1.64	1.64	4.88	1.68

Source: LTES 1:132–37 (table 8-3A).
Notes: Six subdivisions in the original data are grouped into five as follows:
Modern financing: banking, insurance.
Traditional financing: Muzin (mutual loan association), money lending, real estate lending.
Commercial–commodity trade.
Commercial–others: brokerage, *tonya* (wholesale dealer), other intermediary.
Services: restaurants, travelers' inn, and entertainment.
The total includes some others such as warehousing and photographers. A breakdown into corporate (C) and noncorporate (N) is possible only after 1915. Family workers are not included in the number of employes. Data limitations before 1920 prevent a classification by worker status.

small establishments where in many ways they were more like family members living in the proprietor's home and receiving much of their income in kind. As table 6.3 shows, services in 1966 remained small-scale, particularly in retail trade.

Table 6.3. Service Establishments: Distribution by Number of Workers, 1966
(In percent)

Scale (number of workers)	1–9	10–29	30–99	Over 100
Wholesale and retail trade	92.4	6.1	1.3	0.2
Services[a]	88.3	8.2	3.0	0.5
Real estate	97.2	2.1	0.6	0.1
Banking, insurance	53.7	26.5	17.5	2.4
Manufacturing	72.3	18.6	6.9	2.4
All nonprimary	86.2	9.7	3.3	0.8

Source: Sorifu Tokei Kyoku 1969, 6:39.
Notes: An establishment in Japanese statistics is a place of business, such as a specific store location or bank branch. Thus a company may have several establishments, so this table does not indicate distribution by a firm's total employment.

Workers include the proprietor, any unpaid family workers, and employes.
[a] A composite of 20 subcategories including personal and professional services, educators, and miscellaneous.

OUTPUT PER WORKER AND PRODUCTIVITY

Determining whether there has been a convergence of output per worker in the different sectors is a challenging problem. During the early years of development, output per worker in services was considerably higher than in industry, though there may be some over-estimation (see ch. 2, table 2.12). It became equal to that of the industrial sector just before World War I measured in current prices and in 1927–33 for the 1934–36 constant price series. In constant prices, services has continued to decline relative to the industrial sector, but in current prices the pattern was reversed in the 1960s. The evolution of the service sector's composition and the emergence of a national market must have been relevant to the decline of S/N (the ratio of service to industrial output), but their exact impact is beyond direct measurement.

Labor, especially in the traditional subsectors, is services' major input. Since wages in the service sector rose faster than commodity prices in general, S/N in the current-price series could be rising even as the constant price ratio fell. Another factor in the observed decline in S/N is that the nature of productive activity in the service sector makes constant price series productivity data less reliable than for goods-producing sectors.

Table 6.4. Service Output, Labor Employed, and Output per Worker: Average Annual
Growth Rates

(In percent)

		Y	L	y = Y − L	K	k = Y − K
1902–12	(11)	−0.01	1.52	−1.53	4.70	−4.71
1913–19	(7)	5.48	1.59	3.89	6.29	−0.81
1920–28	(9)	−1.59	2.41	−4.00	6.98	−8.57
1929–38	(10)	4.22	1.74	2.48	5.26	−1.04
1902–38	(37)	1.78	1.81	−0.03	5.71	−3.93
1955–62	(8)	8.41	4.63	3.78	5.79	2.62
1963–68	(5)	9.15	4.55	4.60	10.84	−1.69

Source: Authors' calculations.

Notes: The y value (growth rate of output per worker) is calculated simply by subtracting L (growth rate of labor employed) from Y (growth rate of output). Similarly, k = Y − K. Both are calculated from smoothed series (moving averages of seven-year for prewar, five-year for postwar years). Y is at factor costs, net of capital depreciation. A 1962–63 demarcation is tentative, as no clear swing is seen for postwar years.

Because of revisions by the EPA in the source data after it was published, figures in a similar table in Ohkawa and Takamatsu (1975, p. 289) differ from these figures.

Output per Worker

Output (Y) and output per worker (y) growth rates show similar swing patterns in the prewar period (table 6.4). These correspond to swings in aggregate growth rates, turning negative during downswings. However, over the entire 1902–38 period, Y exhibits positive growth while y is almost zero. In other words, the sector's labor force (L) increased at almost exactly the same rate as output (Y). L is counter-cyclical to long swings, demonstrating services' role as an employer of residual labor, as discussed in chapter 2. While the range of the swings may be somewhat overestimated and/or the trend of output per worker growth rate underestimated, a number of conclusions can still be reached. First, the associated swings of Y and y may imply output demand fluctuations played a major role in determining Y, whereas L represents changes in the degree of residual employment. Second, absence of an increasing trend in output per worker may imply there has been little technological progress in the sector.

Output per Unit of Capital

Establishing data for capital is almost impossible because of combined personal and business use of items by the many small proprie-

Table 6.5. Services: Distribution of Fixed-Capital Components, 1902–38
(In percent)

Producers' durable equipment	Buildings	Years
16.2	83.8	1902
18.6	81.4	1912–13
16.2	83.8	1919–20
9.9	90.1	1928–29
8.5	91.5	1938

Source: Ohkawa and Takamatsu 1975, p. 292.

torships, especially in the early period. Further, inventory data, especially important in trade, are not available. Despite the difficulties, the capital stock series in 1934–36 prices compiled by Ishiwata and others is adequate for the purpose of clarifying broad patterns (ch. 9). Table 6.4 gives growth rates for capital stock (K) and output per unit of capital (k). The prewar average of K is much larger than Y, due to the absence of swings in K. Always negative, k thus exhibits drastic prewar swings in phase with those of output growth rates.

Changes in the rate of capital utilization due to demand fluctuation might explain the swing pattern, supporting our earlier suggestion of the importance of demand. Table 6.5 shows buildings constituted most of total fixed capital in the prewar service sector. The absence of swings in K is consistent with the fact many buildings were also the proprietors' homes. There are no reliable indexes of the rate of capital utilization in the service sector for any country, but most observers agree demand influences the formation of long swings in the utilization rate (see the discussion of capital–output ratios, the reciprocal of output per unit of capital, in Ohkawa and Rosovsky 1973, chs. 4 and 8).

The large negative values of k, implying an ever-increasing capital–output ratio, are consistent with structural change in the sector—even excluding financial capital (as this discussion does)—since banks, insurance companies, and large department stores generally involve more capital than the traditional organizations they displaced. Still, the results suggest some overestimation of K.

Total Productivity

The growth rates of output per worker (y) and per unit of capital (k) can be combined to measure the rate of increase in total productivity if appropriate weights can be found. Since historically there has

Table 6.6. Services: Average Annual Growth Rates of Total and Weighted Partial
Productivities and Input

(In percent)

	T	α(Y − K)	β(Y − L)	I
1902–12	−2.26	−1.04	−1.22	2.25
1913–19	2.71	−0.23	2.94	2.77
1920–28	−4.38	−1.11	−3.27	2.77
1929–38	2.02	−0.11	2.11	2.22
1902–38	−0.68	−0.65	0.03	2.40
1955–62	3.43	0.68	2.77	4.98
1963–68	3.08	−0.25	3.33	6.07

Source: Ohkawa and Takamatsu 1975, p. 298. Postwar data have been calculated
from revised EPA data worksheets, so the numbers here differ from those in the source.
Notes: Annual values are calculated based on smoothed series (moving average,
seven-year for prewar, five-year for postwar), and their averages over long swings are
shown. The K series used differs somewhat from that in ch. 9. α is capital's relative
income share, β is labor's. They are derived from our output estimates. I = α K + β L.

not been a competitive factor market for services, the conventional
procedure of using capital and labor's income shares as weights may
not be adequate. However, this approximation is used in table 6.6
because some proportionality can be assumed to exist between factor
prices and marginal productivities.

The annual rate of productivity increase (T) shows long swings as
expected, while the rate of increase in total inputs (I) moves in a very
narrow range during the prewar period. The contrast between I and
T confirms the importance of demand for service sector productivity—
inputs grew almost regardless of general economic conditions, but
output and thus productivity varied with demand, underscoring the
absence of technological progress.

Swings do not appear for the postwar period, but when capital and
labor are already nearly fully utilized, input increases do seem to
increase output and thus total productivity. This is evident in comparing postwar with prewar upswings. In the 1960s, a demand shift
toward services as labor markets tightened led to accelerated capital
investment in the sector. This has contributed to a decline in capital
productivity but a historically high rate of labor productivity increase.

Table 6.7. Services' Share of Output, in Current and Constant Prices, Compared to Industry's

	Output share			Ratio of service to industrial output (S/N)		
	Current	Constant	Ratio[a]	Current	Constant	Ratio[b]
1887	37.5	48.2	1.28	1.88	3.86	2.12
1889	35.1	51.4	1.46	1.50	3.30	2.19
1904	36.4	49.3	1.35	1.41	2.58	1.84
1911	33.4	43.9	1.31	1.07	1.73	1.62
1919	31.8	48.3	1.52	0.83	1.51	1.82
1930	36.7	40.6	1.08	0.85	0.92	1.08
1938	30.0	34.3	1.14	0.58	0.70	1.21
1953	38.3	49.8	1.30	0.96	0.87	0.91
1969	45.4	38.9	0.86	0.99	0.51	0.52

Note: See table 2.1 for the current shares and ratio of services' share of total output to industry's.
[a] Ratio of constant to current output share.
[b] Ratio of constant to current ratio.

TRENDS IN SERVICES' SHARE OF OUTPUT AND LABOR

Because of the peculiar performance of services' output prices relative to other sectors' prices (see ch. 2), it is especially important to distinguish current and constant price output series. While this may seem obvious, some previous studies have failed to do this.

Output Shares in Current Prices

Table 6.7 gives service's share of total output in current prices. (Table 2.1 gives shares for all sectors.) While exhibiting a moderate declining trend in the prewar years, services also had moderate swings, in contrast to the other two sectors. Like Japan, five European countries (the United Kingdom, the Netherlands, Norway, Sweden, and Italy) display a slight prewar decline, followed by a postwar increase. The other two countries for which there are long-term data, Australia and United States, have different patterns. The commonly accepted view is that there is no conspicuous trend in the share of the services sector (see Kuznets 1971, p. 158). Existence of any trend appears to be a matter of judgment.

While data are less complete for other countries, they all display a clear long-term decline in the ratio of service to industrial output and then a reversal of this trend. There thus seems to be a turning point in development at which demand for services becomes largely independent of industry (perhaps through structural changes), and/or the growth elasticity of demand for services by the industrial sector goes from being less than to greater than unity in current prices. Although the Japanese trend of services output is thus similar to other countries, Japan started from higher initial values for both output and labor shares, and the services–industry output ratio had a relatively rapid rate of change.

Relative Prices

Shares in current price series can be decomposed into constant price series and relative price of output. The latter's changes are surprisingly large, particularly for S/N (ratio of service to industrial output) as is shown in table 6.7. In the postwar period the current price S/N and output share increased while the constant price S/N and share dropped steadily except for 1953, reflecting the relatively rapid price increases in services.

Secular changes in sectoral output prices generally can be related to shifts in the supply and demand curves. Services have been characterized by slow shifts of supply curves, primarily because of the slow rate of technological and organizational progress, accentuated by the surplus labor available. The postwar situation may reflect relatively higher wages on the supply side and possibly an acceleration in the pace at which the demand curve shifts. Again, except for the rates themselves, Japan's pattern is similar to that of other developed countries. For all seven nations already mentioned, the share in current prices tended to rise relative to the constant price share from the beginning of the 1950s to the mid 60s.

Labor Shares

Table 6.8 gives an overview of labor in the service and industrial sectors. Only data for Norway, Sweden, Italy, and the United States are available for comparative purposes (Kuznets 1962, pp. 250–54). The initial 15% share for services in Japan is similar to services' share in these countries, but the steady increase to 40% in 1969 exceeds all shares but the United States'. Unlike the European ratios of service sector to industrial labor, which showed a declining trend until the 1960s, the Japanese ratio exhibited some swing in the interwar period and has been almost constant in the postwar years.

Table 6.8. Services: Labor Force Growth Rates and Share of Total Labor Force Compared to the Industrial Sector's
(In percent)

	Labor force share[a]				Labor: rate of increase[c]	
	Services	Industry	Ratio[b]		Services	Industry
1892	14.9	15.2	0.98	1888–96	0.30	0.54
1904	17.0	18.1	0.94	1897–1912	0.54	0.33
1916	21.9	18.1	1.21	1913–20	0.50	1.76
1925	23.0	25.8	0.89	1921–31	0.63	0.46
1936	26.4	26.1	1.01	1932–40	0.52	1.77
1952	27.1	27.7	0.98	1949–54	3.13	1.50
1961	34.0	34.8	0.97	1955–66	1.71	2.09
1969	39.5	40.2	0.98	1967–70	2.24	1.73

Source: Ohkawa 1974, p. 61 (table 3-1) and p. 66 (table 3-2).
[a] Calculated from a five-year moving average, centered on years shown.
[b] Ratio of services' to industry's share of the labor force.
[c] Increase in each sector's labor force as a percentage of the two sector's combined labor force in the previous year.

Japan's pattern is, we believe, indicative of what we call residual employment in the service sector. Labor not absorbed by the modern, mostly industrial, sectors' expansion flows into traditional sectors, mostly services and agriculture. The existence of surplus or under-employed labor in the agriculture sector has frequently been discussed, but in Japan the service sector's role seems more significant. This reflects the already high land–man ratio in agriculture and lack of additional land that could be brought into cultivation. This phe-nomenon also exists in certain contemporary developing economies. Labor force growth rates in the industrial sector vary directly with the long swings, while in services they vary inversely, though the swings are not very pronounced in the prewar period. The very large 1949–54 service figure reflects the sharp drop in industrial demand immediately after the war at the same time that a major portion of about 6 million repatriates and returning soldiers were entering the labor force, mostly in agriculture and services. This bulge in the service sector's share has continued to have significant effects on the sectoral employment pattern.

DATA AND METHODS

LTES 1 provides virtually the first series for services, beyond our interim estimates in GRJE (pp. 100–06) and SIL 3 (pp. 97–104). While the GRJE current price series is an overestimation, its trend is roughly the same as the LTES series. The major change in deflators is the real contrast, and despite a major effort, we are still not fully satisfied with the results. LTES 1 uses a residual method to obtain real output. That is, real GNP in the goods-producing sector is deducted from real GNE, with some adjustments. For the postwar period deflators have been calculated directly, and a comparison of them to the series derived by this method shows it to be a reasonably valid approach.

Output data are from LTES 1, which also describes the estimating procedures (pp. 167–69 in English, pp. 125–48 in Japanese). Briefly, an income approach is used, in contrast to the product or output methods, for each of table 6.1's three groups. Proprietors' income can be estimated directly only for those earning enough to have filed tax returns. For those below that level, the average worker's household income has been used. Wages in the sector are estimated using 1930 benchmark data estimated by Yoko Sano in SIL. These are combined, weighted by the number of units in each group, to obtain total income at factor cost for years since 1899. For 1885–98, indirect estimates using procedures in GRJE (p. 101) are all that are possible.

Labor data are from chapter 14. Umemura has estimated service sector labor for 1905–40 to have a series consistent with the gainfully occupied population (*yugyo jinko*) census classification. The prewar estimates can be linked fairly well with postwar *Labor Force Survey* data (Sorifu). For the pre-1905 period, Takamutsu's estimates are used. There is some discrepancy between the ways output and labor are classified in the sources; services' labor is sometimes put in other sectors. While adjustment has been made for this, the exact extent is indeterminant.

Ishiwata (1975) has revised downward his previous commercial building series to compensate better for use of buildings as residences by proprietors. For producer durables, SIL data are used for 1905–40, but for 1885–1904, the ratio of durables to commercial buildings in 1905–09 is applied to estimates of the latter. Data for the 1940s are unavailable.

REFERENCES

Feldman, Robert A. 1976. "Financial Upheaval and Funds Rechanneling: The Case of Japan from the Panic of 1927 to the End of the Takahashi Era, 1936." Unpublished discussion paper, Yale University.

Fuji Ginko. 1967. *Banking in Modern Japan*, 2d. ed.

GRJE [*Growth Rate of the Japanese Economy*]. Kazushi Ohkawa et al. 1957. Kinokuniya.

Ishiwata, Shigeru. 1975. "Minkan Setsubi Toshi to Minkan Seifu Bumonbetsu Shihon Stokku." In *Kindai Nihon no Kezai Hatten*, edited by Kazushi Ohkawa and Ryoshin Minami. Toyo Keizai Shimposha.

Kravis, Irving B., et al. 1975. *A System of International Comparisons of Gross Product and Purchasing Power*. Johns Hopkins Press.

Kuznets, Simon. 1962. "Quantitative Aspects of the Economic Growth of Nations: VII." *Economic Development and Cultural Change* 10 (1962 Jan.)

——. 1971. *Economic Growth of Nations: Total Output and Production Structure*. Harvard University Press.

LTES [*Estimates of Long-Term Economic Statistics of Japan*]. Series edited by Kazushi Ohkawa, Miyohei Shinohara, and Mataji Umemura. 14 v. 1965–. Toyo Keizai Shimposha.

   1. National Income. 1974. Kazushi Ohkawa et al.

Ohkawa, Kazushi, 1974. *Nihon Keizai no Kozo*. Keiso Shobo.

——, and Henry Rosovsky. 1973. *Japanese Economic Growth: Trend Acceleration in the Twentieth Century*. Stanford University Press.

——, and Nobukiyo Takamatsu. 1975. "Shogyo-Sabisugyo no Junojo no Chiibetsu Yugyosha-su." In *Kindai Nihon no Keizai Hatten*, edited by Kazushi Ohkawa and Ryohei Minami. Toyo Keizai Shimposha.

Patrick, Hugh T. 1967. "Japan, 1868–1914." In *Banking in the Early Stages of Industrialization*, edited by Rondo Cameron. Oxford University Press.

SIL [*Choki Keizai Tokei no Seibi Kaizen ni Kansuru Kenkyu*]. Keizai Kikakucho. 3 v. 1967–69.

Sorifu Tokeikyoku. Annual. *Rodoryoku Chosa* [*Labor Force Survey*]

——. 1969. *Jigyosho Tokeihokoku*.

Yamamura, Kozo. 1972. "Japan, 1868–1930: A Revised View." In *Banking and Economic Development*, edited by Rondo Cameron. Oxford University Press.

7

Trade and Balance of Payments

Ippei Yamazawa and Yuzo Yamamoto

Because of heavy reliance on raw material imports and the need to export processed products to pay for them, foreign trade has been indispensable to Japan's industrial growth. Foreign trade has played a similar role in the growth of the United Kingdom. However, as a late starter in industrialization, Japan assigned imports as well as exports of manufactures a strategic role. This chapter focuses on the interaction between trade and production, including structural changes in both. Trade-oriented industrial growth tends to be restrained by occasional deterioration of the balance of payments, as is readily seen in most contemporary developing economies. How Japan adjusted to this constraint on growth and finally succeeded in overcoming it in the long run is also analyzed. LTES 14, on foreign trade and balance of payment statistics, has not been published as of mid 1978; thus much of the data here are appearing in English for the first time, and some are preliminary. Both trade and balance of payments are for Japan Proper rather than the Empire. Thus trade with Taiwan and Korea, even while under Japanese rule, is included as foreign trade.

Secular Changes in Trade Structure

The ratio of exports or imports to GNP has often been used as a simple measure of the importance of foreign trade in industrial growth. The sharp increase of these ratios until World War II has been noted by several writers (see ch. 1). While the import–GNP ratio reached as high as 16% by 1900, the export–GNP ratio rose from 7.4% in the

Table 7.1. Exports and Imports: Percentage Distribution of Components in Current Price, 1874–1970

Period	Imports (%) Primary products Total	Crude food stuff	Raw materials Fuels	Raw materials Other	Manufactures Total	Textiles	Other light manufactures	Heavy manufactures	Exports (%) Primary products	Manufactures Total	Textiles	Other light manufactures	Heavy manufactures
1874–83	8.8	0.7	5.0	3.1	91.2	54.0	17.8	19.4	42.5	57.5	42.4	6.9	8.2
1877–86	10.3	0.8	6.1	3.4	89.7	49.6	18.7	21.4	39.5	60.5	43.0	7.8	9.7
1882–91	18.7	5.0	6.4	7.3	81.3	37.4	17.4	26.5	33.0	67.0	45.6	9.0	12.4
1887–96	28.3	7.1	5.0	16.1	71.8	28.2	14.6	29.0	26.3	73.7	48.9	11.3	13.5
1892–1901	36.4	9.9	4.5	22.1	63.6	16.8	14.2	32.6	21.0	79.0	52.6	13.2	13.2
1897–1906	43.2	13.8	4.7	24.6	56.9	11.8	12.3	32.8	16.6	83.4	53.6	15.9	13.9
1902–11	45.2	12.5	4.0	28.8	54.8	9.6	10.8	34.4	14.1	85.9	53.8	17.2	14.9
1907–16	50.0	10.3	2.7	37.0	50.0	5.7	9.9	34.4	12.3	87.7	53.6	16.7	17.4
1912–21	52.6	12.5	2.2	37.9	47.4	3.3	8.5	35.6	9.0	91.0	56.4	15.3	19.3
1917–26	54.3	16.1	2.9	35.3	45.7	5.0	9.9	30.8	7.3	92.7	63.6	14.0	15.1
1922–31	56.6	18.8	4.3	33.5	43.4	5.5	11.6	26.3	6.8	93.2	65.8	14.5	12.9
1927–36	61.0	19.0	5.9	36.1	39.0	3.3	10.5	25.2	6.7	93.3	56.8	16.8	19.7
1931–40	58.0	17.5	7.6	33.0	42.0	2.4	8.3	31.3	6.9	93.1	45.7	18.7	28.7
1951–55	87.8	26.9	11.3	49.6	12.2	0.6	1.2	10.4	3.6	96.4	38.6	17.4	40.4
1956–60	77.3	14.8	16.5	46.0	22.7	0.5	2.0	20.2	4.2	95.8	31.6	19.9	44.3
1960–65	73.6	14.9	18.4	40.3	26.4	0.5	3.9	22.0	3.3	96.7	21.1	19.0	56.6
1966–70	70.8	14.4	20.6	35.8	29.2	1.3	4.5	23.4	2.4	97.6	14.4	12.2	68.2

Sources: Appendix tables A26 and A27.
Notes: All figures are percentage shares of total exports or imports calculated from ten-year (prewar) or five-year (postwar) averages of current price series.

1880s to 21.4% in the late 1930s. These ratios were around 10% in the 1960s. Increasing ratios of foreign trade to GNP were seen not only in prewar Japan but also in the process of industrialization of several western nations. However, the increase was most rapid in Japan (LTES 1:27 and Kuznets 1967).

Exports of silk and such primary products as tea and marine products led export growth during early Meiji, helping to finance the beginnings of industrialization. Raw silk is classified here as a manufactured good, though in effect it is a semimanufactured one, first produced through simple processing attached to sericulture. More than two-thirds of silk-manufacture exports was raw silk. Silk was one of the few specialities of resource-poor Japan not requiring any imported inputs.

Major components of trade are given in table 7.1, which shows the expansion of industrial production has been a rapid shift from primary-product to manufactured exports and from manufactured to raw material imports. Imports of crude foodstuff increased steadily, especially from Taiwan and Korea. Under Japanese rule, Taiwan (1896–1945) and Korea (1910–45) were assigned a role of supplying Japan Proper with rice, sugar, and other foods. In the mid 1930s, one-sixth of Japan Proper's total rice consumption was imported, with Korea supplying 58% of the imports, Taiwan 17%. About two-thirds of sugar imports came from Taiwan. The role of imported food provoked debate both in the Diet and among the public (see Hayami 1972 and Yamazawa 1975b).

On a more disaggregate level, table 7.2 shows the shares of three subsectors of manufacturing in output, exports, and imports. The combined share of heavy industries (chemicals, metals, and machinery) started to increase first in imports (1890s), next in output (1900s), and finally in exports (1930s).[1] In the post-World War II period heavy industries continued to increase their share of output and exports but have had a declining share of imports. Before the 1930s, textiles maintained 60 to 70% of manufactured exports, but there was a remarkable shift from silk to cotton. This was the only major structural change in manufactured exports during the period.

1. An increasing share of raw materials in total imports, of manufactures in total exports, and of heavy manufactures in total exports of manufactures is not limited to the Japanese experience, having also been found in the development process of European industrial countries. However, the Japanese experience should be distinguished from the others in the speed of the changes in trade structure (Deane and Cole 1962, pp. 28–33).

Table 7.2. Manufacturing: Structural Changes in Domestic Output and Foreign Trade
(In percent)

	Imports			Output			Exports		
	Heavy[a] manufactures	Textiles	Other[b]	Heavy[a] manufactures	Textiles	Other[a]	Heavy[a] manufactures	Textiles	Other[b]
1874–83	21.3	59.2	19.5	24.0	26.5	49.5	14.4	73.6	12.0
1877–86	23.9	55.3	20.8	22.2	27.8	50.0	16.0	71.1	12.9
1882–91	32.6	45.9	21.5	18.9	33.1	48.0	18.5	68.5	13.0
1887–96	40.3	39.2	20.5	16.9	41.0	42.1	18.2	66.5	15.3
1892–1901	51.4	26.4	22.2	16.1	40.2	43.7	16.7	66.6	16.7
1897–1906	57.9	20.4	21.7	18.6	35.0	46.4	16.6	64.3	19.1
1902–11	62.7	17.4	19.9	20.9	32.6	46.5	17.4	62.7	19.9
1907–16	68.7	11.5	19.8	25.7	33.0	41.3	19.9	61.1	19.0
1912–21	74.2	7.0	18.8	32.5	34.8	32.9	21.2	61.9	16.9
1917–26	68.0	10.1	21.9	29.1	36.5	34.4	16.3	68.7	15.0
1922–31	60.7	12.7	26.6	27.0	35.7	37.3	13.8	70.7	15.5
1927–36	64.6	8.5	26.9	35.6	31.8	32.6	21.1	60.9	18.0
1930–39	74.5	5.7	19.8	49.2	24.3	26.5	30.8	49.2	20.0
1951–55	85.3	4.9	9.8	46.8	18.2	35.0	41.9	39.8	18.3
1956–60	88.6	2.2	9.2	54.1	13.0	32.9	46.2	32.9	20.9
1961–65	83.3	1.9	14.8	56.8	9.6	33.6	58.5	21.8	19.7
1966–70	80.1	4.5	15.4	60.3	8.2	31.5	72.0	15.2	12.7

Sources: Exports and imports: appendix tables A26 and A27; manufacturing output: LTES 10 and *Kogyo Tokeihyo*.

Note: Percentage shares are calculated from overlapping decade average values in current prices.

[a] Chemicals, metals, and machinery.

[b] Includes processed foodstuff, miscellaneous products, wood products (such as lumber and furniture, but excluding logs and wood chips), and ceramics.

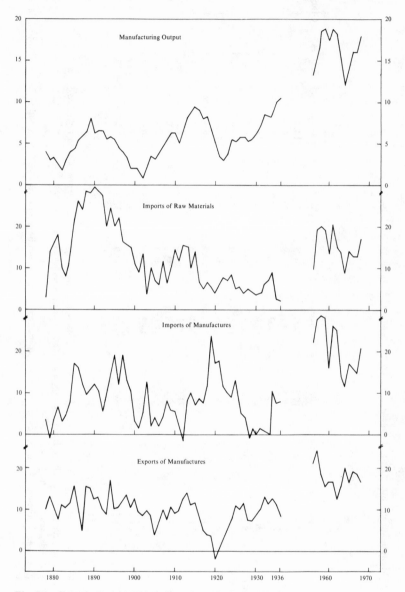

Fig. 7.1. Growth Cycles of Manufacturing Output and Trade

Long Swings in Trade and Production

Long swings have been identified for major variables in Japan's economic growth. Figure 7.1 plots growth cycles for Japan's manufacturing output, trade in manufactures, and imports of raw materials. While the import and export series show considerable fluctuation, long swings in these variables can be recognized with reference to the manufacturing output cycle (also see Shinohara's discussion in ch. 5). Fluctuations are larger and more frequent for imports than for output. The raw material import cycle is synchronous with the output cycle, which is expected since manufacturing output requires raw material input. As to the manufactured imports cycle, if the 1885 and 1896 peaks are associated with the first output cycle peak in 1889 and if the curtailed availability of imports during World War I is taken into consideration, it can also be regarded as synchronous with the output cycle.

Concurrent movement notwithstanding, there has also been a strong decelerating trend in the growth of material imports. The elasticity of material imports with respect to the growth of manufacturing output declined from values in the range of 3.0 to 4.0 before 1900 to between 1.0 and 1.3 in the 1920s and 30s, and to between 0.8 and 0.9 in the post-World War II period. Three factors help explain this. The extraordinarily high values in the early period reflect switching from domestic to imported materials, as was the case in cotton manufacturing in the 1880s and 90s. The declining trend after 1900 reflects the larger share of intermediate products in total gross manufacturing output and material-saving effects from both technological progress and changes in the composition of manufacturing production.

Manufactured exports are synchronous with the output cycle from around 1910 until World War II. Any relation before 1910 is unclear. While export growth rates fluctuated considerably, overall they may be regarded as having maintained fairly steady growth during the prewar period. The export and output cycles have been countercyclical since World War II.

Two channels of interaction are conceivable between output and foreign trade in manufactures. One may be called the income effect—expansion of manufacturing output induces increased imports of manufactured goods for both production and consumption, while manufactured exports lead output expansion as a major component of aggregate demand. This effect tends to produce concurrent movements of output and imports, and of output and exports, especially when output expansion is led by an export boom. The second interaction is the development effect—new industries are introduced for import-substituting production and mature to become exporters, which requires cost reduction through technical progress and scale economies.[2] The domestic price of manufactures has to decline relative to import prices to achieve import substitution, while export growth is promoted by export prices declining relative to competitor's prices in the world market.

For Japan, peaks in the growth cycle of output, imports, and exports of manufactures have usually been accompanied by rapid structural changes, suggesting operation of the development effect. For a single homogenous industry, this effect tends to produce successive peaks, first in imports, then output, and finally exports, but structural changes obscure this for the aggregate of total manufactures. Coefficients of structural changes (the sum of the absolute values of changes in percentage shares among eight individual subsectors) in output, imports, and exports are shown for the whole period in table 7.3. Though these coefficients are only crude measures and are calculated from overlapping-decade averages, they correspond well with the growth cycles in figure 7.1. For manufacturing output, coefficient peaks correspond to those in the growth cycle in 1889, 1915, and 1936, suggesting growth cycle peaks tend to be accompanied by rapid structural change. The first peak reflects rapid expansion of textile production, while the second and third reflect expansion of heavy manufacturing.

Coefficients of structural changes for imports were higher than those for output, but their pattern is similar to that of the growth cycle except the 1920 growth cycle peak was not accompanied by any major structural change. This difference is probably due to the rapid expansion of imports of all commodities as supplies again became available after World War I. The 1885, 1895, and 1934 peaks in the import growth cycle can be identified as contractions of textiles, accompanied in 1934 by expansion of heavy manufactures.

Two series of coefficients of structural changes in manufactured

2. This is the *ganko keitai* (flying geese) hypothesis of industrial growth occasionally cited in studies of Japan's economic growth and foreign trade. This hypothesis is akin to Raymond Vernon's product-cycle hypothesis in explaining the international relocation of comparative advantage of a particular product or industry. However, the ganko keitai hypothesis gives a better explanation for the industrialization catching-up process by a late starter (Yamazawa 1975a).

Table 7.3. Manufacturing: Coefficients of Structural Changes

	Output	Import	Export	Export[a]
1877–86	4.4	9.4	5.6	15.5
1882–91	10.4	19.8	6.8	16.5
1887–96	16.0	15.4	7.4	15.1
1892–1901	5.0	26.6	4.6	15.3
1897–1906	10.4	15.8	6.4	14.8
1902–11	6.0	17.0	5.6	10.5
1907–16	11.0	17.2	5.2	15.6
1912–21	19.2	16.0	6.2	13.1
1917–26	7.0	15.0	13.6	13.5
1922–31	7.2	16.2	5.6	6.5
1927–36	17.4	13.0	19.0	35.2
1930–39	28.0	22.4	23.6	38.6
1956–60	16.0	29.0	31.2	—
1961–65	11.2	19.0	27.0	—
1966–70	8.2	25.2	27.0	—

Source: Calculated from trade data in appendix tables A26 and A27 and output data in LTES 10.

Note: Coefficients of structural changes between periods t and $t-1$ are calculated by

$$Vt = \Sigma_j | S_t^j - s_{t-1}^j |$$

where s_t^j represents the percentage share of the jth sector in total manufactures in period t, which is shown in table 7.2.

Structural change coefficients are not calculated for 1940–55 because of data limitations.

[a] Calculated on the basis of a commodity classification in which silk is separated from other textiles; see text discussion. Postwar silk is not a significant trade item so the series is not computed.

exports are shown in table 7.3, one calculated by using an eight-sector classification and the other by a sector classification distinguishing silk manufactures from other textiles. Changes in product mix are not confined to textile exports alone, but this disaggregation may be justified because the rapid switch from silk to cotton textiles was far more marked in exports than in either output or imports, and silk manufacture was among the few exports made of domestic materials.

The first series shows low rates of structural changes before World War I, whereas the second shows high rates in manufactured exports and imports, which suggests the high growth rates of manufactured exports before World War I involved a switch from silk to cotton textiles. Exports of heavy-industry products began in the 1930s.

Table 7.4. Foreign Trade in Manufacturing: Relative Prices

	Export/domestic[a]	Import/domestic[b]	Material import/domestic[c]	Export/ world trade[d]
1874–83	1.76	1.50	1.34	—
1877–86	1.70	1.36	1.00	2.00
1882–91	1.77	1.23	0.78	2.07
1887–96	1.81	1.15	0.80	2.05
1892–1901	1.63	1.01	0.85	1.96
1897–1906	1.56	0.97	0.83	2.09
1902–11	1.52	1.05	0.73	2.16
1907–16	1.37	1.12	0.70	2.04
1912–21	1.35	1.05	0.84	2.07
1917–26	1.43	0.93	0.90	2.25
1922–31	1.38	0.84	0.95	2.16
1927–36	1.15	0.90	1.02	1.46
1930–39	0.96	0.88	0.95	1.08
1951–55	1.16	1.16	1.27	1.29
1956–60	1.09	1.08	1.14	1.16
1961–65	1.00	0.97	1.01	1.00
1966–70	0.98	1.01	0.98	0.96

Sources: Domestic prices of manufactures, 1874–1939: LTES 10; Nihon Ginko, *Bukka*. World Trade Price of Manufactures, 1875–1939: Lewis 1952; 1953–70: United Nations, *Monthly Bulletin of Statistics.*
Notes: The price indexes are trade weighted, using constant weights from 1934–36 for the 1900–39 period and from 1904 for the 1974–1900 period.
[a] The ratio of export prices to domestic prices for ALL manufactured goods, including those not entering into foreign trade.
[b] The ratio of import prices to domestic prices for ALL manufactured goods, including those not entering into foreign trade.
[c] The ratio of import prices of raw materials to domestic prices of manufactured goods, including those not using imported raw materials.
[d] The ratio of manufactured goods' export prices to world prices.

Changes in relative price in table 7.4 partly support our hypothesis of long-run cost reduction of manufacturing production in the process of industrial development. Export prices declined relative to domestic prices throughout the whole period, while the ratio of export to world trade prices declined after 1920 and in the post-World War II years. On the other hand, the ratio of import to domestic prices does not show any obvious ascending trend, though the rise of import prices for raw materials relative to domestic product prices in the pre-World

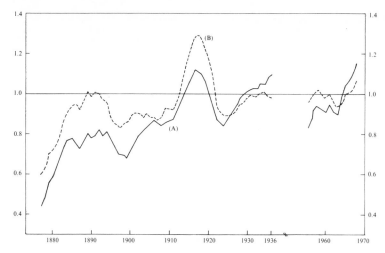

Fig. 7.2. Long Swings in the Balance of Payments

Sources: Calculated from Appendix tables A and B.
Notes: (A) the ratio of current values of exports of manufactures to those of imports of manufactures and raw materials. (B) the ratio of total receipts to total payments in current accounts.
Both series are smoothed by seven-year (five-year for postwar years) moving averages.

War II period had to be offset by productivity improvements. Movements of relative prices in table 7.4 are affected by aggregation. Relative import prices of textiles and metals show clear ascending trends.

Balance of Trade and Other Current Transactions

Changes in the trade balance are primarily determined by the difference in response of export and import growth to output growth. Since import growth fluctuated considerably more than export growth, import changes generally dominated long swings in the industrial trade balance, defined as the excess of value of exports of manufactured goods over those of imports of manufactured goods and raw materials. Exceptions to this are the export booms of World War I and the early 1930s. The long-run decline of the import growth rate combined with the relatively stable rate of exports meant steady improvement in the trade balance, shown by the overall upward trend in the export–import ratio in figure 7.2.

Other items in the current account (primary-product exports, foodstuff imports, and services) appear not to have affected the cyclical pattern of the industrial trade balance, but did tend to weaken the long-run trend in figure 7.2. The service balance changed from persistent deficit to surplus after World War I due to the expansion of transactions with the colonies. Japan excluded foreign vessels from carrying both domestic and colonial trade and also received profit from colonial investment. Rice imports from colonial areas increased rapidly after 1920. In the 1930s the war with China led to increasing military expenditures abroad, including munition imports. Since these are included in government transactions and appear in the service account (rather than in commodity trade) in our data, they are the principal cause of the account's deficits.

Capital Flows and Specie Movements

Major components of the capital account are given in appendix tables A31–A33. Capital movement tended to offset imbalances in current accounts and showed significant long swings inverse to those given in figure 7.2 for the ratio of receipts to current payments. Before World War I the inflow of long-term capital financed current-account deficits and short-term capital moved irregularly and played a minor role. During and after World War I long-term capital turned to an outflow and produced deficits, but it was more than offset by a large inflow of short-term capital in the 1920s. It is widely held foreign capital played only a minor role in financing Japanese economic growth. However, growth was accompanied by a sharply rising net capital inflow to finance the excess demand for goods and services. (For an analysis of the pattern of capital movements, see Key 1970.)

Long-term capital movements presented in appendix table A31 show three cycles in the prewar period. There was a big change in the direction of long-term capital flows about 1912. The two big inflows before World War I represent reparations paid by China after the Sino-Japanese War and loans floated in London and New York during and after the Russo-Japanese War. The two big outflows are capital exports to the Allies and China during World War I and to various parts of the Empire (including Manchuria) after 1931.

Because of the nature of the capital outflows during World War I, Japan cannot be said to have changed from a debtor to a creditor. Treasury bills were bought from Allied governments, but these were really of a short-term, one-shot nature and were redeemed immediately after the war. Japan returned to being a net capital importer from western countries by the early 1920s. Loans to China were primarily for political reasons and in the end were uncollectable. Colonial investment expanded after 1920 and accelerated further after 1931. It was financed with yen and most of it was credit for purchases of Japanese products, including capital goods used in the industrialization of Manchuria. Being within the Yen Bloc, this investment did not directly affect Japan's reserve position with the rest of the world.

No definite pattern appears in the specie balance. The pre-World War I Japanese gold standard actually was operated as a kind of gold exchange system relying heavily on changes in specie held abroad (mostly at the Bank of England) to clear external balances. Therefore, specie movements in appendix table A31 includes both monetary gold flows and changes in specie held abroad. Data for specie held abroad are available only after 1903. For the postwar period (table A33) the specie balance is replaced by changes in foreign exchange reserves.

Abramovitz (1961) found that in 19th century America, regular swings in specie holdings, resulting from changes in current balance and capital inflows, were reflected in the domestic money supply. Further, changes in the growth rate of the money supply and the resulting rate of price change generated the general Kuznets cycle. Specie movements in prewar Japan, however, are not associated with long swings. This relates to the fact balance of payments deficits throughout the period were generally adjusted by expenditure contraction, despite drastic changes in the international monetary system.

The foreign exchange rate was virtually fixed under the prewar international gold standard and the postwar IMF systems, and even during the years of the gold embargo the government tried to maintain the same exchange rates as under the gold standard (table 7.5). Exchange devaluation helped the adjustment of balance of payments

Table 7.5. Chronology of Monetary and Foreign Exchange Systems

Pre-1897	De facto silver standard
1897	Gold standard
1917	Gold embargo
1930	Gold standard restored
1932	Gold embargo again, with successive yen devaluations
1934	Link with pound sterling
1949	Pegged rate under IMF system (360 yen to U.S. dollar).
1971	(Aug.) Floating yen
1971	(Dec.) Revaluation (308 yen to U.S. dollar).
1973	(Feb.) Floating yen

twice, in the 1880s and 90s, when the silver price declined relative to gold, and again beginning in 1932.

In the late 19th century, when adoption of the gold standard by major western countries produced a steady devaluation of silver relative to gold, the exchange rate of Japanese yen for pound sterling, dollars, and other currencies of gold standard countries depreciated in proportion to silver devaluation. This devaluation tended to offset domestic inflation and contributed to Japanese export growth. The 1932 devaluation had a major impact. Export prices in gold fell 71% from 1929 to 1936–38 while the volume of exports increased 68%, helping Japan to be the first country to recover from the depression (Shinohara 1964).

Under a fixed-rate system, theory says an external deficit triggers monetary contraction, which in turn restrains domestic activities. The government resorted to this orthodox adjustment policy repeatedly when there were current-account deficits. However, on several occasions domestic contraction was mitigated by inflows of both of long- and short-term foreign capital. Specie movement was seldom big enough to continue to finance deficits for long.

Balance of Payments Constraint to Industrial Growth

There are two alternative relationships between industrial production and the balance of payments, depending on whether domestic forces or exports initiate the upswing of manufacturing output.[3] In the rising phase of output long swings initiated by some domestic incentive, import growth tends to exceed export growth, decreasing the export–import ratio. The resulting balance of payments deficit triggers monetary contraction, restraining investments and other economic activities and thus slowing output growth. In the long-swing down phase, import growth falls short of export growth, increasing the export–import ratio. The improved balance of payments helps ease credit so investment resumes, initiating a new rising phase in the long swings. Thus, long swings of the export–import ratio lead those

3. Shinohara first analyzed the correspondence between the two variables. He concluded export booms, through improved balance of payments and favorable demand conditions, generated long swings in prewar manufacturing production (Shinohara 1972, p. 30). His explanation is consistent with the second type of correspondence in our analysis but it does not seem able to explain the interaction between production and balance of payments over the whole period.

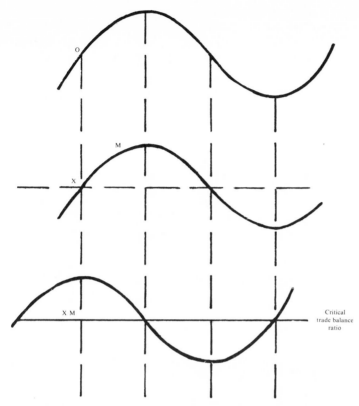

Fig. 7.3. Alternative Correspondence among Domestic Demand-led Output (O), Trade (X and M), and Balance of Payments (X/M)

of manufacturing output by about a quarter cycle, as shown in figure 7.3.

This is essentially what happened in the pre-World War I and post-World War II long swings. In the export boom cases of World War I and the early 1930s, export growth induced output expansion directly. Since export growth also exceeded import growth, increasing the export–import ratio, the balance of payments ran a surplus. Output expansion stopped only after the export boom was ended by exogenous factors, the end of World War I in the first instance, and the worldwide prevalence of bloc economies in the second. Slower export growth compared to imports caused the balance of payments to deteriorate. In this case long swings in the export–import ratio tended to lag

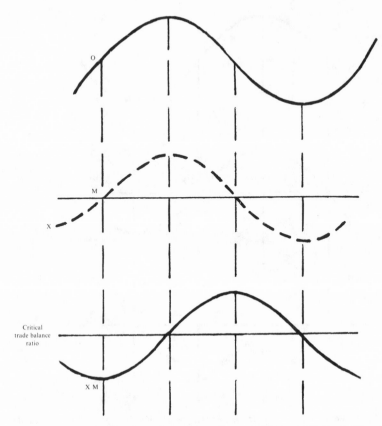

Fig. 7.4. Alternative Correspondence among Export-led Output (O), Trade (X and M), and Balance of Payments (X/M)

behind exports and manufacturing production by about a quarter cycle, as shown in figure 7.4.

In figure 7.2 long swings in the export–import ratio appear to have led the growth cycle of manufacturing output by two to three years before World War I and after World War II, while it was synchronous or tended to lag behind during the interwar period. Decelerating trends for imports of materials and manufactures relative to the high, steady growth of exports produced a strong up trend in the export–import ratio, and this resulted in a persistent surplus during the 1930s and the late 1960s. Accelerated growth of manufacturing production accompanied by long swings corresponded to a strong improvement of balance of payments with long swings.

DATA AND ESTIMATING METHODS

Balance of Payments

Balance of payments statistics are in appendix tables A31–33. These tables have been compiled for preparing the external transactions account of national income for Japan Proper as well as the balance of payments since the beginning of Meiji. Two sources are used, the new Yamamoto estimates for the prewar period and EPA's national income statistics for the postwar period.

All transactions recorded in the balance of payments can be divided into four categories: goods, services, capital, and monetary gold. The Finance Ministry has collected data for trade and specie since early Meiji, and for service and capital items since 1902. These have been published for the period 1902–45 (Okurasho 1950). Compared to other countries, Japan has fairly good data, but they are not without limitations. First, a comprehensive series is not available for years before 1902 because of the lack of data for service and capital items. Second, the data are actually a sequence of five series, each differing in construction and content. Finally, the official statistics cover the Japan Empire, and the dearth of data for the colonies makes it impossible to obtain a series for Japan Proper.

The first two shortcomings have been corrected by Tatemoto, Key, and Yamamoto. Tatemoto filled the first gap by establishing estimates for service and capital for 1868–1901 (Baba and Tatemoto 1968). This estimate, presenting annual data under a version of the IMF format, excels any previous work in scope and has greatly facilitated subsequent research work. The second problem was tackled jointly by Key and Yamamoto (Yamamoto 1969, Key 1970). To correct inconsistency in the official statistics and link them with the Tatemoto estimate, they broke the original data down to the smallest headings and arranged them as nearly as possible in the IMF format.

Since these series cover the Japanese Empire after 1896, when Taiwan was annexed, the major purpose of the Yamamoto estimate in LTES is to extract the balance of payments series for Japan Proper from the Key–Yamamoto estimate for the Empire. For trade and gold movements, there are official statistics (Okurasho *Boeki*; Taiwan Sotokufu; Chosen Sotokufu). The problem is thus to calculate invisible trade. Overall balance of payments between Japan Proper and Taiwan and Korea have been estimated by Yamamoto (1972). With these data, the Japan Proper figures are approximated by adding the

Japan Empire figures to those for Japan–Taiwan and Japan–Korea. This is an overestimate insofar as there were transactions directly between the colonies and third countries, but this trade was probably small and no adjustment has yet been made for this discrepancy.

After World War II the EPA started estimating national income statistics, including external transactions based on the official balance of payments data compiled by the Bank of Japan, using IMF conventions. There are two different sets of EPA figures. The old series covers 1951 to 1963 (Keizai Kikakucho, *Hakusho*, 1958–66). The new series, arranged according to more refined criteria, started in 1964 and has been extended back to 1951 by revising the old series (Keizai Kikakucho, *Nempo*, 1966–70). We have linked the Yamamoto series for 1868–1940 with the new EPA series for 1951–67 using ESB semi-official estimates for 1941–50 (Keizai Kikakucho, *Hakusho*, 1960; pp. 152–57). As the EPA (and ESB) external transactions statistics do not include capital items, we have provided them for years since 1951 from Bank of Japan data (Nihon Ginko).

Statistics published after the war using IMF conventions differ greatly in recording methods from the prewar official statistics on which the Yamamoto estimate relies. IMF statistics cover all international transactions recorded at the time goods are sold or services rendered, while prewar official statistics are confined to transactions requiring foreign exchange settlement and are recorded when purchases or sales of foreign exchange are reported by foreign exchange banks. For merchandise trade, both are based on the customs statistics. But IMF records both exports and imports fob, while prewar imports are cif. There are also many minor conceptual and technical differences which prevent precise comparison of the two series. Our attempts to restate the prewar data in IMF terms have encountered difficulties because of data limitations.

Foreign Trade

Total Value of Exports and Imports

Good foreign trade statistics are available since early Meiji. The basic data sources are Okurasho *Boeki*, Taiwan Sotokufu, and Chosen Sotokufu. Okurasho figures in *Boeki* before 1900 have several deficiencies. Exports and imports were not consistently valued. Imports from gold-standard countries were undervalued because of continued use of the 1874 gold–silver exchange rate until 1890 even though silver depreciated continually against gold during the period. In addition to corrections for these, total values of exports and imports for Japan Proper should include such items as special exports and imports, which consist mainly of the government's external transactions.

Total exports   =   Exports of Japan Proper to foreign countries
of Japan Proper   (including re-exports) 1868–1940
                 + Exports of Japan Proper to Taiwan (including
                   re-exports) 1896–1940
                 + Exports of Japan Proper to Korea (including
                   re-exports) 1910–1940
                 + Packing cost of exports 1869–1903
                 + Special exports 1888–1938

Total imports   =   Imports of Japan Proper from foreign countries
of Japan Proper   (including re-imports) 1868–1940
                 + Imports of Japan Proper from Taiwan (including
                   re-imports) 1896–1940
                 + Imports of Japan.Proper from Korea (including
                   re-imports) 1910–1940
                 + Correction for the depreciation of silver 1874–
                   1889
                 + Freight and insurance costs 1888–1898
                 + Special imports 1888–1938

Inconsistencies remain. For example, Japan Proper's exports to Taiwan and Korea were valued cif while imports were valued fob, and Japan Proper's trade with her other territories was not treated uniformly in the foreign trade statistics. Minami Karafuto (Sakalien) was regarded as domestic trade, while the South Sea Islands (former German territory under Japan's trusteeship after World War I) were treated as colonial trade. Occupied Kwantung (in China) was included in *Boeki* as foreign trade. The first two are not included in our calculation of the foreign trade of Japan Proper. However, these remaining adjustments are small and do not alter the analysis. Total exports and imports defined in the preceding equations coincide with the receipt and payment of the merchandise trade accounts, respectively, in the balance of payments of Japan Proper (appendix table A31) except for special exports and imports which are recorded in the service accounts.

Commodity Classification

Writers analyzing the structure of foreign trade have used both the 17-category classification by commodity characteristics in *Boeki* and the 4-category classification by economic use (foodstuffs, crude materials, semimanufactures, and finished manufactures) published by Toyo Keizai in *Nihon Boeki Seiran*. A more detailed economic use classification was adopted by Brode (1967), and part of his estimates are reproduced by Ohkawa and Rosovsky (1973, p. 303, table 13). However, all three classifications exclude the trade of Japan Proper with Taiwan and Korea and differ from the classification used for domestic manufacturing production. The classification of both domestic output and foreign trade of manufactures by common categories was first started by Shionoya (1968, appendix) and the present work is based partly on his achievement.

For manufacturing production, values at both current and constant prices and price indexes for eight industry groups have been computed by Shinohara in LTES 10. We have adopted his groups for both exports and imports of manufactures. The eight groups are processed food, textiles, wood products, chemicals, ceramics, metals, machinery, and miscellaneous manufactures. Imports of primary products are classified into crude foodstuff and raw materials (including fuel). Since this classification is based on the original Finance Ministry data, such parts of total exports and imports as correction for packing costs, silver depreciation, freight, insurance, special exports and imports, and re-exports are lumped together as classified.

Price Indexes of Exports and Imports

LTES 8 gives three series of export and import price indexes for the pre-World War II period, the *Oriental Economist*'s (1873–1933, by four categories of economic use), Ohkawa–Takamatsu's (1868–1904, by four categories of economic use), and Yamada's (1900–39, by categories of commodity characteristics). None covers the trade of Japan Proper with Taiwan and Korea or corresponds to indexes of domestic prices of manufactures. The present estimate provides export and import price indexes which cover the whole foreign trade of Japan Proper, classified by categories common to domestic manufacturing price indexes.

Price indexes of industry classification should be based on price indexes of individual commodities. Two sets of individual commodity price indexes have been computed, one for 1874–1904 and the other for 1900–39. For the first set, 66 export commodities and 92 import commodities are adopted from *Boeki*, providing a larger coverage of sampling than the Ohkawa–Takamatsu index. For reasons given earlier, values from *Boeki* underestimate, but our price indexes correct for this.[4] For 1900–39 we adopted 135 export and 128 import commodity indexes from Yamada's indexes. Price indexes for 32 commodities were constructed for Taiwan and Korea using official data.

Individual price indexes are aggregated into 19 categories, using as weights the 1900–04 export or import values for the first set and the 1934–36 values for the second set. The two sets are linked at 1900–04. Price indexes of total and subtotal categories are calculated as implicit deflators, obtained by dividing the sum of each subtotal category at current prices by the subtotal at constant prices. Price indexes for the post-World War II period are preliminary and are from *Bukka Shisu Nempo* (Nihon Ginko). Appendix tables A26–A29 show export and import values at current and constant prices and A30 gives price indexes.

Terms of Trade: Comparison with Previous Estimates

An index of net commodity terms of trade is calculated by dividing total export prices by import prices in table A30. The new estimate is below that given in LTES 8 (p. 212) except during World War I. A long-run decline in the terms of trade since the late 1890s has been asserted on the basis of the old estimate, but this is less evident in the new estimates, which instead tend to rise by the 1900s. Differences between the two come from different estimates for export and import price indexes. The LTES 8 series always exceeds ours for export prices, and the gap widens steadily going back to the early years: 16% higher in 1910, 32% in 1900, and 52% in 1890. On the other hand, its import price indexes are usually below the new one, by between 10 and 15% before 1900, somewhat less thereafter. Our new estimate of price indexes for exports and imports by commodity group in LTES 14 supersede the preliminary figures in LTES 8 (pp. 213–17).

---

4. Let V_t be the value of and Q_t the quantity of either exports or imports recorded in *Boeki*, and let $P_t (= V_t/Q_t)$ be the unit price calculated from them. If V_t tends to underestimate the true value $V_t^* (= V_t + E_t)$, but Q_t is the true quantity, then the true unit price P_t^* is $P_t^* = V_t^*/Q_t = P_t(1 + a_t)$, where $a_t = E_t/V_t$. Tatemoto's estimates provide E_t.

There is not much difference between the two in basic statistical procedure. The old series is produced by linking the Ohkawa–Takamatsu 1868–1904 estimate with the Yamada 1900–39 estimate, while the new one is made by linking Yamazawa's 1874–1904 series with the modified Yamada 1900–39 estimate as explained in the preceding section. Both the Ohkawa–Takamatsu estimate and Yamazawa estimate for the period before 1905 are based on *Boeki*, but Yamazawa's adopts twice as many individual commodities as samples and corrects for silver depreciation, freight, insurance, and packing costs. The corrections cause an upward revision of import price indexes before 1900.

After 1900 both the old and new estimates are based on Yamada's price indexes but the new estimate includes price indexes for colonial trade. Although aggregate export and import price indexes are Laspeyres in both estimates, the old estimates are weighted by export or import values for 1928–30 while the new ones use 1934–36 weights. Both the inclusion of colonial trade and the use of later values as weights tend to shift the new estimate downward. Japanese exports of heavy manufactures to protected markets in Taiwan and Korea increased rapidly in the 1930s, giving the new estimate a greater weight for heavy manufactures, whose prices had tended to rise faster than the average. Differences in aggregation methods had a less significant effect on the import price indexes.

These two procedures make our estimation of foreign trade price indexes consistent with other estimates in the LTES series. Shinohara questions inclusion of colonial trade on the grounds Japan's international competitiveness should be measured on the basis of trade with foreign countries. Although Taiwan and Korea cannot be considered perfectly noncompetitive protected markets for Japanese exports, it may be worth reestimating terms of trade with colonial trade excluded. As to the problem of selecting base years, the best solution is to change base year weights more frequently in estimating price indexes for a long period. These improvements are undertaken in LTES 14. In this sense the analysis of this section is preliminary.

Shinohara (1962) associated Japan's rapid export growth with the long-run decline of her terms of trade after the mid 1890s. A long-run decline is less evident in the new estimate. Terms of trade do not reflect correctly the competitiveness of exports. Competitiveness is measured by relative export prices, which are given in table 7.4. Despite increasing relative export prices during World War I, rapid export growth was possible because of reduced competition. An association of declining terms of trade with export growth is evident only for a few years before World War I and in the 1930s. Export growth before 1900 has to be explained by factors other than deteriorating relative prices. Faster growth of world trade has occasionally been mentioned as a major factor in Japanese export growth, but there is clear correspondence between the growth cycle of Japanese exports and that of world trade. The growth of Japanese exports for the pre-1900 period seems to be attributable to such factors as increased supply capacity and diversification of exported items.

REFERENCES

Abramovitz, Moses. 1961. "The Nature and Significance of Kuznets Cycles." *Economic Development and Cultural Change* (1961 Apr.).
———. 1973. "The Monetary Side of Long Swings in the United States Economic Growth." Center for Research on Economic Growth, Stanford University. Mimeo no. 14–6.
Baba, Mosao, and Masahiro Tatemoto. 1968. "Foreign Trade and Economic Growth in Japan: 1868–1937." In *Economic Growth: The Japanese Experience Since the Meiji Era*, edited by Lawrence Klein and Kazushi Ohkawa. Richard D. Irwin.
Brode, John. 1967. "Tables of Japanese Foreign Trade: 1868–1965." Mimeo.
Chosen Sotokufu. *Chosen Boeki Nempyo* (prewar Korean trade annual published by Japanese).
Deane, Phyllis, and Cole, W. A. 1962. *British Economic Growth 1688–1959*. Cambridge University Press.
Hayami, Yujiro. 1972. "Rice Policy in Japan's Economic Development." *American Journal of Agricultural Economics* (1972 Feb.).
Keizai Kikakucho. *Kokumin Shotoku Hakusho* (Annual published 1954–).
Key, Bernard. 1970. "The Role of Foreign Contributions in Prewar Japanese Capital Formation—with Special Reference to the Period 1904–14." Unpublished Ph.D. dissertation, University of California, Berkeley.
Kuznets, Simon. 1967. "Quantitative Aspects of the Economic Growth of Nations: Level and Structure of Foreign Trade: Long-Term Trends" *Economic Development and Cultural Change* (1967 Jan.).
Lewis, W. A. 1952. "World Production, Prices and Trade, 1870–1960." *Manchester School of Economics* (1952 May).
LTES [*Estimates of Long-Term Economic Statistics of Japan*]. Series edited by Kazushi Ohkawa, Miyohei Shinohara, and Mataji Umemura. 14 v. 1965–. Toyo Keizai Shimposha.
   1. National Income. 1974. Kazushi Ohkawa et al.
   8. Prices. 1967. Kazushi Ohkawa et al.
  10. Mining and Manufacturing. 1972. Miyohei Shinohara.

14. Foreign Trade and Balance of Payments. Forthcoming. Ippei Yama-
zawa and Yuzo Yamamoto.
Nihon Ginko, Tokeikyoku. *Bukka Shisu Nempo.*
————. *Kokusai Shushi Nempo.*
Ohkawa, Kazushi, and Henry Rosovsky. 1973. *Japanese Economic Growth:
Trend Acceleration in the Twentieth Century.* Stanford University Press.
Okurasho, Shuzeikyoku. *Nihon Gaikoku Boeki Nempyo* (Annual published
1882–).
————, Daijin Kambo. 1950. *Zaisei Kinyu Tokei Geppo* (monthly; the 1950
no. 5 issue was used in this chapter).
Shinohara, Miyohei. 1962. *Growth and Cycles in the Japanese Economy.*
Kinokuniya.
————. 1964. "Economic Development and Foreign Trade in Prewar Japan."
In *The Economic Development of China and Japan*, edited by C. D. Cowan.
Allen and Unwin.
Shionoya, Yuichi. 1968. "Patterns of Industrial Development." In *Economic
Growth: The Japanese Experience Since the Meiji Era*, edited by Lawrence
Klein and Kazushi Ohkawa. Richard D. Irwin.
Suzuki, Nagatoshi, ed. 1975. *Asian Industrial Development.* Ajiya Keizai
Kenkyujo (1975 Mar.).
Taiwan Sotokufu. *Taiwan Boeki Nempyo* (Annual published on Taiwan by
the Japanese).
Tatemoto, Masahiro. 1966. *Meiji 1–34 nen no Kokusai Shushi Suikei Sagyo
Hokoku.* KIER ser. nos. 6610 and 6612. Kyoto Institute of Economic
Research.
Toyo Keizai Shimposha. 1935. *Nihon Boeki Seiran* (Covers 1868–1933).
Yamamoto, Yuzo. 1969. "Kokusai Shushi Tokei no Choki Sogoka ni tsuite."
Jimbun Gakuho 28 (1969 Mar.).
————. 1972 and 1975. "Shokuminchika Chosen Taiwan no Ikigai Shushi
(Chosenhen)." *Jimbun Gakuho* 35 and 41 (1972 Oct. and 1975 Oct.).
Yamazawa, Ippei. 1975a. "Strategy of Industrial Development: The Japanese
Experience." In *Asian Industrial Development*, edited by Nagatoshi Suzuki.
Institute of Developing Economies.
————. 1975b. "Industrial Growth and Trade Policy in Prewar Japan." *The
Developing Economies* (1975 Apr.).

PART 3: PRODUCT ALLOCATION

8

Consumption

Miyohei Shinohara

The level and structure of consumption from 1874 to 1970 are explored in this chapter. Prewar data are from LTES 6, while official national income estimates are used beginning with 1951. Prewar estimates are based primarily on the commodity flow and retail valuation methods, but the postwar figures rely on family budget surveys, so there is some discontinuity in estimating procedures. Nonetheless the two can be linked to provide long-term perspective.

Research in preparing LTES 6 and since then is one of the few attempts to estimate consumption directly for a long period for any country. The residual after estimating total national product and its other components is often used instead. Adequate historical data are simply lacking in many countries, and even for Japan, in general the earlier the year, the less complete the sources. Despite this and other problems mentioned later in this chapter, the estimates in LTES and here are sufficiently consistent with other data and indirect evidence to give a reasonably comprehensive overview.

Consumption includes expenditures of private nonprofit institutions and business consumption (expense-account entertaining for the most part). The latter is especially important, and it can be argued the rationale for and type of such spending make it classifiable as personal consumption, particularly when considering consumer welfare.

The LTES project has been concerned primarily with establishing series for national income and its components. This means military expenditure for consumption items—primarily food, clothing, and housing—is included under government and is excluded from this discussion. Until after the China Incident (1937), Japan's military forces were not a very large percentage of the population, especially in terms of those stationed domestically. Colonial garrisons (including

Table 8.1. Consumption: Composition of Expenditures in Current Prices
(In percent)

Period	Food[a]	Clothing	Housing[b]	Fuel, and lighting	Medical, and personal care	Transportation	Communication	Social expenses[c]	Education, recreation, and others[d]
1874–83	65.7	7.8	7.2	5.5	3.8	0.2	0.1	5.8	3.9
1877–86	65.4	7.7	7.4	4.9	4.2	0.2	0.1	6.1	4.0
1882–91	63.8	7.9	8.8	4.2	4.7	0.4	0.1	6.0	4.1
1887–96	63.1	9.3	8.9	3.3	4.5	0.7	0.2	6.0	4.0
1892–1901	63.0	9.5	8.0	3.0	4.2	1.0	0.2	7.1	4.0
1897–1906	63.7	8.2	7.9	3.0	3.8	1.3	0.3	7.7	4.1
1902–11	63.2	8.2	8.8	3.3	3.0	1.6	0.4	7.2	4.3
1907–16	61.9	9.2	9.3	3.6	3.0	1.9	0.4	6.1	4.6
1912–21	60.4	13.3	7.5	3.9	3.3	2.2	0.4	3.9	5.1
1917–26	58.9	12.8	8.6	4.0	3.7	2.6	0.4	3.4	5.6
1922–31	56.0	10.9	11.4	4.2	4.2	3.1	0.5	3.4	6.3
1927–36	52.1	11.6	12.7	4.4	5.1	3.3	0.6	2.9	7.3
1931–40	49.5	12.9	12.4	4.4	5.7	3.5	0.7	2.9	8.0
1947–56	54.7	12.8	9.2	4.4	18.9[e]				
1952–61	47.5	13.8	13.1	4.0	21.5[e]				
1957–66	40.4	12.8	16.8	3.5	26.5[e]				
1962–71	35.9	11.1	19.8	2.9	30.1[e]				

Source: Prewar: Reprinted from LTES 6:5 (table 1-2); postwar: ARNIS. Underlying data in appendix tables A34 and A35.

Note: Estimates of prewar data by year and in greater detail are found in LTES 6.

[a] Includes beverages and tobacco, as well as meals eaten out, although some of the latter are included in social expenses.

[b] Includes consumer durables (furniture and appliances) as well as rental costs of dwellings (both direct and imputed to owner-occupied homes). This series may need major revisions; see the discussion in the section on remaining problems.

[c] Includes ceremonial expenses such as weddings and funerals, as well as entertainment by companies (estimated from taxable income for Japanese-type restaurants, which cater to this kind of business).

[d] School uniforms, worn by almost all students, though increasingly less so for postwar college students, are included in clothing. Fees paid by radio and television owners to subsidize public broadcasting are included, as are reading matter, theater, movies, and school fees. See

Manchuria) obtained most food supplies locally, and military uniforms (excluded here) were made in government-owned factories. The impact on domestic consumption, aggregate and per capita, is thus probably not too large though this is an area requiring further study. Two recent studies of living standards are Hazama (1976) and Chubachi and Taira (1976).

Throughout our early work *expenditure* elasticity was used because we were directly estimating consumption expenditure and thus ignored income and its savings component. Income (and hence the savings rate) rose more rapidly than expenditure in the prewar period. Given the mathematics of calculating elasticities, expenditure elasticities are thus *higher* than income elasticities.

MAJOR FINDINGS

Long-Run Perspective

Tables 8.1–8.3 summarize current and constant price consumption by major categories since 1874, except for the war and reconstruction

Table 8.2. Consumption: Composition of Miscellaneous Expenses in Current Prices, 1958–72
(In percent of total consumption expenditure)

Fiscal year	Medical, and health expenses	Transportation, and communication	Recreation, and entertainment	Miscellaneous services
1958	6.1	2.5	5.5	6.0
1959	6.2	2.6	5.6	6.6
1960	6.0	2.7	6.1	7.2
1961	6.6	2.8	6.1	7.5
1962	7.0	2.7	6.8	8.1
1963	7.2	3.2	6.9	8.8
1964	7.4	3.2	7.2	8.8
1965	7.6	3.4	7.2	9.2
1966	7.6	3.8	7.4	9.4
1967	8.1	3.9	7.2	9.3
1968	8.0	4.1	7.5	10.1
1969	8.2	4.4	7.8	9.7
1970	8.3	4.8	8.2	9.5
1971	8.0	5.0	8.0	9.9
1972	8.5	5.2	8.2	9.9

Source: ARNIS 1973.
Note: Postwar data are available only for fiscal years since 1958. The sum of recreation and entertainment plus miscellaneous services is almost identical to social expenses plus education, recreation, and others in table 8.1. Data here are fiscal year (beginning Apr. 1) while in tables 8.1 and 8.3 they are calendar year.

Table 8.3. Consumption: Composition of Expenditures in 1934–46 Prices
(In percent)

Period	Food[a]	Clothing	Housing[b]	Fuel, and lighting	Medical, and personal care	Transportation	Communication	Social expenses[c]	Education, recreation, and others[d]
1874–83	64.9	3.0	12.6	2.6	2.6	0.2	0.0	11.2	2.9
1877–86	65.4	3.1	12.3	2.6	2.9	0.2	0.1	10.4	3.0
1882–91	64.7	3.6	11.5	2.5	3.4	0.3	0.1	9.5	4.4
1887–96	62.7	5.1	10.6	2.4	3.4	0.5	0.1	9.5	5.7
1892–1901	60.9	6.3	10.2	2.3	3.3	1.0	0.2	9.8	6.0
1897–1906	59.9	6.0	11.1	2.4	3.2	1.4	0.2	9.9	5.9
1902–11	59.7	6.2	12.3	2.6	2.7	1.3	0.3	9.3	5.6
1907–16	60.7	7.2	10.8	3.1	2.8	1.3	0.4	8.0	5.7
1912–21	60.5	9.0	9.5	3.7	3.1	1.8	0.4	5.7	6.3
1917–26	58.1	9.4	10.9	3.9	3.5	2.5	0.4	4.1	7.2
1922–31	55.9	9.3	12.0	4.2	3.9	3.0	0.5	3.7	7.5
1927–36	53.1	11.3	12.0	4.3	4.9	3.2	0.6	3.0	7.6
1931–40	50.3	12.0	12.5	4.4	5.7	3.8	0.7	3.0	7.6
1947–56	50.4	9.9	11.6	6.2			21.8[e]		
1952–61	45.4	12.3	12.0	4.9			25.3[e]		
1957–66	39.5	12.6	12.9	4.6			30.3[e]		
1962–71	34.3	11.7	14.6	4.8			34.5[e]		

Source: Reprinted from LTES 6:7 (table 1-4). Underlying data in appendix tables A36 and A37.
Notes: See table 8.1.

Table 8.4. Consumption: Annual Growth Rates of Expenditures in Real Prices
(In percent)

Period		Food	Clothing	Housing	Fuel, and lighting	Medical, and personal care	Transportation	Communication	Social expenses	Education, recreation, and others	Total
1877–86	/1874–83	2.1	3.7	1.0	1.7	6.6	6.2	17.7	−0.8	2.4	1.8
1882–91	/1877–86	2.3	5.7	1.1	1.9	5.4	10.5	9.9	0.7	10.6	2.5
1887–96	/1882–91	2.6	10.5	1.7	2.0	3.3	15.5	10.7	3.3	9.1	3.3
1892–1901	/1887–96	2.1	7.1	1.9	1.9	2.4	16.0	9.7	3.5	3.8	2.7
1897–1906	/1892–1901	1.0	0.5	3.2	2.2	0.4	9.3	7.7	1.5	0.9	1.3
1902–11	/1897–1906	1.2	2.0	3.3	5.7	−2.0	0.4	6.0	0.1	0.3	1.3
1907–16	/1902–11	2.7	5.5	−0.4	5.6	2.9	1.8	6.3	−0.9	2.7	2.3
1912–21	/1907–16	3.3	8.2	1.0	7.1	5.9	11.2	3.8	−3.3	5.8	3.6
1917–26	/1912–21	3.3	3.8	7.1	5.6	6.4	10.8	4.0	−2.4	6.7	4.1
1922–31	/1917–26	1.9	2.6	4.7	4.1	5.0	6.4	8.2	0.5	3.7	2.7
1927–36	/1922–31	0.9	5.8	2.0	2.6	7.0	3.0	7.4	−1.9	2.1	2.0
1931–40	/1927–36	0.7	3.8	3.1	2.4	5.8	6.7	4.6	1.3	2.3	2.1
1952–61	/1947–56	6.9	14.1	9.8	4.0			12.5			9.2
1957–66	/1952–61	5.7	9.2	10.4	7.3			12.6			8.6
1962–71	/1957–66	6.1	7.5	11.8	9.9			12.0			9.1

Source: LTES 6:8 (table 1–6).

Note: Derived by compound interest between decade averages. The simple average of the 12 prewar rates is 2.5% annually; for the postwar 12 it is 9.0%.

Table 8.5. Consumption: Relative Prices

Period	Food	Clothing	Housing	Fuel and lighting	Medical and personal care	Transpor- tation	Communi- cation	Social expenses	Education, recreation, and others
1874–83	101.5	264.3	56.8	208.5	149.7	132.7	184.9	51.8	133.2
1877–86	100.0	245.3	60.4	189.2	144.8	120.3	160.4	58.5	133.5
1882–91	98.6	216.7	76.7	165.6	140.9	129.8	141.9	63.7	93.0
1887–96	100.8	183.3	83.7	140.2	131.8	127.2	135.1	62.8	69.9
1892–1901	103.1	152.3	78.0	132.8	125.7	102.8	128.8	71.8	66.6
1897–1906	106.2	136.8	71.2	125.2	120.9	91.1	123.1	77.4	69.7
1902–11	106.1	132.3	71.7	124.8	112.9	120.0	117.8	77.4	76.4
1907–16	101.8	127.4	86.5	117.5	106.4	146.5	111.7	76.5	79.6
1912–21	99.9	146.7	79.1	108.0	105.9	117.3	108.1	68.7	80.9
1917–26	101.4	136.0	78.4	102.6	108.1	103.0	112.2	83.2	77.5
1922–31	100.4	116.6	94.9	100.1	107.4	103.8	107.8	92.2	83.2
1927–36	98.2	102.6	106.0	100.6	103.4	105.1	104.0	96.5	95.7
1931–40	98.4	107.6	99.3	99.8	100.8	91.9	99.8	96.4	104.6
1947–56	109.4	140.7	81.2	75.2			80.0		
1952–61	105.4	113.5	105.2	82.0			84.0		
1957–66	103.5	102.6	126.8	76.6			86.0		
1962–71	105.5	96.4	133.7	63.5			86.7		

Source: LTES 6:8 (table 1-5) for prewar.

Note: This table is derived by deflating each individual price index (from 1874–1971) by the total implicit consumption deflator. The decade averages are computed after deriving the annual relative price series. This table is equal to table 8.1 divided by table 8.3.

Table 8.6. Consumption: Secular Growth Rates and Crude Expenditure Elasticities
of Expenditures in Real Terms, 1874–1940

	Real consumption expenditures	
	Annual growth rate (%)	Expenditure elasticity
Food		
(1874–1940)	2.12	0.841
Clothing		
(1874–1940)	4.96	1.968
Housing		
(1874–1940)	2.52	1.000
Fuel and Lighting		
(1874–1910)	2.11	0.921
(1911–40)	4.05	1.436
Medical and personal care		
(1875–1900)	4.21	1.565
(1900–1940)	5.99	2.147
Transportation		
(1874–1940)	8.14	3.230
Communication		
(1889–1940)	6.76	2.661
Education, recreation, and others		
(1890–1940)	3.28	1.286
Total		
(1874–1940)	2.52	

Source: LTES 6:12 (table 1-7).
Notes: The expenditure elasticities are crude in that no compensation has been made
for price elasticity effects. Moreover they are derived simply by dividing annual growth
rates of specific real expenditure items by that of total real consumption expenditure,
without any regression calculation.

Annual growth rates are computed by the formula $\log Xi = \log a + bt$ (Xi = real
consumption of each item). Annual growth rates of real consumption in the computation
of expenditure elasticities are:

	1874–1910	1875–1900	1889–1940	1890–1940	1900–40	1911–40
Total real consumption	2.29	2.69	2.54	2.55	2.54	2.82

The prewar periods of measurement differ somewhat among categories because early
years when rates were erratic have been dropped; the analysis is limited to periods
in which slopes of semilogarithmic curves are relatively linear. In two instances the
semilog graphs show some curvature so the period was split and two rates were calculated.

periods. Annual growth rates of total consumption and its subcategories are computed in table 8.4. Relative prices are in table 8.5. Decade averages have been used to eliminate short-term cyclic effects. Secular growth rates, and expenditure elasticities are given in table 8.6.

Specific Items

The relative decline of food expenditure dates from the beginning of rice imports from the colonies in the 1910s. For the 40 years prior to that, food's share was remarkably stable, falling somewhat faster in current than in constant price terms. Saito (1918) surveyed farm households for years between 1890 and 1920, and the results are similar to my nationwide figures for the percentage of expenditure going for food, including beverages and tobacco, as shown in table 8.7. Since most of the population was still rural before 1920, Saito's data help to substantiate a general stability of food's share in current prices. Yokoyama (1949) studied low-income urban workers in 1898 and estimated their Engel coefficient at over 70%. This is probably a good indication of the upper end of the range, but is clearly too high for a nationwide average.

In the postwar period, rapidly rising incomes, permitting greater diversity in consumption, account for most of food's decline. There is

Table 8.7. Food's Share of Consumption in Current Prices, 1890–1920
(In percent)

1890	1899	1906	1911	1920	
65.9	64.1	64.8	65.2	60.8	Saito[a]
66.3	62.4	64.2	62.9	61.8	Shinohara

Source: Saito 1918 and author's calculations.
[a]Saito's data were compiled in 1908 for 1890, 1899, and 1906. He made additional surveys in 1911 and 1912, publishing the results of all five surveys in 1918. The 1920 survey was made by his research group after his death. Tobacco and beverages are included.

Table 8.8. Food's Share of Consumption 1952–72
(In percent)

1952	1955	1960	1965	1968	1970	1972	Relative share in
54.0	51.1	43.1	37.7	35.9	34.3	32.9	Current prices
51.1	49.1	43.9	37.7	35.4	32.9	32.0	1965 prices

Note: Tobacco and beverages are included.

little difference in the food expenditure proportions between the current and constant price series. Except for the lingering influences of the immediate postwar food shortages on the 1952 figures, this pattern is also true when 1965 prices are used for the postwar years (table 8.8).

Kuznets' analysis of long-term changes in food's share in advanced countries suggests, at least over some long period, the logical expectation of a decline in the proportion in real terms, with the current price series share being comparatively stable. This should be true even though cross-section analysis among countries suggests low income elasticity for food. Such a pattern reflects increasing amounts of marketed food, incurring larger processing, transportation, and distribution costs, which Kuznets labels the PTD component. Despite this logical expectation, Kuznets did not find any clear overall pattern in his data (1962, pp. 1–92). For prewar Japan, table 8.9 shows when tobacco and beverages are excluded from food (as is done in Kuznets' analysis) the category is actually quite stable in constant prices, while the current price series declines.

Table 8.10 compares the percentage of real-term food consumption accounted for by PTD expenses for three countries. Aside from problems of comparing different development levels, Japan's percentage is lowest, though by a narrow margin. Ohkawa attributes this in large part to the persistence and development of traditional elements both in consumption preferences and in the production and distribution of

Table 8.9. Food's Share of Consumption 1874–1940
(In percent)

1874–83	1887–96	1902–11	1912–21	1922–31	1931–40	Relative share in
53.9	51.0	50.0	47.1	41.4	37.5	Current prices
42.3	43.0	42.3	42.9	39.5	38.1	1934–36 prices

Note: Tobacco and beverages are excluded.

Table 8.10. Food Consumption in Real Terms: International Comparison of PTD Component
(PTD as percentage of total food expense)

Japan			Sweden		United States	
1885	1935	1961	1871–80	1921–30	1869	1949–57
17	32	47	29	47	29	56

Sources: Japan: Ohkawa 1973, pp. 672–74; others: Kuznets 1962.

food. In part because of the smaller PTD component, there is strong evidence food was cheaper per calorie in Japan than in western countries until at least the late 1960s. Since few people have a diet similar to Japan's there was little competition for traditional Japanese food sources, which were originally mostly domestic (later also colonial) or nearby fishing grounds. Thus as long as Japanese rice (different from other rices in taste and texture) and fish were staples, rather than so-called western foods (meat, eggs, and dairy products) which would have had to be imported at world market prices or grown domestically under less than ideal conditions, Japan had an advantage.

Rice consumption in 1934–36 prices increased about 50% per capita in the 40 years before World War I, but then leveled off for the remainder of the period (table 8.11). In contrast, western items increased over ten times in the period, though the amount remained small. This may be an additional explanation for the stability of food's share in real terms. (For more detailed data see LTES 6:17, table 2-5.)

An important implication of the stability of food share is that the agricultural and traditional food processing sectors were able to increase output without a major change in relative prices. The productivity advances helping to have made this possible are discussed in

Table 8.11. Per Capita Rice and Western Food Expenditure in 1934–36 Prices
(Yen)

1874–83	1892–1901	1912–21	1931–40	
18.28	21.71	28.19	28.99	Rice
0.69	2.05	3.80	7.08	Western foods[a]

[a] Meat, eggs, milk, and other dairy products.

Table 8.12. Health Inspection Data of Public Primary School Students, 1900–60

	Height (cm)				Weight (kg)			
	Seven years old		Twelve years old		Seven years old		Twelve years old	
	Boy	Girl	Boy	Girl	Boy	Girl	Boy	Girl
1900[a]	107.0	105.0	128.0	128.0	17.0	17.0	27.0	27.0
1910	106.7	105.6	128.6	128.4	17.5	17.0	27.1	27.0
1920	107.0	105.8	129.4	129.7	17.6	17.0	27.6	27.4
1930	108.1	106.9	131.4	131.3	17.9	17.3	28.3	28.5
1950	108.6	107.8	131.5	131.7	18.5	17.9	28.7	28.8
1960	111.7	110.6	136.2	138.1	19.1	18.5	30.7	32.3

Source: Prepared by Mataji Umemura from data in Mombusho (1963).
[a] Rounded to nearest integer.

chapter 4. That the agricultural sector was able to obtain the resources to grow as it did even while the manufacturing sector was expanding is important to understanding overall Japanese growth.

Elsewhere (1954; 1963, pp. 311–18) I discuss the relation between the trend stability of the relative price of rice and increasing colonial rice imports, and a pattern of cyclical covariation between the relative price of rice and imports from countries other than the colonies.

Improvement in diet is reflected in figures on height and weight of school children collected by Umemura (table 8.12).

Kelley and Williamson (1974, pp. 156–59) have an extensive discussion of food elasticity in which they use the 0.39 income elasticity of Kaneda (1969, p. 404) in their analysis of the 1878–1922 period. They refer to my computation of 0.71 as too high. In so doing they fail to note two things. First, my figure refers to *expenditure* elasticity, inherently higher than *income* elasticity when the savings rate is rising, as it was at the time. More important, since it calls into question any inferences drawn from using 0.39, Kaneda computed the value from what he calls the Yamada–Noda "agricultural food products available for consumption" series, which he constructed himself from their LTES 9 data. In his article, Kaneda does not define the series' coverage. It excludes not only beverages and tobacco (part of my series) but also processed foods, including western-type and such traditional items as shoyu and miso. In short, precisely those foods displaying the greatest growth are excluded.

Kaneda notes the postwar elasticity of 0.69 "is significantly higher than those [he] computed for the prewar periods. [This] should be interpreted as indicating that the Japanese are not content to eat the same kinds of foods as they used to" (p. 420). My and other data suggest this applied to an important extent in the prewar period as well.

Clothing shows the effects of a two-thirds fall in relative price. The current price share increased about two-thirds before the war but quadrupled in constant prices. Even allowing for an income elasticity of 1.2–1.5, this might suggest a very high price elasticity of clothing demand, since in real terms clothing expenditures increased four times more than total consumption in the prewar period. A more likely explanation is the continuous rapid shift to the right of the textile supply curve due to technological progress. If the supply curve moves to the right faster than the demand curve, the equilibrium price may decrease. Then even if short-run price elasticity of demand is fairly low (the demand curve is steep), ordinary regression analysis on ob-

Table 8.13. Consumer Durables

1952	1958	1961	1963	1968	1971	
—	3.1	—	6.2	7.1	8.1	Consumer durables as a percentage of total consumer expenditure, current prices
117.0	—	100.0	98.0	98.0	98.3	Consumer durables' wholesale price index (Nihon Ginko)

servable prices and quantities may indicate high price elasticity. Prewar industrialization centered on light industry, especially textiles, which as a major export item achieved extensive scale economies. Such rapid expansion having this type of impact on the relative price of textiles and thus on consumption structure is a plausible explanation of the increase of clothing's constant-price share.

Transportation's rising share reflects increased urbanization as does the current-price series for housing. In contrast to its current-price share, the constant-price share for housing was remarkably stable until the late 1960s. One problem in comparing postwar housing figures to the prewar is the inclusion of automobiles and durables such as television sets, which became much more important after the war, obscuring the long-term pattern of basic housing.

Housing has had an upward movement in relative price, reflecting increasing urbanization. Postwar affluence has pushed up the demand for private homes, larger apartments, summer homes, and furniture, so relative prices for the whole category have increased even though many durables have become less expensive. On the other hand, fuel and lighting, affected by improving technology (new energy sources and more efficient use of them), declined almost steadily in relative price, although this has been reversed by the sharp increases in energy prices since 1973. Expenditure elasticities for housing and fuel and lighting have been rising in part because of the move toward smaller households with more appliances. The sharp break between pre- and postwar elasticity for fuel and lighting is mostly due to their historically high relative prices in the immediate postwar years. The abnormally high elasticities of the late 1940s gradually disappeared in the postwar development process.

Official national income statistics since 1958 have categories for consumer durables, nondurables, and services. Durables have increased their share substantially, as table 8.13 shows. The relative price of

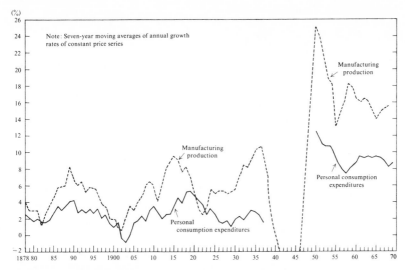

Fig. 8.1. Growth Cycle in Personal Consumption as Contrasted with That of Manufacturing Production

durables has declined in the postwar period, with prices of many electrical appliances actually dropping. Thus durables' share of constant price consumption increased even more, and this increase is undoubtedly a major factor in the acceleration of not only consumption growth, but also economic growth in general.

Social expenditures' decline in the interwar period reflects the general stagnation of the 1920s and the militarization of the 1930s, which tended to hold down business entertaining. The kink in the medical and personal care growth rate might simply be due to the gradual replacement of home care and traditional treatment by a recognizable medical services industry, involving western techniques, doctors, nurses, and hospitals.

Long Swings

Figure 8.1 illustrates seven-year moving averages for both consumption and manufacturing growth rates. There are definite long swings in prewar consumption. The pattern relates to the general stagnation of the 1920s and the increasing militarization of the 1930s. While the general procedure is to relate consumption to income, this comparison to manufacturing has been made because of the importance of the

Table 8.14. Swings in Housing and Stone, Clay, and Glass Output

Peak	Trough	Peak	Trough	
1909	1914	1924	1929	Stone, clay, and glass output
1906	1913	1921	1929	Housing construction

supply curve shift mentioned earlier in connection with textiles, but applicable to other items as well. Postwar the pattern is unclear except, as in the prewar period, production swings lead consumption swings. Growth cycles derived from seven-year moving averages have a duration of just ten years, making them Juglar cycles. Probably, ten-year moving averages need to be used to identify postwar Kuznets cycles, but the initial calculations are counterintuitive and thus require further analysis. Rehabilitation factors are also important in the postwar pattern, probably causing the rates of the late 1940s to be abnormally high.

Data on swings in components in the prewar period show clothing slightly leads total consumption, suggesting the link by which production led consumption, as textiles were a major part of manufacturing output (41% in 1887–96 and still 24% in the 1930s). Housing swings are distinct, with none in the 19th century, while in the 20th century they have been shorter than swings in other components. This relates to swings in stone, clay, and glass output, which are construction-led products (see ch. 5). As table 8.14 shows the troughs are almost identical and housing peaks lead output by three years. (There is a secondary peak in 1924, just after the great Kanto earthquake.) Fuel and light, fairly flat in the 19th century, peaked in the 1910s as electrification spread, then drifted down until leveling in the late 1920s.

DATA AND METHODS

In estimating expenditures for 1874–1940, the commodity-flow and retail-valuation methods have been adopted for commodity consumption. Tokyo retail prices were usually used in applying the retail-valuation method. Because of regional price differences this is a persistent source of upward bias in the prewar current-price estimates, and since the price gap tended to narrow during the period, it is not a consistent bias. Ohkawa adjusted the retail price series downward (but not the 1934–36 constant-price series except for a few specific years for food and clothing) in the incorporation of my aggregate figures into the national income estimates in LTES 1. The components

Table 8.15. Percentage Distribution of Methods Used to Estimate Total Consumption

	Retail valuation	Commodity flow	Others
1885	70	15	15
1935	43	37	20

have not been adjusted, so their sum exceeds the aggregate estimate (LTES 1:161–62 and 178–81; pp. 78–85 in Japanese). Food, fuel, and imputed rent are the items felt to have had the widest regional price differences and thus to be most overestimated.

Personal consumption is estimated by taking output for each commodity, adding imports, subtracting exports, and adjusting for distributor margins and shipping costs. Due to a paucity of inventory data, changes in stocks within the distribution system (and any hoarding by consumers) are usually disregarded. This may account for some short-run erratic movements in the clothing series. However, the use of moving averages in much of our analysis compensates for inventories over the business cycle. (For further discussion on inventory see Shinohara 1962, pp. 163–87.)

Intermediate goods are of course excluded, something relatively easy to do in consumption compared to manufacturing. Since the commodity flow method depends on magnitudes in money terms, distributor margins must be adjusted for when output values are producer prices. In the retail-valuation method, the physical volume of exports, waste, and intermediate use is subtracted and that of imports added to obtain net consumption volume, which is then multiplied by the retail price (or, for farmers' self-consumption, by the farm price). For services, these methods do not work, so a number of others have been used, depending on the item (see LTES 6:92–102 and 6:122–28 for further details).

As the structure of consumption changes, so does the weight of each valuation method, since different methods are used for different items. Table 8.15 gives Ohkawa's calculations of the percentages of total consumption computed by various methods.

Linking Pre- and Postwar Series

LTES 6 stops with 1940, although there is a brief discussion of linkage to the 1950s (6:33–46). Revised official national income statistics cover fiscal years beginning 1951 April 1. The 1951 figures that result from adjusting to the calendar year and converting to 1934–

36 prices using Noda's price index (LTES 8:137) are extrapolated to 1972 using official estimates of personal consumption expenditures in 1965 prices for each category. Total consumption in 1934–36 prices is the sum of these categories.

For interpolating 1946–50 consumption in 1934–36 prices, the indexes of commodity and service supplies, which cover 80 items grouped into food, clothing, fuel and light, housing, and others, adjusted for foreign trade, are used (Keizai Kikakucho 1955). These are in per capita terms, so they have been multiplied by Umemura's population index (computed from data in appendix table A53). The results are fairly reasonable, and the implicit price deflators derived by comparing the current and constant (1934–36) price series are also plausible. This provides a consumption series in 1934–36 prices from 1874 to 1972 except for 1941–45. Extrapolation of expenditures in 1951 current prices to 1946 using the semiofficial national expenditure estimates of the ESB gives the corresponding current price series.

Other Estimates

The semiofficial ESB estimates for the 1930s undoubtedly involve some serious underestimation. In the ESB series, food's share is underestimated because expenditures for food given as gifts (very important in Japan), used for ceremonial purposes, or eaten while traveling or on company expense accounts tend to be omitted. This is an inherent problem in budget survey data.

Much depends on the deflator, and I feel there are errors in the ESB series. For example, it has a value of 189.4 for 1940 (1936 = 100), compared to Morita's 175.0. Morita's index is designed to include black-market prices and thus provide an "effective retail price index." I do not believe the black market was as widespread in 1940 as Morita does, so I think even his index is an overestimate. On the other hand, my deflator is above the *Asahi* cost-of-living index. I have discussed the ESB data in more detail elsewhere (Shinohara 1970, pp. 232–78).

Kuznets (1968, pp. 197–242) has made a number of comments on the LTES 6 estimates as an appendix to his own tentative estimates made before all the LTES estimates were available. My current-price estimates are much higher (by 20 to 50%) than his, but the trend (growth rates) is similar. However, differences in price index movements give the constant-price series substantially different growth rates; mine are much lower, 16 compared to 27% per decade on a per capita basis.

My share for food is smaller in the pre-World War I period. Kuznets considered the food proportion he computed for these years to be unusually high compared to both contemporary LDCs and developed countries in their early development stages.

There is a drastic revision of nonfood items in my series (primarily because of my increase in clothing estimates), which follows the 1874 census rather than the extrapolated-back Noshomusho data. This increase in total consumption makes food's share smaller even though I revised food consumption upward taking into account to some extent Nakamura's research on rice production (1966) and including certain items such as sugar, salt, tofu (bean curd), and beverages omitted by Noshomusho.

REFERENCES

Chubachi, Masayoshi, and Koji Taira. 1976. "Poverty in Modern Japan." In *Japanese Industrialization and its Social Consequences*, edited by Hugh Patrick with Larry Meissner. University of California Press.

Hazama, Hiroshi. 1976. Historical Changes in the Life Style of Industrial Workers." In *Japanese Industrialization and its Social Consequences*, edited by Hugh Patrick with Larry Meissner. University of California Press.

Kaneda, Hiromitsu. 1969. "Long-Term Changes in Food Consumption Patterns in Japan." In *Agriculture and Economic Growth, Japan's Experience*, edited by Kazushi Ohkawa, Bruce F. Johnston, and Hiromitsu Kaneda. Princeton University Press.

Keizai Kikakucho. 1955. *Keizai Hakusho*.

Kelley, Allen C., and Jeffrey G. Williamson. 1974. *Lessons from Japanese Development*. University of Chicago Press.

Kuznets, Simon. 1962. "Quantitative Aspects of the Economic Growth of Nations: VII. The Share and Structure of Consumption." *Economic Development and Cultural Change* (1962 Jan.).

―――. 1968. "Trends in Level and Structure of Consumption." In *Economic Growth: The Japanese Experience Since the Meiji Era*, edited by Lawrence Klein and Kazushi Ohkawa. Richard D. Irwin.

LTES [*Estimates of Long-Term Economic Statistics of Japan*]. Series edited by Kazushi Ohkawa, Miyohei Shinohara, and Mataji Umemura. 14 v. 1965–. Toyo Keizai Shimposha.

   1. National Income. 1974. Kazushi Ohkawa et al.
   6. Personal Consumption Expenditure. 1967. Miyohei Shinohara.
   8. Prices. 1967. Kazushi Ohkawa et al.
   9. Agriculture and Forestry. 1966. Mataji Umemura et al.

Mombusho. 1963. *Mombu Tokei Yoran*.

Noshomusho. *Noshomu Tokeihyo* (Annual published 1883–1923).

Ohkawa, Kazushi. 1973. "Personal Consumption in Dualistic Growth." In *Economic Growth: The Japanese Experience Since the Meiji Era*, edited by Kazushi Ohkawa and Yujiro Hayami. Japan Economic Research Center.

Saito, Mankichi. 1918. *Nihon Noson no Keizaiteki Hensen.* Reprinted in *Noka Keizai Chosa Hokoku*, edited by Taizo Inaba, 1953. See Shinohara 1970, pp. 267–69, for a fuller discussion of Saito's work.

Shinohara, Miyohei. 1954. "Keizai Hatten to Boeki no Kankei." In *Nihon Keizai no Kozo Bunseki.* v. 2, edited by Ichiro Nakayama.

———. 1962. *Growth and Cycles in the Japanese Economy.* Kinokuniya. (See 1963 below.)

———. 1963. *Nihon Keizai no Seicho to Junkan.* Sobunsha. (Although this has the same title as 1962 above, the contents are somewhat different.)

———. 1970. *Structural Change in Japan's Economic Development.* Kinokuniya.

Yokoyama, Gennosuke. 1949. *Nihon no Kasoshakai.* Iwanami. (Reprint of 1898 edition.)

9

Capital Formation and Capital Stock

Much of the analysis of Japanese growth has been concerned with investment patterns and growth. As discussed in chapter 3, here, and by Ishiwata (1975), while net investment and change in capital stock are equivalent, independent estimates of the two have not always given this result. The series in this volume have been made consistent by the editors' judgment of the best available component series. Ohkawa also discusses capital formation in chapter 1.

CAPITAL FORMATION

Koichi Emi

This section briefly covers gross domestic fixed-capital formation (I) and its principal components by type (producers' durable equipment [PDE] and construction, which is divided into nonresidential buildings, structures [nonbuildings], and residences), and by sector (agriculture and nonagriculture; government and private [respectively postscripted g and p]), as well as by military versus nonmilitary within the government sector.

Prewar estimates were made in current prices and have all been converted to 1934–36 prices. Most are taken from LTES 1, where Ohkawa has slightly amended one of my series in LTES 4 and added additional ones. EPA estimates starting with 1952 are published in ARNIS. There are also EPA series for 1930–51 (Keizai Shingicho 1956, pp. 22–23). Appendix tables A38–A41 give the basic data from these sources.

While there were periods of declining investment, the overall prewar movement is one of substantial growth, both in current and constant prices. Moreover, both pre- and postwar rates are higher than GNPs for long-term trends. A plotting of the annual postwar data looks like a flight of steep stairs, with spurts of very rapid growth interspersed with almost flat periods lasting one or two years.

Growth rates are given in chapter 1, tables 1.5–1.8. Most of the series display definite cycles. The exceptions are residential construction after World War I and the agriculture sector. The length and amplitude of the cycles vary considerably. For investment, duration ranges from 4 to 13 years trough to trough, and 9 to 14 years peak to peak.

Private and Government

Capital formation by sectors is given in table 1.10, and growth rates are in table 1.11. They show a steady increase in the government's prewar share, except during the World War I boom period. Further, until the 1930s this was largely for nonmilitary items, as the military share tended to decline after the Sino-Japanese war in the 1890s. The jump in military investment in the 1930s is almost entirely at the expense of other Ig (government investment). Private industrial capital formation maintained a much stabler share than Ip (private investment as a whole), fluctuating around one-half of aggregate investment. PDE investment includes such items as machinery, tools, vehicles, and ships. While it has been primarily private, the government was also important because of involvement in transportation, telecommunications, iron and steel, and arsenals. In addition, during the 1870s the government established pilot plants of various kinds, but most were sold to private enterprises in the 1880s.

Construction is the largest part of Ig. Almost all of this was for structures, including the nationalized railroads, harbors, roads, waterworks, land reclamation and improvement, and afforestation. In the private sector, construction centered on railroads (until nationalization in 1906), the supply of gas and electricity, mining and agricultural works, as well as buildings for industrial, commercial, and residential use. Construction is by type, so part of railroads comes under structures and part under buildings. Cycles in nonmilitary Ig last longer and have larger amplitudes than those of Ip, in part because agriculture and residential construction, the largest Ip components in the 1880s and still important in the 1930s, display little swing. In general Ig swings are determined by spending on structures, and Ip swings by PDE.

Agriculture and Nonagriculture

The nonagriculture sector growth rate has a range of -5 to $+30\%$ in the prewar period, while the agriculture sector rate moves between 0 and 5%. There has been a steady increase in nonagriculture's share, which is expected in an industrializing economy. When residential construction is included, agriculture's share increases one or two percentage points.

Livestock and perennial plants are included as a specific fixed investment item in both pre- and postwar data. Their decline in share from the mid 1890s to the mid 1930s is even more rapid than the agriculture sector's as a whole. Much of this type of investment was for mulberry trees to feed silkworms and for expansion of orchards. Limited arable land constrains the amount that can be invested usefully, and while there are no studies on returns to such investments, the declining share is probably consistent with the limits.

PDE, Construction, and Residences

PDE is more cyclic than the others, and this reflected in the fluctuation of its share. Reconstruction after the 1923 earthquake caused most of the sharp jump in residential construction in the mid 1920s; otherwise this component had a steadily declining share. In real terms residences had only a 1.5% annual growth rate during the prewar period, only somewhat faster than population's 1.2%. Structures' share in the 1920s also reflects rebuilding after the earthquake, as well as government spending on various projects as a partial offset to the general stagnation of the period.

While military equipment is usually treated as consumption, as an important determinant of resource allocation in the prewar period, it is estimated here as part of investment. Most military investment (ordnance, ships, and so forth) is classed as PDE, so including it in the totals increases PDE's share, especially at the turn of the century and in the late 1930s. The only military construction included is of residences. (Examples of excluded military construction are offices, training grounds, and harbors.) Until the late 1930s capital formation including military tended to move in the same direction as the series excluding it, although at different rates.

In the postwar series compiled by the EPA, nonresidential construction and PDE are classed together. Government residential construction is listed separately by the EPA, but its share is small even with the large-scale public housing projects undertaken since the war.

DATA AND METHODS

In view of the decreasing availability of data as one goes back in time, direct estimation of some series is not feasible, especially in the private sector. Indirect methods and estimates both by use and by production have therefore been combined. The results of work by Rosovsky and myself were published in English by Rosovsky (1961) and formed the basis for LTES 4 (1971). The series here are from LTES 4 except, as discussed below, for some additions and one important change (in private PDE) made by Ohkawa in LTES 1 (pp. 162–64).

Construction in the private sector is estimated mostly by the physical-stock approach, which involves converting physical into value series. In LTES 1 Ohkawa extended, primarily by extrapolation, the LTES 4 series on buildings back to 1885, and this is included here. The physical volume of buildings is taken from local public organization records (LTES 4:112–75 in Japanese, 4:211–19 in English). Problems in estimating residential buildings are discussed in Emi (1959) and Rosovsky (1961, p. 215). Many buildings and rooms have multiple uses, for example, workshops by day and sleeping space by night. This complicates distributing construction between residences and nonresidences. Practically no information is available on rural housing, and even in urban areas before 1927 data exist only for the larger cities. Actual value data for major cities begin with 1936. There are EPA estimates beginning in 1930. Both my and the EPA estimates draw heavily on Tokyo statistical yearbooks.

My original (LTES 4) estimates use the commodity-flow method to estimate total PDE, using *Kojo Tokeihyo* as the basic source for 1910–40 and *Kogyo Tokeihyo* for postwar. This method traces production (net of foreign trade) in the machinery and tool industries to its use. Private sector PDE is then taken as the difference between the estimate for total PDE and the (expenditure based) figure for government PDE. Since not all PDE-type items produced actually were used in new capital formation, total and private PDE are over-estimated. To adjust for this Ohkawa used a different approach in LTES 1. For 1905–40, his series uses changes in the level of nonprimary-sector PDE estimated by Ishiwata in LTES 3 (pp. 190–96) as an estimate of total nonmilitary PDE, and then deducts my estimate of nonmilitary government PDE (LTES 4:226–29) to obtain a figure for private PDE. Ohkawa's series is used here.

For the government sector, decomposition into central (since 1868) and local (since 1879), military and nonmilitary, and general and government enterprise categories is possible by analyzing gross expenditures, available from the *Kessansho* (Naikaku Tokeikyoku). Moreover, this approach also permits classification into construction (building and structures) and PDE. Most Ig is in special accounts (see ch. 10).

For mining and for buildings of private nonprofit organizations (schools and hospitals, for example), sufficient data are not available to include series on them. Using capital stock data from LTES 3, Ohkawa has estimated capital formation in the private primary sector. This area is not covered in my own work. Ohkawa has slightly adjusted the series obtained by simply taking year-to-year changes in capital stock. These changes include treating small agricultural implements as current expenditure rather than investment, and reestimating nonresidential buildings and structures, including private land improvement. The latter involves revised assumptions on service life and salvage value.

CAPITAL STOCK

Shigeru Ishiwata

This section summarizes LTES 3 and analysis subsequent to its publication in 1966. A longer discussion of the data in relation to output and labor is found in chapter 2. For real capital stock, trends and changes in shares by sector and type as well as capital–labor ratios are dealt with here. Series are given both including and excluding residential building; however, military assets are excluded entirely.

The work of several people has been incorporated into the aggregate series given here. Thus I have used estimates by Hiromitsu Ishi for residential buildings, by Mataji Umemura and Saburo Yamada for agriculture, and by Minoru Kumazaki for forestry. My own work includes the series for producers' durable equipment and factory buildings. All the other stock series are based on Koichi Emi's work on investment. As already noted (see ch. 3 and Ishiwata 1975), Emi's series for producers' durable equipment series and mine are not consistent.

BASIC CONCEPTS

Three criteria have been adopted in defining what to include in capital stock. An item must be reproducible, tangible, and productive. Capital stock as presented here is thus distinctly narrower than national wealth. Residential structures, while not productive, are included in some series because of their size and importance as a use of investable funds. Unfortunately residential data are less reliable than for other sectors. Net foreign claims are excluded as being intangible. Military assets and consumer durables are omitted as nonproductive. Mineral resources are excluded as nonreproducible. Soil fertility is effectively impossible to measure, but livestock and plants (including planted forests) have been included. Lack of data prevents inclusion of private land improvements such as irrigation and drainage, although some public activity in this area does appear in the category government structures other than buildings. The work of Hayami and Yamada, among others, may help fill this gap (see ch. 4).

Inventories are excluded because they are assumed neutral to the productive capacity being measured. Further, their level is subject to business cycle swings that do not matter to long-term capital stock patterns. In any case, there are little hard data, though Fujino and Akiyama have been collecting and analyzing what data there are (1973; also see Ishiwata 1975).

GROWTH RATES, DISTRIBUTION, AND LEVEL

As table 9.1 shows, the growth rate of aggregate capital stock, both including and excluding residential buildings, accelerated from the 1880s to the 1920s, except for a small decline at the turn of the century. The rate decelerated thereafter, due to the recession after World War I and the worldwide depression in the early 1930s.

Table 9.1. Aggregate Gross Capital Stock: Annual Growth Rates, 1886–1940
(In percent)

Period		Producers' durable equipment	Structures other than buildings[a]	Nonresidential buildings[b]	Subtotal[c]	Residential buildings	Total[d]
1886–90	to 1891–95	5.56	4.42	1.57	2.52	0.84	1.51
1891–95	to 1896–1900	8.93	6.65	2.13	3.88	0.89	2.16
1896–1900	to 1901–05	7.95	2.85	2.53	3.15	0.86	1.91
1901–05	to 1906–10	9.01	5.28	2.88	4.64	0.66	2.62
1906–10	to 1911–15	8.42	6.33	3.39	5.20	1.04	3.30
1911–15	to 1916–20	10.47	4.15	3.15	5.45	1.26	3.75
1916–20	to 1921–25	8.86	5.14	4.04	5.87	1.11	4.17
1921–25	to 1926–30	3.48	5.49	5.17	4.35	1.02	3.31
1926–30	to 1931–35	2.94	4.28	4.26	3.60	1.18	2.92
1931–35	to 1936–40	5.75	4.22	4.31	4.61	1.12	3.73
1886–90	to 1906–10	7.85	4.79	2.28	3.54	0.81	2.05
1906–10	to 1936–40	6.61	4.93	4.05	4.85	1.02	3.73

Source: Computed from data in table A42.

Notes: Geometric means per year measured between quinquennial totals. Secular trends are measured between the first and last quinquennial totals.

[a] Mainly roads, bridges, harbors, and other riparian works financed and owned by the central or local governments. Private irrigation and reclamation are excluded for lack of data.

[b] Factory, commercial, and government buildings, including public schools and warehouses.

[c] Aggregate rate excluding residential buildings.

[d] Aggregate rate including residential buildings.

Table 9.2. Gross Capital Stock in the Private Sector: Annual Growth Rates by Type
(In percent)

Period	Producers' durable equipment	Structures other than buildings[a]	Nonresidential buildings[b]	Subtotal[c]	Residential buildings	Total[d]
1886–90 to 1891–95	5.38	7.09	1.57	2.52	0.84	1.51
1891–95 to 1896–1900	8.58	12.08	2.13	3.88	0.89	2.16
1896–1900 to 1901–05	6.90	0.35	2.53	3.15	0.86	1.91
1901–05 to 1906–10	8.43	−7.91	2.88	4.64	0.66	2.62
1906–10 to 1911–15	7.44	17.49	3.39	5.20	1.04	3.30
1911–15 to 1916–20	11.44	10.47	3.15	5.45	1.26	3.75
1916–20 to 1921–25	8.08	10.15	4.04	5.87	1.11	4.17
1921–25 to 1926–30	1.37	8.26	5.17	4.35	1.02	3.31
1926–30 to 1931–35	1.34	2.83	4.26	3.60	1.18	2.92
1931–35 to 1936–40	6.69	4.89	4.31	4.61	1.12	3.73
1886–90 to 1906–10	7.34	2.62	2.28	3.54	0.81	2.05
1906–10 to 1936–40	6.00	8.91	4.85	4.85	1.02	3.53

Source and Notes: See notes to table 9.1.

Even with rapid expansion of heavy industry, the 1930s' growth rate remained below the level of the 1910s. In part this is because of the larger base in the later period, since the absolute amounts of increases were larger. Shifting resources from capital goods to military production may have been a factor, although military procurement also included some private investment.

Growth rates for aggregate capital stock are in table 9.1 and for sectors by types, in tables 9.2 to 9.5. Changes in the composition of capital stock are shown in table 9.6. Since military assets are not covered, the drop in government share just before World War II is misleading as to the actual extent of government involvement in the economy.

Fei and Ranis hypothesize a process of capital shallowing, a decrease of the capital–labor ratio during development (1963 and 1964a). This is not observable for Japan even with its relatively abundant labor supply (table 9.7). Industrial technology has tended to be labor-saving since most has originated in countries with relatively scarce labor. It thus is doubtful any country, regardless of its factor endowment and factor prices, will experience capital-shallowing in the initial phase of the long-run course of modern economic growth. (See Reubens 1964 and especially Minami 1973 for further discussion.)

Table 9.3. Gross Capital Stock in the Government Sector: Annual Growth Rates by Type

(In percent)

Period	Producers' durable equipment	Structures other than buildings[a]	Nonresidential buildings[b]	Total
1886–90 to 1891–95	7.12	3.65	2.49	3.30
1891–95 to 1896–1900	11.56	4.79	3.48	5.03
1896–1900 to 1901–05	13.76	4.30	4.56	4.59
1901–05 to 1906–10	11.70	8.10	4.16	6.85
1906–10 to 1911–15	12.34	4.27	5.04	5.71
1911–15 to 1916–20	6.75	2.65	4.06	3.71
1916–20 to 1921–25	12.02	3.47	5.30	5.63
1921–25 to 1926–30	9.96	4.26	6.42	6.28
1926–30 to 1931–35	6.45	4.96	4.85	5.32
1931–35 to 1936–40	3.87	3.92	4.83	4.19
1886–90 to 1906–10	11.01	5.22	3.67	4.93
1906–10 to 1936–40	8.52	3.92	5.08	5.14

Source and Notes: See notes to table 9.1.

Table 9.4. Gross Capital Stock in Nonagriculture: Annual Growth Rates by Type
(In percent)

Period		Producers' durable equipment	Structures other than buildings[a]	Nonresidential buildings[b]	Subtotal[c]	Residential buildings	Total[d]
1886–90	to 1891–95	13.20	7.21	3.96	7.94	3.87	4.80
1891–95	to 1896–1900	16.38	12.07	5.45	11.88	6.93	5.61
1896–1900	to 1901–05	9.79	0.05	5.39	5.92	−0.50	4.07
1901–05	to 1906–10	10.60	−8.91	4.87	5.54	2.01	3.34
1906–10	to 1911–15	8.60	18.32	6.15	9.52	2.79	5.69
1911–15	to 1916–20	13.32	10.65	6.43	11.67	3.21	7.60
1916–20	to 1921–25	8.65	10.34	6.83	8.67	2.66	6.29
1921–25	to 1926–30	1.12	6.60	7.80	3.49	1.90	2.93
1926–30	to 1931–35	1.15	4.17	6.19	2.41	2.34	2.25
1931–35	to 1936–40	7.57	4.95	5.90	6.67	2.55	5.49
1886–90	to 1906–10	12.46	2.29	4.91	7.79	3.04	4.46
1906–10	to 1936–40	6.64	9.07	6.55	7.02	2.57	5.03

Source and Notes: See notes to table 9.1.

Table 9.5. Gross Capital Stock in Agriculture: Annual Growth Rates by Type
(In percent)

Period	Livestock and plants	Producers' durable equipment	Structures other than buildings[a]	Nonresidential buildings[b]	Subtotal[c]	Residential buildings	Total[d]
1886–90 to 1891–95	1.17	1.24	0.00	-0.14	0.38	-0.12	0.09
1891–95 to 1896–1900	1.14	0.96	12.47	0.01	0.47	0.02	0.21
1896–1900 to 1901–05	0.79	2.16	15.50	-0.13	0.40	-0.17	0.07
1901–05 to 1906–10	2.17	3.56	12.94	-0.08	1.09	0.00	0.48
1906–10 to 1911–15	1.96	3.12	5.77	0.06	1.10	0.02	0.50
1911–15 to 1916–20	2.08	2.64	6.62	-0.02	1.13	-0.03	0.51
1916–20 to 1921–25	2.36	4.19	5.23	-0.12	1.46	-0.09	0.66
1921–25 to 1926–30	2.73	3.30	11.24	0.22	1.82	0.27	1.05
1926–30 to 1931–35	2.44	2.60	6.42	0.18	1.63	0.08	0.88
1931–35 to 1936–40	1.94	0.12	3.51	-0.36	0.83	-0.42	0.25
1886–90 to 1906–10	1.32	1.97	10.06	-0.08	0.58	-0.07	0.21
1906–10 to 1936–40	2.25	2.65	6.44	-0.01	1.33	-0.03	0.64

Source and Notes: See notes to table 9.1.

Table 9.6. Gross Capital Stock: Sectoral Composition

(In percent)

	Residential buildings included		Residential buildings excluded		Residential buildings included		Residential buildings excluded	
	Private	Government	Private	Government	Primary	Non-primary	Primary	Non-primary
1885	88.98	11.02	70.89	29.11	79.36	20.64	90.34	9.66
1890	87.28	12.72	68.16	31.84	77.99	22.01	83.25	16.75
1895	85.92	14.08	66.68	33.32	74.41	25.59	78.21	21.97
1900	83.58	16.42	64.18	35.82	69.40	30.60	69.66	30.34
1905	81.54	18.46	62.31	37.69	65.41	34.59	64.71	35.29
1910	77.22	22.78	58.14	41.86	62.40	37.60	60.23	39.77
1915	74.91	25.06	57.32	42.68	56.38	43.62	51.79	48.21
1920	76.02	23.98	63.09	36.91	45.87	54.13	36.98	63.02
1925	72.54	27.46	60.03	39.97	42.85	57.15	34.70	65.30
1930	68.51	31.49	56.27	43.73	41.09	58.91	33.74	66.26
1935	65.31	34.69	53.30	46.70	38.36	61.64	32.03	67.97
1940	66.34	33.66	56.76	43.24	31.68	68.32	25.11	74.89
1955	75.5	24.5	62.5	37.5	—	—	20.25	79.75
1960	75.3	24.7	64.2	35.8	—	—	18.21	81.79
1965	73.3	26.7	65.3	34.7	—	—	14.53	85.47
1970	71.8[a]	28.2[a]	66.1	33.9	—	—	12.57	87.43

Note: Figures may not add due to rounding.
[a] 1969.

Table 9.7. Capital–Labor Ratio, Residential Buildings Excluded, 1885–1970
(In yen per person for prewar period, thousand yen per person for postwar period)

	Aggregate K/L	Agriculture sector K_A/L_A	Nonagriculture sector K_N/L_N
1885	322	327	1,119
1890	350	332	1,123
1895	376	343	1,107
1900	429	343	1,245
1905	479	355	1,315
1910	586	396	1,461
1915	703	427	1,615
1920	926	463	1,993
1925	1,107	518	2,232
1930	1,286	552	2,540
1935	1,452	598	2,681
1940	1,772	625	3,166
1955	749	—	—
1960	941	—	—
1965	1,491	—	—
1970	2,404		

Source: Labor: Umemura's figures on gainfully employed given in appendix table A53; Capital: Ishiwata's estimates, given in appendix table A42.

DATA AND METHODS

As one might suspect, the reliability of the data is in general inversely related to distance in time from the present, as sources are increasingly indirect and incomplete in the early years. Three kinds of estimating methods are used according to the nature of assets and availability of data: the perpetual inventory method, the benchmark year method, and the physical stock valuation method.

Perpetual Inventory (PI) Method

This is a well-known method for accumulating capital expenditure less depreciation or quantities of depreciated capital goods, adjusted for changes in costs or prices, to obtain the annual amount of net capital stock. The values thus obtained differ according to the use of different formulas for calculating depreciation allowances. The gross capital is simply obtained by accumulating gross capital formation valued at constant prices for the useful lifetime under the assumption that the assets are kept intact in terms of physical productivity throughout their lifetime followed by sudden death at the time of retirement. This naturally means neglect of possible scrap value of assets. When capital formation series have been continuously available for a period long enough for our purpose, we have tried to apply this method. As a matter of fact, this was what was done in most cases of estimating producers durable equipment.

Benchmark Year (BY) Method

This method obtains annual values of capital stock by adding or subtracting the amount of capital formation to or from the value of capital stock surveyed in a benchmark year or years. When a detailed national wealth survey is available, this method is most advisable. As a matter of fact, the postwar EPA series follow this method and depend on the 1955 National Wealth Survey, the most comprehensive one ever attempted in Japan until the 1975 survey. At the beginning of our project, we tried also to adopt this method as far as possible by depending upon the 1930 National Wealth Survey. But later we found some vagueness of concept and valuation of capital in the survey and it turned out to be rather difficult to link its results with the annual series of capital formation by type of assets. Therefore this method was used to a limited extent.

Physical Stock Valuation (PS) Method

This is adopted mainly in the case of buildings and agricultural assets, where the value of capital stock is thought to be derived most adequately by using a physical series of assets multiplied directly by base-year prices. For example, for residential buildings, the annual gross value is obtained by multiplying the annual series of this asset in terms of *tsubo* (approximately 3.3 square meters—a traditional unit of Japanese construction) and the corresponding construction costs in the base year. Although this method contains some defects, such as the difficulty of evaluating changes in quality over time and of finding adequate prices, it is a workable procedure when assets can be classified into more or less homogeneous groups.

Most of the data are for gross stocks. This is because the gross figures (excluding residences) are better than net for measuring productive capacity, the primary purpose of the estimations. Furthermore, secondhand equipment has been essential to the mechanization of medium and small firms.

Capital can be evaluated either prospectively or retrospectively (Aukrust and Bjerke 1959, pp. 82–87). While prospective evaluation is a better measure of productive capacity, especially for buildings and structures, only retrospective data are available. Market prices can be used with either, but some producers' durables, such as blast furnaces, are made to order and thus have no readily discernible market prices. The prewar estimates have been made primarily by type of capital goods, and division by sectors (public versus private, and agriculture, industry, services) was done later. This is also true of the five-sector classification for 1905–40 published in SIL 3.[1]

In the prewar agriculture sector all assets are assumed to be privately owned, so the private sector figures may be somewhat overstated. In general dividing the various capital goods types between the private and government–public sectors has been a problem, and further research is needed. Some items, owned solely by governments, can be easily classified, but most types are owned by both the private and government sectors. Subdivision can be achieved by estimating capital stock in the government sector based on expenditures for capital goods and the perpetual inventory method, and then deducting the resulting government series from the aggregate. Much of the material on sectoral stocks is new since LTES 3 appeared.

In the prewar period, producers' durable equipment is assumed to have an average useful life of 17 years, and building and structures 50 years (LTES 3:136). A variety of shorter lives are used for equipment in the postwar official series.

Linkage problems between the prewar and postwar periods are crucial. Difficulties arise from changes in the estimation methods adopted, mainly due to differences in quality and scope of the basic sources, including the unavailability of postwar series disaggregated by type. Intensive damage during World War II, as reported by Keizai Antei Honbu (1947), is also a problem. For consistency with the prewar period, postwar private sector data used here are revisions of LTES 3's series H (LTES 3:262). Government sector and residential buildings are based on EPA worksheets in order to utilize as recent data as possible.

---

1. The sectors are: agriculture (including forestry and fishery), mining and manufacturing, facilitating industries, construction, and services. The main difficulty with these estimates is in the assumptions about distribution of PDE among industries.

NATIONAL WEALTH SURVEYS

It is difficult to relate wealth survey data to capital stock estimates since current-price values are used in the surveys and adequate deflators for all the components are not available. Masakichi Ito discusses prewar national wealth surveys and attempts to estimate capital stock from them (GRJE, pp. 151–77). Eight surveys were made between 1905 and 1935.

There are several government estimates of capital stock series for the postwar period based on gross domestic fixed capital formation in the national income accounts and national wealth survey data for the private sector, and on government (enterprise and general) expenditures on capital goods (see LTES 3, ch. 4). Unfortunately all but two private sector estimates are unpublished: Keizai Kenkyujo (1962) and Noda, Kusuda, and Egaitsu (1966). The others have been confined to internal uses such as econometric model building.

Table 9.8 provides a rough comparison between the 1930 national

Table 9.8. National Wealth

(In millions of yen)

	National wealth survey	LTES 3	
		Net	Gross
Harbors and canals	343	279	374
Waterworks	353	428	532
Bridge	483	1,556[a]	2,213[a]
Ships	2,060	1,763	3,632
Vehicles and aircraft	660	591[b]	971[b]
Manufacturing machinery	1,809	2,378[b]	3,965[b]
Railways and tramways	3,598	2,105	2,787
Electricity gas supply	1,905	1,625	2,017
Telegram and telephone	199	—	—
Buildings	22,843	14,355[c]	22,857[c]
Total	34,253	25,080	39,348

Source: National Wealth Survey as given in GRJE, p. 164 (table 2).
Notes: Only comparable categories are included. Since the national wealth data do not cover such things as tools, fixtures, and riparian works included in capital stock, these items are excluded from the capital stock series given here. Because capital stock data for agricultural assets such as trees, livestock, and poultry are not available in 1930 prices, this entire sector is also omitted.
[a] Roads are included in the category.
[b] A series (1908–40).
[c] The base year adjustment from 1934–36 to 1930 was done by the multiplication of a constant coefficient (0.958038).

survey and our estimates. The difference between the two estimates is caused mainly by different estimates for buildings. For comparable categories the survey's total national wealth is 137% of my estimate. This reduces to 106% when buildings are omitted. Even then, the two series are not consistent; there are wide differences in many other items, and in any case the scope is not the same.

REFERENCES

Aukrust, Odd, and Juul Bjerke. 1959. "Real Capital and Economic Growth in Norway 1900–56." *The Measurement of National Wealth*, Income and Wealth Series 8:80–118. National Bureau of Economic Research.

Deane, Phyllis, and William Alan Cole. 1962. *British Economic Growth, 1688–1959: Trends and Structure.* Cambridge University Press.

Emi, Koichi. 1959. "Capital Formation in Residential Real Estate in Japan." *Annals of Hitotsubashi University* 9 (1959 Apr.): 233–43.

———. 1971. "Long-Term Movement of Capital Formation in Japan." *Keizaikenkyu* v. 22, no. 2 (1971 Apr.).

———. 1973. "Long-Term Movements of Gross Domestic Fixed Capital Formation in Japan, 1869–1940." In *Economic Growth, The Japanese Experience Since the Meiji Era*, edited by Kazushi Ohkawa and Yujiro Hayami, v. 1. The Japan Economic Research Center. Tokyo.

Fei, John C. H., and Gustav Ranis. 1963. "Innovation, Capital Accumulation and Economic Development." *American Economic Review* 53 (1963 Jun.): 283–313.

———. 1964a. "Reply (to Reubens 1964)." *American Economic Review* 54 (1964 Dec.): 1063–68.

———. 1964b. *Development of the Labor Surplus Economy: Theory and Policy.* Richard D. Irwin.

Fujino, Shozaboro. 1968. "Construction Cycles and Their Monetary-Financial Characteristics." In *Economic Growth: The Japanese Experience Since the Meiji Era*, edited by Lawrence Klein and Kazushi Ohkawa. Irwin.

———, and Ryoko Akiyama. 1973. *Zaiko Sutokku to Zaiko Toshi: 1880–1940.* Hitotsubashi Daigaku, Keizai Kenkyujo, Tokei Shiryo Shirizu 1.

GRJE [*Growth Rate of the Japanese Economy*]. Kazushi Ohkawa et al. 1957. Kinokuniya.

Ishiwata, Shigeru. 1973. "Capital Stocks." In JERC 1:101–13.

———. 1975. "Minkan Kotei Shihon Toshi." In *Kindai Nihon no Keizai Hatten*, edited by Kazushi Ohkawa and Ryoshin Minami. Toyo Keizai.

Keizai Antei Honbu. 1947. *Senso Higai Chosa Shiryo.*

Keizai Kenkyujo, Keizai Kikakucho. 1962. *Shihon Sutokku to Keizai Seicho.* Keizai Kenkyu Shirizu 11.

Keizai Shingicho. 1956. *National Income and National Economic Accounts of Japan 1930–55.* (English translation of *Nihon Keizai to Kokumin Shotoku*, 1954.)

Kendrick, John W. 1961. *Productivity Trends in the United States*. Princeton University Press.

———. 1970. *Postwar Productivity Trends in the United States*. National Bureau of Economic Research.

LTES [*Estimates of Long-Term Economic Statistics of Japan*]. Series edited by Kazushi Ohkawa, Miyohei Shinohara, and Mataji Umemura. 14 v. 1965–. Toyo Keizai Shimposha.
1. National Income. 1974. Kazushi Ohkawa et al.
3. Capital Stock. 1966. Kazushi Ohkawa, Shigeru Ishiwata, Saburo Yamada, and Hiromitsu Ishi.
4. Capital Formation. 1971. Koichi Emi.
7. Government Expenditure. 1966. Koichi Emi and Yuichi Shionoya.

Minami, Ryoshin. 1973. *The Turning Point in Economic Development: The Japanese Experience*. Kinokuniya.

Naikaku, Tokeikyoku. 1933. *Showa 5-nen Kokufu Chosa Hokoku*.

———. *Kessansho* (Annual prepared 1890–1940).

Noda, Tsutomu, Tadashi Kusuda, and Norio Egaitsu. 1966. "So Shihon Sutokku no Suikei." *Keizai Bunseki* no. 17 (1966 Mar.). Reprinted by Keizai Kikakucho in ERI Reprint Series no. 10, 1969.

Ohkawa, Kazushi, and Henry Rosovsky. 1965. "A Century of Japanese Economic Growth." In *The State and Economic Enterprise in Japan: Essays in the Political Economy of Growth*, edited by William W. Lockwood. Princeton University Press.

———. 1973. *Japanese Economic Growth: Trend Acceleration in the Twentieth Century*. Stanford University Press.

Reubens, Edwin P. 1964. "Capital-Labor Ratio in Theory and History: Comment." *American Economic Review* 54 (1964 Dec.): 1052–61.

Rosovsky, Henry. 1961. *Capital Formation in Japan*. Free Press of Glencoe.

Shinohara, Miyohei. 1954. "Capital Formation in Japan—Estimates by Commodity-Flow Method." *Keizai-kenkyu* v. 4, no. 1 (1954 Jan.).

SIL [*Choki Keizai Tokei no Seibi Kaizen ni Kansufu Kenkyu*]. Keizai Kikakucho, 3 v. 1967–69. Mimeo.

10

Government Accounts

Expenditures by and revenues of all government levels are discussed in this chapter. The Japanese fiscal year begins April 1. It is important in comparing series to know whether they are fiscal or calendar year. Data in LTES 7 (government expenditure) are mostly taken directly from government sources and thus are fiscal. In LTES 1, the government data have been put on a calendar year basis to fit into the national income series. Since much of the source data are at least quarterly, this adjustment generally involves no complicated techniques.

The principal sources for basic data here and in LTES 7 are Nihon Ginko (1966 and *Nenpo*), Okurasho (1972 and *Zaisei*), and Jichicho (*Nenpo*). Nihon Ginko 1966 has fairly detailed English explanatory notes, published separately in two volumes. A general chronological review of monetary and fiscal history and policy, primarily in relation to banking, is Fuji Ginko 1967.

DATA AND METHODS

The EPA has been computing government accounts in a national income framework since 1930. To the extent possible, we have used the same methodology (explained in Keizai Kikakucho 1954) to extend the series back to the mid-19th century. The series on transfers and capital expenditures do not link well, because of what we feel is underestimation by the EPA of local government capital expenditure and interest payments on general revenue bonds (deficit-financing as distinguished from specific-project bonds.).

Central government accounts are divided into a general account and special accounts. In the prewar period the general account covered the regular budgets of the various ministries and general operating funds of government enterprises. Special accounts, first used in 1890, vary in number depending on government policies and since 1909 have covered over half of expenditure. Any series on only the general account cannot be considered representative of government activity, so probably should not be used at all for most analysis. There have been complex transactions among different accounts (LTES 7:162–63).

The flow of funds between the central and local governments is also very complicated. The central government directly controlled many public works, but at the same time it provided various subsidies to promote similar projects which were the responsibility of localities. Duplications between local and central government are fairly easily eliminated. The main difficulty is with payments made on behalf of local units, as it is not always clear whether these have been included in local accounts. It is even more difficult to gather complete data on prefecture subsidies to lower levels and other such local duplication. Fortunately neither of these complications is significant.

Local government expenditures are classed as ordinary and government enterprises. This is sufficiently unlike the central government classification to make combining the two levels difficult even when duplications are eliminated.

EXPENDITURE

Koichi Emi

The actual total of government spending and how its parts fit into the national income accounts are the concern of this section. In current prices, total expenditure jumped in all war periods and remained at a higher level after each war. In constant prices this smooths into a single linear trend. The level of government spending can be related to two phenomena, relative price changes and population growth. The more rapid increase of government's share of GNP in current prices than in constant prices indicates faster inflation for goods and services purchased by the government than for the economy as a whole.

Deflators of government current spending are a weighted average of (for labor costs) a public administration service deflator (LTES 1:236), and (for all other costs) the personal consumption expenditure index (LTES 1:232). The weights are the annual budget expenditure for each group. Labor productivity is assumed constant (LTES 1:90).

To put expenditures into a national income accounting framework, they are divided into five categories: current purchases of goods and services (government consumption), investment purchases (government capital formation), transfers to households, subsidies to enterprises, and transfers to the rest of the world. These series are given in appendix table A44 in current prices for fiscal years. Current and investment purchases as components of GNE are discussed in chapters 1 and 2. Government saving is discussed by Ishi (1974).

SUBSIDIES AND TRANSFERS

Although never large in total amount, the distribution of subsidies indicates areas of government concern. There were three phases of prewar subsidies. The first stage, ending in the 1920s, concentrated on transportation, primarily development of a merchant marine. This reflected the goals of having military transport and preventing foreign companies from controlling Japanese trade. Funds also went to the shipbuilding industry (Blumenthal 1976). In early Meiji private railroads received grants, but when most were nationalized in 1906 these ceased to be important.

In the interwar period commerce and industry became important recipients. Promotion of shipbuilding accounted for the largest share. With the onset of the depression in the late 1920s, money was allocated primarily to agriculture, mostly to maintain stable rice prices and provide relief for farmers. Data covering subsidies in the general account (something over 90% of all subsidies (LTES 7:142)) are given in LTES (7:180–83). An extensive list of subsidies is also given in Mitsubishi (1936, pp. 47–49). By international standards Japanese subsidies were small (Allen 1940, pp. 733–35). Credit and taxation policies were more important as aids to developing industries.

Transfers have increased tremendously in the postwar period, reflecting concern for social welfare. Most transfers are pensions to government employes. There is little unemployment compensation or welfare spending, in part because Japan has relatively less need for such programs than many western countries.

MILITARY SPENDING

Considerable attention, if not careful analysis, has been devoted to the military. Among the better discussions is a series of papers edited by Boulding and Sun (1968). One special problem is that wars were funded mostly from special accounts without fiscal year periods, making construction of historical series difficult. Data are given in appendix table A45.

Military purchase of capital goods can be handled in a number of ways: including it entirely in current consumption on the grounds of nonproductivity (as is done for capital stock in ch. 9) at one extreme, through intermediate positions to treating long-lived items as investment (as is done in some of the capital formation series in ch. 9). It is thus important to know how military expenditures are treated when using any series on government spending.

FUNCTIONAL CLASSIFICATION

Categorizing total government expenditures by purpose for the entire period has yet to be achieved. The principal problems complicating construction of a series are elimination of inter- and intra-government duplications and the decomposition and classification of various accounts, many of which are multipurpose and have changed function through time. The most comprehensive estimates are for selected years up to 1925, plus 1955 and 1960, made by Oshima (1965, pp. 366–89). The unallocated portions are large, even for postwar years. For the central government only, estimates for every fifth fiscal year from 1915 through 1935, cross-classified by national income account, have been computed by Yuichi Shionoya in LTES 7 (pp. 264–75).

An estimate for the general and nonenterprise special accounts for 1900 appears in Emi (1963, pp. 61–72). This is included in Nihon Ginko (1966, p. 144) with an estimate for 1962 of similar categories, but with somewhat different coverage. There is an official series for just the general account covering the postwar years (up to 1963) plus 1934–36 in LTES (7:184–85); more recent years appear annually in the *Japan Statistical Yearbook*. Narrow coverage makes them unrepresentative of total (or even central) government activity and therefore in general *None of the series cited in this paragraph should be used!*

Official figures for local government spending also appear in LTES 7 (pp. 192–95) and in Nihon Ginko's *Nenpo*. However, because of duplication and differences in classification these cannot be combined directly with the central government series. Local government data are discussed briefly by Emi (1963, pp. 105–08).

REVENUE

Hiromitsu Ishi

The LTES project has paid little attention to government revenue, primarily because of the concentration on constructing meaningful GNP estimates and on expanding the supply of statistics available for analysis. Data on government revenue, including debt issue, are among the most reliable and readily available of Japan's long-term statistics. In fact there is little room for estimation errors since the original sources survive. Some processing is required to fit the current revenue figures into the national income framework. One problem is converting the sources' fiscal year data into calendar years for comparability with other components. This is not done here. Little is written on government revenue in English (see Lockwood 1954, Nakayama 1960, and, for the postwar period, Ishi 1973). Revenue is given in appendix table A46 for debt and current revenue components, with the latter divided into national and local taxes, and government enterprise profits.

CURRENT REVENUE

Data on current revenue in national income accounting categories are found in ARNIS for years since 1930. Prior to 1951, there were five categories: personal taxes and nontax revenue, corporate taxes and nontax revenues, indirect business taxes, contributions for social insurance, and surplus of government enterprises and other sources.

In 1951 four new items were added. The total of three of these (other current transfers from households and nonprofit institutions, transfers from the rest of the world, and income from property and entrepreneurship) is assumed to be equivalent to the surplus of government enterprises and other category in the old classification. The fourth new item, interest on public debt, is treated as a charge against revenue. The first four categories of the original classification were unchanged.

LTES 7 (pp. 174–75 and 178) arranges the pre-1930 data somewhat differently, so there is no consistent series for the whole period. On the revenue side, the handling of government enterprise surpluses causes the differences. Transfers and subsidies by government enterprises to the private sector are charged to the enterprise surplus in the main tables of LTES 7 (p. 139). Shionoya does not do this in his section on functional classification (LTES 7:245–75).

Tax revenue at both the national and local level is divided into three categories: personal (including individual income and estate taxes), corporate, and indirect business (for example, land and excise taxes). Nontax revenues includes fees, sales of government assets, and profits of government enterprises.

The type of taxes collected changed considerably over the period. During both the pre- and postwar years the percentage of current revenue collected as taxes declined. This can be attributed to the expansion of government-enterprise activity. Nihon Ginko (1966, pp. 136–37) has a nine-type breakdown with a brief history of each type, but it covers only the central government.

Before 1885 the principal taxes were on land and liquor, and thus relatively inelastic, so taxes as a percentage of GNE probably increased during the Matsukata deflation (1881–85), then dipped to a bottom at the time of the Sino-Japanese war (1895). The next swing peaks around 1910 and bottoms in 1917. New or increased taxes on income, sake, tobacco, soy sauce, drugs, scales, sugar, textiles, beverages, and transportation, as well as custom duties, all contributed to the upswing. Between 1918 and 1932 there is a plateau at a fairly low level. During this period income and liquor taxes were the principal revenue sources. In the 1930s, taxes rapidly increased share. Direct taxes had a tremendous rise, including an excess profits tax instituted in 1935.

Local taxes in the prewar period were collected almost entirely as a surtax on national taxes by prefectual and city and town governments. Japan has never had an extensive system of property taxes collected for school or fire districts as in the United States. The Shoup Mission abolished the surtaxes in 1949. Local governments now rely on direct collection of a variety of income and property taxes.

The economy's rapid growth and decision to stress private sector growth have kept the government's postwar share of national income low—between 14 and 17% since 1952–53. Postwar taxes have been primarily direct, so they have fairly high income elasticities. This has contributed to the stability of the tax share of GNP. In contrast, prewar taxes were relatively income-insensitive, and this rigidity gave rise to the swings already noted.

DEBT

National debt data are available since 1870, and local debt statistics have been officially compiled since 1890. Net new debt issue is given in appendix table A46. Okurasho (1972, pp. 204–05) gives flow data on new issues and redemptions for the central government, and Nihon Ginko (1966) provides data on outstanding national (p. 158) and local (p. 162) debt.

Debt has been important in government policy since the beginning of Meiji. Along with note issue in the 1870s it helped fund the new government until the tax system could be put in place. By the end of that decade, debt equaled half of national income. New debt has fluctuated from negative during Matsukata's redemption policy in the 1880s to being half or more of total revenue during the Russo-Japanese War, expansion into China (late 1930s), and the Pacific War. In 1949, as part of the Dodge plan to curb inflation, a law banning government long-term debt was enacted. It remained in effect until 1965.

There have been four major waves of debt issue by the central government: in the 1870s bonds were issued (some overseas) to commute the stipends and pensions of former samurai; in the 1890s and 1900s, for wars; in 1917–23, to help the economy adjust to World War I, the recession following it, and then the Kanto earthquake of 1923; and lastly, in the 1930s to cover deficits run to help recovery from the depression and (after 1937) for armaments. Local debt has been issued for such things as disaster reconstruction, school construction, public works, and for public enterprises.

REFERENCES

Allen, G. C. 1940. "Japanese Industry." In *The Industrialization of Japan and Manchukuo, 1930–40*, edited by Elizabeth B. Schumpeter. Macmillan.
Blumenthal, Tuvia. 1976. "Japanese Shipbuilding Industry." In *Japanese Industrialization and its Social Consequences*, edited by Hugh Patrick with Larry Meissner. University of California Press.
Boulding, Kenneth, and Norman Sun. 1968. *The Effects of Military Expenditure upon the Economic Growth of Japan*. International Christian University.
Emi, Koichi. 1963. *Government Fiscal Activity and Economic Growth in Japan, 1880–1960*. Kinokuniya.
———. 1973. "The Government Sector in Japan's Development and Growth." In *Economic Growth: The Japanese Experience Since the Meiji Era*, edited

by Kazushi Ohkawa and Yujiro Hayami. The Japanese Economic Research
    Center.
Fuji Ginko. 1967. *Banking in Modern Japan.* 2d. ed.
Ishi, Hiromitsu. 1973. "Cyclical Behavior of Government Revenue and
    Expenditure, A Case Study of Postwar Japan." *Hitotsubashi Journal of
    Economics* 14 (1973 Jun.): 56–83.
Jichicho. *Chiho Zaisei Gaiyo.*
Keizai Shingicho. 1954. *Nihon Keizai to Kokumin Shotoku* (the English version
    is *National Income and National Economic Accounts of Japan, 1930–50*).
LTES [*Estimates of Long-Term Economic Statistics of Japan*]. Series edited
    by Kazushi Ohkawa, Miyohei Shinohara, and Mataji Umemura. 14 v.
    1965–. Toyo Keizai Shimposha.
    4. Capital Formation. 1971. Koichi Emi.
    7. Government Expenditure. 1966. Koichi Emi and Yuichi Shionoya.
Naikaku Tokeikyoku. *Kessansho* (Annual prepared 1890–1940).
Nakayama, Ichiro. 1960. "The Japanese Economy and the Role of Govern-
    ment." *Hitotsubashi Journal of Economics* 1 (1960 Oct.).
Nihon Ginko, Tokeikyoku. 1966. *Honpo Shuyo Keizai Tokei* [*Hundred-Year
    Statistics of the Japanese Economy*). 3 v. including 2 v. of English translation
    of the notes.
Okurasho, Daijin Kambo. *Okurasho Nenpo* (Annual published 1868–1943).
———. 1972. *Okurasho Hyakunen-shi.*
Okurasho, Shukeikyoku Chosaka. *Zaisei Tokei.*
Oshima, Harry T. 1965. "Meiji Fiscal Policy and Agricultural Progress." In
    The State and Economic Enterprise in Japan, edited by William W. Lock-
    wood. Princeton University Press.
Peacock, Alan T. and Jack Wiseman. 1961. *The Growth of Public Expenditure
    in the United Kingdom.* Princeton University Press.
Rosovsky, Henry. 1960. *Capital Formation in Japan, 1868–1940.* Free Press
    of Glencoe.
Toyo Keizai. 1926. *Meiji-Taisho Zaisei Soran.*

PART 4: FACTOR SHARES, PRICES, AND POPULATION

11

Factor Incomes and Shares

Ryoshin Minami and Akira Ono

Most of the LTES and other quantitative studies of Japan have dealt mainly with production and expenditure. Hijikata (1933) and Yamada (1951) are the two principal exceptions. This chapter considers the third aspect of the economy, distribution, by surveying long-term trends in factor incomes and relative shares, using our preliminary estimate (Minami and Ono 1975) for the prewar period and official data for the postwar period. Analysis is confined to the nonagricultural sector (including government) because it is difficult to make any reliable historical estimates of factor incomes in the agricultural sector, although Hayami and Yamada have made preliminary estimates of relative factor shares of labor, capital, and land (see ch. 4). Income means domestic income; that is, net factor income from abroad is not included. Our main concern is to ascertain long-term trends, rather than short-term fluctuations, so all series are seven-year moving averages for the prewar period and five-year moving averages for the postwar period.

DEFINITIONS AND ASSUMPTIONS

Nonagriculture means services (S) and industry (N) combined, with N including manufacturing, mining, construction, and facilitating industries.

Y = nonagriculture sector income = $Y1 + Y2$
$Y1$ = corporate (modern) sector income = $A1 + W1$
$Y2$ = noncorporate (nonmodern) sector income = $A2 + W2$
$A1$ = corporate income and interest payments by the corporate sector

205

W1 = compensation of employes in the corporate sector

A2 = compensation of capital owned by noncorporate enterprises

W2 = compensation to labor supplied by self-employed workers
such as proprietors and their family workers

W = labor income = W1 + W2

A = capital income = A1 + A2

The coexistence of modern and nonmodern sectors is one of the
distinguishing features of the Japanese economy. It is sufficiently
accurate for our analysis to equate these with corporate and noncorporate enterprises respectively. Because of prewar data limitation,
in most of what follows all employes are assigned to the corporate
sector. Thus W = W1 and Y = A1 + W1 + Y2. Estimates have been
made of each of these, as explained in the data and methods section.

Labor's share of income W/Y is the weighted average of labor's
share in the corporate and noncorporate sectors:

$$W/Y = (W1/Y1) (Y1/Y) + (W2/Y2) (Y2/Y)$$

This equation means labor's aggregate share depends on not only the
relative shares for respective sectors but also the sectors' relative
importance in terms of income. Therefore, if W2/Y2 is greater than
W1/Y1, modernization of the employment structure will, other things
being equal, reduce W/Y, and conversely.

There are two imputation methods for dividing Y2 into its components, the labor approach and the capital approach. In the former,
W2 is estimated by imputing the average wage in the noncorporate
sector to labor and then A2 is obtained by subtracting W2 from Y2.
This approach assumes the labor market is fairly competitive at least
during each long swing. In the capital approach, A2 is first estimated
by imputing the profit rate in the corporate sector to capital owned by
noncorporate enterprises, and then W2 is calculated as the residual.

For the postwar period, when capital stock data are available for
noncorporate enterprises, both approaches have been used. Relative
shares shown in table 11.1 reveal large differences between the two
approaches in the service sector, where noncorporate enterprises are
dominant. Presumably there would be fairly large differences in the
two methods' results for the prewar period since the noncorporate
sector is even more important then. Only the labor approach has been
used for the prewar period.

Table 11.1. Labor's Share of Private-Sector Income (W/Y) in the Postwar Period
Using Labor and Capital Approaches
(In percent)

	Industry		Service		Nonagriculture	
	L	C	L	C	L	C
1955	73.2	73.6	71.4	77.1	72.4	74.8
1960	69.3	69.8	68.2	66.1	68.8	68.1
1965	72.0	73.1	66.5	62.9	69.4	68.3
1969	70.2	70.2	63.2	58.6	66.8	64.7

Source: Authors' computation.
Notes: Five-year averages, except 1969 is a three-year average.
L = labor approach; C = capital approach; see explanation in text.

MAJOR FINDINGS

Changes in Factor Incomes

Factor income in the nonagricultural sector for the prewar period can be characterized as growth with large fluctuations, while the postwar period has had a higher growth rate with small fluctuations. This is similar to the GNP pattern studied by Ohkawa and Rosovsky (1968; 1973, ch. 1). Having nothing to add to their analysis of long swings in aggregate incomes, we focus instead on changes in components.

Table 11.2 gives the rate of change in factor incomes by component by swing-periodization. The data show swing-periodization in terms of Y also applies to W1. A1 shows high rates of income in every phase of the long swings, though the rate varies with the phases. This may be associated with the high rate of capital accumulation and of economic growth. Y2 has two components, wages and profits. However, year-to-year fluctuations in Y2 are similar to those of W1. This similarity is not necessarily caused by the procedure for estimating Y2, as the same pattern occurs in the more reliable postwar data. The decrease in the share of Y2 was remarkable, from about 50% in 1909 to 30% in 1937, with most of the decrease offset by the increase of A1. The drop in Y2/Y continued in the postwar period.

One reason for the decline is the modernization of the employment structure. The percentage of proprietors and family workers in the gainfully occupied population decreased from 36% in 1931–40 to 27% in 1953–60. A secondary cause is a change in relative per capita

Table 11.2. Factor Incomes: Growth Rates of Components

(In percent)

	Industry				Services				Nonprimary			
	Y	W1	A1	Y2	Y	W1	A1	Y2	Y	W1	A1	Y2
1909(T)–19(P')	30.0	36.0	42.4	20.6	23.0	24.2	37.2	18.7	26.5	30.5	39.8	19.6
1919(P)–31(T')	3.2	2.7	8.4	1.6	1.7	2.1	2.0	1.1	2.5	2.5	5.3	1.4
1931(T)–37(P')	12.0	12.9	14.8	8.5	4.3	3.1	8.9	3.6	8.8	9.1	12.7	6.0
1955(T)–61(P')	23.5	21.5	31.5	19.8	18.8	18.1	37.4	10.0	21.2	20.0	34.0	12.7
1961(P)–65	19.1	21.2	13.7	20.4	22.7	23.4	25.3	18.5	20.8	22.1	18.9	19.1
1965–68	18.2	17.5	19.6	19.1	20.6	20.2	23.9	17.5	19.4	18.7	21.8	18.1

Source: Calculated from data in appendix tables A47–A49.

Notes: Annual rates of growth calculated from seven-year averages for the prewar period, and from five-year averages for the postwar period.

P and T signify peak and trough in long swings; other abbreviations are explained in the text.

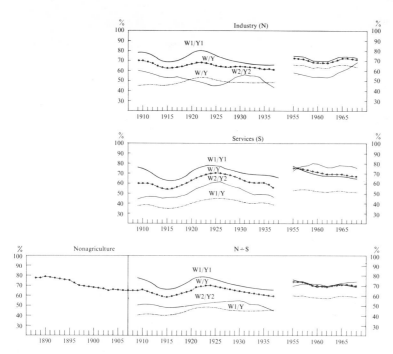

Fig. 11.1. Labor Share of Income

Sources: Authors' estimate. Underlying data are in Minami and Ono 1975 (pp. 615–23).

income between proprietors and employes. The ratio of noncorporate income per proprietor to the average wage level dropped from 1.8 in 1931–40 to 1.4 in 1953–60.

The range of fluctuations in long swings of GNP is narrower in the postwar period than in the prewar period. This is especially reflected in changes in W1 and Y2, which continued growing at about the same rate even after the 1961 peak. This steady increase can be explained by the shift from a labor surplus to a labor shortage economy at the beginning of the 1960s (Minami 1973), which raised the growth rate of money wages and self-employment income.

The share of W1 in N (industrial sector) is larger than in S (service sector), whereas Y2 is smaller in N than in S. This means the N sector is the more modernized in employment structure. However, Y2 in the S sector has sharply decreased during the postwar years, reflecting rapid modernization.

Table 11.3. Growth Rates of Money Wages G(w) and Nominal Labor Productivity G(l)

(In percent)

	Industry		Services		Nonagriculture	
	G(w)	G(l)	G(w)	G(l)	G(w)	G(l)
1909–19	10.31	10.68	10.86	10.59	10.65	10.68
(1909–16)	7.35	8.77	7.67	8.68	7.57	8.76
1919–31	2.23	3.23	0.86	0.41	1.57	1.55
(1916–31)	5.37	5.82	4.60	3.61	5.03	4.48
1931–37	3.63	3.22	−0.33	1.67	2.38	3.67
1955–61	8.30	9.29	8.36	9.62	8.23	9.49
1961–65	11.63	10.11	12.05	12.40	11.22	11.22
1965–68	11.55	12.00	11.22	12.12	11.90	12.06

Source: Authors' estimate.

Changes in Labor's Share of Income

The trend of labor's share (W/Y) from 1888–1969 is shown in figure 11.1. Since there were no substantial changes in hours and days worked per worker, W/Y is equal to the ratio of w (money wage earnings) to l (nominal labor productivity), and labor's share shows a declining trend because l is increasing faster than w. We believe this may be attributed to two main features of the Japanese economy: the existence of surplus labor in the agricultural sector and the steady importation of technology that raises labor productivity. Our analysis suggests labor was in unlimited supply for the nonagricultural sector until the end of the 1950s or the beginning of the 1960s. Although the interwar period was one of substantial flux, until this turning point, the non-agricultural sector could employ unskilled workers at the almost constant real wage level prevailing in the agricultural sector. Since the nonagricultural work force comprises both skilled and unskilled workers, the wage level increased at a slower rate than labor productivity.

As figure 11.1 shows, labor's share in the prewar period decreased between 1910 and 1916, increased until 1924, and then decreased again until data end in 1937. (Data before 1906 are only reliable for assessing broad trends, so discussion of fluctuations is confined to years after 1909.) What brought about these changes?

Growth rates of money wages G(w) and nominal labor productivity G(l) are given in table 11.3 and illustrated in figure 11.2. Both G(w)

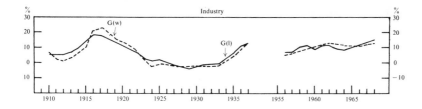

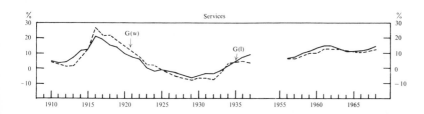

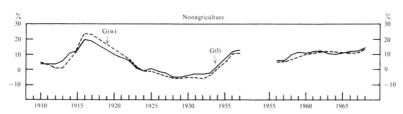

Fig. 11.2. Rates of Growth in Money Wages [G(W)] and Nominal Labor Productivity [G(l)]

Source: Authors' estimates.

and G(l) show patterns of change similar to the long swings; they increased for the years before 1916 and after 1931, and decreased for the interim period. The only deviation, 1917–19, is part of the first upward phase in Ohkawa and Rosovsky's periodization (1973, ch. 1). When G(w) and G(l) increased, G(w) was generally less than G(l), while G(l) was larger during decreases (1915–16 and 1925–29 are exceptions). Thus when labor demand expanded during booms, wage earnings rose, but at a lower rate than nominal labor productivity, while during slumps the rate of increase in wage earnings slowed less than nominal labor productivity.

Wage behavior in boom years relates to surplus labor and in slump years to the downward rigidity of money wages. Downward rigidity of average nominal wages is not inconsistent with an overall labor surplus economy because of a shortage of industrially skilled workers. Large firms invested in employes through on-the-job-training and wished to keep their trained workers, which meant maintaining wages during slowdowns. This is further discussed in chapter 13's section on wage differentials. The association of labor's share with long swings is discussed by Ohkawa (1968) and Umemura (1961, ch. 4).

Labor's share of income is higher in the early postwar period than at the end of the prewar period. This can be attributed to the destruction of capital equipment during the war, which resulted in the marked reduction after the war not only of output per worker but also of real wages. However, the reduction of wages was smaller than that of output per worker, because workers could not be employed at wages below the subsistence wage for any length of time.

During the growth of the late 1950s, wage increases lagged behind productivity increases, causing labor's share to decline from 75% in 1955 to 70% in 1960. However, the decline stopped around 1960 and has remained at about 70% through 1968, the last year for which data are available. The stability of income shares is attributable to the low level of surplus labor in the countryside, requiring entrepreneurs in the nonagricultural sector to increase wages steeply to draw additional workers from the agricultural sector (see Ono 1973, ch. 16).

Changes in W1/Y1 have been similar to and changes in W2/Y2 have been different from, those in W/Y. The rise in W2/Y2 after 1965 can be explained by the sharp increase in wages of unskilled workers, the largest part of the noncorporate sector work force. Our estimates shows W1/Y1 is larger than W2/Y2, although only slightly so in the postwar period. We believe this comes from having assumed all

Table 11.4. Labor's Share of Income: Average for the Years 1953–70
(In percent)

W1/Y1	W2/Y2	
71.5	71.3	All employes assumed to be in corporate sector
70.5	87.0	Calculated using actual distribution of employes between sectors

Table 11.5. Labor's Share of Income 1953–1970
(Average of annual figures for private sectors in percent)

	Industry	Services
Labor approach	71.3	67.8
Capital approach	71.8	67.0

employes belong to the corporate sector. For the prewar period this assumption is necessary because of data limitations, and to obtain continuity of estimates the same procedure has been applied to the postwar period. However, it can be dropped when data are available separately for the corporate and noncorporate sectors, as shown in table 11.4.

A decrease in Y2/Y in the process of industrialization will reduce labor's share, other things being equal. As figure 11.1 shows for the prewar period, W/Y in the industrial sector (N) ranged from 60 to 70%, and in the service sector (S), from 55 to 70%. On average, labor's share was higher in industry than in services, and the range of fluctuations was wider in services than in industry (though the patterns of changes in W/Y were similar).

For the postwar period also, W/Y is higher in industry than in services. These results are the same irrespective of imputation method (see tables 11.1 and 11.5). Labor's share in industry tended to be stable. Its share in services declined because of the excess of G(l) over G(w). A higher growth rate for nominal labor productivity in services is attributable mainly to the remarkable increase in service prices, rather than to any increase in real labor productivity. In the industrial sector, the excess of W1/Y1 over W2/Y2 during both the prewar and postwar periods may be due to estimating assumptions already explained.

INTERNATIONAL COMPARISONS

Table 11.6 presents historical data on labor's share of income for five countries. Several features stand out. Labor's postwar share is higher than its prewar share, except for Germany, where territorial

Table 11.6. Labor's Share of Income: International Comparison
(In percent)

United Kingdom		France		Germany		United States		Japan[a]	
1860–69	54								
				1895	53			1890–99	74.5
						1899–1908	76	1900–09	66.3
1905–14	54	1913	67	1913	60			1910–19	60.9
1920–29		1920–29	71	1925–29	79	1919–28	74	1920–29	67.8
						1929	73	1930–39	61.3
1954–60	75	1954–60	81	1954–60[b]	71	1954–60	81	1954–60	73.0
								1961–70	69.7

Source: Kuznets 1966, ch. 4, for all countries except Japan; authors' estimate for
Japan. Kuznets made estimates using both the labor and capital approaches. For all
countries, only labor-approach figures are given here.
[a] Nonprimary industry.
[b] West Germany.

changes after the war have caused discontinuity in income data. For
the United Kingdom, France, Germany, and the United States there
is an increasing long-term trend, especially in the first two. In contrast,
there is no persistent Japanese trend. However, allowance should be
made for differences in the scope of available data and the arbitrariness
of the method of imputation applied to self-employment income in all
countries.

Long-term data show labor's share of income in the United States
was very stable not only in manufacturing but also in the nonagricultural sector as a whole, whereas in Japan labor's share moves with the
long swings, as already discussed.

OTHER ESTIMATES

Previous series for manufacturing wages and salaries as a percentage
of income (W/Y in our notation) all have a broadly similar trend in
the 1920s and 30s. Hijikata's is the highest mainly because of overestimation of the number of employes (1933, p. 47). He estimated by
components such as wages, noncorporate incomes, and profits.
Yamada multiplied output by the ratio of value added to output, the
ratio being arbitrarily assigned for years before 1929 due to data
limitations (1951, pp. 49, 70–71). This procedure was also followed by
Shinohara (1955, p. 44) and Umemura (1961, p. 79), but there are
differences in their results because of differences in definitions of
incomes. For example, Shinohara and Yamada defined income in the

manufacturing sector as inclusive of miscellaneous expenses such as storage, insurance, and advertising costs.

In the nonagricultural sector both Ohkawa (1968) and the present estimate define labor income as the sum of the compensation of employes and the wage income imputed to the workers engaged in the noncorporate sector. For annual figures our estimates of labor's share of total income (W/Y) range between 53 and 72%, compared to Ohkawa's range of 46 to 78%. This is due to the differences in both estimating procedures and imputing methods, although both use the labor approach. However, both changed in a similar fashion, rising in the 1920s and then slowly declining in the 1930s.

DATA AND METHODS

For 1953–70, income data from ARNIS are used without modification, our own estimation being only for the period 1906–40. For the prewar period, both wage incomes and nonwage incomes have been estimated separately for mining, construction, manufacturing, facilitating industries, and services. For labor's share in the nonagricultural sector as a whole, estimation is extended back to 1885 simply by dividing manufacturing wages (estimated by Umemura [LTES 8:243]) by labor productivity (Ohkawa's figures on income produced [LTES 1:202] divided by Minami's labor force estimates [1973, p. 313]).

W1 is estimated for respective industries by multiplying the number of employes by estimated average wages. Average wages are taken as X(Y/Z), where X is production workers' wages, Y is wages and salaries per employe in electric utilities, and Z is wages of production workers in electric utilities. Data are taken from Umemura's estimate for manufacturing (LTES 8:243); from Noshomusho's *Honpo Kogyo no Susei* for mining; from Minami for railways and electric utilities (LTES 12:218–19); and Yoko Sano for services and the facilitating industries excluding railways and electric utilities (SIL 1(appendix vol.): 51 and 56). Wage data for construction are calculated by adjusting manufacturing wages by the ratio between construction wages and manufacturing wages available for the post-World War II period.

For most industries, data on A1 are available from the *Kaisha Tokeihyo (Shokosho)* for 1921–40. For 1906–20, A1 is calculated by relating it to the increase in reserve funds estimated by Shozaburo Fujino (unpublished). Interest paid by corporate enterprises is taken as the amount of debts multiplied by the rate of interest. Debt is

Table 11.7. NDP and Factor Income Estimates Compared
(In millions of yen)

	Industry		Services		Nonagriculture	
	Income produced	Factor income	Income produced	Factor income	Income produced	Factor income
1910	1,128	1,260	1,201	928	2,329	2,480
1915	1,670	1,815	1,487	1,193	3,157	3,532
1920	4,953	6,077	4,374	3,883	9,327	11,090
1925	5,622	6,998	5,081	4,363	10,703	12,702
1930	5,489	6,562	4,659	4,130	10,148	11,093
1935	7,357	7,695	5,508	4,842	12,865	12,819
1940	18,862	18,764	9,275	8,315	28,137	26,658

Source: Factor income is authors' estimate. Income produced is from LTES 1:202–03.

estimated using Shokosho data for 1921–40, and Fujino's unpublished estimates for 1906–20. The interest rate is available from unpublished work by Shigeru Ishiwata and Konosuke Odaka. Corporate income of railways and electric utilities and interest payments by the Japan National Railways are taken from Minami's estimate (LTES 12: 178–87).

Income from manufacturing and services in the noncorporate sector (Y2) for enterprises filing tax returns is obtained by multiplying the reported figures (Okurasho, *Shuzeikyoku*) by a constant 1.1, based on an assumed 10% rate of tax evasion. For enterprises below the taxation limit, income is estimated by assuming the contribution of proprietors to be the average earnings of salary earners, and the contribution of family workers to be the average earnings of wage earners (or production workers) prevailing in the noncorporate sector (estimated using postwar data).

Due to data limitations, Y2 for other industries is calculated, simply as the number of proprietors multiplied by self-employment income per proprietor. The latter is obtained by adjusting corporate income per company by the postwar ratio of self-employment income per proprietor to corporate income per company.

Table 11.7 compares our factor income estimates with income produced (NDP) for the industry, services, and nonagriculture sectors. Broadly the two are consistent, but some discrepancies, especially in the 1920s, require comment. Income produced is evaluated at market prices, while factor income is at factor cost, so that for rigorous comparisons adjustment with respect to indirect taxes and current subsidies is required. Ohkawa and Takamatsu estimated service sector income produced by adding an adjustment item (indirect taxes minus current subsidies) to their estimate of factor income obtained on the basis of the income approach (LTES 1:207). Therefore the gaps between the LTES 1 estimate and ours come not only from the adjustment item but also from the differences in the procedures of estimating factor income.

Discrepancies in the industrial sector are only partly caused by incompleteness in our income estimates. Estimation of income produced is also based, for the early years, on an indirect method, the income–production ratio, described by Ohkawa in chapter 3, and the results thus depend on both the output data and the estimate of the ratio of value added.

Estimates are lacking for a number of income components, primarily land and house rents (including imputed rents) and imputed interest. The latter need to be estimated to maintain comparability of factor incomes between the prewar and postwar periods. Omission of these items leads to underestimation of total factor incomes and thus to overestimation of labor's share of income. Labor's share is underestimated in the noncorporate sector (W2/Y2) and overestimated in the corporate sector (W1/Y1) because of the assumption all employes are in the corporate sector. Rigorously speaking, division of self-employed income into wages and profit income is necessary for obtaining factor income shares independent of changes in employment structure.

Average wage earnings were estimated using the ratio of wages and salaries per employe to wages of production workers in electric utilities. This is one of the weakest points of our income estimation. Because of the importance of the compensation of employes, this procedure needs to be revised and a more appropriate source of data on salaries found.

REFERENCES

Hijikata, Narumi. 1933. *Kokumin Shotoku no Kosei*. Nippon Hyoron Sha.
Kuznets, Simon. 1966. *Modern Economic Growth: Rate, Structure, and Spread*. Yale University Press.

LTES [*Estimates of Long-Term Economic Statistics of Japan*]. Series edited by Kazushi Ohkawa, Miyohei Shinohara, and Mataji Umemura. 14 v. 1965–. Toyo Keizai Shimposha.
1. National Income. 1974. Kazushi Ohkawa et al.
8. Prices. 1967. Kazushi Ohkawa et al.
12. Railroads and Electric Utilities. 1965. Ryoshin Minami.
Minami, Ryoshin. 1973. *The Turning Point in Economic Development: Japan's Experience*. Kinokuniya.
————, and Akira Ono. 1975. "Hi-ichiji Sangyo no Yoso Shotoku to Bunpairitsu." In *Kindai Nippon no Keizai Hatten*, edited by Kazushi Ohkawa and Ryoshin Minami. Toyo Keizai.
Norinsho. *Noson Bukka Chingin Chosa*.
Noshomusho. *Honpo Kogyo no Susei* (Annual published 1906–; issuing agency has changed several times; postwar, issued by Tsusho Sangyosho).
Ohkawa, Kazushi. 1968. "Changes in National Income Distribution by Factor Share in Japan." In *The Distribution of National Income*, edited by Jean Marchal and Bernard Ducros. Macmillan.
————, and Henry Rosousky. 1968. "Postwar Japanese Economic Growth in Historical Perspective: A Second Look." In *Economic Growth: The Japanese Experience Since the Meiji Era*, edited by Lawrence R. Klein and Kazushi Ohkawa. Irwin.
————, and Henry Rosovsky. 1973. *Japanese Economic Growth: Trend Acceleration in the Twentieth Century*. Stanford University Press.
Okurasho. *Hojin Kigyo Tokei*. Annual.
————. *Shuzeikyoku Nenpo*. Annual.
Ono, Akira. 1973. *Sengo Nihon no Chingin Kettei*. Toyo Keizai.
Sato, Ryuzo. 1968. *Keizai Seicho no Riron*. Keiso Shobo.
Shinohara, Miyohei. 1955. *Shotoku Bunpai to Chingin Kozo*. Iwanami.
Shokosho. *Kaisha Tokeihyo*. Annual.
SIL [*Choki Keizai Tokei no Seibi Kaizen ni Kansuru Kenkyu*]. By Keizai Kikakucho. 3 v. 1967–69. Mimeo.
Umemura, Mataji. 1961. *Chingin, Koyo, Nogyo*. Taimeido.
Woytinsky, W. S. et al. 1953. *Employment and Wages in the United States*. Twentieth Century Fund.
Yamada, Yuzo. 1951. *Kokumin Shotoku Suikei Shiryo*. Toyo Keizai.
Yamada, Saburo, and Yujiro Hayami. 1973. "Agriculture." In *Economic Growth: The Japanese Experience Since the Meiji Era*, edited by Kazushi Ohkawa and Yujiro Hayami. Japan Economic Research Center.

12

Prices

Tsutomu Noda

Price performance from the 1880s to 1972, especially in relation to economic growth and price differentials in a dualistic economy, is summarized in this chapter. From the expenditure side, commodity price indexes for consumers (Pc) and investment goods (Pi) are given, as well as the aggregate price index (P, the GNE deflator). On the production side, indexes for agriculture (Pa), manufacturing (Pn), and services (Pt) are presented. Appendix table A50 gives prewar annual data for the six series, and A51, postwar data for P, Pc, and Pi.

Discussions of price indexes appear in a number of LTES volumes, including those on national income (v. 1), consumption (v. 6), prices (v. 8), and foreign trade (v. 14). In general, concern has been to construct price indexes for calculating constant-price series. The literature in English analyzing the role of prices in Japanese growth is limited.

MAJOR FINDINGS

Prewar

The overall prewar movement of prices is suggested in table 12.1. Except for the Matsukata deflation (1881–85), before the table begins, and the 1920s, the Japanese economy has experienced inflationary growth, with consumer prices increasing much faster than investment goods prices. This is a distinctive feature compared to the relatively stable price patterns of western developed countries, although data for the early stages of western development are not so well developed as in Japan. Between 1879–88 and 1929–38, the GNP deflator in the United States rose about 1.5 times (versus 5.0 times in Japan), and the con-

Table 12.1.　Price Indexes: Annual Growth Rates
(In percent)

Period	GNP deflator	Personal consump- tion	Invest- ment goods	Agri- cultural products	Manufac- tured goods	Commerce– service sector
1887–1920	6.27	5.94	5.25	5.89[a]	5.32	5.97
1920–31	−3.46[b]	−3.76	−6.73	−6.53	−7.82	−0.37[c]
1931–35	1.49	2.83	3.79	7.82	4.37	1.80
1935–40	9.83	18.25	12.13	13.50	11.09	3.16
1887–1935	3.56	3.44	2.34	3.23	2.17	4.17

Source: Appendix table A50.

Notes: Bridge calculations, compound annual growth rates between first and last year in period. In 1920 and 1931 the price indexes reversed direction (except as noted). There was a marked increase in inflation after 1936.

[a] Agriculture prices peaked in 1919. The 1887–1919 rate is 6.83% and the 1919–31 rate is −7.73%.

[b] The GNP trough is in 1932. The 1920–32 rate is −3.2%; 1932–35, 2.28%.

[c] The service trough is in 1932. The 1920–32 rate is −1.35%; 1932–35, 7.30%.

sumer price index in the United Kingdom increased 1.6 times (4.7 in Japan) (LTES 8:12).

A swing pattern can be seen in price changes before World War II. There are several ways to look at swings. One is to consider the direction of the indexes themselves, and another is to look at the changes in the speed with which the index is changing.

Although the prewar trend of the indexes was not steady, prices moved higher until 1920 and then drifted lower until 1931–32. After 1936 inflation became very rapid. Table 12.1 shows growth rates using this periodization. Peaks and troughs determined by using seven-year moving averages of the rate of change in the indexes are given in table 12.2. These periodizations are close to those of GNP and investment growth rates. Changes in relative price are reflected in table 12.3. Export prices (see ch. 7) tended to increase less than domestic prices. Movement of the three product series mirrors their relative productivity changes, with manufacturing having the lowest price increase rate and the most rapid productivity growth.

Because of the role of uncontrollable external factors such as weather, agricultural prices are quite volatile. When smoothed by a seven-year moving average, they tended to rise more rapidly than manufacturing prices (similarly smoothed) in up phases of the long swings and to fall less in downswings (tables 12.1 and 12.3), so there was a secular trend of agricultural prices rising relative to manufacturing.

Table 12.2. Long Swings in Price Index Acceleration
                        (Years of peaks and troughs)

	Peak	Trough	Peak	Trough		Peak	Trough	Peak
Total expenditure	—[a]	—[a]	1895	1902	1907[b]	1916	1929	—[a]
Consumers' goods	—[a]	1886	1895	1902	1907[b]	1916	1929	—[a]
Investment goods	1881	1888	1897	1902		1917	1928	1940
Agricultural products	1878	1885	1895	1902	1912[b]	1916	1928	—[a]
Manufactured goods	1878	1885	1895	1911		1916	1928	1939

Source: LTES 8:8 (table 0-2) with modifications by Ohkawa.
Note: Based on seven-year moving averages of the annual rate of change of the price
index, so this table represents changes in the acceleration of price changes.
[a] Data are such that clear demarcation is not possible.
[b] Price movements were relatively stable between 1900 and 1915, so the trough can be
dated differently depending on the approach used.

Table 12.3. Relative Inflation Rates
                        (In percent)

	Agriculture	Manufacturing and Mining	Services	Consumption	Investment	Exports	Imports
1887–1904	107.7	83.8	94.6	98.1	86.9	88.6	67.3
1897–1919	92.1	81.7	93.1	98.1	68.2	77.4	74.6
1904–30	80.3	69.5	123.0	99.5	72.8	58.0	61.4
1919–38	103.5	83.7	129.1	103.8	100.5	61.3	84.5
1887–1938	111.3	62.7	107.6	100.5	70.0	45.2	47.2

Source: REVISION of LTES 1:59 (table 3-6) to reflect changes in export and import price
indexes.
Notes: The figures are the component's rate of increase as a percentage of the GNE
deflator's rate of increase. Periodization is that of long-swing phases (see ch. 1).

This trend relates to a trade policy protective of domestic agriculture.
Even though development of Taiwan and Korea as sources of Japanese
rice accelerated after the rice riots of 1918, agricultural prices fell less
than manufacturing prices during the 1920s deflation. In part this was
because technological advances in agriculture slowed during the 1920s
(see ch. 4), while textile expansion, with its scale economies (see ch. 5)
and continued productivity increases in other manufacturing areas,
put less cost pressure on prices. Further, the Japanese were slow to
acquire a taste for nontraditional (western-type) foods, although it is
not clear how much this slowness was due to the price structure
(imported foods commanded a premium and little nontraditional food

Table 12.4. Investment Goods Price Indexes

	Aggregate	Producers' durable equipment[a]	Construction goods[b]	Buildings[c]	Residential
Index					
1883	30.8	49.2	24.2	22.8	22.9
1909	60.3	73.4	56.5	58.6	59.6
1935	109.1	110.6	107.3	107.7	106.6
Annual increase[d]					
1883–1909	2.6	1.6	3.3	3.7	3.7
1909–35	2.3	1.6	2.5	2.4	2.3
1883–1935	2.5	1.6	2.9	3.0	3.0

Source: Calculated from LTES 8:158.
Note: Seven-year moving averages centered on year given. 1934–36 = 100.
[a] There are five subgroups in the source. These are machinery and installation, tools and fixtures, rolling stock, wooden ships, and steel ships. Because of data limitations, some substitutions were unavoidable in either the weights or prices. For example, machinery and installation serves as a proxy for steel ships for years before 1915, and as a proxy for tools and fixtures before 1910.
[b] Materials and labor used in buildings and other structures, including both nonresidential and residential. Structures other than buildings are divided into railroads and roads in the underlying data source.
[c] Both residential and nonresidential.
[d] Bridge calculations, annual compound growth rates.

Table 12.5. Consumer Price Indexes
(1934–36 = 100)

	Food	Clothing	Fuel and light	Housing[a]	Miscellaneous[b]	Total
Index						
1883	19.7	50.0	44.9	13.8	19.3	20.4
1909	55.2	64.6	71.5	38.6	44.9	52.2
1935	101.2	99.6	100.6	101.8	99.4	100.7
Annual increase[c]						
1883–09	4.04	0.93	1.81	4.04	3.30	3.68
1909–35	2.36	1.74	1.32	3.80	3.10	2.56
1883–35	3.20	1.33	1.56	3.92	3.20	3.12

Source: Calculated from LTES 6:106.
Note: Seven-year moving averages, centered on year shown. 1934–36 = 100.
[a] Includes rent.
[b] Includes both other consumption goods and services.
[c] Bridge calculations, annual compound growth rates.

Table 12.6. Consumer Price Indexes: Growth Rates
                        (In percent)

	CPI	RCPI	UCPI
1883–90	−1.33	−2.53	−1.46
1890–1900	6.27	5.88	4.75
1900–10	3.92	4.60	2.80
1910–20	7.27	5.82	7.25
1920–30	−1.09	0.24	−2.03
1930–37	1.99	4.46	0.91
1955–60	2.07	1.89	2.21
1960–65	5.27	5.18	5.55
1965–70	5.27	5.10	5.41

Source: Computed by Ryoshin Minami and Akira Ono. Prewar data are from LTES
1:232 (table 30) for CPI; Ono and Watanabe (1976) for rural RCPI; and LTES 8:135–36
(table 2) for urban UCPI. Postwar data: Nihon Ginko.

was produced domestically) and how much was actual unwillingness
to switch from a traditional diet. The spread of beer drinking suggests
prices did play an important role.

The rise in investment prices (table 12.4) is largely because of construction costs, although their weight declined through time. Housing
(representing land and construction costs), food, and services (part of
miscellaneous) account for most of the increase in the consumer price
index (tables 12.5 and 12.6). Urbanization contributed to the rise in
housing and food prices. In contrast, the manufactured components,
producers' durables in the investment index and clothing in the consumer index, have low growth rates.

Investment spurts in long-swing up phases (1885–97, 1909–19, and
the 1930s) induced rates of price increases for investment goods relatively faster than for manufactured goods. Changes in the investment
index were also greater than in the consumption index in upswings, but
less in downswings.

Postwar

This period is characterized by a continuous rise of aggregate
prices.[1] For the 1953–70 period, the average annual rate was 4%, which

1. There are many books in Japanese on postwar prices. One study dealing with the
impact of prices on resource distribution is Ohkawa (1970).

means prices almost doubled in 17 years. Using five-year moving averages to eliminate the influence of trade cycles, the rate of rise declined until 1956–57 but then speeded up. Even in recessionary phases this accelerating tendency has been sustained. In no other peacetime period has the rise in prices continued at such a pace.

The prewar pattern of the investment index increasing faster than the consumption index in upswings and consumption's rate being higher in downswings is found in the postwar period. However, the consumption index rises much more rapidly in downswings than before the war, over 6% a year in 1960–64. This pattern can be attributed to much faster economic growth in postwar declines than in prewar ones, so inflationary pressures continued. Further, there have been structural changes. While the slow price growth of manufactured mass-produced items somewhat mitigated the rise, tighter labor markets in the 1960s induced a rise in relative wages in consumer goods production and distribution, greatly increasing unit labor costs while productivity lagged. This has been especially true of traditional, labor-intensive items.

DATA AND METHODS

The procedures and formulas vary from one index to another, mainly because of differences in data availability, but efforts have been made to use methods as similar as possible. All the indexes are designed to be deflators of components of national income and expenditure. Series for subperiods, each with an appropriate set of weights for its components, are linked to a 1934–36 base using ratios of successive indexes for overlapping years. Implicit deflators are adopted for some indexes, including those for consumer goods, agricultural products, commerce-service, and the GNP deflator.

All the indexes are less reliable as they go back into the 19th century because of the quality and quantity of data. For some indexes, especially consumption, regional variations are important, but lack of consistent data has necessitated disregarding the problem. Over the entire period a number of technical assumptions have been made to overcome data limitations. In part because of the wide prevalence of black and gray markets, no attempt has been made to compute indexes for the World War II price control period.

A brief discussion of each index follows, except for trade prices, which are covered in chapter 7.

Consumer Goods and Services

This index was constructed by Miyohei Shinohara (LTES 6). It is a Paasche formula, implicit deflator type, calculated from the ratio of current values and the 1934–36 constant price series for personal consumption. There is also an index constructed by Noda (LTES 8) to study trends. It uses Tokyo prices only, on the assumption movements for the entire country were roughly parallel.

Investment Goods

The main data source is the series of inflators constructed by the EPA for the historical series in the 1960 national wealth survey (Keizai Kikakucho 1964). In most cases, the survey data depend on input costs instead of output prices, and our indexes derived from them are thus proxies, as is often the case for investment goods price indexes. LTES 8:123 discusses the sources more extensively.

The index is designed to deflate fixed capital formation. A fixed weighting procedure, using proportions of current investment items, is applied. Because of incompleteness of some items such as investment in the primary sector and farm residential construction, an implicit deflator formula cannot be applied to integrate individual indexes, and these two items are excluded from the weighting. Since 1951 a much more elaborate index compiled by the EPA is available. We have tentatively linked our prewar index with the EPA one, although they differ somewhat in scope.

The weights are from gross fixed capital formation data in current prices, most of which can be found in LTES 3. Five sets were made, using five-year averages of investment data centered on 1890, 1900, 1912, 1925, and 1935. These are periods of comparative stability in capital formation long swings.

Agricultural Products

In GRJE a wholesale price index was used. LTES 9 contains overall indexes of prices received by farmers. Weights were calculated for four base periods (1874–76, 1904–06, 1934–36, and 1954–56), and the resulting series were linked to a 1934–36 base. Although the estimates include only 78 of the 96 commodities for which output data have been compiled, 97% of product value is covered for the 1934–36 base. Prices are those received by the farmer at the farm insofar as possible. Data have been weighted for various grades and subgroupings.

Officially compiled nationwide average prices are available for 1949–63 from Norinsho's *Noka Keizai*. These have been adopted without modification. For 1915–40 Norinsho's *Tokeihyo* gives data for both total quantity and value, so an average unit price can be calculated. For years before 1915 four benchmarks were estimated, and intervening years were obtained by interpolation. Quantity and value data for the benchmarks were taken from prefectural-level records. LTES 8:125 more fully describes the data sources.

In constructing indexes by commodity group, weights represent the proportion of an individual item's value to the total value of the group's production. For the aggregate price index the production values of commodities lacking price data were included in calculating the weights. By-products have been included in the value of main products; for example, rice straw comes under rice. Intermediate products have been excluded.

Manufactured Goods

The Bank of Japan's wholesale price data have been the main source, on the assumption they can be a good proxy for domestic producers' prices. Although almost the same as the original data, the LTES index has several advantages. Most important is introducing different weights for subperiods to help adjust for discontinuity and lack of uniformity in the basic data. The subperiods and the years of their weights are 1873–89 (1874), 1887–1903 (1889–91), 1901–15 (1901–03), 1913–33 (1919–29), and 1931–45 (1934–36). LTES 8:127 more fully describes the various data sources, most of which are Bank of Japan publications.

Insofar as possible, when price movements are assumed similar to those of the group, items not included in making price indexes are considered in determining weights. Coverage of the production value of each subgroup ranges from 30% (miscellaneous industries) to 90% (food and metals).

Services

For this sector, a real-term output series is obtained as a residual, essentially by deducting real GNP of the goods-producing sectors from real GNE, with some adjustments. Much effort has been spent gathering data, but there are special difficulties, both conceptual and technical, in making price indexes for service output, and none that can be used with confidence as a deflator was found. Even the postwar official national income accounts do not include indexes of this kind. Rather than a tentative index of doubtful quality, a theoretical identity has been used. Derivation is discussed in chapter 3.

GNE Deflator

The implicit deflator formula is used to derive the series for GNE and its components for 1885–1940. Price indexes are constructed for each GNE item, and these are combined into the overall GNE deflator. The components are personal consumption, general government consumption, gross domestic capital formation, and foreign trade. The last two items were taken from the investment goods price indexes and the export and import price indexes, respectively, using fixed weights for subperiods linked to form a continuous series. The personal consumption component is calculated using the implicit formula. Starting with 1952, the EPA provides a GNE deflator with a 1965 base. It appears in ARNIS.

REMAINING PROBLEMS

For the postwar period there are no indexes for aggregate production. Agricultural prices were estimated for 1949–63, but for manufacturing only the wholesale price index is available. While the EPA publishes GNE deflators, it is still working on indexes for products by industrial group. The largest gap in the price series is the absence of price indexes for government consumption expenditure for any part of the pre- or postwar periods.

REFERENCES

Chubachi, Masayoshi, and Koji Taira. 1976. "Poverty in Modern Japan: Perceptions and Reality." In *Japanese Industrialization and its Social Consequences*, edited by Hugh Patrick with Larry Meissner. University of California Press.
Clark, Colin. 1972. "Investment and Net Stock of Fixed Capital (Nonresidential) in Japan." Submitted to the Second Growth Conference held by the Japan Economic Research Center (1972 Jun. 26–Jul. 1). Mimeo.
GRJE [*Growth Rate of the Japanese Economy*]. Kazushi Ohkawa et al. 1957. Kinokuniya.
Kaneda, Hiromitsu. 1969. "Long-Term Changes in Food Consumption Pat-

terns in Japan." In *Agriculture and Economic Growth: Japan's Experience*, edited by Kazushi Ohkawa, Bruce F. Johnston, and Hiromitsu Kaneda. University of Tokyo Press.

Keizai Kikakucho. 1955. *Keizai Hakusho*.

————. 1964. *Showa 35-nen Kokufu Chosa Hokokusho*.

Kelley, Allen C., and Jeffrey G. Williamson. 1974. *Lessons from Japanese Economic Development*. University of Chicago Press.

Kuznets, Simon. 1962. "Quantitative Aspects of the Economic Growth of Nations: VII, The Share and Structure of Consumption." *Economic Development and Cultural Change* 10 (1962 Jan.).

LTES [*Estimates of Long-Term Economic Statistics of Japan*]. Series edited by Kazushi Ohkawa, Miyohei Shinohara, and Mataji Umemura. 14 v. 1965–. Toyo Keizai Shimposha.
  1. National Income. 1974. Kazushi Ohkawa et al.
  3. Capital Stock. 1966. Kazushi Ohkawa et al.
  6. Personal Consumption Expenditure. 1967. Miyohei Shinohara.
  8. Prices. 1967. Kazushi Ohkawa, Tsutomo Noda, Nobukiyo Takamatsu, Saburo Yamada, Minoru Kumazaki, Yuichi Shionoya, and Ryoshin Minami.
  14. Foreign Trade and Balance of Payments. Forthcoming. Ippei Yamazawa and Yuzo Yamamoto.

Nakamura, James I. 1966. *Agricultural Production and the Economic Development of Japan 1873–1922*. Princeton University Press.

Nihon Ginko, Tokeikyoku. *Keizai Tokei Nempo* (*Economic Statistics Annual*).

Norinsho, *Noka Keizai Chosa* (Annual published 1921–).

————. Norinsho Tokeihyo (Annual published 1933–43, 1946–; issued by Noshomusho until 1933).

Ohkawa, Kazushi, and Henry Rosovsky. 1973. *Japanese Economic Growth: Trend Acceleration in the Twentieth Century*. Stanford University Press.

Ono, Akira, and Tsunehiko Watanabe. 1976. "Changes in Income Inequality in the Japanese Economy." In *Japanese Industrialization and its Social Consequences*, edited by Hugh Patrick with Larry Meissner.

Shinohara, Miyohei. 1954. "Keizai Hatten to Boekino Kankei." In *Nihon Keizaino Kozo Bunseki* v. 2, edited by Ichiro Nakayama.

————. 1961. *Nihon Keizai no Seicho to Junkan*. Sobunsha.

————. 1962. *Growth and Cycles in the Japanese Economy*. Kinokuniya.

————. 1970. *Structural change in Japan's Economic Development*. Kinokuniya.

Yokoyama, Gennosuke. 1949. *Nihon-no Kasoshakai*. Iwanami-bunko. First published in 1899.

13

Wages

Ryoshin Minami and Akira Ono

Long-term changes in nominal wages, real wages, and wage differentials are the topics of this chapter. Discussion is confined to daily wages for production workers grouped into agriculture, industry (including manufacturing, construction, and facilitating industries), and services (excluding almost all personal services) categories. Manufacturing and mining are sometimes treated separately from the industrial sector as a whole. Neither annual wages nor wages of nonproduction workers are dealt with. Wages by occupation, region, scale of firm, age, and so forth are also beyond the scope of this chapter.

Wages by industry group are the most important in understanding the characteristics of the national economy, and fortunately statistics on them are the best among the various wage data available. Unless specified otherwise, all series are moving averages, seven years for the prewar period and five for the postwar.

The following abbreviations are used:

CPI = (national) consumer price index,
RCPI = rural consumer price index, and
UCPI = urban consumer price index.

MAJOR FINDINGS

Wage Levels

Tables 13.1 and 13.2 give growth rates for nominal daily wages. The postwar rates are much higher partly because consumer prices have also risen somewhat faster since the war, but primarily because of the faster growth of the economy in the postwar period, and they

Table 13.1. Consumer Prices and Nominal Daily Wages by Sectors: Long-Term Growth Rates[a]

(In percent)

Wages

	Agriculture	Industry	Mining and manufacturing	Services	Consumer price index
1880–1939[a]	4.17	—	5.54	—	3.73
1905–39[a]	3.40	5.40	5.96	4.18	—
1952–72	10.29	9.46	9.69	8.33	4.21

Note: Annual exponential rates from fitting a regression, ln $w_t = a + bt$, to crude annual figures.

[a] 1940 is the terminal year for agriculture and the consumer price index.

Table 13.2. Nominal Wages: Growth Rates

(In percent)

	Agriculture			Industry	Mining and manufacturing			Services
	Both sexes	Male	Female	Both sexes	Both sexes	Male	Female	Both sexes
1883–90	−1.11	−1.38	−0.59	—	−1.63	−1.20	−2.09	—
1890–1900	7.96	7.45	8.63	—	6.45	6.31	6.23	—
1900–10	2.73	2.56	3.01	—	4.28	3.88	3.73	—
1910–20	10.09	10.33	9.72	11.05	12.56	11.88	11.58	11.68
1920–30	−1.86	−2.04	−1.65	1.70	1.33	2.14	−0.49	−0.97
1930–37	1.16	1.00	1.36	0.68	1.41	0.23	−0.93	−1.02
1955–60	6.45	6.19	6.64	5.41	5.44	5.32	5.87	4.18
1960–65	12.96	13.12	12.89	10.15	10.36	9.24	11.99	8.94
1965–70	11.81	11.97	11.64	13.35	14.25	14.84	14.53	12.76

Notes: All rates are annual exponential growth rates between the two indicated years (seven- and five-year averages in the pre- and postwar years, respectively). Figure for 1937 is five-year average.

Table 13.3. Real Wages by Sector: Long-Term Growth Rates

(In percent)

	Agriculture	Industry	Mining and manufacturing	Services
1880–1939[a]	0.34	—	2.62	—
1905–39[a]	−0.03	3.16	3.71	1.93
1952–72	6.18	5.08	5.30	3.94

[a] Terminal year is 1940 for agriculture.

coincide with changes in the consumer price index (CPI). Growth rates of both wages and the CPI tend to follow the prewar long swings in general economic activity with a lag of three to five years. However, in the postwar years any relationship with long swings is unclear. Ohkawa and Rosovsky (1973, p. 25) put long-swing peaks in 1897, 1917, 1937, and 1962, troughs in 1901, 1931, and 1956.

Table 13.3 presents the growth rates for real wages. Since rural and urban prices grew at different rates, RCPI is used throughout this chapter to deflate agriculture sector wages (on the assumption all such workers have been rural), and UCPI to deflate wages in the nonagriculture sectors. The growth rates of these indexes are given in table 12.6. The prewar pattern follows the long swings fairly closely while the postwar pattern does not.

Noda's CPI series in LTES (8:135–36) does not allow for price differences between rural and urban areas. In estimating current consumption, Ohkawa adjusted for this (LTES 1:19). The implicit deflator for consumption expenditure in LTES 1 is much better than the CPI given in LTES 8; it is used here, together with the RCPI computed from LTES data by Ono and Watanabe (1976).

Wages deflated by CPI relate to what happened to the supply price of labor and to the standard of living. From the standpoint of labor demand, however, wages deflated by industrial output price indexes should be studied. Real wages in this sense, which can be calculated

Table 13.4. Daily Wages Deflated by Output Price Indexes: Annual Growth Rates
(In percent)

	Agriculture	Industry	Mining and manufacturing	Services
1890–1900	1.40	—	1.73	—
1900–10	−0.76	—	1.72	—
1910–20	2.07	2.92	5.08	4.36
1920–30	1.96	5.40	4.96	−2.58
1930–37	−3.89	−2.24	−0.94	−2.26
1955–60	4.87	5.03	6.01	0.75
1960–65[a]	6.31	7.97	9.81	2.80

Sources: See table 13.1 for wages. Output price indexes are estimated by dividing NDP at current prices by NDP at constant prices. NDP figures at current and constant prices are from LTES 1:202, 226, for prewar period and from Ohkawa and Rosovsky (1973, pp. 283, 285) for postwar period.
Notes: See table 13.1.
[a] Figures for this period are tentative.

Table 13.5. Daily Wages Deflated by Consumer Price Indexes: Annual Growth Rates
(In percent)

	Agriculture			Industry		Mining and manufacturing				Services	
	CPI	RCPI			CPI	UCPI	CPI	UCPI			CPI	UCPI
	Both sexes	Both sexes	Male	Female	Both sexes	Both sexes	Both sexes	Both sexes	Male	Female	Both sexes	Both sexes
1883–90	0.30	1.50	1.20	2.02	—	—	−0.26	−0.18	0.28	−0.61	—	—
1890–1900	1.71	2.06	1.57	2.76	—	—	0.18	1.72	1.55	1.53	—	·
1900–10	−1.19	−1.84	−2.05	−1.58	—	—	0.35	1.45	1.09	0.96	—	—
1910–20	2.66	4.08	4.35	3.72	3.55	3.62	5.05	5.12	4.41	4.08	4.16	4.22
1920–30	−0.73	−1.96	−2.14	−1.76	3.03	3.97	2.69	3.64	4.47	1.74	0.24	1.14
1930–37	−1.24	−3.72	−3.87	−3.55	−1.30	−0.39	−0.57	−0.32	−0.82	−1.83	−2.73	−1.76
1955–60	4.26	4.45	4.19	4.64	3.30	3.15	3.30	3.16	3.06	3.53	2.08	1.94
1960–65	7.78	7.84	8.01	7.78	4.85	4.56	5.06	4.78	3.59	6.46	3.62	3.33
1965–70	6.49	6.67	6.80	6.50	7.98	7.84	8.88	8.74	9.40	9.02	7.37	7.24

Sources and Notes: See tables 13.1–13.3.

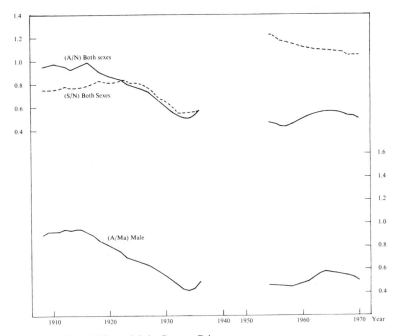

Fig. 13.1. Wage Differentials in Current Prices

Source: Authors' estimates.
A/N: ratio of agricultural to industrial wages
S/N: ratio of services to industrial wages
A/Ma: ratio of agricultural to manufacturing wages

for 1885–1939 and 1953–65, show a pattern of changes rather similar to those in terms of consumer prices. The growth rates in wages deflated by the output price indexes, shown in table 13.4, are much higher than rates deflated by the CPI (table 13.5) in the industry sector as a whole and in manufacturing and mining in the postwar period. Real wages in the service sector are almost constant in the 1950s and rise only slightly in the 1960s. In part this is because personal services, with considerable increases in wages and prices, are excluded from analysis. The increases in industry and in mining and manufacturing sector wages during the 1920s down phase are much larger when deflated by the output price indexes than when deflated by the CPI, which means output prices rose more slowly for these industries than consumer prices.

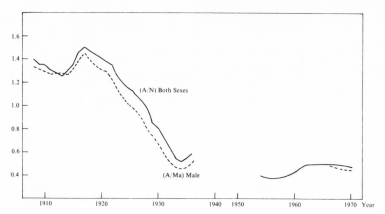

Fig. 13.2. Wage Differentials in 1934–36 Prices

Source: Authors' estimates.
Notes: Moving averages. Wages for A (agriculture) are those deflated by RCPI, while wages for N (industry) and Ma (manufacturing) are those deflated by UCPI.

Wage Differentials

Figures 13.1 and 13.2 shows differentials between various sector pairs. This shows a prewar declining trend for other sectors' wages relative to the industrial sector, and especially compared to mining and manufacturing. Further, the fluctuations are associated with the long swings.

Differentials tended to narrow during upswings and widen during down phases. This is consistent with the view that during booms, demand for labor is focused on unskilled workers, whose wages thus go up faster than those of skilled workers, as happened during the World War I boom in Japan (Taira 1970 for Japan; Reder 1955, Reynolds and Taft 1956 for the United States). This is probably true because skills can be taught to existing workers more readily than new people can be created (Minami 1973, p. 78).

In downswings, skilled workers' nominal wages are sticky and thus might continue to rise in real terms, widening the gap between industrially skilled and other workers, who are available in effectively unlimited numbers. This happened in the 1920s, a period when both nominal and real wages fell in agriculture. Wages for young workers, a proxy for unskilled labor, also decreased, while average wages for factory workers as a whole rose (table 13.6).

Table 13.6. Average Daily Wages in Yen for Skilled and Unskilled Workers, 1924 and
   1927

	Age			
	14–15	16–17	18–19	Factory workers
1924	0.89	1.23	1.59	2.10
1927	0.66	0.93	1.29	2.15

Sources: Rodo Undo 1959, pp. 296–97.

Referring to table 13.2 shows that during the 1920s nominal wages
in manufacturing increased for men but decreased for women. Since
women generally held unskilled jobs, mostly in textiles, the wage
differential by sex is a rough proxy for skill differentials. Further
supporting data are found in series on occupational wages: jobs such
as typesetter and carpenter enjoyed pay increases between 1920 and
1925, while wages declined for groups such as male servants (LTES
8:243–45).[1] This situation is consistent with a two-part labor market.
Skilled industrial workers are supplied within the manufacturing
sector itself, but unskilled workers are drawn from a pool that includes
unskilled agricultural workers. In the postwar period rapid economic
growth has drained this pool and thus put upward pressure on unskilled labor's wages. This turning point came in the late 1950s or
early 60s (Minami 1973).[2]

INTERNATIONAL COMPARISONS

Trend growth rates of annual wages earnings, measured in composite units of consumables as estimated by Phelps-Brown, are given
in table 13.7 for France, Germany, the United Kingdom, and the
United States. Although an exact comparison with Japan cannot be
made since we use series for daily wages, postwar growth in Japan has
been higher than that in the United Kingdom and the United States.
This is attributable to Japan's higher rate of economic growth.

1. Postwar changes in wage differentials are discussed by Ono (1973, pp. 149–206)
while Yasuba (1976) gives a concise account of their emergence and evolution. Also
see Umemura (1961) and Minami (1973, pp. 171–75) for a discussion of the emergence
of differentials during the 1920s.
2. Fei and Ranis (1964) put the point in the 1916–19 period and Jorgensen (1966)
felt at the time he wrote it had still not been reached. The reasons for rejecting these
views are given in Minami (1973, ch. 14).

Table 13.7. Real Wages in Selected Countries: Exponential Growth Rates
(In percent)

	France	Germany	United Kingdom	United States	Japan Agriculture	Nonagriculture	Manufacturing	Services
1860–79	0.72	1.28	1.97	1.41	—	—	—	—
1880–1938[a]	0.94	1.07	1.24	1.38	0.16	—	2.61	—
1905–38[a]	1.00	0.98	1.54	1.26	−0.07	3.17	3.76	2.05
1952–60	3.92	4.30	2.92	2.71	2.64	3.75	3.06	2.16

Sources: Foreign countries: The estimates by Brown for annual wage earnings in the main industries deflated by the cost of living index (Phelps-Brown 1968, appendix 3). Japan: The same as table 13.3. The RCPI is used to deflate agricultural wages, and the UCPI, the other sectors.

Notes: These figures are calculated by fitting a regression, ln w_t = a + bt, to annual statistics.
[a] 1914–24 is excluded because Brown's estimates are not available for this period.

If one assumes agricultural wages in other developed countries were close to their aggregate rates, Japanese wages in this sector lagged far behind. The prewar primary sector was relatively large, which suggests aggregate wage growth rates were lower in Japan. As a rough estimate, by imputing a wage-earner's wages to family workers and using the sectoral composition of employment in 1930 computed by Minami (1973, p. 313), the rate of increase for aggregate wages was 1.28% for 1905–38, excluding the World War I boom-bust of 1914–24 (Minami 1973, p. 313). This is consistent with Ohkawa's conclusion (1972) that growth in per capita consumption in prewar Japan was moderate among developed countries.

It is preferable to compare countries at the same stage of economic development. Unfortunately, reliable wage statistics are not available. Gilboy's study (1934) of the United Kingdom in the 19th century is the principal exception. Her data are largely confined to wages in agriculture and building and cover only four districts. Based on this, Deane and Cole conclude the purchasing power of workers changed little in the last 40 years of the 19th century or even declined slightly and, moreover, claim it was about the same at the beginning and end of the century (1967, p. 21). If this is true, Japan has followed the United Kingdom in having constant wages during the early phase of industrialization.

DATA AND METHODS

Availability and reliability of the data have limited discussion to daily wages for production workers. Almost all prewar official figures for wages are tabulated on a daily basis, and without arbitrary assumptions it is difficult to estimate the number of working days per year and the number of working hours per day. Nonproduction workers (management, accounting, personal services, administration, welfare, research, or study) are excluded here solely because of lack of data (although our tentative estimates are used in ch. 11 on factor incomes).

Our wage concept is a mixture of wage rate and wage earnings, the former because wages are on a daily basis (rather than yearly) and exclude nonproduction workers, the latter because these are not hourly statistics and include irregular payments. The wage rate is usually the best index for the price of labor. That is, enterprises tended to determine the demand for labor and laborers, the supply, in terms of hours by considering the hourly wage rate. This formulation, although true in pure theory, is not applicable to a country such as Japan, where workers seem to be interested more in yearly earnings than hourly wage rates.

There are some differences in wage concept among industries. Almost all series in this study include irregular payments such as bonuses. Postwar wages for the nonagriculture sectors are total cash earnings, and prewar wages for manufacturing, mining, and facilitating industries include irregular payments. However, pre- and postwar wages for agriculture and prewar wages for construction are based on occupational wages and exclude irregular payments.

Wages for daily-contract workers, including board, are used for agriculture. For the prewar period the estimates are from LTES (8:245 and 9:220–21) and for the postwar period from *Noson Bukka Chingin Chosa Hokoku* (Norinsho). While wage laborers are only a small fraction of the agricultural labor force, their wages are an index for the supply price of labor to other sectors (Minami 1973, p. 133).

Postwar wages in the industry sector can be obtained by dividing monthly total cash payments by the number of working days per month, both available from the *Maigetzu Kinro Tokei* (Rodosho). Prewar wages are the weighted averages of the wages for respective subgroups. Weights are Minami's employment figures (1973, pp. 313–15). Wages for the manufacturing subgroup are LTES series C (8:247) for 1899–1939, and for 1880–98 are an extrapolation based on series A (LTES 8:243). In LTES 8 (pp. 243–49) three series for manufacturing wages are given. Series A is daily wage rates by occupation, whereas series B and C are average wage earnings per day. Series A and C are tabulated by nine subindustry groups.

For mining, a ratio of wage payments to the number of employes is used. This was calculated by Yoko Sano using *Honpo Kogyo no Susei* and the *Honpo Kogyo Ippan* (SIL 1 [appendix vol.]:44). For years without such data, we have made estimates on the basis of the ratio of mining to manufacturing wages. Sano's estimates, based on the *Shogyo Chingin Shirabe*, are used for construction (SIL 1 [appendix vol.]:49). These are weighted averages of wages for six occupations: carpenters, plasterers, stone cutters, tile roofers, brick layers, and daily workers. For the facilitating industry, again Sano's estimates are used (SIL 1 [appendix vol.]:51). They are weighted averages for commerce, servants, and miscellaneous occupations given in *Shokugyo Shokai Nenpo*. Postwar wages are from *Maigetsu Kinro Tokei* (Rodosho). However, it provides information for just two groups, finance and insurance, and wholesale and retail trade. This means there is an important difference in coverage between the pre- and postwar periods.

REFERENCES

Deane, Phyllis, and W. A. Cole. 1967 (2d ed.). *British Economic Growth 1688–1959: Trends and Structure.* Cambridge University Press.
Fei, John C. H., and Gustav Ranis. 1964. *Development of the Labor Surplus Economy: Theory and Policy.* Irwin.
Jorgenson, Dale W. 1966. "Testing Alternative Theories of the Development of a Dual Economy." In *The Theory and Design of Economic Development,* edited by Irma Adelman and Erik Thorbecke. Johns Hopkins Press.
Gilboy, Elizabeth W. 1934. *Wages in Eighteenth Century England.* Harvard University Press.
LTES [*Estimates of Long-Term Economic Statistics of Japan*]. Series edited by Kazushi Ohkawa, Miyohei Shinohara, and Mataji Umemura. 14 v. 1965–. Toyo Keizai Shimposha.
    1. National Income. 1974. Kazushi Ohkawa et al.
    8. Prices. 1967. Kazushi Ohkawa et al.
Minami, Ryoshin. 1973. *The Turning Point in Economic Development: Japan's Experience.* Kinokuniya.
————, and Akira Ono. 1977. "Wages and Employment: Japanese Experience." In *Econometric Studies of the Economy of Japan,* edited by Richard F. Kosobud and Ryoshin Minami. University of Illinois Press.
Norinsho. *Noson Bukka Chingin Chosa Hokoku.*
Ohkawa, Kazushi. 1972. *Differential Structure and Agriculture.* Kinokuniya.
————, and Henry Rosovsky. 1968. "Postwar Japanese Growth in Historical Perspective: A Second Look." In *Economic Growth: The Japanese Experience Since the Meiji Era,* edited by Lawrence R. Klein and Kazushi Ohkawa. Irwin.
————. 1973. *Japanese Economic Growth: Trend Acceleration in the Twentieth Century.* Stanford University Press.
Ono, Akira. 1973. *Sengo Nippon no Chingin Kettei.* Japan. Toyo Keizai.
————, and Tsunehiko Watanabe. 1976. "Changes in Income Inequality in the Japanese Economy." In *Japanese Industrialization and Its Social Consequences,* edited by Hugh Patrick with Larry Meissner. University of California Press.
Reder, Melvin W. 1955. "The Theory of Occupational Wage Differentials." *American Economic Review* 45 (1955 Dec.): 833–52.
Phelps-Brown, E. H. 1968. *A Century of Pay.* MacMillan and St. Martin's Press.
Reynolds, Lloyd G., and Cynthia H. Taft. 1956. *The Evolution of Wage Structure.* Yale University Press.
Rodosho. *Maigetsu Kinro Tokei.*

Rodo Undo Shiryo Iinkai. 1962–. *Nihon Rodo Undo Shiryo, Tokeihen.*
Rodo Undo Shiryo Kanko Iinkai. 1959. *Rodo Tokei Jitchi Chosa.*
SIL [*Choki Keizai Tokei no Seibi Kaizen ni Kansuru Kenkyu*]. By Keizai Kikakucho. 3 v. 1967–69. Mimeo.
Taira, Koji. 1970. *Economic Development and the Labor Market in Japan,* Columbia University Press.
Umemura, Mataji. 1961. *Chingin, Koyo, Nogyo Taimei Do.*
Yasuba, Yasukichi. 1976. "The Evolution of Dualistic Wage Structure." In *Japanese Industrialization and Its Social Consequences,* edited by Hugh T. Patrick with Larry Meissner. University of California Press.

14

Population and Labor Force

Mataji Umemura

Providing estimates of total population and the labor force, including its distribution by industry, are the principal concerns of this chapter. LTES 2 (unpublished as of mid 1978) covers this topic in depth. Among the more analytic discussions of demographic transition and the relation between population and industrialization are papers by Umemura, Tussing, Masui, Misawa, and Minami (all in Ohkawa, Johnston, and Kaneda 1969) and work done by Minami (1973) and Ohbuchi (1976).

MAJOR FINDINGS

Background

To place the findings in context, it is appropriate to mention some of the main demographic and economic conditions before and just after the Meiji Restoration (for more details, see Umemura 1969).

A significant positive correlation is found between the regional rate of change in population (excluding samurai) during the period 1721–1834 and the rate of change for kokudaka, the standard output measure for tax purposes. There are two exceptions, Kanto (the Tokyo area) and Tohoku (northeastern Honshu), where there were repeated famines and other population dislocations.

The population, excluding the samurai class, decreased in the second half of the 18th century, but began increasing in the first half of the 19th, although the trends are not very clear. In the Tohoku, Kanto, and Kinai (Kyoto–Osaka area) districts the population continued to decline in the early 19th century. The gradually accelerating

Table 14.1. Population: Annual Growth Rates, 1875–1970
(In percent)

	Growth rate	Birth rate	Death rate
1875	0.70	2.60	1.90
1880	0.90	2.59	1.69
1890	0.90	3.01	2.10
1900	1.23	3.38	2.10
1910	1.31	3.64	2.19
1920	1.32	3.63	2.54
1930	1.56	3.24	1.82
1935	1.35	3.17	1.68
1950	1.61	2.81	1.09
1960	0.93	1.72	0.76
1970	1.25	1.88	0.69

Sources: Author's estimates for 1875–1910 and Koseisho, 1920–70.

upward population trend in the second half of the 19th century, discussed later, is thus a continuation of the late Tokugawa pattern. Further discussion of Tokugawa trends and their continuation into the Meiji period is found in Hanley (1972 and 1974).

Population Growth

Appendix table A53 gives absolute figures for population. Net migration is not significant except for the 1940s, so the total population growth rate is almost equal to the difference between birth and death rates. My estimates show these usually moved in the same direction, although at different rates (table 14.1). Both rose until 1920 and then fell. The death rate in 1920 was abnormally high because of an influenza epidemic.

Underlying data in the early period are weak, leaving room for controversy over not only the levels but also the trend. Demographers following the stage theory of population growth (Notestein 1950) suspect there was a rising death rate. Ohbuchi (1976) and Minami (1973) provide more detailed discussions of the various estimates. Okazaki (1962) and Yasukawa and Hirooka (1972) have attempted to estimate the number of births, deaths, and the total population by taking the 1920 population census (Japan's first modern census) as a benchmark and applying the reverse survival ratio method back to 1870 and 1865, respectively. It is important to note a falling death rate is a basic assumption underlying both Okazaki and Yasukawa's work;

Table 14.2. Gainful Workers: Percentage Composition by Industry in 1872

Agriculture	Industry	Commerce	Other services
77.1	3.7	6.9	12.3

Source: Naikaku 1913, p. 24.

thus, they are not in a position to discuss the real course of the death rate. Of course all these results are still only tentative.

Gainful Workers

Japanese employment statistics for the prewar period are much broader in coverage than in the west. The gainfully occupied concept used in Japan refers to the usual status of an individual. Usual has no precise definition in terms of some minimum number of hours worked in a period. Census takers generally asked for usual occupation, so even those actually unemployed at the time tended to be listed as gainfully occupied. Further, there has been a large number of self-employed and family workers, many only occasional, and they too are often included. All this results in much higher participation rates in Japan than in countries using labor force or employed population concepts. This broad scope and heterogeneous composition of gainfully occupied must be kept in mind when using the data. Postwar data use the labor force concept.

Narumi Hijikata (in GRJE, pp. 245–46) and Henmi (1956, p. 415) were among the first to estimate total gainful workers. Their estimates were made without regard to total population statistics and are quite unreasonable in relation to such data. In 1872 the Bureau of Family Registration made a nationwide population survey. The results (table 14.2) are not comparable with my estimates because of differences in coverage and definition, but they serve as an indication of the situation on the eve of industrialization. If the common practice of peasant families having side occupations is taken into account, the nonagricultural share may increase some (see Smith 1969).

Between 1875 and 1970 gainful workers increased almost 250%, from 21 to 52 million. Table 14.3, column 1, shows three phases of growth. The first is the period up to 1925, with minor fluctuations around a low rate. The interwar period saw acceleration growth, and there has been a high but falling rate since 1950.

For the first phase the mean value of the annual growth rate is about 0.5% for gainful workers and 1.0% for the total population. This

Table 14.3. Gainful Workers: Growth Rates
(Percent per decade)

	Aggregate	Agriculture and forestry	Nonagriculture		
			Total	Industry	Services
1875–85	4.07	0.50	13.57	—	—
1880–90	5.33	0.22	18.83	—	—
1885–95	6.20	0.50	20.23	(42.65)	(10.66)
1890–1900	5.80	1.37	15.65	(23.51)	(7.66)
1895–1905	5.30	1.00	14.13	(11.56)	(7.24)
1900–10	4.50	−0.38	14.02	(13.87)	(17.55)
1905–15	5.30	−4.86	23.71	34.74[a]	28.55[a]
1910–20	6.48	−11.93	37.79	53.34	30.71
1915–25	6.31	−10.62	29.91	31.84	31.50
1920–30	8.65	−0.35	18.41	4.69	31.63
1925–35	11.05	1.43	20.24	12.40	26.97
1930–40	15.39	−2.05	31.13	40.54	27.09
1950–60	22.64	−17.95	57.76	61.73	59.02
1955–65	21.27	−27.78	52.95	65.58	47.49
1960–70	19.55	−29.65	41.69	39.37	46.19

Sources: Author's estimate for 1875–1940, except industry and services for 1885–1905, which are estimated by Takamatsu (the figures in parentheses), (1975, pp. 544–52), and the Census of Population has been used for 1950–70.

Notes: The procedures used in my estimates are given in the data and methods section. The gainful worker approach is used in three successive censuses (1920, 1930, and 1940). The labor force approach has been used since the 1950 census, with unemployed excluded. Thus, data are not strictly comparable between the pre- and postwar periods. Absolute figures on gainful workers are given in appendix table A54. For 1885–1905 industrial employment is the estimate of total nonagricultural employment minus that in services.
[a] 1906–15.

implies a falling participation rate. Responsible factors include the spread of compulsory education (see table 14.4) and a relative decline in the number of peasant households, whose participation rate is high compared to urban families. Cyclic peaks appear in the years 1885–95 and 1910–20, and troughs in 1875–85 and 1900–10. Factors causing this cyclical pattern are not clear at present.

For the second phase the acceleration in total population growth may have caused the acceleration in gainful worker growth. On the other hand, in the first half of the period the economy was in the midst of a worldwide depression, while in the second half it was at a peak, so that simple expansion may have caused increased job opportunities.

In the postwar phase the Japanese economy enjoyed real GNE

Table 14.4. Labor Force Composition by Highest Level of School Completed
(In percent)

	Higher school	Middle school	Primary school	Unschooled
1905	0.2	0.9	41.6	57.3
1925	0.8	4.9	74.3	20.0
1935	1.6	9.2	82.1	7.1

Source: Mombusho 1963, p. 59.

Table 14.5. Growth in Some Selected Industries in the Interwar Period
(Percent per decade)

	1906–16	1910–20	1915–25	1920–30	1925–35	1930–40
Mining	45.7	100.0	−5.1	−26.3	1.0	89.2
Construction	36.6	22.8	20.7	26.4	10.7	−0.5
Manufacturing	35.4	55.6	37.4	3.3	11.8	46.5
Metal	41.2	71.9	23.3	−9.1	25.1	72.7
Machinery	88.8	159.1	117.0	26.7	37.2	318.1
Chemical	26.1	64.3	28.6	9.3	50.3	114.1
Textile	45.0	61.0	51.4	3.8	10.7	−1.5
Clothing	36.8	39.4	17.5	4.6	10.0	0.8
Food and beverages	38.5	35.7	39.5	2.9	−17.1	−24.5
Gas, electricity, and water	64.1	119.5	38.1	35.2	111.1	16.3

Source: Author's estimates.

growth of about 10% a year. At the beginning of the period large numbers of repatriated soldiers and civilians had to be absorbed, and in the 1950s the female participation rate increased. In the 1960s, those born in the postwar baby boom began entering the labor force. All these factors influenced the postwar pattern (for more detail, see Umemura 1963).

Employment by Industry

Table 14.3 also gives growth rates of employment by sector, and growth rates for various industries are in table 14.5.

In the Meiji era regional differences in the movement of agricultural employment are quite evident. It decreased in the west, but increased in Hokkaido, which was still a frontier in the mid-19th century, and in Tohoku. However, overall agricultural employment remains almost stable at about 16 million for the period 1872–1914. Between 1915 and the early 1920s it decreased about 2 million and then remained

Table 14.6. Movement of Gainful Workers
(Thousands per decade)

	Outflow of agricultural working force	Increase of employment in nonagricultural industries	Agricultural contribution rate (%)
1875–85	554	773	71.7
1880–90	807	1,132	71.3
1885–95	900	1,309	68.8
1890–1900	705	1,118	63.1
1895–1905	685	1,099	62.3
1900–10	784	1,158	67.7
1905–15	1,646	2,105	78.2
1910–20	2,950	3,566	82.7
1915–25	2,622	3,285	79.8
1920–30	1,271	2,408	52.8
1925–35	1,330	2,909	45.7
1930–40	2,461	4,848	50.8
1950–60	6,713	11,032	60.9
1955–65	7,534	12,629	59.7
1960–70	6,653	12,563	53.0

Source: See table 14.1.

stable until World War II. Large-scale war destruction of urban industries and repatriation caused about 2.5 million workers to return to agriculture·in the late 1940s. It was 1960 before the prewar low was again reached, and the movement out of agriculture has continued.

Seen from the viewpoint of swings in economic activity in Japan, the nonagricultural employment growth rate has been distinctly higher in upswings and clearly lower in downswings. This is much more evident in the industrial sector. Agricultural employment has been countercyclic. In the service industries the employment growth rate remains stable during downswings, suggesting surplus labor is absorbed in this sector.

Movement out of Agriculture

Table 14.6 shows movement from agriculture into other sectors. At the time of the World War I boom both the increase in nonagricultural employment and the percentage of that increase accounted for by workers shifting out of agriculture jumped. The prolonged deflation of the 1920s and the following depression induced fewer workers to move. The postwar movement reached new highs in absolute numbers, but with an already large nonagricultural population, the contribution rate declined.

DATA AND METHODS

To derive a series of gainful workers, the number of Japanese living in Japan Proper (including Okinawa) is estimated by sex and age group for the years 1872–1920. This is the basis of series A in appendix table A53. These estimates are linked to official figures (series B) beginning in 1920. The two series are not quite comparable since series B includes non-Japanese resident in Japan, while series A excludes them.

Since the first census is for the population as of 1920 October 1, birth and death data are used to adjust the figures back to January 1, and the procedure is repeated back to 1899. (Vital statistics are available for years after 1900, though there is some question about their accuracy.) The 1899 sex and age distribution is then extrapolated using Okazaki's estimates (1962). The total number of Japanese for years before 1899 is obtained by adding estimates of the number of deaths and subtracting the number of births from the estimate of total population at the beginning of 1899. Finally, a tentative adjustment is made for net emigration.

The second step was to use 1920 census data to compute, for each prefecture, regressions between the gainful worker participation rate by sex and age group, and the ratio of peasant family members to the total population. Applying these regressions to my estimates of total population and data (developed by Minami [1973]) on the number of peasant family members provides a series of gainful worker participation rates by sex and age group for the years back to 1872. A second series of gainful worker participation rates was made using regressions derived from 1930 census data. For 1921–29 the average of the two series is used, while for 1930–39 the 1930 regressions are used. Akasaka (1964) has estimated the number of students by sex back to 1878 using Mombusho data. Census data have been used to estimate participation rates for those not in school.

Next the industrial distribution of gainful workers by sex was estimated for 1906–40 by using the industrial distribution of dead gainful workers by sex (available for 1906–36 from *Teikoku Shiin Tokei*) to extrapolate 1920, 1930, and 1940 census data. In doing this, it was assumed the relative death rates of gainful workers between industries remained stable. For 1937–39, a linear interpolation between 1936 and 1940 was made.

Finally gainful workers in agriculture and forestry are estimated by sex back to 1872 by extrapolating the corresponding estimates for 1906, using estimates of the number of peasant households, with some minor adjustments. A more complete explanation will appear in LTES 2.

Minami's estimates (1973, p. 102) of agriculture and forestry workers are lower than mine before 1920 and higher in the interwar period, so they show a much more gradual declining trend in the prewar period and near stability in the 1885–1930 period. This results from differences in methodology and in assumptions about relations between different series, as Minami primarily has used as a starting point the data I developed for the LTES project.

REFERENCES

Akasaka, Keiko. 1964. *Danjo Nenrei betsu Jinko no Suikei, 1872–98*. Hito-tsubashi Daigaku Keizai Kenkyujo. Unpublished.
Deane, Phyllis, and W. A. Cole. 1962. *British Economic Growth 1688–1959*. Cambridge University Press.
Deldycke, T., H. Gelders, and J. M. Limbor. 1968. *The Working Population and its Structure, International Historical Statistics*, v. 1.
Hanley, Susan B. 1972. "Toward an Analysis of Demographic and Economic Change in Tokugawa Japan: A Village Study." *Journal of Asian Studies* 31 (1972 May): 515–37.
———. 1974. "Fertility, Mortality, and Life Expectancy in Pre-modern Japan." *Population Studies* 28 (1974 May): 127–42.
Henmi, Kenzo. 1956. "Nogyo Yugyo Jinko no Suikei." In *Nippon no Keizai to Nogyo*, v. 1, edited by Seiichi Tobata and Kazushi Ohkawa. Iwanami.
GRJE [*Growth Rate of the Japanese Economy since 1878*]. Edited by Kazushi Ohkawa. 1957. Kinokuniya.
ILO (International Labor Organization). 1956. *The World's Working Population*.
Koseisho, Daijin Kambo, Tokeichosabu. 1920–. *Jinko Dotai Tokei* [*Vital Statistics*].
LTES [*Estimates of the Long-Term Economic Statistics of Japan*]. Series edited by Kazushi Ohkawa, Miyohei Shinohara, and Mataji Umemura. 14 v. 1965–. Toyo Keizai Shimposha.
    2. Population and Labor Force. Forthcoming, Mataji Umemura.
Minami, Ryoshin. 1973. *The Turning Point in Japanese Economic Development*. Kinokuniya.

Mombusho. 1963. *Mombu Tokei Yoran.*
Naikaku, Tokeikyoku. 1913. Genju Jinko Seitai ni Kansuru Tokei Zairyo.
Notestein, F. W. 1950. "The Population of the World in the Year 2000." *Journal of the American Statistical Association* (1950 Sep).
Ohbuchi, Hiroshi. 1976. "Demographic Transition in the Process of Japanese Industrialization." In *Japanese Industrialization and its Social Consequences* edited by Hugh Patrick with Larry Meissner. University of California Press.
Okazaki, Yoichi. 1962. "Meiji Shonen iko Taisho 9-nen ni itaru Danjo Nenrei betsu Jinko Suikei ni tsuite." Institute of Population Problems Research Series no. 145.
Smith, Thomas C. 1969. "Farm Family By-Employments in Preindustrial Japan." *Journal of Economic History* (1969 Dec.)
Umemura, Mataji. 1963. *Sengo Nihon no Rodoryoku.* Iwanami.
————. 1969. "Agriculture and Labor Supply in the Meiji Era." In *Agriculture and Economic Growth: Japan's Experience.* Kazushi Ohkawa, Bruce F. Johnston, and Hiromitsu Kaneda. Princeton University Press and Tokyo University Press.
Takamatsu, Nobukiyo. 1975. "Shogyo to Sabisugyo no Jugyojo no Chiibetsu Yugyoshasu." In *Kindai Nihon no Keizai Hatten* edited by Kazushi Ohkawa and Ryoshin Minami. Toyo Keizai.
Yasukawa, Masaaki, and Keijiro Hirooka. 1972. "Meiji-Taisho Nenkan no Jinko Suikei to Jinko Dotai." *Mita Gakkai Zasshi* 65 (1972 Mar.).

Appendix Tables

Table A1. Gross National Expenditure in Current Prices, 1885–1940

(In millions of yen)

	Personal consumption expenditure	General government consumption expenditure	Gross domestic fixed capital formation	Surplus on current account	Exports of goods and services and factor income received from abroad	Less: imports of goods and services and factor income paid abroad	Gross national expenditure at market prices
1885	652	60	97	−3	42	45	806
1886	630	63	101	6	55	49	800
1887	664	62	100	−8	59	67	818
1888	677	62	133	−6	74	80	866
1889	755	59	141	−0	78	78	955
1890	869	66	153	−32	65	97	1,056
1891	903	63	160	13	89	76	1,139
1892	888	70	153	14	102	88	1,125
1893	970	66	165	−4	100	104	1,197
1894	1,009	124	220	−15	125	140	1,338
1895	1,160	148	251	−7	150	157	1,552
1896	1,308	118	303	−68	135	203	1,666
1897	1,545	111	402	−101	191	292	1,957
1898	1,808	131	426	−171	200	371	2,194
1899	1,776	150	376	12	257	245	2,314
1900	1,914	183	391	−74	259	333	2,414

Table A1 (continued)

	Personal consumption expenditure	General government consumption expenditure	Gross domestic fixed capital formation	Surplus on current account	Exports of goods and services and factor income received from abroad	Less: imports of goods and services and factor income paid abroad	Gross national expenditure at market prices
1901	1,898	201	379	6	310	304	2,484
1902	1,984	202	335	16	332	316	2,537
1903	2,103	241	366	−14	370	384	2,696
1904	2,259	546	364	−141	383	524	3,028
1905	2,278	626	517	−337	401	738	3,084
1906	2,312	485	540	−35	540	575	3,302
1907	2,787	338	634	−16	617	633	3,743
1908	2,884	307	663	−88	506	594	3,766
1909	2,880	320	597	−17	539	556	3,780
1910	2,967	338	689	−69	587	656	3,925
1911	3,295	407	860	−99	619	718	4,463
1912	3,657	370	857	−110	727	837	4,774
1913	3,920	339	861	−107	844	951	5,013
1914	3,595	354	806	−17	799	816	4,738
1915	3,616	366	793	216	1,004	788	4,991
1916	4,147	361	1,035	605	1,646	1,041	6,148
1917	5,416	423	1,816	937	2,356	1,419	8,592
1918	7,756	582	2,702	799	3,016	2,217	11,839
1919	11,302	881	2,937	333	3,242	2,909	15,453
1920	11,326	1,085	3,596	−111	2,984	3,095	15,896

Table A1 (continued)

	Personal consumption expenditure	General government consumption expenditure	Gross domestic fixed capital formation	Surplus on current account	Exports of goods and services and factor income received from abroad	Less: imports of goods and services and factor income paid abroad	Gross national expenditure at market prices
1921	11,171	1,120	2,868	−273	2,065	2,338	14,886
1922	11,590	1,198	2,975	−190	2,388	2,578	15,573
1923	11,796	1,164	2,500	−536	2,184	2,720	14,924
1924	12,149	1,187	2,929	−689	2,665	3,354	15,576
1925	12,740	1,073	2,704	−252	3,272	3,524	16,265
1926	12,359	1,133	2,862	−379	2,985	3,364	15,975
1927	12,141	1,391	2,892	−131	2,981	3,112	16,293
1928	12,210	1,688	2,743	−135	3,033	3,168	16,506
1929	11,782	1,612	2,815	77	3,300	3,223	16,286
1930	10,850	1,452	2,322	47	2,486	2,439	14,671
1931	9,754	1,685	1,946	−76	2,029	2,105	13,309
1932	9,804	1,839	2,030	−13	2,466	2,479	13,660
1933	10,850	2,046	2,466	−15	3,092	3,107	15,347
1934	12,097	2,005	2,923	−59	3,580	3,639	16,966
1935	12,668	2,117	3,346	167	4,158	3,991	18,298
1936	13,328	2,183	3,622	191	4,580	4,389	19,324
1937	15,121	2,609	5,661	−568	5,401	5,969	22,823
1938	16,012	3,046	7,977	−641	5,283	5,924	26,394
1939	17,912	3,402	9,822	94	6,298	6,204	31,230
1940	20,290	4,821	11,698	42	7,192	7,150	36,851

Source: Reprinted from LTES 1:178 (table 1).
Note: Inventory changes are not explicitly estimated in investment.

Table A2. Gross National Expenditure in Current Prices, 1930–71
(1930–44, in millions of yen; 1946–71, in billions of yen)

	Private consumption expenditure	General government consumption expenditure	Gross domestic fixed capital formation	Increase in stocks	Exports of goods and services and factor income received from abroad	Less: imports of goods and services and factor income paid abroad	Gross national expenditure at market prices
1930	10,572	1,624	1,177	278	2,701	2,502	13,850
1931	9,103	1,939	888	406	2,344	2,160	12,520
1932	9,504	2,217	1,379	−16	2,441	2,482	13,043
1933	10,186	2,464	1,797	7	3,006	3,126	14,334
1934	10,610	2,421	2,246	582	3,478	3,665	15,672
1935	10,833	2,637	2,374	735	4,247	4,092	16,734
1936	11,443	2,723	2,616	974	4,471	4,427	17,800
1937	12,809	4,714	3,949	1,845	6,110	6,001	23,426
1938	13,886	6,699	5,303	1,049	5,775	5,919	26,793
1939	16,475	7,126	7,453	1,481	6,621	6,073	33,083
1940	19,155	9,646	8,299	2,247	7,275	7,226	39,396
1941	20,701	13,495	9,308	2,414	6,117	7,139	44,896
1942	23,734	17,118	10,187	4,416	5,031	6,102	54,384
1943	26,001	22,855	14,158	1,716	4,889	5,795	63,824
1944	26,554	27,672	17,390	3,265	3,950	4,328	74,503
1946	333	55	78	28	5	24	475
1947	915	102	263	83	28	82	1,309
1948	1,741	282	516	236	81	191	2,665
1949	2,261	394	623	208	217	327	3,376
1950	2,397	437	639	368	469	364	3,946
1951	3,018	552	1,093	570	908	699	5,442

Table A2 (continued)

	Private consumption expenditure	General government consumption expenditure	Gross domestic fixed capital formation	Increase in stocks	Exports of goods and services and factor income received from abroad	Less: imports of goods and services and factor income paid abroad	Gross national expenditure at market prices
1952	3,861	668	1,277	385	788	720	6,259
1953	4,665	780	1,549	142	789	870	7,055
1954	5,162	864	1,698	140	854	882	7,836
1955	5,529	894	1,705	421	979	904	8,624
1956	6,012	936	2,290	507	1,189	1,208	9,726
1957	6,597	1,009	2,946	740	1,334	1,549	11,077
1958	7,057	1,105	2,941	252	1,318	1,150	11,523
1959	7,722	1,209	3,435	418	1,531	1,390	12,925
1960	8,823	1,382	4,682	551	1,774	1,713	15,499
1961	10,106	1,607	6,370	1,382	1,860	2,199	19,126
1962	11,747	1,864	7,136	459	2,142	2,148	21,200
1963	13,769	2,200	7,875	884	2,349	2,613	24,464
1964	15,945	2,554	9,404	1,083	2,889	3,036	28,839
1965	17,929	2,949	9,767	776	3,563	3,197	31,787
1966	20,586	3,328	11,344	1,037	4,164	3,665	36,794
1967	23,554	3,733	13,965	2,296	4,467	4,472	43,543
1968	27,296	4,277	17,327	2,366	5,528	5,087	51,707
1969	31,320	4,925	20,938	2,228	6,818	5,989	60,240
1970	36,292	5,853	24,921	3,132	8,272	7,488	70,982
1971	41,266	6,884	27,179	1,624	9,896	7,807	79,042

Source: Reprinted from LTES 1:179 (table 1A). The original sources are various issues of ARNIS: the 1962 issue for 1930–51; the 1969 revised issue for 1952–62; and the 1973 issue for 1963–71.

Note: Figures for 1945 are not available; 1946–51 data are for fiscal years.
Figures for 1930–44 and 1946–51 are not revised to be consistent with those for the years since 1952 but are listed for reference.

Table A3. Gross National Expenditure in 1934–36 Prices, 1885–1940
(In millions of yen)

	Personal consumption expenditure	General government consumption expenditure	Gross domestic fixed-capital formation	Surplus on current account	Exports of goods and services and factor income received from abroad	Less: imports of goods and services and factor income paid abroad	Gross national expenditure at market prices
1885	3,284	283	346	−23	101	124	3,890
1886	3,466	311	362	5	127	122	4,114
1887	3,765	320	361	−38	131	169	4,408
1888	3,837	315	412	−35	169	204	4,529
1889	4,096	292	434	−36	167	203	4,786
1890	3,992	299	458	−110	134	244	4,639
1891	4,342	298	481	−16	182	198	5,105
1892	4,291	324	445	−44	191	235	5,016
1893	4,610	315	463	−65	187	252	5,323
1894	4,522	575	574	−117	215	332	5,554
1895	4,791	657	581	−132	232	364	5,897
1896	4,976	459	665	−222	225	447	5,878
1897	4,972	383	777	−382	277	659	5,750
1898	5,278	421	800	−472	282	754	6,027
1899	5,388	476	711	−184	335	519	6,391
1900	5,270	538	703	−244	364	608	6,267

Table A3 (continued)

	Personal consumption expenditure	General government consumption expenditure	Gross domestic fixed-capital formation	Surplus on current account	Exports of goods and services and factor income received from abroad	Less: imports of goods and services and factor income paid abroad	Gross national expenditure at market prices
1901	5,349	603	696	−143	439	582	6,505
1902	5,346	584	668	−179	427	606	6,419
1903	5,363	671	698	−247	429	676	6,485
1904	5,515	1,428	632	−435	449	884	7,140
1905	5,202	1,574	842	−750	427	1,177	6,868
1906	5,169	1,178	866	−399	551	950	6,814
1907	5,840	729	926	−329	598	927	7,166
1908	5,936	710	1,035	−380	542	922	7,301
1909	6,051	740	991	−235	597	832	7,547
1910	6,305	754	1,146	−244	673	917	7,961
1911	6,223	839	1,389	−280	663	943	8,171
1912	6,402	736	1,271	−501	750	1,251	7,908
1913	6,604	672	1,297	−462	966	1,428	8,111
1914	6,430	727	1,272	−223	898	1,121	8,206
1915	6,806	769	1,176	−16	1,141	1,151	8,735
1916	7,193	731	1,252	205	1,498	1,293	9,381
1917	7,521	750	1,598	237	1,563	1,326	10,106
1918	7,949	821	2,038	99	1,627	1,528	10,907
1919	8,697	994	2,283	−504	1,377	1,881	11,470
1920	8,566	1,026	2,471	−564	1,234	1,798	11,499

Table A3 (continued)

	Personal consumption expenditure	General government consumption expenditure	Gross domestic fixed-capital formation	Surplus on current account	Exports of goods and services and factor income received from abroad	Less: imports of goods and services and factor income paid abroad	Gross national expenditure at market prices
1921	9,132	1,039	2,649	−1,028	1,095	2,123	11,792
1922	9,698	1,113	2,381	−1,233	1,199	2,432	11,959
1923	9,867	1,097	1,883	−1,343	1,056	2,399	11,504
1924	10,073	1,113	2,052	−1,398	1,306	2,704	11,840
1925	10,271	1,000	2,225	−975	1,549	2,524	12,521
1926	10,417	1,079	2,338	−1,218	1,643	2,861	12,616
1927	10,718	1,303	2,395	−1,118	1,857	2,975	13,298
1928	11,030	1,594	2,368	−1,074	1,967	3,043	13,918
1929	10,956	1,532	2,504	−1,089	2,186	3,275	13,903
1930	11,005	1,476	2,430	−774	2,211	2,985	14,137
1931	11,247	1,843	2,197	−1,093	2,269	3,362	14,194
1932	11,085	1,982	2,302	−687	2,728	3,415	14,682
1933	11,842	2,175	2,565	−611	2,911	3,522	15,971
1934	12,589	2,062	2,955	−275	3,569	3,826	17,349
1935	12,580	2,103	3,355	344	4,259	3,951	18,382
1936	12,910	2,135	3,559	271	4,508	4,237	18,875
1937	13,567	2,442	4,327	−726	4,608	5,334	19,610
1938	13,057	3,029	5,386	−743	4,439	5,182	20,729
1939	13,433	2,529	6,907	−598	4,127	4,725	22,217
1940	13,389	3,377	7,070	−658	4,276	4,934	23,178

Source: REVISION of LTES 1:213 (table 18). The figures for trade, and thus for GNE, are revised by use of the new price index in table A30.

Table A4. Gross National Expenditure in Constant Prices, 1930–1971 (1930–51: 1934–36 prices, in millions of yen; 1952–71: 1965 prices, in billions of yen)

	Private consumption expenditure	General government consumption expenditure	Gross domestic fixed capital formation	Increase in stocks	Exports of goods and services and factor income received from abroad	Less: imports of goods and services and factor income paid abroad	Gross national expenditure at market prices
1930	10,899	1,674	1,213	287	2,524	3,128	13,469
1931	10,837	2,308	1,083	489	2,894	3,724	13,887
1932	10,800	2,519	1,604	−18	2,872	3,704	14,073
1933	10,836	2,621	1,815	7	2,976	3,593	14,662
1934	11,052	2,522	2,364	606	3,478	3,778	16,244
1935	10,726	2,611	2,398	735	4,205	4,051	16,624
1936	11,003	2,618	2,468	928	4,471	4,340	17,148
1937	11,540	4,247	3,109	1,550	5,407	4,546	21,307
1938	11,382	5,491	3,958	820	4,978	4,661	21,968
1939	10,839	4,688	5,002	981	5,225	4,672	22,093
1940	9,723	4,896	4,610	1,189	5,684	5,474	20,628
1941	9,410	6,134	4,607	1,316	4,433	4,992	20,908
1942	8,956	6,460	3,901	2,071	3,246	3,814	20,820
1943	8,469	7,445	4,771	820	2,910	3,330	21,085
1944	7,006	7,301	4,723	1,218	2,310	2,445	20,113
1946	6,826	1,123	2,545	812	102	534	10,874
1947	7,410	828	2,965	1,273	247	757	11,966
1948	8,391	1,360	2,973	1,734	352	889	13,921
1949	9,297	1,619	2,756	1,230	753	1,186	14,469
1950	10,077	1,838	2,741	1,277	1,614	1,307	16,240
1951	11,040	2,022	2,929	2,009	2,187	1,757	18,430

Table A4 (continued)

	Private consumption expenditure	General government consumption expenditure	Gross domestic fixed capital formation	Increase in stocks	Exports of goods and services and factor income received from abroad	Less: imports of goods and services and factor income paid abroad	Gross national expenditure at market prices
1952	6,305	1,780	1,817	363	798	556	10,506
1953	7,104	1,806	2,091	45	798	743	11,101
1954	7,454	1,848	2,255	153	855	781	11,783
1955	8,041	1,840	2,291	499	977	790	12,859
1956	8,672	1,832	2,798	474	1,150	1,037	13,888
1957	9,217	1,822	3,323	658	1,304	1,326	14,997
1958	9,885	1,905	3,462	273	1,389	1,113	15,801
1959	10,660	2,004	3,968	443	1,563	1,380	17,258
1960	11,743	2,094	5,225	559	1,799	1,720	19,699
1961	12,753	2,222	6,700	1,359	1,924	2,193	22,766
1962	13,972	2,409	7,422	380	2,243	2,199	24,228
1963	15,342	2,619	8,158	856	2,409	2,601	26,785
1964	17,136	2,775	9,551	1,062	2,908	2,980	30,453
1965	18,112	2,943	9,765	705	3,563	3,197	31,891
1966	19,599	3,103	10,920	949	4,114	3,582	35,104
1967	21,598	3,272	12,895	2,090	4,374	4,382	39,847
1968	23,748	3,499	15,751	2,180	5,356	4,946	45,589
1969	25,973	3,722	18,437	2,110	6,430	5,656	51,016
1970	27,942	3,981	20,966	2,842	7,463	6,830	56,363
1971	29,944	4,279	22,512	1,379	8,788	7,061	59,841

Source: Reprinted from LTES 1:214 (table 18A); same issues of ARNIS as table A2.
Note: Figures for 1945 are not available; 1946–51 data are for fiscal years.

Table A5. Savings in Current Prices, 1885–1940

(in millions of yen)

	Series A							Series B			
	Gross national savings	Net lendings to the rest of the world	Net national savings	Provisions for the consumption of fixed capital	Private savings	Corporate	Government savings	Gross national savings	Net national savings	Private savings	Military capital formation
1885	87	−3	11	76	−22	—	33	145	69	36	7
1886	103	7	26	77	0	—	26	167	90	64	5
1887	88	−7	−1	89	−27	—	26	142	53	27	5
1888	124	−4	35	89	8	—	27	117	28	1	6
1889	135	1	41	94	10	—	31	116	22	−9	7
1890	115	−30	19	96	−1	—	20	229	133	113	8
1891	169	17	73	96	54	—	19	108	12	−7	8
1892	164	18	59	105	35	—	24	185	80	56	7
1893	159	0	49	110	16	—	33	128	18	−15	6
1894	185	−10	66	119	103	—	−37	235	116	153	25
1895	345	118	212	133	264	—	−52	317	184	236	24
1896	309	23	155	154	177	—	−22	229	75	97	22
1897	292	−57	109	183	150	—	−41	244	61	102	53
1898	323	−40	127	196	151	—	−24	561	365	389	63
1899	340	28	135	205	133	—	2	219	14	12	64
1900	280	−51	61	219	57	—	4	351	132	128	60

Table A5 (continued)

	Series A							Series B			
	Gross national savings	Net lendings to the rest of the world	Net national savings	Provisions for the consumption of fixed capital	Private savings	Corporate	Government savings	Gross national savings	Net national savings	Private savings	Military capital formation
1901	351	16	131	220	105	—	26	381	161	135	44
1902	331	26	115	216	50	—	65	244	28	−37	30
1903	327	−6	99	228	79	—	20	434	206	186	33
1904	174	−131	−65	239	259	—	−324	74	−165	159	59
1905	113	−326	−159	272	208	—	−367	62	−210	157	78
1906	452	−24	159	293	300	15	−141	645	352	493	64
1907	568	4	233	335	133	19	100	765	430	330	70
1908	520	−63	191	329	15	20	176	731	402	226	80
1909	536	4	215	321	29	8	186	635	314	128	65
1910	552	−73	216	336	10	1	206	531	195	−11	64
1911	684	−99	326	358	133	20	193	751	393	200	77
1912	669	−108	258	411	−7	32	265	918	507	242	80
1913	681	−99	248	433	−63	31	311	902	469	158	81
1914	707	−13	277	430	12	25	265	757	327	62	86
1915	939	220	466	473	215	33	251	1,006	533	282	74
1916	1,584	624	975	609	633	125	342	1,988	1,379	1,037	75
1917	2,636	959	1,765	871	1,351	329	414	2,784	1,913	1,499	139
1918	3,309	834	2,202	1,107	1,812	34	390	3,090	1,983	1,593	228
1919	3,026	379	1,719	1,307	1,266	−145	453	3,278	1,971	1,518	290
1920	3,145	−74	1,345	1,800	1,048	−99	297	2,751	951	654	377

	Series A							Series B			
	Gross national savings	Net lendings to the rest of the world	Net national savings	Provisions for the consumption of fixed capital	Private savings	Corporate	Government savings	Gross national savings	Net national savings	Private savings	Military capital formation
1921	2,191	248	618	1,573	229	−26	389	2,544	971	582	429
1922	2,444	−175	821	1,623	143	45	678	2,417	794	116	356
1923	1,741	−518	32	1,709	−663	−114	695	2,609	900	205	241
1924	2,097	−640	352	1,745	−430	104	782	3,117	1,372	590	192
1925	2,225	−236	636	1,589	−271	102	907	3,181	1,592	685	243
1926	2,286	−377	743	1,538	−157	14	905	3,011	1,473	568	199
1927	2,564	−126	1,006	1,558	290	−11	716	2,480	922	206	202
1928	2,399	−124	794	1,605	277	64	517	2,909	1,304	787	220
1929	2,716	88	1,085	1,631	457	32	628	3,682	2,051	1,423	187
1930	2,192	43	798	1,394	382	−168	416	1,993	599	183	173
1931	1,689	−81	475	1,214	478	−173	−3	1,412	198	201	176
1932	1,763	42	393	1,370	695	−34	−302	2,416	1,046	1,348	309
1933	2,153	43	583	1,570	1,047	181	−464	2,982	1,412	1,876	356
1934	2,502	6	898	1,604	1,122	317	−224	2,561	957	1,181	427
1935	3,114	234	1,440	1,674	1,615	350	−175	2,992	1,318	1,493	466
1936	3,336	232	1,531	1,805	1,592	366	−61	4,033	2,228	2,289	518
1937	3,492	−562	1,064	2,428	1,628	626	−564	4,088	1,660	2,224	1,607
1938	4,260	−560	1,512	2,748	3,948	570	−2,436	5,135	2,387	4,823	3,157
1939	6,376	171	3,236	3,140	6,105	640	−2,869	9,066	5,926	8,795	3,617
1940	7,628	125	3,758	3,870	7,261	1,221	−3,503	10,495	6,625	10,128	4,195

Source: Reprinted from LTES 1:190 (table 6).

Notes: Tentatively estimated by two series: A, disregarding the statistical discrepancies and B, counting them.

Private savings (fifth column) are tentatively estimated by deducting government savings (seventh column) and capital depreciation allowances (fourth column) from gross national savings (first column). For 1895–98, the indemnity from the Sino-Japanese War is treated as a transfer in the second (net lendings) column. Corporate savings for 1906–29 are tentative and are based on Yuzo Yamada's estimates.

Table A6. Savings in Current Prices, 1930–71

(1930–44, in millions of yen; 1946–71, in billions of yen)

	Gross national savings	Net lendings to the rest of the world	Net national savings[a]	Provisions for the consumption of fixed capital	Private savings	Corporate	Government savings	Statistical discrepancies
1930	1,689	234	963	726	521	−168	291	151
1931	1,508	214	820	688	833	−173	−100	87
1932	1,408	45	531	877	1,208	−34	−368	−309
1933	1,778	−26	608	1,170	1,565	181	−496	−461
1934	2,743	−85	1,596	1,147	1,641	317	−134	89
1935	3,372	263	2,139	1,233	2,628	350	−188	−301
1936	3,720	130	2,369	1,351	2,974	366	−19	−586
1937	5,987	193	4,425	1,562	3,577	626	−747	1,595
1938	6,297	−55	4,484	1,813	4,324	570	−2,999	3,159
1939	9,531	597	7,123	2,408	6,636	640	−2,826	3,313
1940	10,701	155	7,919	2,782	8,710	1,221	−3,792	2,938
1941	10,846	−876	7,689	3,157	11,850	1,781	−7,043	2,882
1942	13,689	−914	10,023	3,666	13,550	2,176	−8,404	4,877
1943	15,297	−577	11,025	4,272	16,643	2,519	−11,403	5,785
1944	21,053	398	15,796	5,257	23,106	2,986	−15,450	8,140
1946	100	−6	76	24	7	−1	−23	92
1947	352	7	295	57	−44	−4	148	191
1948	773	21	665	108	−6	2	317	354
1949	905	75	747	158	−5	38	552	200
1950	1,179	171	972	207	602	192	351	19
1951	1,821	158	1,541	280	933	215	452	156

Table A6 (continued)

	Gross national savings	Net lendings to the rest of the world	Net national savings[a]	Provisions for the consumption of fixed capital	Private savings	Corporate	Government savings	Statistical discrepancies
1952	1,745	81	1,311	434	595	153	453	263
1953	1,617	−74	1,064	553	608	214	403	53
1954	1,819	−18	1,118	701	849	300	370	−101
1955	2,207	82	1,416	791	1,074	222	377	−35
1956	2,785	−12	1,851	934	1,225	274	504	122
1957	3,462	−223	2,418	1,044	1,774	555	738	−94
1958	3,287	95	2,158	1,129	1,691	443	619	−152
1959	3,983	130	2,683	1,300	2,025	478	761	−103
1960	5,285	52	3,695	1,590	2,820	956	1,094	−219
1961	7,398	−354	3,561	2,037	3,452	1,050	1,543	367
1962	7,577	−18	5,164	2,413	3,657	966	1,746	−238
1963	8,479	−281	5,624	2,855	3,933	916	1,849	−158
1964	10,313	−173	6,800	3,513	4,315	1,163	1,946	539
1965	10,878	335	6,854	4,024	4,765	956	1,937	151
1966	12,832	450	8,071	4,761	5,787	1,449	2,092	193
1967	16,192	−69	10,686	5,506	7,808	2,290	2,599	279
1968	20,071	377	13,401	6,670	9,882	3,273	3,251	268
1969	23,931	763	15,832	8,099	11,280	3,724	4,271	280
1970	28,764	709	19,193	9,571	14,067	4,758	5,410	−285
1971	30,805	2,002	20,819	10,642	14,958	4,457	5,861	−656

Source: Reprinted from 1:191 (table 6A); same issues of ARNIS as table A2.

Note: Figures for 1945 are not available; 1946–51 data are for fiscal years.

[a] Net national savings (third column) equals gross national savings (first column) minus depreciation allowances (fourth column).

Table A7. Net Domestic Product, Gross National Product, and Personal Disposable Income, in Current Prices, 1885–1940
(In millions of yen)

	Net domestic product at market prices	Net factor income from abroad	Net national product at market prices	Provisions for the consumption of fixed capital	Statistical discrepancies	Gross national product at market prices	Discrepancy ratio[a]	Personal disposable income
1885	789	−1	788	76	−58	806	−7.2	631
1886	789	−2	787	77	−64	800	−8.0	629
1887	785	−2	783	89	−54	818	−6.6	636
1888	772	−2	770	89	7	866	0.8	682
1889	844	−2	842	94	19	955	2.0	763
1890	1,077	−3	1,074	96	−114	1,056	−10.8	866
1891	985	−3	982	96	61	1,139	5.4	952
1892	1,044	−3	1,041	105	−21	1,125	−1.9	919
1893	1,058	−2	1,056	110	31	1,197	2.6	983
1894	1,270	−1	1,269	119	−50	1,338	−3.7	1,107
1895	1,392	−1	1,391	133	28	1,552	1.8	1,299
1896	1,434	−2	1,432	154	80	1,666	4.8	1,394
1897	1,727	−1	1,726	183	48	1,957	2.5	1,651
1898	2,236	0	2,236	196	−238	2,194	−10.8	1,828
1899	1,990	−2	1,988	205	121	2,314	5.2	1,894
1900	2,274	−8	2,266	219	−71	2,414	−2.9	1,948

Table A7 (continued)

	Net domestic product at market prices	Net factor income from abroad	Net national product at market prices	Provisions for the consumption of fixed capital	Statistical discrepancies	Gross national product at market prices	Discrepancy ratio[a]	Personal disposable income
1901	2,300	−6	2,294	220	−30	2,484	−1.2	1,992
1902	2,240	−6	2,234	216	87	2,537	3.4	2,024
1903	2,582	−7	2,575	228	−107	2,696	−4.0	2,174
1904	2,702	−13	2,689	239	100	3,028	3.3	2,509
1905	2,787	−26	2,761	272	51	3,084	1.7	2,475
1906	3,271	−69	3,202	293	−193	3,302	−5.8	2,586
1907	3,656	−51	3,605	335	−197	3,743	−5.3	2,880
1908	3,705	−57	3,648	329	−211	3,766	−5.6	2,854
1909	3,613	−55	3,558	321	−99	3,780	−2.6	2,880
1910	3,628	−60	3,568	336	21	3,925	0.5	2,980
1911	4,236	−64	4,172	358	−67	4,463	−1.5	3,408
1912	4,674	−62	4,612	411	−249	4,774	−5.2	3,615
1913	4,860	−59	4,801	433	−221	5,013	−4.4	3,818
1914	4,418	−60	4,358	430	−50	4,738	−1.1	3,578
1915	4,640	−55	4,585	473	−67	4,991	−1.3	3,793
1916	5,966	−23	5,943	609	−404	6,148	−6.6	4,635
1917	7,859	10	7,869	871	−148	8,592	−1.7	6,416
1918	10,475	38	10,513	1,107	219	11,839	1.8	9,490
1919	14,350	48	14,398	1,307	−252	15,453	−1.6	12,666
1920	13,671	31	13,702	1,800	394	15,896	2.5	12,435

Table A7 (continued)

	Net domestic product at market prices	Net factor income from abroad	Net national product at market prices	Provisions for the consumption of fixed capital	Statistical discrepancies	Gross national product at market prices	Discrepancy ratio[a]	Personal disposable income
1921	13,614	52	13,666	1,573	−353	14,886	−2.4	11,400
1922	13,859	64	13,923	1,623	27	15,573	0.2	11,672
1923	14,018	65	14,083	1,709	−868	14,924	−5.8	11,230
1924	14,786	65	14,851	1,745	−1,020	15,576	−6.6	11,567
1925	15,575	57	15,632	1,589	−956	16,265	−5.9	12,351
1926	15,119	43	15,162	1,538	−725	15,975	−4.5	12,185
1927	14,586	65	14,651	1,558	84	16,293	0.5	12,438
1928	15,364	47	15,411	1,605	−510	16,506	−3.1	12,413
1929	15,561	60	15,621	1,631	−966	16,286	−5.9	12,196
1930	13,062	43	13,105	1,394	199	14,698	1.4	11,431
1931	11,771	47	11,818	1,214	277	13,309	2.1	10,410
1932	12,888	55	12,943	1,370	−653	13,660	−4.8	10,478
1933	14,591	15	14,606	1,570	−829	15,347	−5.4	11,658
1934	15,374	47	15,421	1,604	−59	16,966	−0.3	12,837
1935	16,432	70	16,502	1,674	122	18,298	0.7	13,867
1936	18,097	119	18,216	1,805	−697	19,324	−3.6	14,513
1937	20,890	101	20,991	2,428	−596	22,823	−2.6	16,110
1938	24,478	123	24,601	2,748	−955	26,394	−3.6	19,309
1939	30,676	104	30,780	3,140	−2,690	31,230	−8.6	23,300
1940	35,641	207	35,848	3,870	−2,867	36,851	−7.8	26,247

Source: Reprinted from LTES 1 : 200 (table 8).

Notes: Provisions for consumption of fixed capital were originally estimated in constant prices and then inflated by the investment goods price index in LTES 8 (pp. 158–59, table 7).

The statistical discrepancies are conventionally expressed in terms of GNE − GNP actually estimated.

[a] Statistical discrepancies as a percentage of GNP.

Table A8. Gross National Product in Current Prices, 1930–71
(1930–44, in millions of yen; 1946–71, in billions of yen)

	Net domestic product at factor cost	Net factor income from abroad	Net national product at factor cost	Indirect taxes	Less: current subsidies	Provisions for the consumption of fixed capital	Statistical discrepancies	Gross national product at market prices	Personal disposable income
1930	11,765	−25	11,740	1,235	2	726	151	13,850	11,226
1931	10,540	−23	10,517	1,225	0	688	90	12,520	10,079
1932	11,370	−38	11,332	1,147	4	877	−309	13,043	10,660
1933	12,470	−53	12,417	1,213	5	1,170	−461	14,334	11,476
1934	13,158	−27	13,131	1,309	4	1,147	89	15,672	11,832
1935	14,455	−15	14,440	1,362	0	1,233	−301	16,734	13,003
1936	15,522	24	15,546	1,491	2	1,351	−586	17,800	13,965
1937	18,612	8	18,620	1,651	2	1,562	1,595	23,426	15,676
1938	19,968	40	20,008	1,819	6	1,813	3,159	26,793	17,551
1939	25,337	17	25,354	2,025	17	2,408	3,313	33,083	22,422
1940	30,973	70	31,043	2,710	77	2,782	2,938	39,396	26,538
1941	35,575	259	35,834	3,173	150	3,157	2,882	44,896	30,624
1942	41,759	367	42,126	4,242	545	3,666	4,895	54,384	34,951
1943	48,100	348	48,448	6,094	775	4,272	5,785	63,824	39,796
1944	56,772	165	56,937	6,002	1,833	5,257	8,140	74,503	45,898
1946	361	−0.5	361	24	26	24	91	474	341
1947	969	−0.6	968	129	37	57	192	1,309	875
1948	1,962	−0.5	1,962	353	110	108	354	2,666	1,733
1949	2,738	−0.5	2,737	490	211	158	201	3,375	2,218
1950	3,384	−2.2	3,382	408	68	207	19	3,947	2,782
1951	4,528	−2.5	4,525	519	37	280	157	5,444	3,729

Table A8 (continued)

	Net domestic product at factor cost	Net factor income from abroad	Net national product at factor cost	Indirect taxes	Less: current subsidies	Provisions for the consumption of fixed capital	Statistical discrepancies	Gross national product at market prices	Personal disposable income
1952	4,967	46	5,013	603	49	434	262	6,263	4,304
1953	5,799	43	5,842	687	81	553	53	7,055	5,059
1954	6,534	32	6,566	717	52	701	−101	7,831	5,711
1955	7,087	25	7,113	776	21	791	−35	8,624	6,382
1956	7,836	18	7,855	840	25	934	122	9,726	6,964
1957	9,200	10	9,210	963	42	1,044	−94	11,080	7,815
1958	9,558	3	9,561	1,005	22	1,129	−152	11,522	8,305
1959	10,592	−7	10,585	1,165	21	1,300	−103	12,926	9,269
1960	12,833	−16	12,817	1,364	53	1,590	−219	15,499	10,686
1961	15,193	−37	15,156	1,657	91	2,037	367	19,126	12,508
1962	17,397	−50	17,348	1,775	98	2,413	−238	21,199	14,437
1963	19,961	−66	19,895	1,993	121	2,855	−158	24,464	16,785
1964	22,883	−98	22,785	2,239	156	3,513	539	28,921	19,180
1965	25,636	−99	25,537	2,436	187	4,024	151	31,962	21,914
1966	29,446	−99	29,346	2,750	254	4,761	193	36,796	24,925
1967	35,021	−107	34,914	3,206	360	5,506	279	43,545	29,073
1968	41,642	−150	41,492	3,830	551	6,670	268	51,708	33,907
1969	48,141	−169	47,972	4,486	595	8,099	280	60,242	38,877
1970	57,333	−159	57,174	5,294	769	9,571	−285	70,985	45,602
1971	64,291	−115	64,176	5,750	870	10,642	−656	79,042	59,420

Source: Reprinted from LTES 1:201 (table 8A); same issues of ARNIS as table A2.

Note: Figures for 1945 are not available; 1946–51 data are for fiscal year.

Table A9. Net Domestic Product, Net National Product, and Gross National Product,
in 1934–36 Prices, 1885–1940

(In millions of yen)

	Net domestic product at market prices	Net factor income from abroad	Net national product at market prices	Provisions for the consumption of fixed capital	Statistical discrepancies	Gross national product at market prices	Adjustment item
1885	3,909	− 5	3,904	274	− 280	3,890	− 8
1886	4,215	− 6	4,209	276	− 329	4,114	− 42
1887	4,411	− 6	4,405	281	− 291	4,408	13
1888	4,216	− 6	4,210	288	36	4,529	− 5
1889	4,438	− 7	4,431	295	96	4,786	− 36
1890	4,830	− 8	4,822	303	− 501	4,639	15
1891	4,598	− 8	4,590	310	276	5,105	− 71
1892	4,904	− 8	4,896	316	− 95	5,016	− 101
1893	4,913	− 8	4,905	327	138	5,323	− 47
1894	5,487	− 4	5,483	335	− 205	5,554	− 59
1895	5,542	− 6	5,536	342	106	5,897	− 87
1896	5,240	− 6	5,234	355	282	5,878	7
1897	5,336	− 2	5,334	372	144	5,750	− 100
1898	6,349	1	6,350	385	− 651	6,027	− 57
1899	5,876	− 5	5,871	395	332	6,391	− 207
1900	6,120	− 13	6,107	407	− 182	6,267	− 65
1901	6,342	− 13	6,329	416	− 78	6,505	− 162
1902	5,998	− 12	5,986	432	218	6,419	− 217
1903	6,533	− 14	6,519	442	− 259	6,485	− 217
1904	6,581	− 24	6,557	456	236	7,140	− 109
1905	6,350	− 47	6,303	471	117	6,868	− 23
1906	7,176	− 122	7,054	488	− 395	6,814	− 333
1907	7,405	− 81	7,324	509	− 380	7,166	− 287
1908	7,486	− 96	7,390	536	− 409	7,301	− 216
1909	7,481	− 96	7,385	559	− 196	7,547	− 201
1910	7,556	− 104	7,452	584	40	7,961	− 115
1911	7,896	− 104	7,792	615	− 123	8,171	− 113
1912	8,092	− 95	7,997	647	− 411	7,908	− 325
1913	8,174	− 88	8,086	680	− 357	8,111	− 298
1914	7,881	− 97	7,784	706	− 90	8,206	− 194
1915	8,608	− 94	8,514	723	− 114	8,735	− 388
1916	9,970	− 36	9,934	754	− 619	9,381	− 688
1917	10,298	13	10,311	804	− 172	10,106	− 837
1918	10,391	35	10,426	867	196	10,907	− 582
1919	11,429	35	11,464	939	− 184	11,470	− 749
1920	10,663	21	10,684	1,011	287	11,499	− 483

Table A9 (continued)

	Net domestic product at market prices	Net factor income from abroad	Net national product at market prices	Provisions for the consumption of fixed capital	Statistical discrepancies	Gross national product at market prices	Adjustment item
1921	11,791	38	11,829	1,068	−283	11,792	−822
1922	11,854	48	11,902	1,115	24	11,959	−1,082
1923	11,898	49	11,947	1,145	−667	11,504	−921
1924	12,319	49	12,368	1,185	−781	11,840	−932
1925	12,764	43	12,807	1,221	−789	12,521	−768
1926	12,778	35	12,813	1,263	−568	12,616	−892
1927	12,869	53	12,922	1,312	66	13,298	−1,002
1928	13,960	40	14,000	1,356	−431	13,918	−1,007
1929	14,426	51	14,477	1,400	−820	13,903	−1,154
1930	13,279	42	13,321	1,439	198	14,137	−821
1931	13,378	51	13,429	1,471	298	14,194	−1,004
1932	14,502	59	14,561	1,505	−705	14,682	−679
1933	15,962	15	15,977	1,554	−862	15,971	−698
1934	15,938	48	15,986	1,616	−52	17,349	−201
1935	16,339	70	16,409	1,688	129	18,382	156
1936	17,591	116	17,707	1,764	−680	18,875	84
1937	18,410	90	18,500	1,853	−510	19,610	−233
1938	19,682	99	19,781	1,939	−746	20,729	−245
1939	22,702	75	22,777	2,060	−1,911	22,217	−709
1940	23,321	140	23,461	2,199	−1,808	23,178	−674

Source: REVISION of LTES 1:225 (table 23). Revisions are from changes in the export and import price indexes.

Notes: Net income received from abroad is tentatively deflated by the implicit deflator for total expenditure.

The adjustment item is for treating overseas current surplus, which comes from estimating the real net product of the services sector as a residual. See ch. 6.

Table A10. Net Domestic Product at Market Prices by Industry, in Current Prices, 1885–1940
(In millions of yen)

	Agriculture, forestry, and fishery	Manufacturing and mining	Construction	Facilitating industry	Commerce-services	Subtotal	Imputed house rent	Total = net domestic product
1885	339	86	24	18	283	750	39	789
1886	332	93	24	19	280	748	41	789
1887	314	100	31	19	277	741	44	785
1888	296	106	28	20	275	725	47	772
1889	315	128	34	20	295	792	52	844
1890	496	121	36	21	350	1,024	53	1,077
1891	414	117	38	22	338	929	56	985
1892	440	127	33	23	364	987	57	1,044
1893	430	142	34	24	370	1,000	58	1,058
1894	548	160	41	30	436	1,215	55	1,270
1895	567	193	48	39	482	1,329	63	1,392
1896	548	218	64	42	489	1,361	73	1,434
1897	638	272	95	53	594	1,652	75	1,727
1898	971	319	100	61	708	2,159	77	2,236
1899	749	353	92	68	642	1,904	86	1,990
1900	858	365	97	85	772	2,177	97	2,274

Table A10 (continued)

	Agriculture, forestry, and fishery	Manufacturing and mining	Construction	Facilitating industry	Commerce–services	Subtotal	Imputed house rent	Total = net domestic product
1901	866	370	99	84	777	2,196	104	2,300
1902	800	360	90	80	811	2,141	99	2,240
1903	1,016	390	99	85	877	2,467	115	2,582
1904	1,042	404	72	108	958	2,584	118	2,702
1905	877	477	86	144	1,085	2,669	118	2,787
1906	1,122	610	114	170	1,130	3,146	125	3,271
1907	1,328	695	176	194	1,126	3,519	137	3,656
1908	1,325	669	158	203	1,188	3,543	162	3,705
1909	1,181	700	156	209	1,192	3,438	175	3,613
1910	1,119	741	157	230	1,201	3,448	180	3,628
1911	1,487	774	171	257	1,358	4,047	189	4,236
1912	1,713	852	188	278	1,436	4,467	207	4,674
1913	1,747	960	194	285	1,471	4,657	203	4,860
1914	1,348	957	186	300	1,425	4,216	202	4,418
1915	1,289	1,130	197	343	1,487	4,446	194	4,640
1916	1,593	1,677	190	462	1,843	5,765	201	5,966
1917	2,173	2,250	244	595	2,380	7,642	217	7,859
1918	3,307	3,112	344	769	2,701	10,233	242	10,475
1919	5,032	3,755	478	767	4,043	14,075	275	14,350
1920	4,036	3,218	669	1,066	4,374	13,363	308	13,671

Table A10 (continued)

	Agriculture, forestry, and fishery	Manufacturing and mining	Construction	Facilitating industry	Commerce–services	Subtotal	Imputed house rent	Total = net domestic product
1921	3,855	2,851	673	1,201	4,668	13,248	366	13,614
1922	3,480	3,013	761	1,276	4,846	13,376	483	13,859
1923	3,628	2,957	820	1,304	4,783	13,492	526	14,018
1924	3,941	3,110	823	1,402	4,930	14,206	580	14,786
1925	4,193	3,187	852	1,583	5,081	14,896	679	15,575
1926	3,571	3,125	862	1,641	5,236	14,435	684	15,119
1927	3,406	3,093	820	1,519	5,070	13,908	678	14,586
1928	3,214	3,543	844	1,605	5,440	14,646	718	15,364
1929	3,182	3,879	836	1,655	5,241	14,793	768	15,561
1930	2,163	3,166	727	1,596	4,659	12,311	751	13,062
1931	1,823	2,945	616	1,535	4,103	11,002	749	11,771
1932	2,236	3,371	626	1,445	4,451	12,129	759	12,888
1933	2,736	3,794	890	1,394	5,031	13,845	746	14,591
1934	2,491	4,256	892	1,525	5,480	14,644	730	15,374
1935	2,844	4,765	985	1,607	5,508	15,709	723	16,432
1936	3,283	5,150	1,429	1,664	5,802	17,328	769	18,097
1937	3,725	6,286	1,719	1,830	6,547	20,107	783	20,890
1938	3,969	8,814	1,822	1,931	7,088	23,624	854	24,478
1939	5,893	11,506	2,264	2,183	8,001	29,847	829	30,676
1940	6,527	13,758	2,661	2,443	9,275	34,664	977	35,641

Source: Reprinted from LTES 1:202 (table 9).
Note: Imputed house rent is adjusted for regional rent levels.

Table A11. Net Domestic Product at Factor Cost by Industry, in Current Prices, 1930–71
(1930–44, in millions of yen; 1946–71, in billions of yen)

	Agriculture, forestry, and fishery	Manufacturing and mining	Manufacturing	Construction	Facilitating industry	Commerce–services A	Net domestic product
1930	1,983	2,742	2,520	456	1,586	4,998	11,765
1931	1,832	2,364	2,219	436	1,286	4,622	10,540
1932	2,193	2,627	2,480	425	1,261	4,864	11,370
1933	2,669	3,107	2,889	415	1,195	5,084	12,470
1934	2,443	3,540	3,276	437	1,389	5,349	13,158
1935	2,858	4,019	3,683	458	1,518	5,602	14,455
1936	3,262	4,350	3,979	473	1,566	5,871	15,522
1937	3,722	5,119	4,655	508	1,802	7,461	18,612
1938	4,047	6,308	5,677	575	2,074	6,964	19,968
1939	6,116	7,969	7,252	760	2,341	8,151	25,337
1940	7,465	10,164	9,277	964	2,715	9,665	30,973
1941	7,092	12,736	11,711	1,266	2,842	11,639	35,575
1942	8,233	15,241	14,187	1,603	3,391	13,291	41,759
1943	8,315	18,088	16,879	1,876	4,168	15,653	48,100
1944	10,104	20,740	19,340	2,243	5,134	18,551	56,772
1946	140	70	59	25	16	110	361
1947	343	229	200	48	36	313	969
1948	625	521	454	83	105	628	1,962
1949	751	778	709	102	202	905	2,738
1950	879	938	840	137	250	1,180	3,384
1951	1,128	1,293	1,126	172	331	1,604	4,528

Table A11 (continued)

	Agriculture, forestry, and fishery	Manufacturing and mining	Manufacturing	Construction	Facilitating industry	Commerce–services A	Net domestic product
1952	1,146	1,348	1,194	190	425	1,857	4,967
1953	1,238	1,494	1,344	232	531	2,303	5,799
1954	1,460	1,696	1,552	278	581	2,519	6,534
1955	1,634	1,729	1,592	301	630	2,793	7,087
1956	1,568	2,069	1,912	351	715	3,133	7,836
1957	1,720	2,622	2,432	407	840	3,611	9,200
1958	1,699	2,650	2,466	468	913	3,829	9,558
1959	1,768	3,021	2,827	566	1,033	4,204	10,592
1960	1,906	3,953	3,743	701	1,184	5,089	12,833
1961	2,122	4,778	4,559	889	1,449	5,955	15,193
1962	2,277	5,355	5,115	1,115	1,625	7,026	17,397
1963	2,432	6,046	5,830	1,303	1,881	8,298	19,961
1964	2,548	6,898	6,674	1,610	2,111	9,716	22,883
1965	2,881	7,375	7,154	1,802	2,188	11,390	25,636
1966	3,250	8,444	8,211	2,107	2,568	13,077	29,446
1967	3,994	10,268	10,015	2,493	2,903	15,362	35,021
1968	4,189	15,221	12,241	2,981	3,287	18,643	41,642
1969	4,220	14,753	14,415	3,489	3,823	21,856	48,141
1970	4,450	17,478	17,131	4,327	4,575	26,503	57,333
1971	4,254	19,366	18,985	5,091	5,190	30,391	64,291

Source: Reprinted from LTES 1:203 (table 9A); same issues of ARNIS as table A2.

Note: Figures for 1945 are not available; 1946–51 data are for fiscal years. For Commerce–services A, see Notes on table A23.
Factor costs are estimated by the income approach. Figures in market prices, estimated by the production approach, are available in ARNIS and Keizai Antei Honbu (*Nihon Keizai to Kokumin Shotoko* [Gakuyo Shobo 1954]).

Table A12. Gross Domestic Product at Market Prices by Industry, in 1934–36 Prices, 1885–1940
(In millions of yen)

	Agriculture, forestry, and fishery	Manufacturing and mining	Construction	Facilitating industry	Commerce–services A	Gross domestic product[a]	Gross domestic product[b]
1885	1,590	266	88	54	1,716	3,774	3,850
1886	1,747	307	87	58	1,842	4,041	4,178
1887	1,810	328	116	60	1,903	4,217	4,354
1888	1,754	331	99	65	1,777	4,026	4,164
1889	1,606	374	115	67	2,081	4,243	4,385
1890	1,848	369	127	73	2,222	4,639	4,783
1891	1,808	376	139	74	2,012	4,409	4,555
1892	1,864	379	111	77	2,282	4,713	4,861
1893	1,814	399	115	83	2,315	4,726	4,876
1894	1,960	438	128	98	2,678	5,302	5,454
1895	1,987	480	130	117	2,661	5,375	5,529
1896	1,808	511	163	127	2,463	5,072	5,228
1897	1,731	569	206	153	2,521	5,180	5,337
1898	2,175	659	211	157	2,991	6,193	6,354
1899	1,976	663	204	167	2,710	5,720	5,883
1900	2,071	669	197	190	2,839	5,966	6,131
1901	2,173	701	205	199	2,902	6,180	6,348
1902	1,888	683	200	201	2,880	5,852	6,023
1903	2,300	731	214	206	2,823	6,274	6,447
1904	2,371	731	164	239	2,814	6,319	6,494
1905	1,963	785	185	278	3,003	6,214	6,389
1906	2,241	925	226	339	3,317	7,048	7,224
1907	2,380	1,036	308	385	3,168	7,277	7,454
1908	2,406	1,038	275	444	3,161	7,324	7,504
1909	2,410	1,097	291	455	3,056	7,309	7,490
1910	2,294	1,162	296	490	3,182	7,424	7,608

Table A12 (continued)

	Agriculture, forestry, and fishery	Manufacturing and mining	Construction	Facilitating industry	Commerce–services A	Gross domestic product[a]	Gross domestic product[b]
1911	2,444	1,187	314	519	3,371	7,835	8,022
1912	2,439	1,277	325	535	3,545	8,121	8,313
1913	2,476	1,429	339	558	3,449	8,251	8,447
1914	2,713	1,464	348	609	2,859	7,993	8,190
1915	2,691	1,703	352	587	3,420	8,753	8,953
1916	2,944	1,966	291	629	4,304	10,134	10,338
1917	2,867	2,061	282	667	4,603	10,480	10,688
1918	2,775	2,175	306	737	4,595	10,588	10,799
1919	3,003	2,179	359	852	5,291	11,684	11,898
1920	2,984	2,034	349	1,075	4,495	10,937	11,155
1921	2,693	2,152	420	1,373	5,527	12,165	12,386
1922	2,758	2,372	476	1,516	5,000	12,122	12,347
1923	2,682	2,291	495	1,545	5,123	12,136	12,362
1924	2,771	2,356	511	1,702	5,135	12,475	12,707
1925	3,018	2,455	594	1,900	5,026	12,993	13,227
1926	2,794	2,630	641	2,018	5,028	13,111	13,348
1927	2,993	2,767	629	1,946	4,965	13,300	13,541
1928	2,937	3,061	671	2,043	5,689	14,401	14,644
1929	2,982	3,504	674	2,152	5,547	14,859	15,106
1930	3,130	3,520	729	2,236	4,141	13,756	14,006

Table A12 (continued)

	Agriculture, forestry, and fishery	Manufacturing and mining	Construction	Facilitating industry	Commerce–services A	Gross domestic product[a]	Gross domestic product[b]
1931	2,762	3,748	678	2,236	4,447	13,871	14,126
1932	3,082	3,713	677	2,136	5,442	15,050	15,309
1933	3,397	4,083	893	2,109	6,067	16,549	16,813
1934	2,892	4,507	954	2,236	5,986	16,575	16,844
1935	3,052	5,012	1,208	2,485	5,452	17,029	17,304
1936	3,281	5,301	1,427	2,419	5,861	18,289	18,567
1937	3,361	5,407	1,502	2,473	6,428	19,171	19,454
1938	3,267	6,811	1,424	2,595	6,369	20,466	20,752
1939	3,519	8,057	1,515	2,805	7,837	23,733	24,023
1940	3,419	8,773	1,408	2,993	7,839	24,432	24,727

Source: Reprinted from LTES 1 : 227 (table 25).

Note: Imputed house rent is not included. For Commerce–services A, see Notes on table A23.

[a]Sum of first five columns.

[b]Sum of first five columns plus depreciation allowances for residential buildings and riparian works.

Table A13. Gross Domestic Product by Industry, in Current Prices, 1953–70
(In billions of yen)

	Agriculture, forestry, and fishery	Manufacturing and mining	Construction	Facilitating industries	Commerce–services	Gross domestic product
1953	1,350	2,134	334	681	2,404	6,903
1954	1,492	2,241	345	791	2,747	7,596
1955	1,802	2,387	346	895	3,169	8,599
1956	1,725	2,847	439	1,033	3,638	9,682
1957	1,858	3,345	566	1,156	4,168	11,093
1958	1,852	3,211	538	1,222	4,470	11,293
1959	1,952	3,999	672	1,407	5,130	13,160
1960	2,098	5,218	856	1,648	5,986	15,806
1961	2,360	6,428	1,138	2,023	7,171	19,120
1962	2,561	7,063	1,332	2,293	8,387	21,636
1963	2,654	8,291	1,545	2,718	9,867	25,075
1964	2,889	9,440	1,857	3,071	11,392	28,649
1965	3,153	9,904	2,022	3,361	13,082	31,522
1966	3,545	11,694	2,372	3,984	15,285	36,880
1967	4,255	14,465	2,857	4,372	17,661	43,610
1968	4,472	17,659	3,552	4,911	21,290	51,894
1969	4,619	20,863	3,951	5,522	24,375	59,330
1970	4,691	24,795	4,859	6,418	29,533	70,296

Source: ARNIS.
Notes: At market prices. Estimated using the output approach.
Estimates using an income approach thus differ slightly from the series here.

Table A14. Gross Domestic Product by Industry, in 1965 Prices, 1953–70
(In billions of yen)

	Agriculture, forestry, and fishery	Manufacturing and mining	Construction	Facilitating industries	Commerce–services	Gross domestic product
1953	2,077	2,107	545	825	5,213	10,767
1954	2,285	2,287	689	920	5,182	11,361
1955	2,833	2,491	560	1,023	5,852	12,759
1956	2,666	2,824	652	1,152	6,428	13,722
1957	2,741	3,235	790	1,251	6,785	14,802
1958	2,810	3,300	777	1,370	7,165	15,422
1959	3,008	4,135	943	1,584	7,877	17,547
1960	2,997	5,363	1,130	1,856	8,708	20,054
1961	3,069	6,560	1,346	2,235	9,403	22,613
1962	3,121	7,288	1,512	2,509	10,186	24,616
1963	3,033	8,452	1,679	2,945	10,000	26,109
1964	3,130	9,565	1,921	3,159	12,201	29,976
1965	3,153	9,904	2,022	3,361	12,920	31,360
1966	3,258	11,443	2,234	3,929	14,182	35,046
1967	3,643	13,842	2,535	4,307	15,475	39,802
1968	3,739	16,748	3,038	4,625	17,355	45,505
1969	3,575	19,229	3,189	5,185	18,885	50,063
1970	3,508	21,904	3,667	5,888	20,749	55,716

Source: Tokei Kenkyukai: *Keizai Keikaku no tame no Keiryo Moderuni Kansuru Kenkyu.* (1974, pp. 41–42). No official data are available for services, so we have estimated them by applying the same residual method used in the prewar series.
Note: At market prices.

Table A15. Per Capita Gross National Product and Personal Disposable Income in
Current Prices, 1885–1940 and 1952–70
(In yen)

Disposable income	GNP	Disposable income	GNP	Disposable income (In thousands of yen)	GNP
Population series A		Population series B		Population series C	
1885	16.7	21.3	1920	222	284	1952	50	73
1886	16.5	21.0	1921	201	263	1953	58	81
1887	16.6	21.4	1922	203	271	1954	65	89
1888	17.7	22.4	1923	193	257	1955	71	97
1889	19.5	24.4	1924	196	265	1956	77	108
1890	21.9	26.7	1925	207	272	1957	86	122
1891	23.8	28.6	1926	201	263	1958	91	126
1892	22.9	28.0	1927	202	264	1959	100	140
1893	24.3	29.6	1928	198	264	1960	114	166
1894	27.1	32.8	1929	192	257	1961	133	203
1895	31.5	37.7	1930	177	228	1962	152	223
1896	33.5	40.0	1931	159	203	1963	175	254
1897	39.2	46.5	1932	158	206	1964	197	298
1898	43.0	51.6	1933	173	228	1965	223	325
1899	44.0	53.7	1934	188	248	1966	252	372
1900	44.8	55.5	1935	200	264	1967	290	435
1901	45.2	56.4	1936	207	276	1968	335	510
1902	45.3	56.8	1937	228	323	1969	379	588
1903	48.0	59.6	1938	272	372	1970	440	684
1904	54.7	66.0	1939	326	438			
1905	53.4	66.5	1940	365	512			
1906	55.3	70.6						
1907	61.1	79.4						
1908	59.9	79.0						
1909	59.7	78.4						
1910	61.0	80.3						
1911	68.9	90.2						
1912	72.0	95.1						
1913	75.0	98.4						
1914	69.2	91.7						
1915	72.4	95.3						
1916	87.3	115.8						
1917	119.3	159.8						
1918	174.7	217.8						
1919	231.5	282.4						
1920	226.0	288.8						

Sources: Calculated from GNP and disposable income data in table A7 and population
figures in table A53.

Table A16. Agriculture: Production and Output in Current Prices at the Farm Gate, 1874–1940 and 1950–71 (1874–1940, in millions of yen; 1950–71, in billions of yen)

	Field crops			Cocoon	Livestock	Total production	Agricultural intermediate products	Total output	Current inputs	Gross value added
	Rice	Other crops	Total							
1874	186	103	289	15	2	306	—	—	—	—
1875	218	103	321	19	2	342	—	—	—	—
1876	145	105	250	14	3	267	—	—	—	—
1877	155	115	270	24	2	296	—	—	—	—
1878	165	124	289	30	3	322	39	283	45	238
1879	278	148	426	37	4	467	71	396	61	335
1880	344	191	535	36	4	575	75	500	85	415
1881	357	179	536	60	5	601	67	534	85	449
1882	286	174	460	45	5	510	48	462	67	395
1883	202	145	347	31	5	383	37	346	47	299
1884	149	144	293	27	6	326	35	291	43	248
1885	219	154	373	27	6	406	50	356	43	313
1886	200	154	354	39	7	400	46	354	45	309
1887	187	152	339	42	7	388	40	348	51	297
1888	171	150	321	32	9	362	36	326	55	271
1889	180	161	341	33	8	382	39	343	55	288
1890	347	199	546	35	9	590	65	525	62	463
1891	243	203	446	47	10	503	58	445	64	381
1892	273	200	473	46	12	531	57	474	67	407
1893	252	208	460	56	13	529	60	469	71	398
1894	340	236	576	58	15	649	64	585	76	509
1895	328	235	563	76	17	656	63	593	75	518
1896	322	242	564	63	18	645	62	583	89	494
1897	372	276	648	76	20	744	79	665	94	571
1898	666	334	1,000	75	21	1,096	109	987	110	877
1899	414	320	734	97	25	856	91	765	105	660

Table A16 (continued)

| | Field crops | | | | | | Agricultural | | | Gross |
	Rice	Other crops	Total	Cocoon	Livestock	Total production	intermediate products	Total output	Current inputs	value added
1901	506	327	833	92	25	950	84	866	105	761
1902	444	323	767	101	28	896	94	802	108	694
1903	637	385	1,022	116	32	1,170	117	1,053	124	929
1904	646	420	1,066	109	39	1,214	129	1,085	136	949
1905	466	423	889	116	43	1,048	119	929	144	785
1906	647	429	1,076	140	41	1,257	96	1,161	144	1,017
1907	768	485	1,253	192	49	1,494	116	1,378	173	1,205
1908	786	486	1,272	141	49	1,462	118	1,344	159	1,185
1909	636	490	1,126	144	44	1,314	109	1,205	165	1,040
1910	591	492	1,083	147	48	1,278	105	1,173	183	990
1911	895	587	1,482	168	50	1,700	123	1,577	217	1,360
1912	1,043	694	1,737	176	51	1,964	162	1,802	225	1,577
1913	1,042	691	1,733	202	51	1,986	161	1,825	251	1,574
1914	746	563	1,309	191	49	1,549	112	1,437	234	1,203
1915	694	550	1,244	165	53	1,462	99	1,363	199	1,164
1916	827	609	1,436	293	63	1,792	118	1,674	227	1,447
1917	1,104	820	1,924	468	73	2,465	183	2,282	334	1,948
1918	1,824	1,205	3,029	576	100	3,705	282	3,423	469	2,954
1919	2,891	1,655	4,546	837	132	5,515	354	5,161	720	4,441
1920	2,348	1,429	3,777	396	156	4,329	307	4,022	736	3,286
1921	2,018	1,272	3,290	439	171	3,900	217	3,683	443	3,240
1922	1,621	1,153	2,774	629	171	3,574	213	3,361	468	2,893
1923	1,771	1,110	2,881	712	181	3,764	224	3,540	531	3,009
1924	2,214	1,214	3,428	590	191	4,209	253	3,956	552	3,404
1925	2,134	1,345	3,479	869	196	4,544	268	4,276	622	3,654

Table A16 (continued)

| | Field crops | | | | | | Agricultural | | | Gross |
	Rice	Other crops	Total	Cocoon	Livestock	Total production	intermediate products	Total output	Current inputs	value added
1926	1,836	1,169	3,005	697	192	3,894	219	3,675	610	3,065
1927	1,764	1,136	2,900	520	196	3,616	179	3,437	531	2,906
1928	1,633	1,142	2,775	583	209	3,567	218	3,349	558	2,791
1929	1,585	1,113	2,698	690	210	3,598	215	3,383	570	2,813
1930	1,118	854	1,972	319	179	2,470	162	2,308	417	1,891
1931	913	712	1,625	290	155	2,070	130	1,940	352	1,588
1932	1,235	815	2,050	315	152	2,517	146	2,371	375	1,996
1933	1,434	862	2,296	522	171	2,989	160	2,829	391	2,438
1934	1,385	949	2,334	222	177	2,733	169	2,564	428	2,136
1935	1,611	1,004	2,615	371	190	3,176	182	2,994	498	2,496
1936	1,865	1,169	3,034	410	216	3,660	204	3,456	562	2,894
1937	2,072	1,348	3,420	445	233	4,098	247	3,851	645	3,206
1938	2,173	1,481	3,654	368	274	4,296	271	4,025	752	3,273
1939	2,874	2,091	4,965	917	339	6,221	343	5,878	946	4,932
1940	2,554	2,533	5,087	895	456	6,438	413	6,025	877	5,148
1950	368	326	694	24	48	766	—	—	—	—
1951	457	433	890	38	68	996	68	928	185	743
1952	580	478	1,058	50	98	1,206	69	1,137	191	946
1953	585	495	1,080	50	130	1,260	78	1,182	227	955
1954	634	550	1,184	44	135	1,363	78	1,285	262	1,023
1955	862	580	1,442	50	145	1,637	89	1,548	275	1,273
1956	735	579	1,314	46	170	1,530	80	1,450	283	1,167
1957	803	609	1,412	51	185	1,648	88	1,560	323	237
1958	836	595	1,431	42	195	1,668	85	1,583	302	1,281
1959	873	624	1,497	49	219	1,765	81	1,684	326	1,358
1960	898	688	1,586	59	259	1,904	86	1,818	401	1,417

Table A16 (continued)

	Field crops			Cocoon	Livestock	Total production	Agricultural intermediate products	Total output	Current inputs	Gross value added
	Rice	Other crops	Total							
1961	903	819	1,722	64	314	2,100	103	1,997	433	1,564
1962	1,053	907	1,960	67	398	2,425	103	2,322	494	1,828
1963	1,115	863	1,978	80	458	2,516	88	2,428	545	1,883
1964	1,243	990	2,233	63	521	2,817	109	2,708	613	2,095
1965	1,345	1,091	2,436	73	602	3,111	138	2,973	676	2,297
1966	1,508	1,214	2,722	98	692	3,512	127	3,385	780	2,605
1967	1,867	1,328	3,195	124	749	4,068	137	3,931	847	3,084
1968	1,976	1,340	3,316	111	859	4,286	115	4,171	908	3,263
1969	1,941	1,572	3,513	105	951	4,569	129	4,440	990	3,450
1970	1,766	1,655	3,421	126	1,014	4,561	129	4,432	1,080	3,352
1971	1,545	1,564	3,109	103	1,152	4,364	123	4,241	1,127	3,114

Sources:

Norinsho. 1973. *Showa 46 nendo, Nogyo oyobi Noka no Shakai Kanjo.*

Norinsho. 1971. *Norinsho Tokeihyo.*

Sorifu, Tokeikyoku. 1968 and 1971. *Rodoryoku Chosa Hokoku.*

Agricultural production (cols. 1–6): The 1874–1963 data are from LTES 9:146–47 (table 1) with revisions of rice production explained in ch. 4; 1964–69 data are from Norinsho 1973 (pp. 40–41, table 17) excluding changes in plant and livestock inventory. The 1970–71 data are from Norinsho 1971 (pp. 80–81).

Agricultural intermediate products (col. 7): The 1878–1963 data are from LTES 9:183–84 (table 16, col. 6); 1964–69 data are from Norinsho 1973 (table 17, pp. 40–41); 1970–71 data are estimated by multiplying total agricultural production by the ratio of intermediate products to total production in 1969.

Total output (col. 8): Total production (col. 6) minus agricultural intermediate products (col. 7).

Current inputs (col. 9): Current inputs in agriculture supplied from nonagricultural sector. The 1878–1963 data are from LTES 9:183–84 (col. 12); 1964–71 data are the total of the inputs of fertilizers, agricultural chemicals, fuels, feeds, and miscellaneous items in Norinsho 1971 (pp. 84–85, table 15).

Gross value added (col. 10): Total output (col. 8) minus nonfarm current inputs (col. 9).

Note: In principle the data are for Japan Proper, including Okinawa before 1945 but not since 1945.

Table A17. Agriculture: Production and Output in 1934–36 Constant Prices at the Farm Gate, 1874–1971
(In millions of yen)

	Field crops				Livestock	Total production	Agricultural intermediate products	Total output	Gross value added ratio	Gross value added
	Rice	Other crops	Total	Cocoon						
1874	920	408	1,328	33	8	1,369	162	1,207	84.4%	1,019
1875	970	414	1,384	35	8	1,427	168	1,259	84.4	1,063
1876	922	420	1,342	37	9	1,388	164	1,224	84.4	1,033
1877	953	432	1,385	40	9	1,434	169	1,265	84.4	1,068
1878	886	435	1,321	41	9	1,371	173	1,198	84.1	1,008
1879	1,016	464	1,480	43	10	1,533	176	1,357	84.6	1,148
1880	1,000	501	1,501	52	11	1,564	171	1,393	83.0	1,156
1881	972	474	1,446	59	11	1,516	183	1,333	84.1	1,121
1882	975	514	1,489	59	12	1,560	185	1,375	85.5	1,176
1883	984	508	1,492	49	13	1,554	185	1,369	86.4	1,183
1884	889	537	1,426	51	18	1,495	179	1,316	85.2	1,121
1885	1,023	548	1,571	48	21	1,640	176	1,464	87.9	1,287
1886	1,087	584	1,671	49	23	1,743	176	1,567	87.3	1,368
1887	1,144	597	1,741	54	21	1,816	173	1,643	85.3	1,401
1888	1,086	597	1,683	52	30	1,765	174	1,591	83.1	1,322
1889	919	594	1,513	52	21	1,586	174	1,412	84.0	1,186
1890	1,184	617	1,801	52	21	1,874	175	1,699	88.2	1,499
1891	1,049	632	1,681	69	23	1,773	178	1,595	85.6	1,365
1892	1,138	619	1,757	66	25	1,848	175	1,673	85.9	1,437
1893	1,024	629	1,653	75	26	1,754	181	1,573	84.7	1,332
1894	1,150	675	1,825	80	31	1,936	181	1,755	87.0	1,527
1895	1,098	682	1,780	99	33	1,912	181	1,731	87.4	1,513
1896	996	653	1,649	81	33	1,763	182	1,581	84.7	1,339
1897	908	662	1,570	94	35	1,699	186	1,513	85.9	1,300
1898	1,302	713	2,015	89	36	2,140	186	1,954	88.9	1,737
1899	1,091	693	1,784	108	40	1,932	189	1,743	86.3	1,504

Table A17 (continued)

| | Field crops | | | | | | Agricultural | | Gross | |
	Rice	Other crops	Total	Cocoon	Livestock	Total production	intermediate products	Total output	value added ratio	Gross value added
1901	1,289	754	2,043	112	41	2,196	189	2,007	87.9	1,764
1902	1,015	692	1,707	113	44	1,864	190	1,674	86.5	1,448
1903	1,277	730	2,007	114	48	2,169	189	1,980	88.2	1,746
1904	1,413	746	2,159	124	56	2,339	189	2,150	87.5	1,881
1905	1,019	754	1,773	120	48	1,941	181	1,760	84.5	1,487
1906	1,272	778	2,050	130	45	2,225	179	2,046	87.6	1,792
1907	1,348	827	2,175	150	49	2,374	186	2,188	87.5	1,915
1908	1,427	823	2,250	153	49	2,452	188	2,264	88.2	1,997
1909	1,441	816	2,257	156	52	2,465	187	2,278	86.3	1,966
1910	1,281	819	2,100	168	62	2,330	195	2,135	84.3	1,800
1911	1,421	867	2,288	181	66	2,535	197	2,338	86.2	2,015
1912	1,380	892	2,272	190	66	2,528	199	2,329	87.5	2,038
1913	1,381	931	2,312	196	64	2,572	200	2,372	86.2	2,045
1914	1,567	954	2,521	189	63	2,773	197	2,576	83.7	2,156
1915	1,537	972	2,509	199	69	2,777	198	2,579	85.4	2,202
1916	1,606	997	2,603	241	81	2,925	201	2,724	86.4	2,354
1917	1,500	970	2,470	266	79	2,815	202	2,613	85.4	2,232
1918	1,503	922	2,425	284	75	2,784	195	2,589	86.3	2,234
1919	1,671	973	2,644	299	78	3,021	199	2,822	86.1	2,430
1920	1,737	980	2,717	263	82	3,062	194	2,868	81.7	2,343
1921	1,516	946	2,462	260	95	2,817	190	2,627	87.9	2,309
1922	1,668	938	2,606	254	99	2,959	190	2,769	86.1	2,384
1923	1,524	879	2,403	282	105	2,790	194	2,596	84.9	2,204
1924	1,571	873	2,444	298	115	2,857	187	2,670	86.1	2,299
1925	1,641	972	2,613	341	119	3,073	188	2,885	85.4	2,464

Table A17 (continued)

	Field crops			Cocoon	Livestock	Total production	Agricultural intermediate products	Total output	Gross value added ratio	Gross value added
	Rice	Other crops	Total							
1926	1,528	932	2,460	348	117	2,925	187	2,738	83.4	2,283
1927	1,707	951	2,658	365	122	3,145	178	2,967	84.5	2,507
1928	1,657	939	2,596	376	137	3,109	184	2,925	83.3	2,437
1929	1,637	939	2,576	408	150	3,134	180	2,954	83.1	2,455
1930	1,838	981	2,819	423	148	3,390	187	3,203	81.9	2,623
1931	1,517	937	2,454	388	158	3,000	186	2,814	81.8	2,302
1932	1,660	957	2,617	359	184	3,160	185	2,975	84.1	2,502
1933	1,946	1,042	2,988	404	186	3,578	189	3,389	86.1	2,918
1934	1,425	1,012	2,437	348	186	2,971	185	2,786	83.2	2,318
1935	1,579	1,041	2,620	329	196	3,145	188	2,957	83.3	2,463
1936	1,851	1,077	2,928	331	201	3,460	183	3,277	83.7	2,743
1937	1,822	1,135	2,957	342	209	3,508	191	3,317	83.2	2,760
1938	1,810	1,087	2,897	300	207	3,404	191	3,213	81.2	2,609
1939	1,895	1,174	3,069	359	215	3,643	193	3,450	83.9	2,895
1940	1,673	1,148	2,821	346	221	3,388	192	3,196	85.4	2,729
1941	1,514	1,045	2,559	277	173	3,009	194	2,815	82.0	2,308
1942	1,835	1,048	2,883	222	136	3,241	193	3,048	82.0	2,499
1943	1,728	987	2,715	215	128	3,058	178	2,880	82.0	2,362
1944	1,609	968	2,577	159	108	2,844	182	2,662	82.0	2,183
1945	1,648	815	2,463	90	64	2,617	160	2,457	82.0	2,015
1946	1,687	878	2,565	71	69	2,705	152	2,553	82.0	2,093
1947	1,612	872	2,484	57	74	2,615	129	2,486	82.0	2,039
1948	1,826	989	2,815	67	84	2,966	135	2,831	82.0	2,321
1949	1,554	1,040	2,594	65	112	2,771	146	2,625	82.0	2,153
1950	1,768	1,146	2,914	83	161	3,158	171	2,987	82.0	2,449

Table A17 (continued)

	Field crops			Cocoon	Livestock	Total production	Agricultural intermediate products	Total output	Gross value added ratio	Gross value added
	Rice	Other crops	Total							
1951	1,656	1,202	2,858	97	188	3,143	219	2,924	80.1	2,342
1952	1,818	1,359	3,177	107	271	3,555	222	3,333	83.2	2,773
1953	1,509	1,220	2,729	97	314	3,140	237	2,903	80.8	2,346
1954	1,670	1,300	2,970	106	357	3,433	289	3,144	79.5	2,499
1955	2,269	1,469	3,738	120	409	4,267	268	3,999	82.1	3,283
1956	1,997	1,494	3,491	113	445	4,049	246	3,803	80.3	3,054
1957	2,100	1,528	3,628	125	488	4,241	255	3,986	79.1	3,153
1958	2,197	1,494	3,691	122	542	4,355	268	4,087	80.6	3,294
1959	2,290	1,595	3,885	116	591	4,592	255	4,337	80.3	3,483
1960	2,356	1,681	4,037	117	623	4,777	276	4,501	77.6	3,493
1961	2,275	1,704	3,979	120	759	4,858	321	4,537	78.0	3,539
1962	2,383	1,671	4,054	108	903	5,065	294	4,771	78.4	3,740
1963	2,347	1,511	3,858	110	956	4,924	235	4,689	77.2	3,620
1964	2,307	1,639	3,946	111	1,083	5,140	215	4,925	77.4	3,812
1965	2,275	1,663	3,938	105	1,145	5,188	196	4,992	77.3	3,859
1966	2,335	1,712	4,047	105	1,219	5,371	194	5,177	77.0	3,986
1967	2,649	1,757	4,406	114	1,316	5,836	193	5,643	78.5	4,430
1968	2,647	1,867	4,514	121	1,377	6,012	190	5,822	78.2	4,553
1969	2,566	1,723	4,289	114	1,535	5,938	200	5,738	77.8	4,464
1970	2,326	1,701	4,027	111	1,689	5,827	218	5,609	75.6	4,240
1971	1,998	1,743	3,741	107	1,760	5,608	240	5,368	73.4	3,940

Table A17 (continued)

Sources: See table A16 for bibliographic data.

Agricultural production (cols. 1–6): The 1874–1963 data are from LTES 9:152–53 (table 4) with revisions of rice production explained in the text. Straw products are included in (col. 2) other crops. The 1964–71 data are extended by commodity groups from the 1963 data by the Index of Agricultural Production (1970 = 100) prepared by Norinsho (1971, pp. 332–33).

Agricultural intermediate products (col. 7): Current inputs in agriculture produced within the agricultural sector, including seeds, silkworm eggs, feed produced within domestic agriculture, green manure and forage crops, and others. The 1878–1963 data are from LTES 9:186–87 (table 16, col. 6); 1874–77 data are the series of total agricultural production multiplied by the 1878–82 average ratio of agricultural intermediate products to total agricultural production; for 1964–71, the figures are the difference between total production (col. 6) and total output (col. 8).

Total output (col. 8): For 1874–1963, total production (col. 6) minus agricultural intermediate products (col. 7). The 1964–71 data are extended from the 1963 data by the Index of Total Agricultural Output (1970 = 100) prepared by Norinsho (1971, p. 330).

Gross value added ratio (col. 9): Ratio of gross value added to total output in current prices. Data from table A16 for cols. 8 and 10. The 1874–77 data are the 1878–82 average. The 1941–50 data are the 1933–37 and 1953–57 average.

Gross value added (col. 10): Total output (col. 8) multiplied by gross value added ratio (col. 9).

Note: In principle the data are for Japan Proper, including Okinawa before 1945 but not since 1945.

	Labor (1,000 workers)			Arable land (1,000 hectares)			Fixed capital (million yen, 1934–36 prices)				Nonfarm current inputs		
	Male	Female	Total	Paddy field	Upland field	Total	Livestock and plants	Machinery and implements	Building	Total	Fertilizer	Others	Total
1874	8,284	7,212	15,496	2,738	1,900	4,638	667	534	1,450	2,651	—	—	—
1875	8,284	7,219	15,503	2,744	1,908	4,652	686	538	1,462	2,686	—	—	—
1876	8,299	7,227	15,526	2,750	1,915	4,665	708	543	1,476	2,727	—	—	—
1877	8,309	7,236	15,545	2,759	1,923	4,682	735	547	1,494	2,776	—	—	—
1878	8,318	7,244	15,562	2,759	1,932	4,691	774	552	1,512	2,838	27	52	79
1879	8,327	7,252	15,579	2,782	1,939	4,721	796	556	1,530	2,882	31	55	86
1880	8,336	7,260	15,596	2,802	1,947	4,749	815	561	1,546	2,922	30	55	85
1881	8,339	7,263	15,602	2,805	1,951	4,756	834	565	1,560	2,959	30	59	89
1882	8,338	7,263	15,601	2,804	1,966	4,770	836	569	1,560	2,965	27	63	90
1883	8,340	7,263	15,603	2,817	1,981	4,798	844	574	1,566	2,984	27	63	90
1884	8,346	7,270	15,616	2,818	1,986	4,804	818	578	1,554	2,950	31	63	94
1885	8,338	7,263	15,601	2,824	1,990	4,814	841	582	1,566	2,989	27	62	89
1886	8,335	7,260	15,595	2,828	2,004	4,832	860	586	1,576	3,022	28	62	90
1887	8,338	7,262	15,600	2,839	2,021	4,860	860	590	1,578	3,028	27	63	90
1888	8,338	7,263	15,601	2,848	2,041	4,889	860	594	1,578	3,032	28	63	91
1889	8,343	7,264	15,607	2,852	2,048	4,900	879	598	1,592	3,069	27	64	91
1890	8,356	7,275	15,631	2,858	2,064	4,922	907	602	1,608	3,117	27	65	92
1891	8,364	7,284	15,648	2,863	2,082	4,945	926	608	1,620	3,154	30	67	97
1892	8,371	7,287	15,658	2,865	2,099	4,964	958	612	1,638	3,208	28	72	100
1893	8,366	7,278	15,644	2,869	2,108	4,977	975	615	1,648	3,238	32	71	103
1894	8,366	7,278	15,645	2,870	2,133	5,003	976	621	1,650	3,247	32	73	105
1895	8,385	7,290	15,675	2,877	2,157	5,034	1,013	626	1,670	3,309	32	72	104
1896	8,416	7,315	15,731	2,878	2,181	5,059	1,046	634	1,690	3,370	32	75	107
1897	8,417	7,313	15,730	2,880	2,210	5,090	1,066	638	1,702	3,406	33	77	110
1898	8,444	7,333	15,777	2,890	2,232	5,122	1,091	644	1,712	3,447	32	79	111
1899	8,474	7,354	15,828	2,897	2,278	5,175	1,075	651	1,712	3,438	35	80	115
1900	8,483	7,361	15,844	2,905	2,295	5,200	1,071	655	1,714	3,440	39	82	121

294 *Appendix Tables*

Table A18 (continued)

	Labor (1,000 workers)			Arable land (1,000 hectares)			Fixed capital (million yen, 1934–36 prices)				Nonfarm current inputs		
	Male	Female	Total	Paddy field	Upland field	Total	Livestock and plants	Machinery and implements	Building	Total	Fertilizer	Others	Total
1901	8,477	7,356	15,833	2,913	2,311	5,224	1,092	659	1,726	3,477	45	84	129
1902	8,495	7,371	15,866	2,914	2,329	5,243	1,114	666	1,736	3,516	49	85	134
1903	8,487	7,363	15,850	2,922	2,322	5,244	1,136	681	1,754	3,571	54	88	142
1904	8,489	7,366	15,855	2,929	2,353	5,282	1,121	697	1,750	3,568	45	89	134
1905	8,476	7,355	15,831	2,936	2,364	5,300	1,158	713	1,770	3,641	54	84	138
1906	8,619	7,462	16,081	2,947	2,373	5,320	1,220	729	1,818	3,767	59	84	143
1907	8,572	7,452	16,024	2,956	2,444	5,400	1,287	747	1,844	3,878	73	90	163
1908	8,547	7,429	15,976	2,972	2,468	5,440	1,293	764	1,854	3,911	81	95	176
1909	8,473	7,416	15,839	2,994	2,539	5,533	1,336	782	1,882	4,000	99	100	199
1910	8,495	7,288	15,783	3,007	2,572	5,579	1,372	798	1,906	4,076	97	103	200
1911	8,568	7,326	15,894	3,021	2,610	5,631	1,388	816	1,916	4,120	117	108	225
1912	8,604	7,280	15,884	3,037	2,647	5,684	1,402	832	1,930	4,164	113	110	223
1913	8,669	7,192	15,861	3,049	2,659	5,708	1,416	850	1,942	4,208	139	113	252
1914	8,685	7,157	15,842	3,059	2,677	5,736	1,420	867	1,950	4,237	129	113	242
1915	8,239	6,820	15,059	3,072	2,705	5,777	1,447	883	1,950	4,280	120	114	234
1916	8,157	6,706	14,863	3,086	2,740	5,826	1,462	900	1,976	4,338	123	118	241
1917	8,204	6,730	14,934	3,102	2,776	5,878	1,476	918	1,988	4,382	143	119	262
1918	7,565	6,469	14,034	3,110	2,831	5,941	1,483	935	1,998	4,416	161	121	282
1919	7,725	6,368	14,093	3,118	2,853	5,971	1,498	953	1,998	4,449	207	126	333
1920	7,577	6,342	13,919	3,136	2,862	5,998	1,486	970	2,012	4,468	175	127	302

Table A18 (continued)

	Labor (1,000 workers)			Arable land (1,000 hectares)			Fixed capital (million yen, 1934–36 prices)				Nonfarm current inputs		
	Male	Female	Total	Paddy field	Upland field	Total	Livestock and plants	Machinery and implements	Building	Total	Fertilizer	Others	Total
1921	7,630	6,394	14,024	3,141	2,860	6,001	1,497	983	2,026	4,506	171	131	302
1922	7,633	6,304	13,937	3,161	2,846	6,007	1,497	997	2,032	4,526	171	136	307
1923	7,369	6,090	13,459	3,176	2,788	5,964	1,519	1,014	2,048	4,581	198	146	344
1924	7,398	6,263	13,661	3,185	2,742	5,927	1,520	1,034	2,056	4,610	194	158	352
1925	7,395	6,132	13,527	3,199	2,715	5,914	1,537	1,055	2,070	4,662	201	161	362
1926	7,360	6,118	13,478	3,209	2,702	5,911	1,549	1,074	2,080	4,703	246	163	409
1927	7,408	6,147	13,555	3,228	2,690	5,920	1,575	1,094	2,098	4,767	248	166	414
1928	7,467	6,234	13,701	3,246	2,690	5,936	1,598	1,118	2,116	4,832	258	170	428
1929	7,592	6,303	13,895	3,262	2,680	5,942	1,619	1,139	2,130	4,888	276	183	459
1930	7,579	6,365	13,944	3,274	2,688	5,962	1,646	1,163	2,150	4,959	269	161	430
1931	7,691	6,355	14,046	3,282	2,717	5,999	1,665	1,189	2,164	5,018	279	191	470
1932	7,827	6,444	14,271	3,290	2,747	6,037	1,668	1,212	2,174	5,054	250	178	428
1933	7,698	6,411	14,109	3,296	2,778	6,074	1,670	1,231	2,182	5,083	246	173	419
1934	7,649	6,284	13,933	3,293	2,794	6,087	1,662	1,250	2,186	5,098	266	199	465
1935	7,531	6,141	13,672	3,290	2,814	6,104	1,660	1,271	2,194	5,125	289	187	476
1936	7,432	6,260	13,692	3,288	2,842	6,130	1,671	1,289	2,206	5,166	342	204	546
1937	6,978	6,494	13,472	3,288	2,854	6,142	1,651	1,303	2,200	5,154	323	203	526
1938	6,562	6,730	13,292	3,280	2,844	6,124	1,660	1,310	2,210	5,180	366	210	576
1939	6,221	6,957	13,178	3,280	2,843	6,123	1,701	1,328	2,234	5,263	357	219	576
1940	6,362	7,183	13,545	3,277	2,845	6,122	1,723	1,351	2,250	5,324	335	178	513

Table A18 (continued)

	Labor (1,000 workers)			Arable land (1,000 hectares)			Fixed capital (million yen, 1934–36 prices)				Nonfarm current inputs		
	Male	Female	Total	Paddy field	Upland field	Total	Livestock and plants	Machinery and implements	Building	Total	Fertilizer	Others	Total
1941	6,290	7,330	13,620	3,273	2,828	6,101	1,648	1,328	2,220	5,196	326	159	485
1942	5,880	7,410	13,290	3,273	2,804	6,077	1,586	1,305	2,198	5,089	326	131	457
1943	5,580	7,600	13,180	3,263	2,780	6,043	1,477	1,271	2,144	4,892	262	107	369
1944	5,390	7,940	13,330	3,232	2,734	5,966	1,301	1,249	2,060	4,610	201	83	284
1945	6,130	7,640	13,770	3,153	2,588	5,741	1,114	1,247	1,968	4,329	88	43	131
1946	6,950	7,430	14,380	3,170	2,596	5,766	1,044	1,218	1,932	4,194	113	36	149
1947	7,250	7,760	15,010	3,186	2,604	5,790	1,061	1,225	1,972	4,258	222	72	294
1948	7,870	7,980	15,850	3,201	2,611	5,812	1,091	1,268	2,010	4,369	273	99	372
1949	7,890	8,890	16,780	3,216	2,619	5,835	1,144	1,323	2,056	4,523	382	134	516
1950	7,720	8,280	16,000	3,231	2,627	5,858	1,164	1,357	2,080	4,601	434	144	578
1951	7,410	7,830	15,240	3,244	2,634	5,878	1,233	1,409	2,138	4,780	403	211	614
1952	7,570	7,990	15,560	3,258	2,635	5,893	1,195	1,461	2,198	4,854	372	226	598
1953	7,480	7,960	15,440	3,267	2,637	5,904	1,343	1,504	2,228	5,075	560	296	856
1954	7,370	7,910	15,280	3,282	2,653	5,935	1,413	1,567	2,280	5,260	587	335	922
1955	7,350	8,060	15,410	3,302	2,680	5,982	1,521	1,652	2,356	5,529	633	362	995
1956	7,150	7,870	15,020	3,320	2,693	6,013	1,095	1,773	2,430	5,298	677	384	1,061
1957	6,990	7,720	14,710	3,335	2,709	6,044	1,629	1,881	2,484	5,994	672	437	1,109
1958	6,610	7,430	14,040	3,345	2,719	6,064	1,700	2,025	2,564	6,289	656	471	1,127
1959	6,490	7,310	13,800	3,364	2,708	6,072	1,748	2,229	2,656	6,633	712	558	1,270
1960	6,230	7,160	13,390	3,382	2,690	6,072	1,851	2,496	2,786	7,133	776	672	1,448

	Labor (1,000 workers)			Arable land (1,000 hectares)			Fixed capital (million yen, 1934–36 prices)				Nonfarm current inputs		
	Male	Female	Total	Paddy field	Upland field	Total	Livestock and plants	Machinery and implements	Building	Total	Fertilizer	Others	Total
1961	5,990	7,040	13,030	3,389	2,697	6,086	1,989	2,783	2,924	7,696	751	764	1,515
1962	5,840	6,890	12,730	3,393	2,689	6,082	2,067	3,242	3,098	8,407	772	907	1,679
1963	5,530	6,520	12,050	3,399	2,662	6,061	2,344	4,005	3,414	9,763	804	1,007	1,811
1964	5,240	6,370	11,610	3,392	2,650	6,042	2,419	4,528	4,076	11,023	836	1,213	2,049
1965	5,030	6,140	11,170	3,391	2,614	6,005	2,576	4,793	3,812	11,181	861	1,304	2,165
1966	4,890	5,920	10,810	3,396	2,600	5,996	2,724	5,105	3,959	11,788	953	1,538	2,491
1967	4,760	5,770	10,530	3,415	2,524	5,939	2,802	6,537	4,382	13,721	1,021	1,693	2,714
1968	4,710	5,560	10,270	3,435	2,462	5,897	3,142	7,631	4,540	15,313	956	1,784	2,740
1969	4,630	5,300	9,930	3,441	2,411	5,852	3,528	7,724	4,498	15,750	982	2,291	3,273
1970	4,350	4,970	9,320	3,415	2,381	5,796	3,753	8,062	4,791	16,606	934	2,515	3,449
1971	3,980	4,510	8,490	3,364	2,377	5,741	3,410	8,234	4,428	16,072	923	2,639	3,562

Sources: See table A16 for bibliographic data.

Labor (cols. 1–3): The 1878–1920 data are Umemura's estimates of the number of gainful workers in agriculture and forestry in table A53 multiplied by the ratio of the number of workers in agriculture to the number in agriculture and forestry in the 1920 Population Census. The 1921–40 data are estimated by multiplying the Umemura series by ratios of the number of agricultural and forestry workers to the number of agricultural and forestry workers that have been estimated by interpolating between the ratios in 1920, 1930, and 1940 calculated from population census data. The 1941–63 data are from LTES 9:218–19 (table 33, cols. 1–3); 1964–67 data are from Sorifu 1968 (pp. 42 and 46) from which 1968–71 data are extrapolated based on Sorifu 1971 (pp. 73–74).

Land (cols. 4–6): The 1874–1963 data are from LTES 9:216–17 (table 32, cols. 10–12, which give the data in *cho*); 1964–71 data are from Norinsho 1971.

Fixed capital (cols. 7–10): The 1878–1962 data are from LTES 9:210–11 (table 28), with col. 7 as revised by Kazushi Ohkawa and Nobukiyo Takamatsu for LTES 1. The 1963–71 data are obtained by deflating the current values of the fixed capital items (Norinsho 1973, pp. 76, 77, 92 and 93) and splicing to the LTES series at 1960–62.

Nonfarm current inputs (cols. 11–13): The 1878–1963 data are from LTES 9:186–87 (table 16, col. 12); 1964–71 data are the nonfarm current inputs in current prices in table A16, col. 9, deflated by a price index calculated from the data prepared by the price index for agricultural production goods of the Ministry of Agriculture and Forestry (Norinsho 1971, pp. 144–45), which are spliced with the LTES series at 1961–63.

Note: In principle the data are for Japan Proper, including Okinawa before 1945 but not since 1945.

Table A19. Manufacturing: Value of Production in Current Prices, 1874–1940
(In thousands of yen)

	Food products	Textiles	Lumber and wood products	Chemicals	Stone, clay, and glass products	Iron and steel[a]	Non-ferrous metals[a]	Machinery[b]	Printing and publishing	Others	Total
1874	59,746	40,806	7,132	29,671	3,450	1,806	2,833	3,449	267	10,269	159,429
1875	70,192	38,976	8,033	33,110	3,636	1,799	3,833	3,654	321	10,859	174,413
1876	68,637	41,779	8,937	35,776	4,118	1,300	4,740	4,038	378	10,745	180,448
1877	69,087	40,558	9,839	41,290	4,513	1,787	6,135	4,871	507	12,260	190,847
1878	77,041	58,002	10,742	43,307	4,953	2,186	5,881	5,831	530	13,571	222,044
1879	98,275	81,204	11,645	53,368	5,789	2,239	6,263	6,012	890	16,645	282,330
1880	114,760	94,895	17,551	67,951	8,347	2,494	7,303	9,090	936	17,202	340,529
1881	123,777	102,161	22,432	61,398	9,041	2,668	9,013	10,829	1,161	18,596	361,076
1882	124,217	95,628	18,751	50,794	7,435	1,904	8,549	9,032	1,122	19,180	336,612
1883	110,212	76,117	15,583	40,605	5,879	1,458	9,075	7,894	1,146	16,416	284,385
1884	115,573	74,526	12,643	39,477	4,409	1,332	7,519	6,442	1,162	16,509	279,592
1885	119,721	82,124	10,560	40,054	3,649	1,277	7,288	5,180	1,126	17,772	288,751
1886	122,019	103,217	11,130	43,619	4,594	1,846	7,295	5,729	1,326	17,446	318,221
1887	135,632	113,103	12,186	48,888	6,620	2,599	7,292	7,288	1,093	19,295	353,996
1888	135,685	127,703	11,787	51,578	7,646	4,086	11,412	8,524	1,084	20,808	380,313
1889	153,650	185,389	12,072	52,675	8,713	2,951	10,939	9,412	1,828	22,162	459,791
1890	156,085	160,003	11,558	59,702	7,886	2,792	11,404	9,162	1,454	23,498	443,544
1891	152,593	172,840	13,328	59,696	7,626	2,225	11,118	8,775	1,938	24,116	454,255
1892	166,534	220,681	12,900	64,175	10,352	1,434	11,622	9,841	1,727	28,150	527,416
1893	179,712	260,337	13,784	71,061	11,139	2,372	11,546	10,511	1,796	31,421	593,679
1894	200,911	288,219	16,810	76,486	10,652	3,539	12,783	14,042	1,739	32,586	657,767
1895	219,022	370,674	21,548	83,496	13,716	3,672	12,519	17,007	2,700	39,783	784,137
1896	262,509	357,525	27,113	96,361	14,491	6,299	14,950	22,329	3,343	39,891	844,811
1897	317,116	392,911	34,304	108,848	16,162	6,712	15,208	25,405	4,299	45,129	966,094
1898	395,340	418,751	39,956	109,704	16,776	6,210	16,542	32,217	5,007	48,922	1,089,425
1899	375,296	496,729	40,898	119,313	19,053	6,719	21,544	32,680	5,317	49,816	1,167,325
1900	429,065	428,468	46,833	127,602	23,341	5,286	25,805	47,872	7,384	54,743	1,196,399

Table A19 (continued)

	Food products	Textiles	Lumber and wood products	Chemicals	Stone, clay, and glass products	Iron and steel[a]	Non-ferrous metals[a]	Machinery[b]	Printing and publishing	Others	Total
1901	463,206	400,060	49,602	129,956	24,274	6,758	25,436	43,312	8,501	59,236	1,210,341
1902	407,259	407,965	45,548	132,770	25,106	7,021	22,409	46,261	9,285	65,221	1,168,845
1903	456,563	407,141	47,290	147,098	24,533	9,029	26,135	51,466	9,597	58,334	1,237,186
1904	470,931	381,093	53,197	156,663	25,034	16,078	26,829	69,306	10,629	54,313	1,264,073
1905	494,282	458,808	52,513	166,018	26,985	21,288	36,559	101,653	13,710	65,503	1,437,319
1906	587,407	563,087	52,370	201,575	39,529	22,278	38,158	96,634	17,697	85,306	1,704,041
1907	672,242	608,479	58,564	219,351	45,678	24,179	38,258	121,594	18,206	90,501	1,897,052
1908	676,721	563,488	61,274	205,658	43,852	25,695	28,622	115,891	19,869	90,466	1,831,536
1909	697,098	619,617	56,309	226,242	47,156	25,895	29,344	105,118	19,873	88,762	1,915,414
1910	707,623	700,305	60,818	237,527	51,048	37,722	32,703	136,007	23,344	95,407	2,082,504
1911	753,305	765,947	64,928	257,422	57,035	43,736	39,783	165,420	26,895	98,678	2,273,149
1912	798,539	838,595	66,869	286,163	63,472	53,755	46,660	212,045	30,523	99,269	2,495,890
1913	879,826	907,925	75,402	309,591	67,309	63,680	50,158	233,485	34,225	109,916	2,731,517
1914	815,335	830,482	71,006	312,192	61,203	77,737	50,332	204,487	38,010	100,209	2,560,993
1915	784,431	955,129	68,238	339,455	68,380	130,541	110,677	268,802	47,679	125,574	2,888,906
1916	929,091	1,441,174	75,829	442,487	101,123	255,523	282,271	549,628	59,798	155,776	4,292,700
1917	1,203,407	1,928,695	103,827	589,580	145,661	549,998	361,335	1,233,110	74,982	188,588	6,379,183
1918	1,623,055	2,906,688	152,858	984,584	216,719	659,230	376,794	1,627,503	94,026	259,081	8,900,538
1919	2,111,416	4,598,674	257,427	1,091,508	293,047	459,031	380,464	1,472,115	117,883	377,724	11,159,289
1920	2,285,882	3,286,932	257,169	1,189,122	279,360	441,605	181,790	1,390,222	147,817	319,338	9,579,237
1921	2,332,650	3,185,485	306,609	855,680	247,465	301,984	172,249	936,936	145,905	332,380	8,817,343
1922	2,380,938	3,184,413	255,628	813,272	284,138	268,117	238,822	933,259	133,340	323,702	8,815,629
1923	2,378,716	3,398,567	315,502	910,964	292,760	325,166	199,483	670,622	155,457	391,634	9,038,871
1924	2,560,090	3,673,186	290,812	996,482	305,701	386,469	200,657	723,951	218,207	321,027	9,676,582
1925	2,582,793	3,974,725	284,223	1,021,965	307,161	449,254	197,406	731,914	217,977	333,011	10,100,434

Table A19 (continued)

	Food products	Textiles	Lumber and wood products	Chemicals	Stone, clay, and glass products	Iron and steel[a]	Non-ferrous metals[a]	Machinery[b]	Printing and publishing	Others	Total
1926	2,597,040	3,663,107	308,903	1,058,860	326,435	501,223	177,639	838,716	230,438	343,526	10,045,887
1927	2,543,928	3,484,829	302,180	1,088,715	305,250	473,910	219,902	937,579	287,903	330,947	9,975,143
1928	2,657,089	3,688,717	313,540	1,188,549	277,192	548,279	271,213	968,828	256,563	366,267	10,536,237
1929	2,482,380	3,773,277	324,952	1,308,123	302,568	672,573	254,289	1,007,758	272,409	345,354	10,743,683
1930	2,206,441	2,708,502	265,167	1,134,351	228,357	547,386	219,785	994,390	251,988	281,505	8,837,872
1931	2,010,264	2,561,673	261,696	997,069	210,894	414,704	197,100	694,341	272,583	256,263	7,876,587
1932	1,986,919	2,858,953	288,562	1,167,844	239,549	574,560	264,041	848,818	282,984	301,314	8,813,544
1933	2,259,137	3,627,958	333,994	1,532,428	308,746	909,848	357,882	1,177,870	290,786	367,239	11,165,888
1934	2,345,604	4,097,713	390,223	1,772,534	348,528	1,232,762	330,624	1,730,775	313,012	453,566	13,015,341
1935	2,461,086	4,355,625	409,192	2,149,137	391,353	1,494,948	426,445	2,445,941	344,251	489,895	14,967,873
1936	2,589,730	4,562,198	451,506	2,484,695	427,204	1,764,371	480,794	2,598,879	366,516	554,057	16,279,950
1937	2,738,598	5,604,397	615,564	3,385,794	496,154	2,812,521	720,378	3,520,718	431,704	746,443	21,072,271
1938	3,360,365	5,607,166	715,085	4,113,024	472,548	3,652,373	1,008,953	5,061,320	441,413	813,096	25,245,343
1939	3,925,281	5,551,600	1,108,795	5,014,175	678,655	4,503,754	1,004,155	7,348,815	502,872	1,093,738	30,731,840
1940	4,057,730	5,578,982	1,477,105	5,528,112	789,954	4,658,065	782,804	8,599,590	527,889	1,251,988	33,252,219

Source: Reprinted from LTES 10:140–43 (table 1).

Notes: Output covers all factories regardless of number of employees, and also includes government factories.

Series B in the source is given here for iron and steel, nonferrous metals, and machinery. A fuller explanation is given in LTES 10 (p. 271, notes to table 1-4).

[a] LTES 10's series B, which is adjusted to be consistent with the 1874 production census (the *Zenfuken Bussanhyo*).

[b] LTES 10's series B, which includes some fabricated metal products in the machinery category.

Table A20. Manufacturing: Value of Production in Current Prices, 1952–70
(In billions of yen)

	Food products	Textiles	Lumber and wood products	Chemicals	Stone, clay, and glass products	Iron and steel	Non-ferrous metals	Machinery	Printing and publishing	Others	Total
1952	908.7	969.9	217.7	865.2	163.2	623.5	240.2	751.0	150.8	94.5	4,985
1953	1,051.8	1,009.2	257.7	1,063.9	191.6	720.0	269.6	917.5	193.0	85.1	5,759
1954	1,317.2	986.0	315.2	1,140.7	219.4	655.3	278.5	998.4	216.9	100.3	6,228
1955	1,420.6	1,181.8	337.8	1,326.2	232.7	837.5	314.7	999.7	229.9	135.3	7,016
1956	1,522.1	1,455.4	406.4	1,601.7	291.5	1,229.5	452.2	1,552.6	261.1	172.8	8,945
1957	1,709.2	1,590.9	496.1	1,852.4	352.4	1,542.8	479.1	2,211.4	291.4	207.1	10,733
1958	1,794.1	1,443.6	493.3	1,845.5	346.2	1,213.2	409.5	2,258.3	313.2	233.2	10,350
1959	1,920.0	1,624.7	568.3	2,285.4	409.2	1,627.3	555.3	2,804.2	336.7	288.9	12,420
1960	2,219.0	1,922.7	711.0	2,775.8	537.5	2,189.4	745.9	4,012.1	401.2	394.5	15,909
1961	2,718.4	2,162.8	897.2	3,118.0	692.7	2,835.2	891.5	5,140.7	486.2	481.9	19,425
1962	3,043.0	2,350.4	1,034.5	3,465.0	729.2	2,735.0	900.7	5,862.3	573.6	565.9	21,260
1963	3,534.8	2,726.6	1,197.4	4,093.2	853.7	3,065.0	991.2	6,308.8	756.2	731.5	24,258
1964	3,934.0	2,924.3	1,350.8	4,722.8	977.1	3,592.8	1,235.4	7,492.1	871.6	886.3	27,987
1965	4,356.2	3,043.3	1,459.2	5,138.4	1,032.7	3,901.0	1,339.1	7,862.0	929.4	990.3	30,053
1966	4,964.0	3,407.2	1,738.1	5,843.9	1,222.2	4,451.1	1,720.1	9,119.5	1,104.9	1,209.6	34,781
1967	5,570.7	3,816.4	2,064.8	6,805.6	1,492.7	5,643.8	1,978.8	11,694.3	1,291.9	1,392.9	41,777
1968	6,195.6	4,158.8	2,422.7	7,805.3	1,781.8	6,306.9	2,345.7	14,832.9	1,487.7	1,638.6	49,029
1969	6,997.6	4,700.7	2,802.4	9,211.6	2,106.4	7,969.4	2,953.5	18,361.9	1,761.7	1,968.1	58,957
1970	7,966.7	5,346.6	3,241.1	10,765.6	2,469.7	9,840.9	3,515.1	22,335.8	2,020.8	2,210.8	69,967

Source: Tsusho Sangyosho: *Kogyo Tokeihyo*, 1971 edition.

Table A21. Manufacturing: Value of Production in 1934–36 Prices, 1874–1940
(In thousands of yen)

	Food products	Textiles	Lumber and wood products	Chemicals	Stone, clay, and glass products	Iron and steel[a]	Non-ferrous metals[a]	Machinery[b]	Printing and Publishing	Others	Total
1874	422,801	59,991	44,243	72,492	16,829	2,128	4,586	4,300	855	57,497	685,722
1875	457,545	64,063	51,312	75,576	17,314	2,293	6,128	4,911	988	62,516	742,646
1876	447,409	57,177	58,259	80,269	17,230	1,906	7,694	6,184	1,189	67,156	744,473
1877	454,909	65,862	58,185	96,449	17,095	2,757	10,832	8,298	1,636	73,501	789,524
1878	469,619	84,922	55,514	89,755	17,079	3,440	9,912	10,106	1,657	75,985	817,989
1879	493,200	110,362	49,343	96,506	16,125	3,548	9,624	10,224	2,600	82,319	873,851
1880	512,504	117,955	51,169	108,774	14,747	3,952	9,258	16,408	2,734	73,955	911,456
1881	510,484	118,544	50,751	100,258	13,084	4,406	10,189	19,407	3,315	67,426	897,864
1882	544,286	103,966	50,816	96,917	12,350	3,260	9,664	16,819	2,936	75,157	916,171
1883	538,618	112,366	50,430	96,518	11,998	2,826	11,648	14,979	2,938	74,686	917,007
1884	577,490	120,964	50,171	100,145	11,078	2,866	13,127	14,347	3,041	84,531	977,760
1885	454,005	129,738	53,604	99,119	10,577	3,185	13,798	12,246	3,215	98,405	877,892
1886	551,573	163,733	58,579	107,410	14,867	4,372	14,389	14,541	3,966	104,592	1,038,022
1887	618,731	196,769	56,157	114,011	16,633	5,394	15,407	15,343	4,291	106,250	1,148,986
1888	623,352	225,027	50,372	109,021	17,497	7,429	17,848	15,814	5,237	112,780	1,184,377
1889	696,352	280,213	50,937	103,732	18,859	5,243	20,531	18,061	8,831	119,472	1,322,231
1890	668,917	300,419	48,360	111,969	18,087	5,281	21,763	17,653	6,766	130,111	1,329,326
1891	676,477	366,419	55,766	123,313	16,542	4,277	21,336	17,585	8,694	138,837	1,429,246
1892	711,623	402,335	49,049	137,243	23,743	2,735	22,239	20,459	7,483	152,575	1,529,484
1893	767,967	409,206	53,634	148,044	25,965	4,183	20,007	21,539	7,782	161,714	1,620,041
1894	810,746	468,878	59,610	154,611	25,182	5,930	21,007	28,953	7,802	155,914	1,734,633
1895	835,962	509,938	64,515	153,881	32,502	5,897	20,513	31,789	10,601	163,447	1,829,045
1896	891,765	539,823	65,490	147,296	32,202	9,531	19,596	39,037	13,125	138,751	1,896,616
1897	921,126	549,449	76,915	162,971	29,493	9,777	18,360	41,376	15,431	142,363	1,967,261
1898	1,018,760	569,962	82,045	158,394	28,974	8,319	18,990	52,815	17,972	147,489	2,103,720
1899	969,381	606,137	83,465	171,156	30,930	8,001	21,234	47,778	20,240	144,604	2,102,926

Table A21 (continued)

	Food products	Textiles	Lumber and wood products	Chemicals	Stone, clay, and glass products	Iron and steel[a]	Non-ferrous metals[a]	Machinery[b]	Printing and Publishing	Others	Total
1901	1,080,439	490,510	89,052	211,655	32,066	7,256	23,672	64,936	26,699	158,005	2,184,290
1902	937,327	515,433	88,788	203,385	36,491	7,645	24,609	70,952	29,161	179,623	2,093,414
1903	996,775	511,998	88,891	213,836	35,452	9,988	26,737	79,178	30,141	159,383	2,152,379
1904	947,204	469,038	96,023	229,442	36,334	15,644	25,498	98,028	32,564	144,873	2,094,648
1905	903,640	545,551	90,540	209,091	37,741	20,890	30,282	136,264	41,011	167,270	2,182,280
1906	1,047,632	611,852	91,237	230,450	49,722	21,498	27,093	127,654	45,377	194,452	2,446,967
1907	1,164,378	665,732	91,793	243,129	54,770	25,544	41,785	148,830	46,361	182,241	2,664,563
1908	1,110,726	642,078	93,979	255,730	53,938	27,393	46,669	159,410	50,596	184,361	2,624,880
1909	1,109,340	719,230	93,848	284,510	64,333	29,621	47,544	155,730	50,606	199,241	2,754,003
1910	1,150,251	804,394	97,621	270,933	70,588	44,902	53,664	196,826	59,445	210,891	2,959,515
1911	1,191,863	822,626	98,525	286,566	75,244	50,773	66,683	238,357	68,487	209,463	3,108,587
1912	1,242,572	942,136	101,163	307,339	83,626	58,360	64,067	272,202	77,726	208,548	3,357,739
1913	1,343,595	1,079,578	110,237	337,650	82,285	66,368	70,082	307,217	87,153	213,346	3,697,511
1914	1,300,085	986,438	108,572	357,731	75,559	79,616	79,401	263,175	94,318	199,064	3,543,959
1915	1,356,302	1,133,550	106,789	427,579	79,052	89,100	145,436	326,216	110,470	254,921	4,029,415
1916	1,462,168	1,324,487	114,373	446,551	94,596	98,289	247,454	519,989	138,550	268,117	4,714,574
1917	1,551,302	1,417,741	122,149	487,055	95,893	131,362	301,288	844,018	165,523	265,430	5,381,761
1918	1,704,639	1,505,510	136,116	510,941	116,079	150,115	345,556	930,002	161,473	293,676	5,854,107
1919	1,641,643	1,689,509	152,866	523,204	148,378	119,964	395,123	955,299	170,771	303,539	6,100,296
1920	1,798,505	1,498,966	110,278	514,781	112,509	198,366	225,742	899,238	142,722	187,879	5,688,986
1921	1,925,153	1,769,911	154,697	543,116	132,689	170,661	258,554	748,950	140,876	209,782	6,074,389
1922	2,074,982	1,849,897	129,366	556,426	152,516	194,203	323,651	765,594	154,543	210,360	6,411,538
1923	2,113,757	1,898,429	174,793	590,270	154,084	209,177	254,280	553,318	189,929	268,077	6,406,114
1924	2,153,381	1,907,455	161,832	674,255	182,290	278,055	241,290	581,020	256,956	224,825	6,661,359
1925	2,175,079	2,044,822	172,256	675,322	211,252	382,246	225,555	664,169	236,726	255,710	7,043,137

Table A21 (continued)

	Food products	Textiles	Lumber and wood products	Chemicals	Stone, clay, and glass products	Iron and steel[a]	Non-ferrous metals[a]	Machinery[b]	Printing and Publishing	Others	Total
1926	2,267,622	2,343,639	193,670	739,841	233,669	448,441	223,249	822,271	225,285	279,153	7,776,840
1927	2,282,799	2,513,581	202,262	829,750	249,795	441,751	293,516	932,914	281,403	274,624	8,302,395
1928	2,343,029	2,588,210	215,640	902,536	226,464	479,139	232,818	566,894	250,770	386,213	8,491,713
1929	2,378,100	2,817,560	251,706	1,114,150	242,637	663,614	280,270	997,945	266,258	285,417	9,257,657
1930	2,359,754	2,601,077	271,688	1,189,671	223,879	618,166	335,601	1,097,561	251,335	312,610	9,261,342
1931	2,158,812	3,035,158	292,071	1,180,662	224,355	593,027	389,757	971,106	298,754	322,790	9,466,492
1932	2,008,592	3,317,806	332,828	1,350,890	247,980	855,764	388,181	986,998	307,524	357,855	10,154,418
1933	2,261,897	3,670,536	324,897	1,675,884	311,550	880,101	412,022	1,193,384	312,707	386,608	11,429,586
1934	2,352,568	4,239,744	393,370	1,768,114	348,528	1,224,679	358,361	1,715,337	297,795	456,717	13,155,213
1935	2,474,572	4,363,042	418,825	2,153,660	389,019	1,536,590	425,085	2,480,670	353,259	499,180	15,093,902
1936	2,567,012	4,455,271	437,930	2,463,997	430,649	1,729,097	449,803	2,585,949	376,107	540,280	16,036,095
1937	2,617,737	5,089,354	466,690	2,990,456	467,629	1,638,235	548,149	2,495,193	412,246	594,681	17,320,370
1938	2,775,601	4,892,388	443,051	3,248,064	412,706	1,956,174	789,478	3,412,893	385,783	545,812	18,861,950
1939	2,821,264	4,098,332	556,066	3,406,832	531,861	2,412,165	798,660	4,942,041	439,497	613,735	20,620,453
1940	2,634,667	3,454,264	560,146	3,342,268	544,796	2,494,813	556,206	5,580,526	444,052	598,465	20,210,203

Source: Reprinted from LTES 10:144–47 (table 2).
Notes: See notes to table A19.

Table A22. Value of Production in Manufacturing: 1934–36 Prices, 1940–70
(In millions of yen)

	Food products	Textiles	Lumber and wood products	Chemicals	Lime, clay, and glass products	Iron and steel	Nonferrous metals	Machinery	Printing and publishing	Others	Total
1940	2,634.7	3,454.3	560.1	3,342.3	544.8	2,494.8	556.2	5,580.5	444.1	598.5	20,210.3
1941	2,316.6	2,792.7	572.0	3,315.7	491.3	2,389.3	545.6	5,735.1	353.9	488.7	19,000.9
1942	2,140.1	2,207.3	503.7	2,654.1	407.5	2,326.3	652.6	5,518.6	367.5	443.8	17,221.5
1943	1,837.4	1,277.1	417.9	2,268.3	369.7	2,377.5	831.0	5,550.5	338.6	372.3	15,640.3
1944	1,603.3	759.5	337.0	1,917.3	293.7	2,095.4	950.5	5,973.4	197.0	230.2	14,357.3
1945	1,132.3	289.9	191.3	739.3	112.0	788.5	347.9	2,593.3	63.0	93.3	6,351.5
1946	1,155.5	508.0	213.6	460.7	133.9	208.4	197.1	679.8	171.3	107.4	3,835.7
1947	1,046.8	680.8	282.2	586.5	163.7	275.3	267.2	816.3	261.5	163.9	4,544.2
1948	1,278.4	772.6	326.7	827.4	249.8	459.2	368.6	1,249.9	432.9	271.2	6,236.7
1949	1,950.8	1,030.3	328.4	1,175.7	330.2	789.3	421.1	1,563.0	483.1	302.7	8,374.6
1950	2,179.5	1,467.3	344.2	1,791.5	389.8	1,110.2	486.9	1,616.6	503.1	315.2	10,204.4
1951	2,780.2	2,081.9	516.2	2,445.0	541.1	1,496.4	592.6	2,609.4	604.2	378.6	14,045.6
1952	2,860.2	2,363.2	549.1	2,677.7	562.5	1,520.7	625.7	2,676.5	644.1	403.6	14,883.3
1953	3,449.4	2,448.3	513.4	3,513.2	676.7	1,970.8	757.8	3,321.5	731.7	386.7	17,769.5
1954	4,078.7	2,644.5	571.1	3,976.4	776.2	1,859.8	824.7	3,642.7	754.2	451.3	19,579.6
1955	4,484.8	3,322.7	700.7	4,753.0	866.2	2,316.0	914.2	3,715.0	745.2	611.9	22,429.6
1956	4,939.6	3,977.3	810.5	5,620.5	1,125.0	2,633.8	1,068.8	5,462.7	836.7	801.2	27,276.2
1957	5,451.6	4,724.1	876.4	6,348.9	1,259.4	3,088.5	1,316.6	7,290.8	923.0	983.2	32,262.5
1958	5,866.3	4,648.5	903.9	6,798.7	1,257.2	3,007.9	1,314.7	7,644.1	965.5	1,190.7	33,597.5
1959	6,272.5	5,073.9	1,011.5	8,458.9	1,505.2	3,891.4	1,653.2	9,247.3	968.7	1,450.6	39,533.2
1960	7,107.7	6,066.4	1,219.1	8,919.5	1,931.0	5,325.5	2,190.1	13,837.5	1,102.1	1,913.2	49,612.1

Table A22 (continued)

	Food products	Textiles	Lumber and wood products	Chemicals	Lime, clay, and glass products	Iron and steel	Nonferrous metals	Machinery	Printing and publishing	Others	Total
1961	8,617.9	6,794.3	1,291.6	11,760.6	2,446.8	6,998.2	2,731.3	18,063.6	1,265.7	2,307.5	62,277.5
1962	9,704.8	7,607.3	1,468.4	13,477.0	2,433.3	7,168.5	2,868.4	20,833.8	1,404.8	2,758.8	69,725.1
1963	10,954.7	8,056.3	1,660.6	15,983.3	2,859.7	8,135.7	3,262.0	22,718.0	1,806.1	3,576.6	79,013.0
1964	12,284.7	8,902.3	1,856.6	18,138.9	3,276.5	9,419.2	3,722.5	27,227.9	2,016.0	4,382.2	91,226.8
1965	13,560.4	9,514.4	2,031.3	19,713.4	3,484.1	10,285.9	3,680.0	28,518.0	2,039.9	4,803.6	97,630.9
1966	15,210.7	10,620.4	2,267.9	22,865.1	4,038.7	11,569.4	3,900.2	33,116.2	2,077.9	5,741.2	111,407.7
1967	16,984.1	11,213.6	2,484.3	26,790.6	4,755.3	14,258.0	5,035.3	42,392.9	2,386.4	6,756.3	133,056.8
1968	18,265.4	12,746.9	2,760.0	31,168.7	5,576.5	15,089.8	5,892.6	53,800.1	2,669.8	7,948.3	155,266.2
1969	19,838.6	13,746.9	3,057.6	37,150.7	6,454.0	20,080.7	6,730.4	66,783.8	2,830.2	9,546.6	186,219.4
1970	21,717.7	14,713.5	3,320.1	42,332.1	7,257.8	23,093.2	7,752.9	80,281.3	2,944.8	10,723.6	214,137.0

Source: Tsusho Sangyosho: *Kogyo Tokeihyo*, 1971 edition.

Notes: For 1941–51 the data are interpolations using indexes of industrial production by subsectors prepared by MITI. For 1952–70 the value of output in each industry is deflated by its wholesale price index, with 1934–36 = 1.

Table A23. Commerce–Services: Net Domestic Product in Current Prices, 1885–1940
(In millions of yen)

| | Total | Commerce–services A | | | Commerce–services B | Adjustment item |
		Public administration	Professionals	Domestic servants, etc.		
1885	283	24	14	17	208	20
1886	280	28	13	17	200	22
1887	277	30	13	17	196	21
1888	275	32	14	17	195	17
1889	295	32	14	19	209	21
1890	350	33	17	23	255	22
1891	338	33	17	22	244	22
1892	364	33	19	25	261	26
1893	370	34	19	25	263	29
1894	436	61	21	27	296	31
1895	482	71	23	30	323	35
1896	489	49	26	33	339	42
1897	594	45	32	42	429	46
1898	708	51	36	48	518	55
1899	642	53	34	45	444	66
1900	772	61	40	52	544	75
1901	777	73	41	53	535	75
1902	811	78	43	56	557	77
1903	877	110	47	62	576	82
1904	958	157	48	64	590	99
1905	1,085	180	48	68	649	140
1906	1,130	160	52	73	688	157
1907	1,126	112	58	76	702	178
1908	1,188	104	65	91	745	183
1909	1,192	109	70	91	726	196
1910	1,201	120	68	92	717	204

Table A23 (continued)

	Total	Commerce–services A			Commerce–services B	Adjustment item
		Public administration	Professionals	Domestic servants, etc.		
1911	1,358	128	75	97	796	262
1912	1,436	132	78	104	862	260
1913	1,471	130	84	111	893	253
1914	1,425	137	83	120	849	236
1915	1,487	144	91	127	918	207
1916	1,843	153	103	140	1,239	208
1917	2,380	161	138	173	1,644	264
1918	2,701	183	192	267	1,694	365
1919	4,043	244	310	412	2,610	467
1920	4,374	337	359	386	2,721	570
1921	4,668	403	441	457	2,755	612
1922	4,846	434	468	456	2,720	768
1923	4,783	441	480	449	2,647	766
1924	4,930	453	498	399	2,844	736
1925	5,081	492	508	412	2,880	789
1926	5,236	538	521	445	2,909	823
1927	5,070	577	540	441	2,654	858
1928	5,440	600	568	464	2,895	913
1929	5,241	613	578	383	2,717	950
1930	4,659	589	541	313	2,544	672

Table A23 (continued)

| | | Commerce–services A | | | | |
	Total	Public administration	Professionals	Domestic servants, etc.	Commerce–services **B**	Adjustment item
1931	4,103	555	531	301	2,135	581
1932	4,451	556	558	272	2,537	528
1933	5,031	575	598	303	3,009	546
1934	5,480	551	640	334	3,333	622
1935	5,508	556	678	352	3,256	666
1936	5,802	571	722	345	3,440	724
1937	6,547	766	806	323	3,835	817
1938	7,088	780	896	329	4,160	923
1939	8,001	848	1,073	322	4,697	1,061
1940	9,275	977	1,245	324	5,167	1,562

Source: Reprinted from LTES 1:207 (table 13).

Notes: All items are in terms of factor costs, estimated by the income approach.

Commerce–services A (first column) is the total of the other five columns.

B (fifth column) includes all commerce–services other than public administration, professionals, and domestic servants.

The adjustment item (col. 6) for converting the totals into a market price series is indirect taxes minus current subsidies.

Table A24. Commerce–Services B: Net Domestic Product in Current Prices, 1885–1940
(In millions of yen)

	Commerce–services B	Principal workers						Side workers	Less: Interest received from other industries
		Enterprises					Wages received by employes		
		Total	Incorporated	Unincorporated					
				Total	Tax paying	Tax exempt			
1885	208	183	—	—	—	—	—	28	3
1886	200	178	—	—	—	—	—	26	4
1887	196	175	—	—	—	—	—	25	4
1888	195	175	—	—	—	—	—	25	5
1889	209	188	—	—	—	—	—	27	6
1890	255	232	—	—	—	—	—	29	6
1891	244	220	—	—	—	—	—	30	6
1892	261	235	—	—	—	—	—	33	7
1893	263	240	—	—	—	—	—	33	10
1894	296	272	—	—	—	—	—	35	11
1895	323	299	—	—	—	—	—	38	14
1896	339	316	—	—	—	—	—	40	17
1897	429	393	—	—	—	—	—	51	15
1898	518	480	—	—	—	—	—	57	19
1899	444	415	11	372	141	231	32	54	25
1900	544	512	18	457	173	284	37	61	29

Table A24 (continued)

	Commerce–services B	Principal workers						Wages received by employes	Side workers	Less: Interest received from other industries
		Enterprises								
		Total	Incorporated	Unincorporated						
				Total	Tax paying	Tax exempt				
1901	535	499	17	443	168	275	38	63	27
1902	557	521	18	462	175	287	41	65	29
1903	576	541	19	478	180	298	44	67	32
1904	590	554	20	488	185	303	46	68	32
1905	649	625	25	549	207	342	51	59	35
1906	688	674	28	591	223	368	55	63	49
1907	702	681	25	593	224	369	63	70	49
1908	745	718	27	621	235	386	70	74	47
1909	726	700	25	602	227	375	73	74	48
1910	717	695	25	594	225	369	76	76	54
1911	796	776	30	660	252	408	86	82	62
1912	862	842	37	709	268	441	96	89	69
1913	893	874	41	732	276	456	101	93	74
1914	849	835	40	696	263	433	99	89	75
1915	918	905	48	754	285	469	103	91	78
1916	1,239	1,224	84	1,014	383	631	126	108	93
1917	1,644	1,649	184	1,319	498	821	146	123	128
1918	1,694	1,718	170	1,347	510	837	202	164	188
1919	2,610	2,619	312	1,991	754	1,237	316	251	260

Table A24 (continued)

	Commerce–services B	Principal workers							Less: Interest received from other industries
		Enterprises					Wages received by employes	Side workers	
		Total	Incorporated	Unincorporated					
				Total	Tax paying	Tax exempt			
1920	2,721	2,727	385	1,959	740	1,219	383	272	278
1921	2,755	2,761	310	2,004	758	1,246	447	302	308
1922	2,720	2,765	330	2,002	757	1,245	434	275	320
1923	2,647	2,720	281	1,980	749	1,231	459	275	348
1924	2,844	2,949	362	2,122	803	1,319	466	259	364
1925	2,880	3,025	372	2,179	824	1,355	474	246	391
1926	2,909	3,080	351	2,227	843	1,384	502	241	412
1927	2,654	2,808	294	2,021	739	1,282	493	217	371
1928	2,895	3,032	357	2,171	740	1,431	504	202	339
1929	2,717	2,863	317	2,050	726	1,324	496	180	326
1930	2,544	2,693	281	1,936	611	1,325	481	154	308
1931	2,135	2,291	185	1,593	468	1,125	513	145	301
1932	2,537	2,677	259	1,816	518	1,298	602	153	293
1933	3,009	3,123	362	2,062	604	1,458	699	161	275
1934	3,333	3,435	457	2,171	715	1,456	807	166	268
1935	3,256	3,354	412	2,072	717	1,355	870	169	267
1936	3,440	3,544	464	2,129	779	1,350	951	172	276
1937	3,835	3,953	523	2,307	874	1,433	1,123	190	308
1938	4,160	4,285	545	2,422	964	1,458	1,317	209	334
1939	4,697	4,879	680	2,670	1,140	1,530	1,529	229	411
1940	5,167	5,401	715	2,872	1,414	1,458	1,814	257	491

Source: Reprinted from LTES 1:208 (table 14); originally from SIL 3, sec. 2.
Notes: For estimating procedures, see ch. 6.

Table A25. Commerce–Services A : Net Domestic Product in 1934–36 Prices, 1885–1940
(In millions of yen)

	Total	Public administration	Pro- fessional	Domestic servants etc.	Commerce– services B	Adjustment item
1885	1,689	100	88	125	1,314	62
1886	1,809	124	89	130	1,390	76
1887	1,883	138	91	132	1,454	68
1888	1,752	144	94	138	1,320	56
1889	2,058	143	97	139	1,612	67
1890	2,189	148	104	153	1,719	65
1891	1,989	152	106	154	1,510	67
1892	2,247	148	108	158	1,747	86
1893	2,285	160	109	160	1,762	94
1894	2,642	292	113	169	1,970	98
1895	2,629	341	115	171	1,902	100
1896	2,434	200	119	175	1,831	109
1897	2,483	171	124	181	1,900	107
1898	2,943	187	125	184	2,327	120
1899	2,672	183	125	177	2,038	149
1900	2,798	204	123	185	2,133	153
1901	2,856	242	132	192	2,133	157
1902	2,834	250	139	202	2,087	156
1903	2,772	335	146	213	2,025	159
1904	2,768	480	146	213	1,748	186
1905	2,953	554	134	215	1,796	254
1906	3,259	450	135	206	2,190	278
1907	3,103	311	148	211	2,146	287
1908	3,093	292	164	262	2,072	305
1909	2,988	296	174	249	1,927	342
1910	3,119	291	156	236	2,082	354
1911	3,300	310	169	253	2,142	426
1912	3,478	320	175	268	2,316	399
1913	3,363	320	188	289	2,188	378
1914	2,776	340	189	316	1,601	381
1915	3,340	352	202	323	2,111	352
1916	4,211	370	220	357	2,941	323
1917	4,522	386	278	433	3,096	329
1918	4,506	413	324	598	2,829	342
1919	5,191	504	433	835	3,080	339
1920	4,396	461	404	594	2,550	387

Table A25 (continued)

	Total	Public administration	Pro-fessional	Domestic servants etc.	Commerce–services B	Adjustment item
1921	5,437	454	453	503	3,568	459
1922	4,891	474	487	483	2,863	584
1923	5,031	493	505	488	2,959	586
1924	5,075	504	520	488	3,003	560
1925	4,895	532	519	437	2,806	601
1926	4,896	579	534	472	2,652	659
1927	4,837	585	534	438	2,583	697
1928	5,490	612	567	477	3,064	770
1929	5,394	602	568	374	3,032	818
1930	3,997	572	539	304	1,932	650
1931	4,297	541	534	289	2,259	638
1932	5,267	533	557	266	3,344	567
1933	5,798	569	603	299	3,763	564
1934	5,807	547	643	331	3,655	631
1935	5,274	558	682	354	3,023	657
1936	5,666	573	719	344	3,328	702
1937	6,237	789	780	315	3,629	724
1938	6,156	705	760	280	3,664	747
1939	7,607	708	841	254	5,036	768
1940	7,600	928	1,110	291	4,215	1,056

Source: Reprinted from LTES 1:231 (table 29).

Notes: The output of commerce–services B is estimated as a residual (see chs. 3 and 6), but the incomes of public administrative services, professionals, and domestic servants are deflated by their respective deflators. The adjustment item is deflated by the aggregate expenditure price index.

Table A26. Exports of Major Commodity Groups in Current Prices 1874–1940 and 1953–70
(1874–1940 in millions of yen; 1953–70 in billions of yen)

	Processed food	Textiles	Wood products	Chemicals	Ceramics	Metals	Machinery	Other manufactures	Total manufactures	Primary products	Total commodity
1874	0.5	5.7	0.0	0.8	0.1	0.7	0.0	0.5	8.3	10.5	18.8
1875	0.4	5.8	0.1	0.7	0.1	0.5	0.0	0.6	8.2	9.9	18.1
1876	0.4	13.8	0.1	0.7	0.1	0.3	0.0	0.6	16.0	11.2	27.2
1877	0.6	10.0	0.0	0.9	0.1	0.7	0.0	0.8	13.1	9.8	22.9
1878	0.4	8.6	0.0	0.9	0.2	1.1	0.0	1.1	12.3	13.5	25.8
1879	0.5	11.2	0.1	1.4	0.3	1.2	0.0	1.1	15.8	12.0	27.8
1880	0.6	10.1	0.0	1.9	0.5	1.1	0.0	1.3	15.5	12.6	28.1
1881	0.6	12.9	0.0	1.9	0.8	1.4	0.0	1.4	19.0	11.7	30.7
1882	0.4	18.8	0.1	1.9	0.6	1.3	0.0	1.3	24.4	13.1	37.5
1883	0.5	16.6	0.1	1.9	0.6	1.2	0.0	1.3	24.2	11.8	36.0
1884	0.6	13.5	0.1	1.8	0.6	1.7	0.0	1.5	19.8	13.1	32.9
1885	0.9	15.0	0.1	1.9	0.7	2.3	0.0	1.8	22.7	13.5	36.2
1886	0.6	21.2	0.0	2.4	1.0	2.6	0.0	2.3	30.1	17.6	47.7
1887	0.7	23.7	0.1	3.3	1.4	3.1	0.1	3.2	35.6	16.1	51.7
1888	0.8	30.9	0.1	3.1	1.4	4.3	0.1	3.5	44.2	21.0	65.2
1889	0.9	32.6	0.2	4.1	1.5	3.7	0.0	3.6	46.6	22.7	69.3
1890	0.7	21.0	0.1	5.0	1.4	6.3	0.1	4.1	38.7	17.2	55.9
1891	0.8	37.5	0.1	5.4	1.4	5.8	0.1	5.0	56.1	22.8	78.9
1892	1.0	49.1	0.3	5.6	1.7	5.7	0.1	5.8	69.3	21.4	90.7
1893	1.1	42.1	0.2	7.5	1.9	5.5	0.2	7.4	65.9	22.9	88.8
1894	1.6	60.7	0.3	8.1	1.8	6.0	0.2	8.5	87.2	25.4	112.6
1895	2.0	72.9	0.3	9.5	2.4	6.5	0.3	12.3	106.2	29.1	135.3
1896	1.7	52.9	0.4	9.9	2.4	6.7	0.3	13.6	87.9	29.2	117.1
1897	2.3	91.0	0.6	11.4	2.2	7.3	0.4	17.4	132.6	33.0	165.6
1898	2.9	87.4	0.7	12.2	2.5	8.8	0.4	16.1	131.0	36.4	167.4
1899	4.1	124.1	1.1	13.1	3.1	13.2	0.6	19.0	178.3	43.6	221.9
1900	6.0	103.3	1.4	15.5	3.8	14.4	0.8	21.3	166.5	42.9	209.8

Table A26 (continued)

	Processed food	Textiles	Wood products	Chemicals	Ceramics	Metals	Machinery	Other manufactures	Total manufactures	Primary products	Total commodity
1901	8.1	141.4	1.5	18.5	3.9	16.2	1.2	22.5	213.3	45.5	258.8
1902	8.5	146.1	1.9	20.0	4.1	13.1	1.9	24.0	219.6	45.7	265.3
1903	8.8	159.9	2.9	22.4	5.4	18.4	2.4	25.9	246.1	51.4	297.5
1904	11.8	184.5	2.3	25.4	6.1	16.8	2.5	28.1	277.5	47.7	325.2
1905	21.9	171.1	4.1	24.9	8.3	19.6	3.7	32.9	286.5	44.4	330.9
1906	26.0	227.5	7.0	30.3	13.0	30.6	4.5	42.1	381.0	53.3	434.3
1907	17.9	229.7	10.8	31.5	11.1	35.9	9.5	40.3	386.7	60.8	447.5
1908	18.3	205.1	7.5	28.6	8.9	27.4	7.7	34.3	337.8	56.4	394.2
1909	20.5	234.5	6.3	33.5	7.6	28.2	4.4	36.2	371.2	59.6	430.8
1910	23.6	280.0	9.0	35.5	11.5	30.1	5.8	42.3	437.8	65.7	503.5
1911	24.7	278.5	8.5	35.9	11.4	28.9	6.8	39.3	434.0	69.7	503.7
1912	28.8	331.7	8.8	43.7	12.2	35.6	9.1	52.4	522.4	77.3	599.7
1913	39.1	405.7	10.3	49.3	14.1	39.3	10.5	55.5	623.8	80.4	704.2
1914	33.9	372.7	8.8	48.0	12.6	39.9	7.4	48.4	571.7	82.6	654.3
1915	36.3	388.5	10.3	65.5	17.8	76.6	10.6	69.9	675.5	94.2	769.7
1916	51.6	589.9	13.6	115.9	28.8	142.1	35.5	91.4	1,068.8	112.0	1,180.8
1917	92.2	807.2	17.4	143.3	36.8	211.7	124.3	99.9	1,532.8	152.9	1,685.7
1918	110.4	1,099.3	20.0	191.1	49.2	172.8	131.7	111.7	1,886.2	183.9	2,070.1
1919	87.7	1,456.6	27.8	176.5	55.5	124.2	54.2	138.7	2,121.2	171.8	2,293.0
1920	109.7	1,257.0	32.5	179.9	71.9	102.3	69.8	151.6	1,974.7	157.3	2,132.0
1921	70.3	926.2	19.8	101.4	45.7	60.5	39.0	76.4	1,339.3	109.2	1,448.5
1922	67.4	1,249.5	19.6	113.3	43.5	54.9	35.6	107.8	1,691.6	116.0	1,807.6
1923	58.5	1,107.9	17.6	102.8	46.6	51.5	30.3	99.9	1,515.1	112.9	1,628.0
1924	87.1	1,431.8	19.5	124.6	49.4	56.2	35.6	100.0	1,904.2	131.7	2,035.9
1925	114.5	1,794.7	24.3	155.8	65.8	66.4	41.7	114.1	2,377.3	181.5	2,558.8

Table A26 (continued)

	Processed food	Textiles	Wood products	Chemicals	Ceramics	Metals	Machinery	Other manufactures	Total manufactures	Primary products	Total commodity
1926	128.0	1,572.6	24.1	150.2	63.0	64.1	48.3	114.8	2,165.1	147.5	2,312.6
1927	122.2	1,515.8	22.7	144.6	65.5	70.8	54.1	111.6	2,107.3	158.3	2,265.6
1928	147.3	1,481.9	24.9	162.1	68.5	84.0	68.2	117.2	2,154.1	151.6	2,305.7
1929	145.7	1,629.2	28.3	171.5	74.0	94.4	80.9	132.6	2,356.6	156.8	2,513.4
1930	120.2	1,007.3	21.6	160.3	61.8	103.7	74.7	115.5	1,665.1	134.5	1,799.6
1931	92.1	809.5	15.9	115.0	46.1	75.0	61.5	96.5	1,311.6	114.5	1,426.1
1932	109.9	1,014.5	17.5	132.8	53.4	92.9	72.2	113.5	1,606.7	113.2	1,719.9
1933	159.3	1,257.8	24.8	197.3	75.1	148.1	113.9	171.0	2,147.3	131.1	2,278.4
1934	158.0	1,427.4	32.8	250.7	91.5	203.3	186.9	187.3	2,537.9	175.5	2,713.4
1935	200.1	1,620.6	40.2	313.7	101.6	255.9	230.9	216.2	2,979.2	206.4	3,185.6
1936	207.2	1,699.4	45.4	362.0	109.1	294.9	290.3	242.5	3,250.8	240.9	3,491.7
1937	242.0	1,952.7	59.4	407.1	129.5	384.2	363.3	293.5	3,831.7	262.1	4,093.8
1938	320.6	1,570.5	71.1	429.2	108.0	417.6	443.8	322.1	3,682.9	241.3	3,924.2
1939	392.2	1,936.3	147.5	543.6	136.2	515.3	647.6	368.3	4,687.0	395.9	5,082.9
1940	307.1	1,832.6	176.6	623.5	176.0	524.0	823.3	339.0	4,802.1	418.4	5,220.5
1953	27.5	148.7	5.3	22.4	20.7	72.6	75.0	29.0	401.2	17.3	418.5
1954	24.1	218.0	11.8	28.4	24.9	96.4	80.9	39.4	523.9	20.8	544.7
1955	24.8	248.9	15.9	33.7	30.6	146.7	99.3	52.2	652.1	20.2	672.3
1956	43.2	293.7	19.9	38.4	41.2	131.9	190.0	69.6	827.9	34.8	862.7
1957	40.8	344.5	19.8	45.3	41.9	126.0	244.3	83.1	945.1	36.3	982.0
1958	51.9	307.3	19.9	49.6	38.9	144.1	246.6	86.5	940.8	46.0	986.8
1959	60.0	356.8	27.5	59.9	45.4	158.0	318.2	121.7	1,147.5	50.7	1,198.2
1960	55.8	411.6	22.5	60.9	52.2	220.3	367.4	147.0	1,331.4	58.7	1,390.1

Table A26 (continued)

	Processed food	Textiles	Wood products	Chemicals	Ceramics	Metals	Machinery	Other manufactures	Total manufactures	Primary products	Total commodity
1961	50.4	384.4	21.1	67.9	50.9	223.5	441.3	151.3	1,390.8	62.8	1,453.6
1962	73.1	411.0	33.6	94.3	67.7	267.4	502.5	196.1	1,645.7	68.8	1,714.5
1963	61.6	405.4	33.2	113.7	76.5	340.0	599.8	210.6	1,840.8	64.2	1,905.0
1964	67.4	484.2	34.3	138.0	87.1	432.9	775.8	249.1	2,248.8	72.5	2,321.5
1965	73.3	513.5	35.7	196.9	95.4	618.4	1,043.4	292.3	2,868.9	75.4	2,944.3
1966	69.4	579.7	41.0	241.0	102.4	640.0	1,309.6	337.0	3,320.1	108.0	3,428.1
1967	77.9	563.2	40.0	246.3	106.9	641.2	1,514.4	395.1	3,585.1	92.6	3,677.7
1968	102.6	711.8	50.9	299.9	118.6	844.9	2,036.1	293.4	4,458.2	85.7	4,543.9
1969	103.5	817.4	53.2	365.7	140.0	1,056.7	2,564.2	331.2	5,431.9	143.4	5,575.3
1970	113.1	886.7	46.3	444.4	134.1	1,370.0	3,218.9	361.5	6,575.0	149.3	6,723.4

Source: Ippei Yamazawa and Yuzu Yamamoto's estimates for LTES 14.

Notes: Figures show the trade of the Japan Proper not only with foreign countries but also with Taiwan and Chosen under Japanese rule.

Total manufactures are divided into eight subcategories (the first eight columns) and the imports of primary products are divided into crude foodstuff and raw materials. Figures for total commodities exclude unclassified items such as correction for silver depreciation, packing costs, freight, and insurance, all of which are included in exports and imports in the balance of payment statistics (tables A31 and A32). On the other hand, part of special imports and exports excluded from tables A31 and A32 is included here.

Industry classification corresponds to that adopted by Shinohara in his estimates for manufacturing production (LTES 10:140–43).

Table A27. Imports of Major Commodity Groups in Current Prices 1874-1940 and 1953-70 (1874-1940 in millions of yen; 1953-70 in billions of yen)

	Manufactures									Primary products			
	Processed food	Textiles	Wood products	Chemicals	Ceramics	Metals	Machinery	Other manufactures	Total	Crude foodstuff	Raw materials	Total	Total
1874	3.3	12.9	0.1	1.5	0.2	1.4	1.2	1.3	21.9	0.0	1.9	1.9	23.8
1875	4.1	16.0	0.0	3.0	0.2	1.6	3.2	1.1	29.2	0.1	1.6	1.7	30.9
1876	3.4	13.8	0.0	1.6	0.3	1.5	1.3	1.0	22.9	0.1	1.4	1.5	24.4
1977	3.4	14.6	0.0	2.3	0.2	2.0	2.8	1.0	26.3	0.0	1.6	1.6	27.9
1878	3.6	18.9	0.0	2.5	0.2	2.4	1.6	1.1	30.3	0.0	3.0	3.0	33.3
1879	4.1	18.2	0.1	2.2	0.2	2.0	1.2	1.0	29.0	0.7	3.2	3.9	32.9
1880	4.4	20.4	0.1	2.8	0.3	2.7	1.8	1.0	33.5	0.7	2.6	3.3	36.8
1881	4.5	17.9	0.1	2.1	0.2	2.3	0.1	0.7	27.9	0.2	2.1	2.3	30.2
1882	5.2	14.8	0.0	1.9	0.1	2.0	1.0	0.7	25.7	0.2	3.5	3.7	29.4
1883	5.1	13.8	0.1	1.8	0.2	2.2	1.8	0.4	25.4	0.1	3.4	3.5	28.9
1884	6.1	12.5	0.0	1.9	0.2	2.1	4.6	0.5	27.9	0.3	3.0	3.3	31.2
1885	5.5	12.2	0.0	2.1	0.2	2.6	4.3	0.5	27.4	0.3	3.3	3.6	31.0
1886	6.6	12.7	0.1	2.7	0.3	3.2	2.4	0.7	28.7	0.1	4.1	4.2	32.9
1887	7.2	19.4	0.0	4.2	0.3	4.3	4.7	1.4	41.5	0.7	4.2	4.9	46.4
1888	8.5	27.6	0.1	5.4	0.6	7.3	8.1	1.4	59.0	0.7	6.9	7.6	66.6
1889	7.7	26.1	0.0	4.9	0.7	6.2	8.0	1.3	54.9	1.1	11.6	12.7	67.6
1890	9.9	24.4	0.1	5.3	0.6	6.8	9.0	1.1	57.2	14.3	11.8	26.1	83.3
1891	9.3	16.4	0.0	5.6	0.4	5.2	6.2	1.0	44.1	6.1	14.2	20.3	64.4
1892	11.1	20.5	0.0	7.0	0.3	5.0	7.0	1.0	51.9	5.0	17.3	22.3	74.2
1893	13.3	23.0	0.0	7.6	0.5	6.8	6.8	1.2	59.2	7.2	22.6	29.8	89.0
1894	15.8	24.5	0.0	8.9	0.4	11.0	15.9	1.3	77.8	11.9	27.7	39.6	117.4
1895	14.3	30.1	0.0	12.6	0.5	13.1	14.5	2.3	87.4	7.8	33.8	41.6	129.0
1896	17.2	47.2	0.0	16.1	0.9	18.5	23.8	2.2	125.9	10.6	43.9	54.5	180.4
1897	25.6	35.3	0.1	18.0	1.6	20.3	40.4	2.2	143.5	29.4	56.7	86.1	229.6
1898	41.5	36.8	0.1	27.3	1.3	23.4	38.6	2.7	171.7	57.8	59.4	117.2	288.9
1899	28.4	29.8	0.1	27.5	1.6	20.0	22.8	2.5	132.7	18.6	80.6	99.2	231.9
1900	35.1	52.0	0.0	34.7	1.6	39.3	44.0	2.8	209.5	19.8	86.5	106.3	315.8

Table A27 (continued)

| | Manufactures | | | | | | | | | Primary products | | | |
Year	Processed food	Textiles	Wood products	Chemicals	Ceramics	Metals	Machinery	Other manufactures	Total	Crude foodstuff	Raw materials	Total	Total
1901	41.1	27.2	0.1	30.3	1.8	26.4	46.2	3.0	176.1	23.5	88.0	111.5	287.6
1902	24.4	33.4	0.1	36.5	2.3	24.7	33.8	2.6	157.8	31.6	107.3	138.9	296.7
1903	37.4	27.8	0.1	38.7	2.1	28.5	20.2	3.1	157.9	75.0	95.9	170.9	328.8
1904	42.6	30.4	0.1	37.6	1.6	34.7	26.4	3.0	176.4	78.5	125.2	203.7	380.1
1905	35.9	61.4	0.1	67.7	2.7	61.6	38.7	3.2	271.3	74.2	153.6	227.8	499.1
1906	46.4	56.7	0.2	66.8	4.2	49.7	65.1	5.2	294.3	51.2	122.7	173.9	468.2
1907	38.1	50.7	0.4	79.9	4.7	66.5	47.4	5.4	293.1	56.9	165.9	222.8	515.9
1908	36.8	43.4	0.3	80.4	3.1	57.8	53.0	5.0	279.8	51.6	131.5	183.1	462.9
1909	43.2	38.9	0.2	75.6	3.5	42.0	31.3	4.5	239.2	41.8	149.9	191.7	430.9
1910	54.2	41.9	0.3	77.5	3.6	53.0	26.9	5.0	262.4	45.3	215.1	260.4	522.8
1911	52.6	43.7	0.3	95.1	3.5	72.2	51.6	5.7	324.7	54.5	202.1	256.6	581.3
1912	52.0	36.0	0.4	96.8	4.2	93.6	62.0	4.5	349.5	74.0	270.1	344.1	693.6
1913	74.0	39.7	0.5	115.1	4.2	88.1	81.0	4.1	406.7	115.4	309.2	424.6	831.3
1914	56.3	26.8	0.2	103.6	3.1	61.7	38.1	3.1	292.9	83.1	306.7	389.8	682.7
1915	55.4	15.6	0.2	97.8	1.6	61.0	16.6	4.2	252.4	64.5	313.6	378.1	630.5
1916	68.8	20.5	0.5	130.2	3.6	151.0	34.4	6.0	415.0	54.0	406.0	460.0	875.0
1917	85.4	23.7	1.5	156.2	5.6	274.9	48.4	4.6	600.3	77.9	511.6	589.5	1,189.8
1918	101.6	41.8	3.9	234.9	4.8	395.9	84.0	5.7	872.6	251.9	765.7	1,017.6	1,890.2
1919	167.3	62.3	2.3	343.2	6.6	360.9	136.2	7.7	1,086.5	454.7	941.9	1,396.6	2,483.1
1920	232.5	93.7	7.9	413.1	8.4	381.0	163.4	16.9	1,316.9	263.8	1,060.6	1,324.4	2,641.3
1921	183.0	98.3	17.8	250.2	8.6	233.3	186.2	12.6	990.0	291.4	676.9	968.3	1,958.3
1922	186.5	159.7	39.4	275.8	10.0	262.0	167.6	15.6	1,116.6	368.0	721.5	1,089.5	2,206.1
1923	202.6	188.4	43.8	283.0	12.8	204.0	167.6	18.7	1,120.9	375.0	853.4	1,228.4	2,349.3
1924	239.8	201.5	59.7	317.0	19.4	302.6	235.1	24.1	1,399.2	541.0	1,033.2	1,574.2	2,973.4
1925	224.3	185.8	34.9	303.6	13.1	183.9	177.6	19.2	1,142.6	613.2	1,359.8	1,973.0	3,115.6

Table A27 (continued)

| | Manufactures | | | | | | | | | Primary products | | | |
	Processed food	Textiles	Wood products	Chemicals	Ceramics	Metals	Machinery	Other manufactures	Total	Crude foodstuff	Raw materials	Total	Total
1926	223.2	133.7	47.3	347.0	14.3	230.8	178.3	21.6	1,196.2	583.5	1,136.9	1,720.4	2,916.6
1927	220.6	139.6	52.0	297.3	13.3	216.8	147.9	16.5	1,104.0	554.9	1,051.6	1,606.5	2,710.5
1928	238.6	129.0	54.8	301.2	17.3	246.4	171.4	20.0	1,178.7	524.0	1,020.9	1,544.9	2,723.6
1929	235.1	105.2	43.8	323.6	16.8	250.7	191.1	24.0	1,190.3	496.9	1,052.8	1,549.7	2,740.0
1930	219.9	76.6	24.3	243.0	14.4	154.9	128.2	17.4	878.7	370.6	732.4	1,103.0	1,961.7
1931	182.7	80.8	17.7	192.2	9.9	92.1	83.0	18.5	676.9	355.3	629.8	985.1	1,662.0
1932	174.8	63.5	15.4	197.4	10.6	125.6	95.9	15.4	698.6	410.6	806.3	1,216.9	1,915.5
1933	184.0	76.0	16.9	232.9	13.4	232.0	108.5	15.9	879.6	431.1	1,125.8	1,556.9	2,436.5
1934	198.9	60.6	15.1	272.4	14.3	315.4	146.2	18.5	1,041.4	538.3	1,358.1	1,896.4	2,937.8
1935	218.7	63.0	16.9	320.3	16.6	394.2	163.0	20.8	1,213.5	592.2	1,430.7	2,022.9	3,236.4
1936	237.6	66.4	16.3	369.8	17.1	376.4	157.6	21.1	1,262.3	656.0	1,674.2	2,330.2	3,592.5
1937	260.2	80.9	22.8	493.2	18.7	853.3	248.8	25.7	2,003.6	662.4	2,046.4	2,708.8	4,712.4
1938	226.1	62.8	6.0	392.5	16.4	669.8	319.4	23.8	1,716.6	704.4	1,337.2	2,041.6	3,758.2
1939	276.1	102.5	6.1	474.1	19.1	870.5	298.9	32.4	2,079.7	624.2	1,390.1	2,014.3	4,094.0
1940	232.8	127.0	7.0	608.6	23.8	919.7	282.5	47.4	2,248.8	772.9	1,560.5	2,333.5	4,582.3
1953	4.8	6.8	—	24.9	1.1	14.1	61.4	5.9	119.0	220.3	506.9	727.2	846.2
1954	5.0	3.8	—	23.0	1.3	16.3	68.1	4.1	121.6	230.4	454.9	685.3	806.9
1955	5.7	4.0	—	28.8	1.3	15.0	51.9	3.9	110.6	214.7	534.4	749.1	859.7
1956	5.0	5.5	11.2	58.8	1.6	47.4	65.0	5.5	200.0	196.0	754.0	950.0	1,150.0
1957	3.9	9.0	14.6	66.0	2.4	153.1	111.4	9.6	370.0	203.9	954.4	1,158.3	1,528.3
1958	5.3	4.9	4.3	59.8	—	19.4	131.2	7.8	232.7	185.2	650.4	835.6	1,068.3
1959	10.3	5.2	6.6	79.5	—	35.0	134.9	8.9	280.4	168.9	817.9	986.7	1,267.1
1960	12.2	6.5	10.3	95.4	—	69.0	155.3	11.4	360.1	184.7	1,038.6	1,223.3	1,583.4

Table A27 (continued)

| | Manufactures | | | | | | | | | Primary products | | | |
	Processed food	Textiles	Wood products	Chemicals	Ceramics	Metals	Machinery	Other manufactures	Total	Crude foodstuff	Raw materials	Total	Total
1961	17.4	6.4	11.4	120.9	—	108.9	230.4	15.4	510.8	222.9	1,311.0	1,533.9	2,044.7
1962	21.4	7.9	25.1	108.1	8.4	76.4	296.6	14.0	557.9	245.7	1,198.7	1,444.4	2,002.3
1963	23.3	14.0	29.2	132.9	14.7	78.1	315.3	24.5	632.0	381.9	1,383.4	1,765.3	2,397.3
1964	32.8	19.0	28.6	164.9	17.8	155.0	321.6	31.9	771.6	467.6	1,557.2	2,024.8	2,796.4
1965	33.3	17.8	58.0	146.9	21.0	139.7	277.6	37.6	679.7	495.9	1,680.7	2,176.6	2,856.3
1966	28.1	21.2	74.7	178.9	29.0	178.3	300.2	43.9	854.3	577.0	1,957.8	2,534.8	3,389.1
1967	35.1	36.8	85.8	219.8	32.5	345.1	384.6	54.6	1,193.4	615.7	2,321.6	2,937.3	4,130.7
1968	40.1	58.1	85.8	248.4	38.8	336.0	477.7	25.0	1,309.9	636.3	2,603.0	3,239.3	4,547.2
1969	43.3	72.0	90.8	281.7	48.0	431.6	588.5	35.3	1,591.2	727.9	2,917.8	3,645.7	5,236.9
1970	45.5	113.2	122.6	360.2	58.6	429.1	827.2	53.4	2,009.8	880.7	3,635.5	4,516.2	6,526.0

Source and Notes: See table A26.

Table A26. Exports of Major Commodity Groups in Constant Prices 1874–1939 and 1953–70
(1874–1939 in millions of yen at 1934–36 prices; 1953–70 in billions of yen at 1965 prices)

	Processed food	Textiles	Wood products	Chemicals	Ceramics	Metals	Machinery	Other manufactures	Total manufactures	Primary products	Total commodity
1874	15	106	0	31	1	13	0	12	178	204	382
1875	13	128	0	28	1	8	0	16	194	211	405
1876	14	198	0	27	2	5	0	20	266	283	549
1877	20	181	0	35	2	12	0	6	256	262	518
1878	12	159	0	34	2	21	0	9	237	381	618
1879	13	191	0	49	3	23	0	8	287	279	566
1880	18	171	0	74	3	21	0	27	314	328	642
1881	18	212	0	40	4	26	0	15	315	299	614
1882	11	325	0	40	3	25	0	18	422	334	756
1883	12	352	0	45	4	23	0	13	449	359	808
1884	16	252	0	47	5	37	0	15	372	433	805
1885	25	276	0	47	7	59	0	26	440	435	875
1886	17	321	0	62	10	68	0	29	507	593	1,100
1887	22	367	0	87	11	76	0	48	611	539	1,150
1888	24	528	0	92	10	69	0	58	781	707	1,488
1889	26	492	0	110	11	75	0	62	776	710	1,486
1890	17	277	0	125	10	132	0	68	629	527	1,156
1891	18	565	0	139	10	120	0	78	930	688	1,618
1892	20	684	0	137	13	123	0	90	1,067	627	1,694
1893	22	560	0	161	14	108	0	119	984	677	1,661
1894	34	793	0	171	12	109	0	115	1,234	701	1,935
1895	40	879	0	187	18	106	0	139	1,369	730	2,099
1896	30	675	7	183	20	104	2	162	1,183	768	1,951
1897	37	1,113	8	219	11	103	3	193	1,687	720	2,407
1898	40	1,037	10	234	13	117	3	200	1,664	694	2,358
1899	53	1,261	14	240	21	145	5	238	1,977	917	2,894
1900	79	1,354	17	260	25	137	7	247	2,126	814	2,940

Table A28 (continued)

	Processed food	Textiles	Wood products	Chemicals	Ceramics	Metals	Machinery	Other manufactures	Total manufactures	Primary products	Total commodity
1901	104	1,915	17	307	24	157	11	256	2,791	874	3,665
1902	95	1,457	23	316	30	147	18	320	2,406	1,007	3,413
1903	97	1,501	34	321	38	195	22	319	2,527	924	3,451
1904	125	1,811	26	401	43	168	23	343	2,940	872	3,812
1905	200	1,421	47	352	76	165	33	436	2,730	795	3,525
1906	250	1,796	77	445	97	253	42	541	3,501	936	4,437
1907	177	1,578	109	446	79	384	89	449	3,311	1,024	4,335
1908	159	1,738	78	445	66	313	76	420	3,295	929	4,224
1909	212	2,065	58	551	59	353	50	429	3,777	999	4,776
1910	353	2,622	84	552	115	382	66	501	4,675	1,107	5,782
1911	320	2,562	77	523	93	436	81	459	4,551	1,158	5,709
1912	360	3,090	79	609	102	555	122	342	5,259	1,292	6,551
1913	491	3,631	88	637	125	752	126	373	6,223	1,379	7,602
1914	465	3,358	76	697	122	763	89	415	5,985	1,364	7,349
1915	408	3,857	97	966	182	1,001	165	573	7,249	1,502	8,751
1916	610	4,251	120	1,337	252	1,256	536	693	9,055	1,685	10,740
1917	936	4,837	147	1,168	226	1,185	280	645	9,424	1,764	11,188
1918	902	5,528	121	1,262	236	649	376	616	9,690	1,476	11,166
1919	541	5,267	113	999	251	657	165	661	8,654	1,086	9,740
1920	564	4,557	102	918	252	573	264	629	7,859	959	8,818
1921	473	4,424	97	704	204	412	152	401	6,867	816	7,683
1922	544	5,362	104	782	204	440	162	629	8,227	852	9,079
1923	466	4,395	91	689	230	408	120	593	6,992	877	7,869
1924	658	5,989	93	798	274	391	155	616	8,974	1,007	9,981
1925	828	7,057	119	986	369	484	195	727	10,764	1,354	12,118

Table A28 (continued)

	Processed food	Textiles	Wood products	Chemicals	Ceramics	Metals	Machinery	Other manufactures	Total manufactures	Primary products	Total commodity
1926	1,025	7,452	112	1,078	386	516	197	751	11,517	1,213	12,730
1927	999	8,370	118	1,187	443	631	258	787	12,793	1,327	14,120
1928	1,234	8,410	154	1,309	489	712	556	871	13,735	1,233	14,968
1929	1,271	9,335	168	1,489	557	817	751	1,002	15,390	1,263	16,653
1930	1,192	8,281	158	1,678	532	1,063	729	1,060	14,693	1,322	16,015
1931	1,124	8,795	144	1,460	410	942	764	1,112	14,751	1,210	15,961
1932	1,257	10,725	155	1,696	493	1,128	922	1,393	17,769	1,259	19,028
1933	1,583	10,835	214	2,102	696	1,487	1,298	1,815	20,032	1,419	21,451
1934	1,603	14,426	261	2,652	850	1,994	1,517	1,879	25,182	1,867	27,049
1935	2,085	16,892	428	3,116	1,037	2,562	2,520	2,168	30,808	2,101	32,909
1936	1,963	16,166	562	3,453	1,154	3,002	3,406	2,409	32,115	2,258	34,373
1937	2,046	15,997	593	3,614	1,328	2,687	4,064	2,575	32,904	2,035	34,939
1938	2,481	13,849	626	3,677	1,069	2,308	4,418	2,619	30,984	1,995	32,979
1939	2,355	12,516	1,061	4,037	1,137	2,276	4,581	2,532	30,495	2,811	33,306
1953	28.2	127.6	5.7	16.6	20.5	63.4	59.1	28.5	340.3	20.5	372.7
1954	23.8	195.2	12.1	17.8	24.6	92.3	65.7	37.3	452.4	22.3	504.8
1955	26.9	236.4	15.5	22.5	30.9	121.7	84.8	44.2	560.7	23.4	620.2
1956	47.4	279.7	21.1	30.0	42.7	91.0	160.9	64.5	696.3	41.8	762.8
1957	45.6	347.6	20.8	38.6	43.6	89.7	200.4	83.5	811.8	43.8	896.8
1958	57.8	339.2	20.7	49.6	42.0	132.2	204.6	100.6	894.3	52.8	989.8
1959	64.0	367.8	25.1	66.2	49.9	138.2	265.4	128.8	1,288.1	57.0	1,106.5
1960	57.6	410.0	21.4	57.5	58.4	193.4	320.3	145.5	1,229.4	65.4	1,334.1

Table A28 (continued)

	Processed food	Textiles	Wood products	Chemicals	Ceramics	Metals	Machinery	Other manufac-tures	Total manufac-tures	Primary products	Total commodity
1961	50.7	392.2	20.0	68.1	55.3	209.3	424.7	150.4	1,359.5	66.5	1,453.6
1962	74.3	429.0	30.5	101.3	72.3	269.6	504.5	199.3	1,675.9	71.9	1,769.3
1963	63.5	390.9	30.5	128.2	80.1	346.9	603.4	216.7	1,857.5	67.9	1,920.4
1964	68.1	448.1	32.8	142.7	88.5	432.0	776.6	258.7	2,248.8	73.8	2,307.7
1965	73.3	513.5	35.7	196.9	95.4	618.4	1,043.4	292.3	2,868.9	75.4	2,944.3
1966	65.5	600.7	37.1	262.5	103.3	629.9	1,295.4	329.7	3,330.1	93.2	3,424.7
1967	73.1	566.0	35.4	282.8	104.5	786.7	1,489.1	387.7	3,570.8	82.2	3,659.4
1968	96.8	700.6	42.9	382.0	113.5	786.7	1,982.6	285.4	4,418.4	76.0	4,498.9
1969	91.5	757.0	44.4	461.7	130.1	983.9	2,463.2	316.3	5,248.2	119.4	5,376.4
1970	90.8	858.4	37.2	576.5	113.5	1,160.0	2,986.0	329.5	6,093.6	104.8	6,185.3

Source: Ippei Yamazawa and Yuzo Yamamoto's estimates for LTES 14.

Notes: Figures in each subcategory are derived by dividing figures at current prices (tables A26 and A27) by the subcategory's price index (not included in this book); such aggregates as total manufactures, primary products, and total commodity are sums of figures at constant prices of related subcategories.

Table A29. Imports of Major Commodity Groups in Constant Prices, 1874–1939 and 1953–70 (1874–1939 in millions of yen at 1934–36 prices; 1953–70 in billions of yen at 1965 prices)

	Manufactures									Primary products			Total
	Processed food	Textiles	Wood products	Chemicals	Ceramics	Metals	Machinery	Other	Total	Crude foodstuff	Raw materials	Total	
1874	71	329	0	29	5	17	35	11	497	0	50	50	547
1875	86	394	0	73	6	22	101	11	693	2	33	35	728
1876	79	377	0	32	8	23	47	18	584	2	31	33	617
1877	63	295	0	29	7	30	112	9	545	0	28	28	573
1878	61	462	0	32	7	39	65	7	673	0	46	46	719
1879	74	409	0	24	7	39	48	6	607	19	60	79	686
1880	84	482	0	33	12	40	76	9	736	18	58	76	812
1881	81	403	0	15	8	36	4	5	552	4	47	51	603
1882	95	368	0	12	3	31	44	11	564	4	68	72	636
1883	100	360	0	13	7	37	80	7	604	3	73	76	680
1884	138	307	0	15	7	40	240	9	756	9	75	84	840
1885	125	318	0	16	7	50	238	10	764	8	83	91	855
1886	135	327	0	22	12	65	143	13	717	3	96	99	816
1887	171	466	0	40	13	86	232	29	1,037	22	110	132	1,169
1888	193	689	0	52	27	152	352	32	1,497	23	173	196	1,693
1889	161	670	0	49	34	127	370	31	1,442	26	296	322	1,764
1890	207	631	0	51	27	129	405	27	1,477	330	289	619	2,096
1891	208	419	0	52	18	110	291	24	1,122	161	399	560	1,682
1892	242	539	0	63	12	100	340	24	1,320	127	532	659	1,979
1893	254	542	0	59	20	134	325	28	1,362	184	617	791	2,153
1894	282	476	0	58	14	191	768	26	1,815	279	691	970	2,785
1895	314	586	0	81	20	236	633	46	1,916	185	891	1,076	2,992

Table A29 (continued)

| | Manufactures | | | | | | | | | Primary products | | | |
	Processed food	Textiles	Wood products	Chemicals	Ceramics	Metals	Machinery	Other	Total	Crude foodstuff	Raw materials	Total	Total
1896	312	893	0	123	30	331	975	48	2,712	217	1,048	1,265	3,977
1897	451	734	1	140	50	336	1,548	48	3,310	540	1,333	1,873	5,183
1898	672	741	2	213	39	372	1,490	58	3,587	868	1,423	2,291	5,878
1899	517	618	1	199	40	258	773	65	2,471	343	2,102	2,445	4,916
1900	619	960	0	222	36	435	1,472	67	3,811	339	1,617	1,956	5,767
1901	703	473	1	197	38	330	1,610	74	3,426	409	1,675	2,084	5,510
1902	463	662	1	254	49	318	1,203	55	3,005	548	2,138	2,686	5,691
1903	697	514	1	267	51	372	719	51	2,672	1,228	1,889	3,117	5,789
1904	726	585	1	233	41	454	866	51	2,957	1,327	2,128	3,455	6,412
1905	451	857	1	378	64	744	1,187	51	3,733	1,279	2,946	4,225	7,958
1906	628	782	2	413	97	641	1,967	90	4,620	845	2,276	3,121	7,741
1907	498	577	4	466	110	783	1,343	98	3,879	871	2,809	3,680	7,559
1908	431	533	3	536	72	712	1,704	91	4,082	836	2,281	3,117	7,199
1909	433	511	2	453	79	493	917	85	2,973	751	2,728	3,479	6,452
1910	525	460	4	320	83	638	915	94	3,039	726	3,544	4,270	7,309
1911	594	454	4	460	85	850	1,767	106	4,320	767	2,554	3,321	7,641
1912	509	425	5	469	96	1,059	2,083	44	4,690	1,423	4,250	5,673	10,363
1913	574	448	5	622	91	1,020	2,841	44	5,645	2,142	4,696	6,838	12,483
1914	526	338	2	691	72	738	961	31	3,359	1,392	4,626	6,018	9,377
1915	586	214	2	675	20	689	433	45	2,664	1,297	5,295	6,592	9,256
1916	629	189	4	736	43	1,203	887	46	3,737	957	6,173	7,130	10,864
1917	742	140	10	799	29	1,600	1,123	39	4,482	1,030	5,603	6,633	11,115
1918	859	208	18	1,185	21	1,378	1,473	42	5,184	2,184	5,655	7,839	13,023
1919	1,101	297	12	1,632	24	1,580	1,981	65	6,692	3,028	6,340	9,368	16,060
1920	733	391	35	1,659	46	1,918	2,389	146	7,317	1,785	6,245	8,030	15,347

Table A29 (continued)

| | Manufactures | | | | | | | | | Primary products | | | |
	Processed food	Textiles	Wood products	Chemicals	Ceramics	Metals	Machinery	Other	Total	Crude foodstuff	Raw materials	Total	Total
1921	1,012	592	146	1,981	44	1,568	2,624	111	6,078	2,731	6,974	9,705	17,783
1922	1,392	853	340	2,276	71	2,621	2,379	161	10,093	3,203	7,514	10,717	20,810
1923	1,247	1,097	343	2,120	130	2,038	2,383	200	9,558	3,429	7,732	11,161	20,719
1924	1,534	1,138	454	2,285	175	2,848	3,257	234	11,925	4,068	7,984	12,052	23,977
1925	1,585	883	291	1,474	95	1,639	2,275	169	8,811	4,079	9,432	13,511	22,322
1926	1,731	804	451	1,953	141	2,443	2,588	213	10,324	4,366	10,114	14,480	24,804
1927	1,716	984	530	2,061	149	2,451	2,321	184	10,396	4,640	10,888	15,528	25,924
1928	2,024	848	595	2,449	196	2,839	2,582	219	11,752	4,633	9,776	14,409	26,161
1929	2,481	724	463	2,747	177	2,844	3,106	280	12,822	4,478	10,533	15,011	27,833
1930	2,119	796	325	2,768	188	2,032	2,161	233	10,622	4,010	9,635	13,645	24,269
1931	2,263	1,082	284	3,050	147	1,538	1,359	270	9,993	5,406	11,164	16,570	26,563
1932	2,189	708	197	2,936	130	1,772	1,072	140	9,144	5,055	12,201	17,256	26,400
1933	1,752	736	133	2,811	143	2,631	1,070	139	9,415	5,384	12,820	18,204	27,619
1934	2,030	663	153	2,837	145	3,263	1,529	187	10,807	6,213	13,860	20,073	30,880
1935	2,278	608	169	3,143	131	3,920	1,667	201	12,117	5,678	14,237	19,915	32,032
1936	2,239	631	159	3,621	228	3,661	1,478	214	12,231	5,997	16,467	22,464	34,695
1937	2,211	698	147	3,498	226	9,741	2,348	209	19,078	5,540	17,503	23,043	42,121
1938	1,968	583	34	3,052	67	6,396	2,516	189	14,805	5,760	12,308	18,068	32,893
1939	2,297	531	33	3,202	93	4,958	2,271	232	13,617	4,595	13,246	17,841	31,188

Table A29 (continued)

| | Manufactures | | | | | | | | | Primary products | | | |
	Processed food	Textiles	Wood products	Chemicals	Ceramics	Metals	Machinery	Other	Total	Crude foodstuff	Raw materials	Total	Total
1953	—	—	—	25.4	—	13.2	—	—	114.6	162.1	409.8	573.0	686.9
1954	—	—	—	23.6	—	15.5	—	—	118.4	192.5	367.2	558.1	785.7
1955	—	—	—	26.3	—	14.0	—	—	100.5	181.5	412.3	591.7	721.2
1956	4.6	—	8.8	39.1	—	42.5	—	—	160.0	166.5	607.6	776.1	965.6
1957	2.2	—	12.7	46.1	—	151.3	—	—	312.8	178.2	715.4	902.8	1,280.0
1958	5.1	—	4.2	43.6	—	23.6	—	—	215.9	179.8	568.5	750.1	1,013.6
1959	11.4	—	6.6	57.9	—	41.3	—	—	267.3	173.6	793.2	971.2	1,243.5
1960	13.5	7.6	10.1	71.7	—	86.1	165.9	—	363.7	186.9	929.8	1,129.5	1,569.3
1961	18.4	7.1	10.9	97.6	—	131.7	243.0	—	517.5	222.5	1,295.5	1,518.7	2,020.5
1962	24.0	8.5	25.5	95.7	—	92.8	310.3	—	584.2	253.3	1,201.1	1,457.5	2,039.0
1963	26.7	14.3	29.4	129.3	—	87.6	327.1	—	666.0	318.0	1,373.8	1,666.9	2,373.6
1964	35.7	18.8	28.4	166.6	—	165.1	330.2	—	801.2	380.2	1,541.8	1,895.9	2,725.5
1965	33.3	17.8	58.0	146.9	—	139.7	277.6	—	679.7	495.9	1,680.7	2,176.6	2,856.3
1966	28.8	20.9	74.6	182.6	—	162.7	296.9	—	853.4	565.1	1,925.1	2,490.0	3,319.4
1967	36.9	34.2	86.8	227.1	—	304.9	378.4	—	1,187.5	598.9	2,307.8	2,902.5	4,089.8
1968	42.6	51.0	87.9	252.4	—	284.0	465.1	—	1,283.0	633.8	2,549.5	3,188.3	4,606.3
1969	39.9	62.2	87.6	284.5	—	314.8	565.3	—	1,461.2	695.2	2,855.0	3,543.0	5,045.2
1970	34.6	91.7	103.7	358.4	—	298.6	790.1	—	1,743.1	774.6	3,688.0	4,236.6	6,082.0

Source and Notes: See table A28.

Table A30. Exports and Imports: Price Indexes and Terms of Trade
(1934–36 = 100 for 1874–1939; 1965 = 100 for 1953–70)

	Exports	Imports	Terms of trade		Exports	Imports	Terms of trade
1874	49.3	43.5	113.3	1916	109.9	80.5	136.5
1875	44.8	42.5	105.4	1917	150.7	107.0	140.8
1876	49.5	39.6	125.0	1918	185.4	145.1	127.8
1877	44.2	48.7	90.8	1919	235.4	154.6	152.3
1878	41.8	46.3	90.3	1920	241.8	172.1	140.5
1879	49.1	48.0	102.3	1921	188.5	110.1	171.2
1880	43.8	45.3	96.7	1922	199.1	106.0	187.8
1881	50.0	50.1	99.8	1923	206.9	113.4	182.5
1882	49.6	46.2	107.4	1924	204.0	124.0	164.5
1883	44.6	42.5	104.9	1925	211.2	139.6	151.3
1884	40.9	37.1	110.2	1926	181.7	117.6	154.5
1885	41.4	36.3	114.0	1927	160.5	104.6	153.4
1886	43.4	40.3	107.7	1928	154.0	104.1	147.9
1887	45.0	39.7	113.4	1929	150.9	98.4	153.4
1888	43.8	39.3	111.5	1930	112.4	81.7	137.6
1889	46.6	38.3	121.7	1931	89.4	62.6	142.8
1890	48.4	39.7	121.9	1932	90.4	72.6	124.5
1891	48.8	38.3	127.4	1933	106.2	88.2	120.4
1892	53.5	37.5	142.7	1934	100.3	95.1	105.5
1893	53.5	41.3	129.5	1935	96.8	101.0	95.8
1894	58.2	42.2	137.9	1936	101.6	103.6	98.1
1895	64.5	43.1	149.7	1937	117.2	111.9	104.7
1896	60.0	45.4	132.2	1938	119.0	114.3	104.1
1897	68.8	44.3	155.3	1939	152.6	140.7	108.5
1898	71.0	49.2	144.3	1953	112.3	123.2	91.2
1899	76.7	47.2	162.5	1954	107.9	118.3	91.2
1900	71.2	54.8	129.9	1955	108.4	119.2	90.9
1901	70.6	52.2	135.2	1956	113.1	119.1	95.0
1902	77.7	52.1	149.1	1957	109.5	119.4	91.7
1903	86.2	56.8	151.8	1958	99.7	105.4	94.6
1904	85.3	59.3	143.8	1959	103.8	101.9	101.9
1905	93.9	62.7	149.8	1960	104.2	100.9	103.3
1906	97.9	60.5	161.8	1961	100.0	101.2	98.8
1907	103.2	68.3	151.1	1962	96.9	98.2	98.7
1908	93.3	64.4	144.9	1963	99.2	101.0	98.2
1909	90.2	66.8	135.0	1964	100.6	102.6	98.1
1910	87.1	71.5	121.8	1965	100.0	100.0	100.0
1911	93.3	71.0	131.4	1966	100.1	102.1	98.0
1912	96.9	66.9	144.8	1967	100.5	101.0	99.5
1913	92.6	66.6	139.0	1968	101.0	101.5	99.5
1914	89.0	72.8	122.3	1969	103.7	103.8	99.9
1915	88.0	68.1	129.2	1970	108.7	107.3	101.3

Source: Figures for 1874–1939 derived as implicit deflator by dividing figures for total commodity at current prices (in appendix tables A26 and A27) by those at constant prices (appendix tables A28 and A29).

Figures for 1953–70 are derived from Bank of Japan export and import price indexes, using 1964 as a base. (LTES 8:212 uses 1960 as a base. The two series are thus not directly comparable.)

Note: This table SUPERSEDES LTES 8:212 for the prewar period.

Table A31. Balance of Payments, 1868–1940

(In millions of yen)

	Exports of goods and services, and factor income from abroad			Imports of goods and services, and factor income paid abroad			Net exports and net factor income from abroad	Net transfers from abroad (excluding reparations)[a]	Surplus on current account (excluding reparations)[a]	Net long-term capital inflow (including reparations)[a]	Net short-term capital inflow and errors and omissions[b]	Net exports of monetary gold	Net decrease in specie held abroad
	Merchandise (fob)	Other services	Income from abroad	Merchandise (cif)	Other	Income from abroad							
1868	15.9	1.0	—	12.6	0.2	0.4	3.7	-0.1	3.6	0.4	-4.0	—	—
1869	13.2	0.8	—	24.5	0.7	0.9	-12.1	-0.7	-12.8	-0.4	13.2	—	—
1870	14.8	1.0	—	40.0	2.2	1.6	-28.0	-0.6	-28.6	4.0	24.6	—	—
1871	18.3	1.3	—	25.9	1.5	1.3	-9.1	-0.6	-9.7	-0.2	9.9	—	—
1872	17.4	1.0	—	31.0	2.5	1.4	-16.5	-0.6	-17.1	-3.1	19.4	0.8	—
1873	22.1	1.3	—	34.0	2.7	2.0	-15.3	-0.6	-15.9	11.1	2.8	2.0	—
1874	19.7	1.4	—	29.2	8.0	2.2	-18.3	-2.1	-20.4	-0.5	8.0	12.9	—
1875	19.0	1.6	—	37.5	5.8	2.5	-25.2	0.2	-25.0	-0.7	10.5	15.2	—
1876	28.3	1.7	—	31.2	4.1	2.2	-7.5	-0.6	-8.1	-0.7	5.6	3.2	—
1877	23.8	1.6	—	35.3	3.7	2.3	-15.9	-0.5	-16.4	-0.8	9.2	8.0	—
1878	26.5	1.7	—	43.9	3.0	2.5	-21.2	-0.6	-21.8	-0.8	15.7	6.9	—
1879	28.8	1.9	—	43.8	2.9	2.8	-18.8	-0.7	-19.5	-0.9	10.0	10.4	—
1880	29.0	2.5	0.1	48.8	3.4	3.0	-23.6	-0.1	-23.7	-1.0	13.9	10.8	—
1881	31.7	2.7	0.2	41.3	2.7	3.8	-13.2	0.0	-13.2	-1.3	8.5	6.0	—
1882	38.5	3.2	0.2	38.2	2.4	3.2	-1.9	0.8	-1.1	-1.0	3.6	-1.5	—
1883	37.0	3.2	0.2	36.8	3.9	2.9	-3.2	0.9	-2.3	-0.5	4.9	-2.1	—
1884	34.6	3.1	0.3	37.5	6.4	2.3	-8.2	0.2	-8.0	-0.5	8.9	-0.4	—
1885	37.9	3.6	0.7	37.3	5.9	2.3	-3.3	0.5	-2.8	-0.5	6.6	-3.3	—

Table A31 (continued)

	Exports of goods and services, and factor income from abroad			Imports of goods and services, and factor income paid abroad			Net exports and net factor income from abroad	Net transfers from abroad (excluding reparations)[a]	Surplus on current account (excluding reparations)[a]	Net long-term capital inflow (including reparations)[a]	Net short-term capital inflow and errors and omissions[b]	Net exports of monetary gold	Net decrease in specie held abroad
	Merchandise (fob)	Other services	Income from abroad	Merchandise (cif)	Other	Income from abroad							
1886	50.0	4.4	0.5	41.3	5.2	2.2	6.2	0.7	6.9	-0.6	-6.5	0.2	—
1887	53.5	5.0	0.6	59.3	5.5	2.3	-8.0	1.0	-7.0	-0.7	5.8	1.9	—
1888	67.1	6.0	0.7	74.4	2.5	2.6	-5.7	1.5	-4.2	-0.7	5.8	-0.9	—
1889	71.5	6.1	0.5	73.4	2.3	2.8	-0.4	1.2	0.8	-0.8	9.0	-9.0	—
1890	57.8	6.6	0.4	91.4	2.0	3.2	-31.8	2.0	-29.8	-0.8	18.0	12.6	—
1891	81.2	7.2	0.5	69.7	2.9	2.9	13.4	3.1	16.5	-0.8	-3.3	-12.4	—
1892	93.0	8.0	0.7	78.4	6.3	3.0	14.0	4.1	18.1	-1.0	-3.9	-13.2	—
1893	91.6	8.2	0.5	98.6	2.8	2.8	-3.9	4.1	0.2	-1.2	-0.1	1.1	—
1894	115.6	8.9	0.6	132.6	5.9	1.9	-15.3	4.8	-10.5	-1.6	4.5	7.6	—
1895	138.9	10.2	0.6	142.2	11.9	2.6	-7.0	124.6	117.6	-1.9	-137.1	21.4	—
								(5.5)	(-1.5)	(117.2)			
1896	120.3	13.8	0.9	188.8	11.5	3.0	-68.3	91.7	23.4	-1.8	5.9	-27.5	—
								(7.2)	(-61.1)	(82.7)			
1897	170.2	18.7	2.6	243.3	45.6	3.5	-100.9	43.5	-57.4	42.5	77.1	-62.2	—
								(8.5)	(-92.4)	(77.5)			
1898	173.4	22.7	4.4	315.5	51.5	4.1	-170.6	130.6	-40.0	—	-6.2	46.2	—
								(11.4)	(-159.2)	(119.2)			
1899	227.4	24.9	4.1	224.1	14.6	6.1	11.6	16.5	28.1	97.9	-116.9	-9.1	—
1900	217.1	40.1	2.2	291.7	32.2	8.7	-73.2	22.6	-50.6	—	4.9	45.7	—

Table A31 (continued)

	Exports of goods and services, and factor income from abroad			Imports of goods and services, and factor income paid abroad			Net exports and net factor income from abroad	Net transfers from abroad (excluding reparations)[a]	Surplus on current account (excluding reparations)[a]	Net long-term capital inflow (including reparations)[a]	Net short-term capital inflow and errors and omissions[b]	Net exports of monetary gold	Net decrease in specie held abroad
	Merchandise (fob)	Other services	Income from abroad	Merchandise (cif)	Other	Income from abroad							
1901	266.3	41.2	2.4	263.2	31.7	8.8	6.2	10.1	16.3	—	−20.1	3.8	—
1902	272.9	55.0	3.8	279.2	27.2	9.7	15.6	9.9	25.5	15.2	−9.2	−31.5	—
1903	306.7	59.8	3.9	326.9	46.4	11.1	−14.3	8.2	−6.1	33.5	−19.6	−7.8	—
1904	329.4	47.6	6.0	381.8	122.8	18.9	−140.5	9.9	−130.6	101.8	7.0	73.5	−51.7
1905	335.0	54.5	11.6	502.2	198.0	37.4	−336.5	10.3	−326.2	592.1	120.5	−14.5	−371.9
1906	439.4	90.8	9.8	437.0	59.6	78.5	−35.1	10.8	−24.3	131.2	−85.3	−23.1	1.5
1907	452.2	149.4	15.1	512.1	55.2	65.6	−16.2	20.3	4.1	25.3	−79.5	9.8	40.3
1908	399.2	93.0	13.7	460.7	61.8	71.1	−87.7	24.8	−62.9	67.3	−60.0	−15.3	70.9
1909	437.1	81.8	19.9	430.5	50.0	75.0	−16.7	20.9	4.2	132.8	−63.2	−74.3	0.5
1910	501.9	65.3	20.1	520.5	55.9	79.9	−69.0	−4.5	−73.5	110.5	−34.4	5.0	−7.6
1911	522.9	76.3	20.2	581.1	52.5	84.4	−98.6	−0.9	−99.5	0.7	−16.1	9.3	105.6
1912	618.2	82.9	26.0	684.1	65.6	87.7	−110.3	1.9	−108.4	45.0	39.2	7.7	16.5
1913	716.5	94.7	33.5	794.9	63.9	92.5	−106.6	7.1	−99.5	99.1	17.1	14.8	−31.5
1914	670.8	97.2	31.2	670.9	54.1	91.3	−17.1	3.6	−13.5	−11.0	−17.6	8.5	33.6
1915	792.6	175.6	36.2	635.7	61.5	91.1	216.1	3.5	219.6	−75.0	15.3	6.8	−166.7
1916	1,233.9	355.1	57.1	878.6	82.7	80.1	604.7	19.5	624.2	−451.0	23.9	−89.5	−107.6
1917	1,752.1	509.7	93.9	1,201.0	134.4	83.9	936.4	22.8	959.2	−378.2	−175.6	−248.8	−156.6
1918	2,159.0	737.2	120.4	1,901.5	232.9	82.9	799.3	34.8	834.1	−538.4	206.2	−10.3	−491.6
1919	2,379.2	726.2	137.2	2,500.6	319.4	89.3	333.3	45.6	378.9	−97.4	251.7	−325.2	−208.0
1920	2,200.3	663.6	119.9	2,681.0	324.7	89.4	−111.3	37.6	−73.7	−353.7	570.2	−423.6	280.8

Year	Exports of goods and services, and factor income from abroad			Imports of goods and services, and factor income paid abroad			Net exports and net factor income from abroad	Net transfers from abroad (excluding reparations)[a]	Surplus on current account (excluding reparations)[a]	Net long-term capital inflow (including reparations)[a]	Net short-term capital inflow and errors and omissions[b]	Net exports of monetary gold	Net decrease in specie held abroad
	Merchandise (fob)	Other services	Income from abroad	Merchandise (cif)	Other	Income from abroad							
1921	1,502.8	422.7	139.9	1,940.4	309.0	88.7	-272.7	24.9	-247.8	-185.5	372.7	-146.6	207.2
1922	1,879.9	373.2	135.3	2,215.5	289.0	72.6	-189.5	14.1	-175.4	-172.0	110.8	-3.0	239.6
1923	1,686.2	341.6	156.1	2,392.9	235.2	91.6	-535.8	17.7	-518.1	39.1	308.7	-0.7	171.0
1924	2,105.5	399.5	159.5	2,971.2	288.1	94.6	-689.4	49.0	-640.4	221.7	308.0	-8.1	118.8
1925	2,670.1	430.5	171.5	3,105.2	304.3	114.8	-252.2	16.5	-235.7	43.0	105.6	18.7	68.4
1926	2,414.4	408.8	162.5	2,917.8	328.0	118.5	-378.6	1.3	-377.3	-82.2	405.3	27.3	26.9
1927	2,382.9	424.0	174.2	2,712.0	291.0	109.2	-131.1	4.7	-126.4	-185.5	231.5	36.2	44.2
1928	2,400.1	466.9	165.6	2,744.7	304.6	118.4	-135.2	11.1	-124.1	-151.8	206.6	-2.5	71.8
1929	2,604.3	503.6	192.0	2,764.8	325.7	132.3	77.1	11.3	88.4	-164.6	219.6	-2.6	-140.8
1930	1,871.2	441.5	172.9	2,005.5	303.8	129.5	46.8	-3.5	43.3	-303.7	-135.4	274.5	121.3
1931	1,479.5	386.1	164.1	1,686.1	301.9	117.4	-75.7	-5.8	-81.5	-372.0	36.8	370.8	45.9
1932	1,802.1	464.7	199.3	1,936.3	398.7	144.1	-13.0	54.8	41.8	-258.0	137.4	102.8	-24.0
1933	2,350.8	561.5	180.0	2,463.8	478.0	165.3	-14.8	58.0	43.2	-215.3	90.3	7.7	74.1
1934	2,788.5	595.0	196.4	2,969.7	519.2	149.8	-58.8	64.5	5.7	-262.4	270.1	-22.5	9.1
1935	3,276.0	651.1	230.7	3,272.3	558.3	160.7	166.5	67.4	233.9	-549.3	295.8	18.5	1.1
1936	3,585.0	724.6	270.0	3,641.0	596.4	151.3	191.0	41.0	231.9	-353.0	150.6	-28.4	-1.1
1937	4,188.0	929.9	283.4	4,765.0	1,021.8	182.3	-567.8	5.5	-562.3	-870.1	565.0	866.9	0.5
1938	3,939.0	997.3	346.6	3,794.0	1,906.6	223.8	-641.5	81.0	-560.5	-305.7	185.0	676.3	4.9
1939	5,163.0	738.6	396.9	4,165.0	1,746.5	292.8	94.2	76.9	171.1	-1,265.1	411.3	686.7	-4.0
1940	5,418.0	1,268.5	505.4	4,653.0	2,198.3	298.4	42.2	83.1	125.3	-1,417.7	939.8	351.1	1.5

[a] Reparation in this table means an indemnity gained from China as a result of the Sino-Japanese War.
[b] Net short-term capital is calculated as a residual of current balance, specie balance, and long-term capital balance.

Table A32. Balance of Payments, 1941–50

(In millions of yen)

Year[a]	Exports of goods and services, and factor income from abroad			Imports of goods and services, and factor income paid abroad			Net exports and net factor income from abroad	Net transfers from abroad (excluding reparations)	Surplus on current account (excluding reparations)
	Merchandise (fob)	Other services	Income from abroad	Merchandise (cif)[b]	Other	Income paid abroad			
1941	4.6	1.1	0.4	4.1	2.9	0.1	−1.0	0.1	−0.9
1942	3.6	1.0	0.4	2.9	3.1	0.1	−1.1	0.2	−0.9
1943	3.2	1.2	0.5	2.9	2.8	0.1	−0.9	0.3	−0.6
1944	1.5	2.0	0.5	1.9	2.1	0.3	−0.4	0.8	0.4
1946	4.8	0	—	21.5	2.6	—	−19.3	13.8	−5.5
1947	27.5	0.2	—	67.4	14.1	0.5	−53.8	60.8	7.0
1948	75.0	6.1	—	154.7	35.9	0.6	−109.5	130.7	21.2
1949	193.0	23.5	—	262.1	64.2	0.5	−110.3	184.9	74.6
1950	332.6	136.5	—	319.0	43.1	2.2	104.8	66.6	171.4

Note: All figures are tentative. For more details see ch. 7. Estimates for capital and specie flows are not available.

[a] Merchandise figures for 1941–44 are on calendar-year basis; those for 1946–50 are fiscal year. 1945 has not been estimated.

[b] Figures for 1941–44 are on a cif basis; those for 1946–50 are fob.

Table A33. Balance of Payments, 1951–67

(In billions of yen)

	Exports of goods and services, and factor income from abroad			Imports of goods and services, and factor income paid abroad			Net exports and net factor income from abroad	Net transfers from abroad	Surplus on current account	Net long-term capital inflow	Net short-term capital inflow[a]	Net decrease in foreign exchange reserves	Errors and omissions
	Merchandise (fob)	Other services	Income from abroad	Merchandise (cif)	Other	Income paid abroad							
1951	571.0	198.6	0.4	592.3	113.5	7.2	57.1	61.6	118.6	7.9	−129.6	—	3.1
1952	465.9	266.5	56.5	612.5	97.2	10.7	68.6	12.3	80.9	−22.0	−59.0	—	0.1
1953	453.7	270.6	64.6	737.9	110.8	21.6	−81.4	7.5	−73.9	−49.7	67.0	56.2	0.4
1954	581.0	212.7	59.9	734.6	119.5	28.1	−28.5	10.1	−18.3	18.0	−34.6	30.6	4.3
1955	722.9	198.8	57.7	741.9	130.1	32.4	74.5	7.0	81.6	0.7	−64.1	−11.2	−7.0
1956	893.6	236.7	58.7	940.6	227.0	40.4	−19.1	6.9	−12.1	26.6	45.0	−63.7	4.0
1957	1,027.6	250.5	60.3	1,172.3	326.2	50.5	−210.6	−12.7	−223.2	20.1	51.5	150.1	1.5
1958	1,033.7	236.0	48.4	900.5	204.0	45.4	168.2	−73.1	95.2	41.4	−28.4	−121.3	13.1
1959	1,228.9	253.6	48.8	1,098.8	235.2	55.9	141.5	−11.4	130.1	−77.0	92.9	−166.0	20.0
1960	1,432.3	282.5	59.1	1,335.8	302.1	75.2	60.6	−9.0	51.6	−19.8	137.2	−180.7	11.7
1961	1,493.7	301.1	65.1	1,694.6	401.9	102.0	−338.6	−15.1	−353.7	−3.6	228.6	121.7	7.0
1962	1,749.9	320.5	71.2	1,605.1	422.3	120.8	−6.6	−10.9	−17.6	61.9	81.7	−127.8	1.8
1963	1,940.8	328.9	79.7	2,000.4	466.8	146.2	−264.1	−16.4	−280.5	168.1	110.2	−13.3	15.5
1964	2,413.1	388.6	87.7	2,278.0	572.8	185.6	−147.0	−25.9	−172.9	38.5	174.2	−43.6	3.8
1965	3,000.0	451.9	111.1	2,315.6	671.7	209.7	366.1	−30.9	335.1	−149.0	−128.9	−38.9	−18.3
1966	3,469.9	563.5	131.4	2,651.6	783.4	230.6	499.1	−48.7	450.4	−291.2	−155.5	11.9	−15.6
1967	3,682.3	633.0	152.5	3,265.3	948.1	259.5	−5.0	−64.1	−69.1	−287.6	361.4	24.9	−29.6

[a] Entered under this item are all short-term capital flows excluding changes in foreign exchange reserves.

Table A34. Personal Consumption Expenditures in Current Prices, 1874–1940
(In thousands of yen)

	Food[a]	Clothing	Housing	Fuel and light	Medical and personal care	Transportation	Communication	Social expenses	Education, recreation, and miscellaneous	Total
1874	267,129	35,382	39,285	23,245	14,955	907	—	20,358	16,201	417,462
1875	332,326	36,932	42,142	29,539	16,760	930	61	26,613	19,335	504,638
1876	294,629	30,869	38,030	32,911	18,231	1,194	78	20,604	18,082	454,628
1877	314,203	33,342	39,675	29,187	19,805	1,291	382	20,849	19,190	477,924
1878	341,480	43,697	39,828	26,003	21,034	1,402	447	27,226	20,722	521,839
1879	453,673	63,954	45,763	26,618	22,632	1,623	584	40,226	26,086	681,159
1880	588,818	70,781	49,571	34,343	27,534	1,804	696	51,141	32,442	857,130
1881	594,783	76,835	52,432	50,777	31,866	1,946	812	60,094	34,779	904,324
1882	542,221	57,825	50,822	54,065	35,331	2,011	865	54,084	32,549	829,773
1883	430,750	46,108	56,292	40,611	34,379	2,031	852	47,950	27,565	686,538
1884	440,904	40,896	61,143	33,348	35,487	1,747	1,006	46,848	29,194	690,573
1885	485,846	52,270	66,351	32,786	38,746	1,767	654	47,707	31,581	757,708
1886	472,719	58,763	67,388	24,426	35,608	1,911	903	37,160	28,845	727,723
1887	485,715	63,778	73,187	28,824	37,094	2,358	1,020	49,792	31,032	772,800
1888	482,492	79,821	79,230	31,221	38,998	3,269	982	42,556	32,431	791,000
1889	538,023	85,277	85,995	31,479	42,963	4,829	1,158	57,763	36,370	883,857
1890	664,027	72,445	87,967	33,097	44,374	5,600	1,391	52,245	40,266	1,001,412
1891	678,422	86,587	91,786	33,263	45,083	6,042	1,515	56,292	41,643	1,040,633
1892	651,286	86,900	97,366	35,965	46,264	6,854	1,655	59,603	41,326	1,027,219
1893	718,299	100,148	99,715	35,698	47,728	7,595	1,947	63,405	44,725	1,119,260
1894	748,068	110,594	95,214	35,926	50,156	8,912	2,515	63,895	46,824	1,162,104
1895	836,107	142,741	111,003	43,359	59,324	11,710	2,867	81,556	53,921	1,342,588

Table A34 (continued)

	Food[a]	Clothing	Housing	Fuel and light	Medical and personal care	Transportation	Communication	Social expenses	Education, recreation, and miscellaneous	Total
1896	927,763	168,119	129,047	48,210	63,817	13,472	3,125	108,536	59,982	1,522,071
1897	1,130,706	174,714	133,064	54,281	76,173	17,147	3,665	122,640	71,410	1,783,800
1898	1,346,804	193,459	137,296	57,355	81,791	19,226	4,088	158,410	82,855	2,081,284
1899	1,279,857	210,669	153,073	58,153	82,246	23,501	5,233	156,220	81,897	2,050,849
1900	1,366,053	221,935	173,844	67,543	91,603	26,244	6,033	168,630	90,969	2,212,854
1901	1,383,655	164,350	182,526	66,301	91,738	27,147	6,123	181,040	88,674	2,191,554
1902	1,452,617	169,741	176,771	70,336	91,190	29,462	6,626	184,690	93,355	2,275,288
1903	1,561,864	151,481	201,305	70,352	92,369	31,891	7,242	191,990	97,947	2,406,441
1904	1,667,934	127,855	205,542	70,854	89,830	31,955	8,510	198,560	102,660	2,503,700
1905	1,610,380	202,407	208,972	79,854	87,931	38,001	9,665	189,800	107,394	2,534,404
1906	1,635,863	247,407	228,337	86,389	86,387	43,944	9,260	191,260	115,705	2,644,552
1907	1,782,097	270,991	248,808	100,511	86,987	50,597	10,322	194,180	127,619	2,872,112
1908	2,113,351	265,157	289,715	113,208	82,812	52,072	10,829	223,380	141,116	3,291,640
1909	2,029,043	283,562	313,201	118,266	75,226	53,669	11,573	237,980	139,799	3,262,319
1910	2,060,322	311,273	326,111	117,688	85,915	60,006	12,978	239,440	145,279	3,359,012
1911	2,341,738	341,039	347,226	121,286	97,100	69,543	14,478	229,220	159,090	3,721,539
1912	2,641,854	341,596	379,104	141,818	105,069	74,784	15,288	235,060	178,969	4,113,542
1913	2,874,809	361,709	377,756	149,133	111,361	79,367	16,307	241,630	192,126	4,404,198
1914	2,282,444	318,289	377,623	146,436	124,249	79,836	16,664	245,280	174,808	3,765,629
1915	2,267,904	348,035	377,176	159,045	144,902	82,508	18,657	195,640	190,392	3,784,259
1916	2,468,390	569,830	403,444	173,665	175,556	99,206	22,134	204,400	228,805	4,345,430
1917	3,324,080	760,978	457,389	222,129	223,314	120,664	26,445	218,270	302,688	5,655,957
1918	4,851,582	1,226,527	553,173	305,395	271,083	163,227	31,017	251,850	430,497	8,084,351
1919	6,993,351	2,217,007	688,837	400,736	322,726	218,368	39,840	295,650	596,182	11,772,697
1920	7,298,770	1,473,313	754,383	542,781	391,178	283,775	41,904	376,680	654,161	11,816,945

Table A34 (continued)

	Food[a]	Clothing	Housing	Fuel and light	Medical and personal care	Trans-portation	Commu-nication	Social expenses	Education, recreation, and miscellaneous	Total
1921	6,908,428	1,589,105	836,995	498,849	412,154	306,949	46,526	438,000	616,711	11,653,717
1922	7,029,304	1,463,369	1,046,520	527,000	443,053	335,930	47,485	549,690	655,023	12,097,374
1923	7,120,583	1,414,379	1,130,570	505,177	661,085	350,223	44,891	433,620	676,297	12,336,825
1924	7,375,183	1,494,529	1,265,240	488,797	492,004	374,763	50,921	400,040	742,705	12,684,182
1925	7,843,201	1,352,810	1,421,993	502,264	474,891	381,486	62,885	448,950	787,658	13,276,138
1926	7,404,949	1,327,313	1,446,093	535,374	507,387	389,081	66,952	427,780	782,478	12,887,407
1927	7,090,207	1,338,211	1,461,458	546,389	511,124	402,847	70,988	427,780	820,993	12,669,997
1928	6,922,667	1,498,080	1,522,050	542,285	527,202	424,391	70,024	402,960	834,468	12,744,127
1929	6,703,726	1,238,853	1,590,462	520,974	521,965	423,202	71,839	401,500	818,338	12,290,859
1930	6,056,933	1,101,207	1,548,997	493,777	490,761	389,245	68,779	373,760	801,740	11,325,199
1931	5,119,953	1,131,267	1,517,675	483,588	456,519	363,507	68,742	309,520	747,595	10,198,366
1932	5,171,283	1,129,975	1,456,742	476,195	454,724	350,084	72,905	285,430	756,781	10,154,119
1933	5,731,599	1,249,041	1,472,076	502,819	700,756	374,303	78,515	290,540	828,193	11,227,842
1934	6,222,434	1,620,528	1,525,768	530,380	862,010	397,163	81,048	317,550	957,771	12,514,652
1935	6,575,148	1,671,278	1,533,579	559,439	869,285	417,044	86,616	344,560	1,024,476	13,081,425
1936	6,894,026	1,879,465	1,647,561	578,710	717,902	447,689	93,213	375,950	1,087,512	13,722,028
1937	7,522,214	2,471,387	1,786,841	648,158	869,082	486,287	108,984	408,800	1,281,159	15,582,912
1938	8,113,751	3,089,420	1,937,679	755,718	990,118	559,356	115,418	449,680	1,424,562	17,435,702
1939	9,129,037	1,915,388	2,122,199	792,375	1,071,134	701,692	121,852	544,580	1,515,240	17,913,497
1940	9,955,110	2,246,723	2,655,686	915,604	1,159,019	837,634	129,163	730,000	1,727,993	20,356,932

Source: Reprinted from LTES 6:132–35 (table 1).

Notes: The difference between the consumption total in this table and Ohkawa's estimate in table A1 widens as one goes back in time because of his increasing downward adjustment of the implicit price deflator, taking into account the wider regional differential of consumer prices, while Shinohara's estimate (given in this table) mostly depends on Tokyo prices. For table A1, Ohkawa also amended this table's 1938–40 clothing expenditures, and food expenditures to correct for unreasonable movements around 1907.

[a]Includes beverages and tobacco.

Table A35. Personal Consumption Expenditures in Current Prices, 1946–72
(In billions of yen)

	Food	Clothing	Housing	Fuel and light	Others	Total
1946	243.1	23.8	22.2	19.5	37.8	346.4
1947	626.4	83.4	50.4	52.9	131.2	944.3
1948	1,121.5	148.7	151.1	88.2	290.5	1,800.0
1949	1,480.0	206.9	186.1	116.9	354.4	2,344.3
1950	1,526.2	291.3	227.1	130.4	387.8	2,562.8
1951	1,774.6	476.7	261.0	153.2	484.1	3,149.6
1952	2,084.3	605.4	349.3	188.6	634.3	3,861.9
1953	2,446.8	698.3	469.5	220.0	830.2	4,664.7
1954	2,704.5	717.5	527.7	233.7	978.8	5,162.0
1955	2,824.7	744.5	603.5	235.2	1,121.3	5,529.2
1956	2,983.8	833.5	706.1	245.7	1,242.9	6,012.0
1957	3,202.6	921.6	797.0	267.0	1,408.6	6,596.9
1958	3,370.7	939.1	924.8	268.2	1,554.0	7,056.8
1959	3,545.6	995.5	1,141.2	275.6	1,764.3	7,722.1
1960	3,807.0	1,208.1	1,388.3	320.2	2,099.4	8,823.0
1961	4,189.1	1,380.3	1,687.0	365.0	2,484.0	10,105.6
1962	4,717.8	1,616.2	1,919.5	420.7	3,072.2	11,746.5
1963	5,413.1	1,822.6	2,309.6	477.3	3,745.9	13,768.5
1964	6,047.6	2,025.4	2,925.4	525.7	4,514.4	16,038.5
1965	6,825.3	2,182.5	3,298.6	589.9	5,201.7	18,098.0
1966	7,644.7	2,357.5	3,881.3	651.3	6,084.9	20,619.7
1967	8,632.0	2,608.9	4,601.9	718.3	7,033.2	23,594.3
1968	9,724.0	2,941.2	5,490.6	772.1	8,337.7	27,265.6
1969	10,976.7	3,265.1	6,539.8	852.8	9,747.9	31,382.2
1970	12,449.6	3,700.7	7,868.7	963.0	11,558.8	36,340.8
1971	13,873.2	4,246.8	8,930.6	1,099.1	13,089.2	41,238.9
1972	15,537.2	4,831.0	10,179.9	1,184.1	15,433.3	47,165.5

Source: 1951–64: ARNIS 1969 revised issue; 1965–72: ARNIS 1974. The 1946 period
was extrapolated from the ESB's semiofficial data in ARNIS 1961, based on the official
1951 estimates.

Table A36. Personal Consumption Expenditures in 1934–36 Prices, 1874–1940
(In thousands of yen)

	Food	Clothing	Housing	Fuel and light	Medical and personal care	Transportation	Communication	Social expenses	Education, recreation and miscellaneous	Total
1874	1,823,279	80,855	369,941	79,549	60,659	3,669	—	345,051	75,564	2,838,567
1875	1,905,840	79,750	387,430	79,805	65,719	4,122	177	350,171	83,920	2,956,934
1876	1,948,553	63,687	398,367	80,353	71,844	4,532	226	349,220	72,248	2,989,030
1877	2,010,647	80,149	401,604	81,474	73,999	4,974	1,107	353,372	77,885	3,085,211
1878	1,986,380	101,858	402,362	82,006	77,479	5,351	1,321	353,584	78,390	3,088,731
1879	2,094,582	133,127	405,277	82,795	81,868	6,069	1,726	359,161	95,024	3,259,629
1880	2,293,083	125,565	412,498	83,896	86,865	6,665	1,783	360,148	119,073	3,489,576
1881	2,173,150	98,544	410,037	86,937	91,851	6,942	1,877	362,012	124,434	3,355,784
1882	2,234,610	86,877	409,729	88,688	98,664	7,281	2,175	365,432	107,011	3,400,467
1883	2,189,437	92,290	407,690	90,393	105,268	7,663	2,594	368,862	98,709	3,362,906
1884	2,372,121	88,043	420,072	92,554	116,730	7,585	3,236	377,806	92,667	3,570,814
1885	2,231,290	107,397	428,744	94,204	127,076	7,408	2,127	298,169	95,707	3,392,122
1886	2,388,119	133,887	426,755	95,229	125,586	8,700	3,224	285,846	112,571	3,579,917
1887	2,540,396	132,650	437,354	96,362	130,848	10,073	3,640	363,445	174,890	3,889,658
1888	2,556,353	165,056	447,772	97,622	138,148	12,320	3,574	340,448	202,039	3,963,332
1889	2,666,277	182,802	452,351	101,163	146,481	15,211	3,979	440,939	221,020	4,230,223
1890	2,591,074	170,219	458,622	103,444	143,476	17,109	4,371	365,350	269,423	4,123,088
1891	2,836,706	222,189	463,866	104,466	150,267	19,802	5,069	396,423	286,146	4,484,934
1892	2,756,212	224,200	477,187	107,660	152,590	22,390	5,359	419,739	267,413	4,432,750
1893	3,002,809	242,724	485,926	108,208	156,074	24,523	6,224	446,514	289,222	4,762,224
1894	2,890,991	261,947	493,312	110,799	160,851	30,551	7,803	431,723	283,062	4,671,039
1895	3,032,284	318,405	505,252	112,215	163,596	37,584	8,143	474,163	296,972	4,948,614

Table A36 (continued)

	Food	Clothing	Housing	Fuel and light	Medical and personal care	Transportation	Communication	Social expenses	Education, recreation and miscellaneous	Total
1896	3,098,021	353,117	520,139	124,497	168,035	43,121	8,230	553,755	270,920	5,139,835
1897	3,095,484	355,326	522,635	117,009	173,390	55,738	8,443	498,537	308,680	5,135,242
1898	3,218,220	399,957	534,578	119,440	176,801	61,002	8,685	559,753	372,765	5,451,201
1899	3,339,045	387,472	546,186	120,966	178,588	65,926	11,885	561,942	353,889	5,565,899
1900	3,254,221	365,265	558,061	123,073	184,580	73,101	12,156	530,283	342,908	5,443,648
1901	3,421,230	288,131	565,673	128,038	187,860	74,051	12,648	548,606	299,453	5,525,690
1902	3,369,165	307,446	583,252	131,605	182,162	73,367	13,168	559,667	302,022	5,521,854
1903	3,256,662	267,776	740,517	135,607	172,308	78,345	13,713	561,374	312,854	5,539,156
1904	3,421,930	216,008	762,348	139,249	165,265	87,061	15,756	580,585	308,376	5,696,578
1905	3,173,268	319,758	627,220	145,479	157,911	103,651	17,152	521,429	307,708	5,373,576
1906	3,122,687	368,330	643,856	148,725	153,601	88,440	16,124	486,667	311,164	5,339,594
1907	3,215,008	378,585	689,198	153,310	146,544	63,957	16,227	495,357	324,375	5,482,561
1908	3,714,871	404,080	753,401	157,145	142,405	61,888	17,602	535,683	344,621	6,131,696
1909	3,673,754	445,642	811,334	165,526	132,476	66,036	19,569	600,960	335,456	6,250,753
1910	3,907,202	444,676	798,332	173,224	150,385	71,853	21,874	598,600	346,890	6,513,036
1911	3,896,684	466,985	754,623	186,271	162,816	82,258	22,739	489,786	366,135	6,428,297
1912	4,075,621	469,483	672,884	216,647	170,179	88,069	22,736	503,340	393,564	6,612,523
1913	4,242,372	491,787	660,155	211,994	176,766	93,320	23,555	505,502	416,333	6,821,784
1914	4,059,314	440,966	638,533	231,424	205,697	95,745	26,127	560,000	384,475	6,642,281
1915	4,404,613	508,229	618,418	253,759	250,803	103,186	31,558	471,422	387,689	7,029,677
1916	4,536,025	687,039	640,001	268,083	272,111	121,183	34,359	441,469	429,391	7,429,661
1917	4,677,976	686,432	709,708	286,997	279,115	144,720	32,636	422,186	529,427	7,769,197
1918	4,828,289	820,638	815,864	314,669	255,639	164,492	27,773	414,909	568,446	8,210,718
1919	5,261,367	1,128,018	858,287	335,366	232,362	193,895	26,461	360,549	587,486	8,983,791
1920	5,296,432	789,938	920,943	357,204	269,637	207,794	26,645	349,101	630,084	8,847,778

Table A36 (continued)

	Food	Clothing	Housing	Fuel and light	Medical and personal care	Transportation	Communication	Social expenses	Education, recreation and miscellaneous	Total
1921	5,654,211	1,009,982	841,941	370,366	301,293	230,454	33,112	381,533	609,572	9,432,464
1922	5,718,695	1,043,252	1,072,681	383,866	334,048	256,580	34,469	449,093	724,701	10,017,385
1923	5,867,261	835,773	1,171,567	388,224	500,860	273,474	32,646	384,415	737,605	10,191,825
1924	5,936,834	887,277	1,310,306	411,605	367,302	300,030	36,623	357,819	797,249	10,405,045
1925	6,037,237	813,329	1,377,976	435,510	354,583	311,933	45,124	401,925	831,330	10,608,947
1926	6,089,139	917,667	1,308,879	457,583	397,302	325,114	51,237	394,995	818,107	10,760,023
1927	6,154,708	1,032,730	1,266,267	465,593	408,662	345,078	55,795	481,192	861,513	11,071,538
1928	6,252,475	1,187,162	1,313,706	486,560	437,155	371,671	57,676	419,313	867,657	11,393,375
1929	6,245,159	1,009,330	1,384,750	501,074	442,062	382,317	60,772	422,632	868,516	11,316,612
1930	6,162,307	1,113,117	1,416,822	507,824	474,777	364,253	66,007	386,515	876,480	11,368,102
1931	6,322,409	1,334,986	1,424,864	528,548	489,451	350,423	73,348	324,444	797,331	11,645,804
1932	6,118,978	1,346,651	1,430,445	531,338	475,459	345,648	77,148	294,866	829,283	11,449,816
1933	6,616,029	1,307,212	1,447,999	517,047	718,890	369,965	80,877	297,990	875,779	12,231,788
1934	6,625,302	1,639,215	1,542,416	531,600	885,282	394,608	82,609	319,145	984,103	13,004,280
1935	6,494,981	1,678,158	1,506,605	556,270	869,515	418,246	86,642	341,487	1,042,007	12,993,911
1936	6,573,495	1,850,778	1,670,788	569,843	706,336	449,226	91,457	367,789	1,055,368	13,335,080
1937	6,609,629	2,185,714	1,765,934	596,230	780,963	488,065	99,329	390,822	1,097,740	14,014,426
1938	6,655,301	2,164,369	1,792,346	624,871	820,517	563,397	96,415	405,848	1,060,948	14,184,012
1939	6,965,921	1,099,913	1,726,999	627,097	819,693	702,099	94,753	495,073	1,058,196	13,589,744
1940	6,447,466	1,045,133	1,971,182	638,749	827,993	831,434	93,834	610,879	1,132,589	13,599,259

Source: Reprinted from LTES 6:138–39 (table 3).

Notes: The footnotes in table A34 are mostly applicable here. However, in real terms, there is no major difference between this table's total and table A3, except such slight changes as Ohkawa multiplying the total here by 0.968.

Table A37. Personal Consumption Expenditures in 1934–36 Prices, 1946–72
(In millions of yen)

	Food	Clothing	Housing	Fuel and light	Others	Total
1946	3,633	340	709	552	1,263	6,497
1947	4,279	405	850	619	1,425	7,578
1948	4,626	411	1,025	649	1,568	8,279
1949	4,990	446	1,072	678	1,746	8,932
1950	5,408	680	1,149	747	2,086	10,070
1951	5,878	1,045	1,226	774	2,428	11,351
1952	6,607	1,577	1,589	833	2,732	13,338
1953	7,336	1,817	1,750	870	3,280	15,053
1954	7,541	1,864	1,859	886	3,659	15,809
1955	8,082	1,997	1,992	889	4,101	17,061
1956	8,711	2,229	2,103	917	4,453	18,413
1957	9,040	2,458	2,206	924	4,975	19,605
1958	9,652	2,549	2,410	945	5,456	21,012
1959	10,122	2,732	2,766	994	6,014	22,628
1960	10,539	3,259	3,142	1,101	6,927	24,968
1961	10,998	3,589	3,521	1,204	7,833	27,145
1962	11,638	4,004	3,828	1,353	9,020	29,843
1963	12,356	4,300	4,285	1,519	10,365	32,825
1964	13,372	4,614	5,001	1,665	12,002	36,654
1965	13,978	4,827	5,258	1,852	12,868	38,783
1966	15,130	5,034	5,782	2,030	14,068	42,044
1967	16,400	5,416	6,522	2,245	15,738	46,321
1968	17,187	5,860	7,530	2,392	17,773	50,742
1969	18,187	6,217	8,607	2,631	19,992	55,634
1970	18,845	6,480	9,485	2,923	22,136	59,869
1971	19,779	6,826	10,499	3,200	23,675	63,979
1972	21,390	7,348	11,445	3,392	26,232	69,807

Notes: For 1951–72 the conversion of current price data to 1934–36 prices is made as follows: First, based on LTES 8 (p. 137, table 3) the 1934–36 constant-price consumption in each category is derived for 1951. Second, this is extrapolated to 1972 utilizing 1965 constant-price consumption in each category. For 1941–50 the interpolation is made by the ESB per capita indexes of commodity and service supplies for national livelihood after multiplying it by total population.

Table A38. Gross Domestic Fixed-Capital Formation in Current Prices, 1885–1940
(In millions of yen)

Private sector

	Primary industry				Nonprimary industry		
	Livestock and perennial plants	Producers' durable equipment	Structures other than residential buildings	Total	Producers' durable equipment	Structures other than residential buildings	Total
1885	21	9	6	36	6	2	8
1886	23	9	6	38	9	4	13
1887	20	11	5	36	14	4	18
1888	20	12	5	37	30	8	38
1889	25	11	7	43	23	10	33
1890	29	12	7	48	28	13	41
1891	29	12	6	47	34	10	44
1892	35	11	8	54	28	6	34
1893	34	10	7	51	41	7	48
1894	32	12	7	51	59	11	70
1895	43	13	10	66	65	15	80
1896	47	15	11	73	88	16	104
1897	47	16	12	75	98	40	138
1898	49	16	12	77	94	43	137
1899	47	18	10	75	49	30	79
1900	49	16	11	76	62	29	91
1901	52	16	13	81	48	29	77
1902	52	18	12	82	29	24	53
1903	60	21	14	95	34	33	67
1904	47	22	10	79	73	27	100
1905	59	25	17	101	156	35	191
1906	70	27	25	122	138	61	199
1907	76	29	22	127	157	57	214
1908	59	30	20	109	154	49	203
1909	67	30	26	123	109	46	155
1910	68	31	26	125	129	98	227
1911	60	32	26	118	181	158	339
1912	63	36	29	128	242	74	316
1913	62	35	32	129	247	61	308
1914	59	35	31	125	210	73	283
1915	65	35	29	129	223	64	287
1916	62	42	53	157	411	74	485
1917	76	56	41	173	914	194	1,108
1918	101	76	48	225	1,406	319	1,725
1919	139	107	60	306	1,203	442	1,645
1920	129	134	105	368	1,249	565	1,814

Private sector, all industries

Livestock and perennial plants	Producers' durable equipment	Structures other than residential buildings	Total	Residential buildings			Total	
				Farm	Nonfarm	Total	Total	
21	15	8	44	19	11	30	74	1885
23	17	10	50	19	15	34	84	1886
20	25	8	54	19	9	27	81	1887
20	42	13	75	21	19	39	114	1888
25	34	17	76	22	22	43	119	1889
29	40	19	88	21	18	39	128	1890
29	46	16	91	22	13	35	126	1891
35	39	13	88	22	14	36	123	1892
34	51	14	99	20	16	37	136	1893
32	72	18	121	27	21	49	170	1894
43	78	25	146	31	24	55	202	1895
47	103	27	177	35	32	68	245	1896
47	114	51	213	37	41	78	290	1897
49	110	55	214	44	42	87	301	1898
47	67	40	154	44	44	87	242	1899
49	78	40	167	43	38	81	248	1900
52	65	42	158	38	47	85	245	1901
52	47	36	135	41	42	83	217	1902
60	56	47	162	37	42	79	242	1903
47	94	38	179	28	30	57	236	1904
59	181	52	292	40	32	72	364	1905
70	165	85	321	46	27	73	393	1906
76	186	79	341	55	35	90	431	1907
59	184	69	312	52	45	97	410	1908
67	139	72	278	52	40	92	370	1909
68	160	124	352	49	46	95	447	1910
60	213	184	457	48	59	107	564	1911
63	278	103	444	50	71	121	565	1912
62	282	93	347	53	79	132	569	1913
59	244	104	408	50	65	114	521	1914
65	257	94	416	46	79	125	540	1915
62	453	127	642	57	90	146	789	1916
76	970	235	1,281	68	106	174	1,454	1917
101	1,482	367	1,950	90	147	237	2,186	1918
139	1,309	502	1,951	113	160	273	2,223	1919
129	1,383	670	2,182	160	224	384	2,566	1920

Table A38 (continued)

Private sector

	Primary industry				Nonprimary industry		
	Livestock and perennial plants	Producers' durable equipment	Structures other than residential buildings	Total	Producers' durable equipment	Structures other than residential buildings	Total
1921	147	151	103	401	498	436	934
1922	131	117	106	354	557	483	1,040
1923	150	136	115	401	362	268	630
1924	134	119	114	367	432	679	1,111
1925	142	113	115	370	322	550	872
1926	129	102	121	352	304	716	1,020
1927	137	101	121	359	329	726	1,055
1928	135	104	123	362	395	485	880
1929	126	101	124	351	477	498	975
1930	109	90	109	308	366	434	800
1931	87	76	106	269	183	373	556
1932	73	83	94	250	206	275	481
1933	83	101	106	290	439	329	768
1934	80	93	97	270	770	426	1,196
1935	85	90	86	261	914	551	1,465
1936	101	92	88	281	1,071	565	1,636
1937	81	109	74	264	1,749	841	2,590
1938	125	115	88	328	2,637	701	3,338
1939	182	137	123	442	3,650	844	4,494
1940	220	223	194	637	4,222	1,008	5,230

Government sector

	Producers' durable equipment		Structures other than residential buildings		Total including military	Total excluding military
	Including military	Excluding military	Including military	Excluding military		
1885	9	4	14	12	23	16
1886	6	2	12	10	18	12
1887	6	2	12	11	18	13
1888	7	2	13	12	20	14
1889	8	2	14	13	22	16
1890	8	3	17	15	25	18

Private sector, all industries

Livestock and perennial plants	Producers' durable equipment	Structures other than residential buildings	Total	Residential buildings			Total	
				Farm	Nonfarm	Total		
147	650	539	1,335	105	268	373	1,708	1921
131	674	589	1,394	127	283	410	1,804	1922
150	498	383	1,031	140	250	390	1,421	1923
134	551	793	1,478	138	256	394	1,872	1924
142	435	665	1,242	129	221	350	1,592	1925
129	406	837	1,372	120	218	338	1,709	1926
137	430	847	1,414	126	151	276	1,690	1927
135	499	608	1,242	121	162	283	1,524	1928
126	578	622	1,326	116	179	294	1,620	1929
109	456	543	1,109	97	124	221	1,329	1930
87	259	479	825	100	133	233	1,058	1931
73	288	369	731	96	146	241	971	1932
83	540	435	1,058	84	168	25?	1,310	1933
80	862	523	1,466	84	167	250	1,715	1934
85	1,004	637	1,726	86	194	280	2,006	1935
101	1,164	652	1,917	83	210	292	2,209	1936
81	1,857	916	2,854	88	253	341	3,195	1937
125	2,752	789	3,666	81	200	281	3,947	1938
182	3,787	967	4,936	116	231	347	5,284	1939
220	4,445	1,202	5,867	189	311	500	6,367	1940

All sectors

Livestock and perennial plants	Producers' durable equipment		Structures other than residential buildings		Residential buildings	Grand total		Less: duplication between (3) and (19)	
	Including military	Excluding military	Including military	Excluding military		Including military	Excluding military		
21	24	19	22	20	30	97	90	—	1885
23	24	19	22	20	34	101	96	—	1886
20	31	28	21	19	27	100	95	—	1887
20	49	44	26	25	39	133	128	—	1888
25	42	37	31	30	43	141	134	—	1889
29	48	43	36	34	39	153	145	—	1890

Table A38 (continued)

	Government sector					
	Producers' durable equipment		Structures other than residential buildings		Total including military	Total excluding military
	Including military	Excluding military	Including military	Excluding military		
1891	10	4	24	22	34	26
1892	10	4	20	18	30	23
1893	9	4	20	19	29	23
1894	28	4	23	21	51	25
1895	27	5	22	21	49	26
1896	22	7	40	34	62	41
1897	51	11	61	48	112	59
1898	66	14	59	48	125	62
1899	69	15	65	55	134	70
1900	65	19	78	64	143	83
1901	55	23	79	67	134	90
1902	46	23	72	64	118	87
1903	53	25	71	66	124	91
1904	78	23	50	46	128	69
1905	97	22	55	53	152	75
1906	85	26	62	58	147	84
1907	91	34	113	100	204	134
1908	92	43	162	131	254	174
1909	90	43	139	121	229	164
1910	101	46	143	134	244	180
1911	121	53	177	167	298	220
1912	131	63	163	150	294	213
1913	132	64	161	148	293	212
1914	141	64	144	136	285	200
1915	131	63	123	116	254	179
1916	135	69	112	104	247	172
1917	211	82	152	141	363	223
1918	330	119	187	171	517	290
1919	425	163	290	262	715	425
1920	535	195	500	464	1,035	659
1921	606	209	560	528	1,166	737
1922	527	191	650	631	1,177	822
1923	437	211	647	632	1,084	843
1924	427	246	637	626	1,064	872
1925	488	253	631	623	1,119	876

All sectors

Livestock and perennial plants	Producers' durable equipment		Structures other than residential buildings		Residential buildings	Grand total		Less: duplication between (3) and (19)	
	Including military	Excluding military	Including military	Excluding military		Including military	Excluding military		
29	56	50	39	38	35	160	152	—	1891
35	49	43	33	32	36	153	146	—	1892
34	60	55	34	33	37	165	159	—	1893
32	99	76	40	39	49	220	195	—	1894
43	105	83	48	46	55	251	227	—	1895
47	125	110	67	61	68	308	286	—	1896
47	165	126	112	99	78	402	349	—	1897
49	176	124	114	103	87	426	363	—	1898
47	136	83	105	95	87	376	312	—	1899
49	143	97	117	104	81	391	331	—	1900
52	119	88	121	109	85	379	335	—	1901
52	93	70	108	100	83	335	305	—	1902
60	108	80	119	114	79	366	333	—	1903
47	173	117	87	83	57	364	305	0	1904
59	278	203	107	104	72	517	439	0	1905
70	250	191	146	142	73	540	476	1	1906
76	277	220	191	177	90	634	564	1	1907
59	276	227	230	200	97	663	583	1	1908
67	229	182	210	192	92	597	532	2	1909
68	261	206	266	257	95	689	625	1	1910
60	334	266	360	351	107	860	783	1	1911
63	409	341	265	252	121	857	777	1	1912
62	414	346	253	241	132	861	780	1	1913
59	386	308	247	239	114	806	720	1	1914
65	389	320	216	208	125	793	719	1	1915
62	588	522	238	230	146	1,035	960	1	1916
76	1,181	1,052	386	275	174	1,816	1,677	1	1917
101	1,812	1,601	552	537	237	2,702	2,475	1	1918
139	1,735	1,473	791	763	273	2,937	2,647	1	1919
129	1,918	1,578	1,168	1,128	384	3,596	3,219	6	1920
147	1,255	859	1,093	1,061	373	2,868	2,439	6	1921
131	1,201	865	1,232	1,213	410	2,975	2,619	7	1922
150	935	708	1,025	1,011	390	2,500	2,259	5	1923
134	978	797	1,423	1,413	394	2,929	2,737	7	1924
142	923	687	1,290	1,282	350	2,704	2,461	6	1925

Table A38 (continued)

Government sector

	Producers' durable equipment		Structures other than residential buildings		Total including military	Total excluding military
	Including military	Excluding military	Including military	Excluding military		
1926	484	294	679	670	1,163	964
1927	486	299	728	712	1,214	1,011
1928	484	282	751	734	1,235	1,015
1929	465	294	745	730	1,210	1,023
1930	432	270	578	567	1,010	837
1931	413	247	489	480	902	726
1932	567	270	526	514	1,093	784
1933	616	283	578	558	1,194	840
1934	675	278	562	531	1,237	810
1935	729	291	625	596	1,354	887
1936	791	311	636	599	1,427	909
1937	1,893	334	589	542	2,482	875
1938	3,467	380	577	507	4,044	887
1939	3,951	434	606	507	4,557	941
1940	4,309	485	1,059	688	5,368	1,173

Source: Reprinted from LTES 1:183–86 (table 4).
Notes: Composed of Ishiwata's estimates of changes in private nonagricultural industry producers' durable equipment (1905–40, from LTES 3:68), Ohkawa's estimates of private agricultural investment (LTES 1:188–89, table 5), and Emi's series for the other items (LTES 4:226–29).

All sectors

Livestock and perennial plants	Producers' durable equipment		Structures other than residential buildings		Resi-dential build-ings	Grand total		Less: dupli-cation between (3) and (19)	
	Includ-ing military	Exclud-ing military	Includ-ing military	Exclud-ing military		Includ-ing military	Exclud-ing military		
129	890	700	1,506	1,497	338	2,862	2,663	10	1926
137	916	729	1,564	1,548	276	2,892	2,690	12	1927
135	983	780	1,342	1,326	283	2,743	2,523	16	1928
126	1,043	872	1,352	1,337	294	2,815	2,628	15	1929
109	888	726	1,104	1,093	221	2,322	2,149	17	1930
87	672	505	953	944	233	1,946	1,770	15	1931
73	856	558	860	849	241	2,030	1,721	34	1932
83	1,156	823	973	952	252	2,466	2,110	40	1933
80	1,538	1,141	1,056	1,026	250	2,923	2,496	29	1934
85	1,733	1,296	1,247	1,219	280	3,346	2,880	14	1935
101	1,954	1,474	1,274	1,237	292	3,622	3,104	14	1936
81	3,751	2,191	1,489	1,442	341	5,661	4,054	16	1937
125	6,219	3,132	1,351	1,281	281	7,977	4,820	14	1938
182	7,738	4,221	1,554	1,455	347	9,822	6,205	19	1939
220	8,754	4,931	2,224	1,853	500	11,698	7,503	37	1940

Table A39. Gross Domestic Fixed-Capital Formation in 1934–1936 Prices, 1885–1940
(In millions of yen)

Private sector

	Primary industry				Nonprimary industry		
	Livestock and perennial plants	Producers' durable equipment	Structures other than residential buildings	Total	Producers' durable equipment	Structures other than residential buildings	Total
1885	70	28	27	125	13	8	21
1886	76	29	25	130	19	15	34
1887	67	29	22	118	27	17	44
1888	66	29	22	117	49	26	75
1889	78	28	27	133	41	28	69
1890	83	29	28	140	48	33	81
1891	79	31	27	137	60	29	89
1892	87	29	30	146	51	18	69
1893	82	28	26	136	74	23	97
1894	73	33	24	130	112	32	144
1895	91	33	31	155	107	38	145
1896	91	35	31	157	136	38	174
1897	87	34	28	149	142	75	217
1898	86	34	28	148	137	80	217
1899	75	34	·23	132	63	58	121
1900	78	36	24	138	78	54	132
1901	91	35	29	155	64	53	117
1902	89	37	28	154	39	51	90
1903	95	43	33	171	46	65	111
1904	71	41	24	136	90	53	143
1905	79	45	37	161	202	66	268
1906	93	46	49	188	181	105	286
1907	97	47	40	184	183	86	269
1908	82	50	37	169	216	78	294
1909	89	52	49	190	168	80	248
1910	91	53	49	193	182	171	353
1911	80	53	48	181	255	261	516
1912	80	56	51	187	294	116	410
1913	81	55	57	193	325	100	425
1914	76	57	56	189	290	131	421
1915	89	55	52	196	252	108	360
1916	82	56	84	222	377	111	488
1917	85	59	53	197	686	191	877
1918	80	62	47	189	1,039	253	1,292
1919	83	71	48	202	1,071	307	1,378
1920	69	79	60	208	1,046	350	1,396

Private sector, all industries

Livestock and perennial plants	Producers' durable equipment	Structures other than residential buildings	Total	Residential buildings			Total	
				Farm	Nonfarm	Total	Total	
70	41	35	146	84	43	127	273	1885
76	48	40	164	83	60	143	306	1886
67	56	39	162	85	56	141	303	1887
66	78	48	192	85	77	162	354	1888
78	69	55	202	85	84	169	371	1889
83	77	61	221	88	75	163	385	1890
79	91	56	226	94	58	152	378	1891
87	80	48	215	84	55	139	354	1892
82	102	49	223	79	64	143	375	1893
73	145	56	274	95	75	170	441	1894
91	140	69	300	93	72	165	465	1895
91	171	69	331	100	86	186	518	1896
87	178	103	366	85	96	181	548	1897
86	171	108	365	97	93	190	555	1898
75	97	81	253	98	99	197	451	1899
78	114	78	270	91	80	171	440	1900
91	99	82	272	82	95	177	448	1901
89	76	79	244	95	98	193	437	1902
95	89	98	282	84	94	178	459	1903
71	131	77	279	64	69	133	407	1904
79	247	103	429	86	68	154	582	1905
93	227	154	474	90	53	143	617	1906
97	230	126	453	100	64	164	617	1907
82	266	115	463	93	80	173	635	1908
89	220	129	438	97	76	173	612	1909
91	235	220	546	93	87	180	726	1910
80	308	309	697	89	108	197	894	1911
80	350	167	597	90	128	218	815	1912
81	380	157	618	94	140	234	852	1913
76	347	187	610	91	119	210	820	1914
89	307	160	556	84	144	228	784	1915
82	433	195	710	91	144	235	945	1916
85	745	244	1,074	88	137	225	1,298	1917
80	1,101	300	1,481	91	149	240	1,721	1918
83	1,142	355	1,580	93	132	225	1,805	1919
69	1,125	410	1,604	94	132	226	1,831	1920

Table A39 (continued)

Private sector

	Primary industry				Nonprimary industry		
	Livestock and perennial plants	Producers' durable equipment	Structures other than residential buildings	Total	Producers' durable equipment	Structures other than residential buildings	Total
1921	82	102	66	250	692	272	964
1922	77	85	66	228	523	277	800
1923	90	96	71	257	297	174	471
1924	82	86	72	240	340	387	727
1925	90	85	79	254	318	431	749
1926	86	86	86	258	317	498	815
1927	93	87	90	270	351	526	877
1928	95	90	93	278	396	389	785
1929	94	92	98	284	458	431	889
1930	98	96	106	300	459	429	888
1931	94	94	108	296	239	383	622
1932	80	95	97	272	234	282	516
1933	89	98	106	293	418	321	739
1934	84	91	98	273	749	419	1,168
1935	87	91	86	264	934	529	1,463
1936	94	90	87	271	1,074	536	1,610
1937	70	87	67	224	1,140	710	1,850
1938	97	86	66	249	1,701	548	2,249
1939	109	93	78	280	2,451	1,042	3,493
1940	100	95	100	295	2,849	477	3,326

Government sector

	Producers' durable equipment		Structures other than residential buildings		Total	
	Including military	Excluding military	Including military	Excluding military	Including military	Excluding military
1885	22	9	52	45	74	53
1886	16	7	40	36	56	42
1887	15	6	42	39	58	45
1888	14	5	43	41	58	46
1889	17	5	47	44	63	49
1890	19	7	55	49	74	56

Private sector, all industries

Livestock and perennial plants	Producers' durable equipment	Structures other than residential buildings	Total	Residential buildings			Total	
				Farm	Nonfarm	Total	Total	
82	794	338	1,214	69	169	238	1,452	1921
77	608	343	1,028	81	180	261	1,289	1922
90	393	245	728	87	156	243	971	1923
82	426	459	967	96	166	262	1,229	1924
90	403	510	1,003	102	163	265	1,268	1925
86	403	584	1,073	94	170	264	1,337	1926
93	438	616	1,147	100	120	220	1,367	1927
95	486	482	1,063	102	136	238	1,302	1928
94	550	529	1,137	103	160	263	1,436	1929
98	555	535	1,188	103	131	234	1,422	1930
94	333	491	918	105	139	244	1,162	1931
80	329	379	788	100	153	253	1,041	1932
89	516	427	1,032	84	169	253	1,284	1933
84	840	517	1,441	87	174	261	1,703	1934
87	1,025	615	1,727	85	192	277	2,004	1935
94	1,164	623	1,881	80	204	284	2,165	1936
70	1,227	777	2,074	76	221	297	2,372	1937
97	1,787	614	2,498	60	148	208	2,706	1938
109	2,544	1,120	3,773	72	143	215	3,988	1939
100	2,944	577	3,621	86	142	228	3,849	1940

All sectors

Livestock and perennial plants	Producers' durable equipment		Structures other than residential buildings		Residential buildings	Grand total		Less: duplication between (3) and (19)	
	Including military	Excluding military	Including military	Excluding military		Including military	Excluding military		
70	63	50	86	79	127	346	327	—	1885
76	64	55	80	75	143	362	348	—	1886
67	71	62	82	78	141	361	348	—	1887
66	92	83	91	88	162	412	399	—	1888
78	86	74	102	98	169	434	419	—	1889
83	96	84	117	110	163	458	440	—	1890

Table A39 (continued)

	Government sector					
	Producers' durable equipment		Structures other than residential buildings		Total	
	Including military	Excluding military	Including military	Excluding military	Including military	Excluding military
1891	23	10	79	73	103	83
1892	24	10	67	61	91	71
1893	21	9	67	62	88	71
1894	62	9	71	66	134	75
1895	55	9	62	57	117	67
1896	43	12	104	88	147	100
1897	89	18	140	110	229	128
1898	114	22	131	107	245	129
1899	111	22	149	125	259	148
1900	97	26	165	136	263	163
1901	82	32	165	140	247	172
1902	70	33	161	145	232	177
1903	82	36	157	145	239	182
1904	116	31	110	101	225	133
1905	133	28	128	122	261	150
1906	120	32	130	122	250	154
1907	112	40	197	173	309	213
1908	125	56	275	221	400	277
1909	134	60	249	218	382	278
1910	150	64	272	245	422	309
1911	181	74	316	299	498	373
1912	176	80	282	258	457	338
1913	176	80	271	249	447	329
1914	196	83	257	242	452	324
1915	181	72	213	201	394	273
1916	145	63	163	157	309	220
1917	136	55	164	153	300	208
1918	156	65	163	149	318	214
1919	272	109	207	185	479	294
1920	365	130	277	256	643	386
1921	867	167	335	317	1,201	484
1922	702	159	394	383	1,096	541
1923	531	202	384	375	915	577
1924	442	210	385	379	827	589
1925	535	223	426	421	961	644

All sectors

Livestock and perennial plants	Producers' durable equipment		Structures other than residential buildings		Resi-dential build-ings	Grand total		Less: dupli-cation between (3) and (19)	
	Includ-ing military	Exclud-ing military	Includ-ing military	Exclud-ing military		Includ-ing military	Exclud-ing military		
79	114	101	135	129	152	481	461	—	1891
87	104	90	115	109	139	445	425	—	1892
82	123	111	116	111	143	463	446	—	1893
73	207	154	128	122	170	574	516	—	1894
91	195	149	132	127	165	581	531	—	1895
91	214	183	174	158	186	665	618	—	1896
87	265	194	244	214	181	777	676	—	1897
86	285	193	240	216	190	800	684	—	1898
75	208	119	230	207	197	711	598	—	1899
78	211	140	243	214	171	703	602	—	1900
91	181	131	247	222	177	696	620	—	1901
89	147	109	240	223	193	668	614	—	1902
95	171	125	255	243	178	698	641	—	1903
71	247	162	187	179	133	632	540	0	1904
79	380	275	229	223	154	842	731	1	1905
93	347	259	283	275	143	866	770	1	1906
97	342	270	322	299	164	926	830	1	1907
82	391	322	389	334	173	1,035	912	1	1908
89	354	280	375	345	173	991	887	3	1909
91	385	299	490	463	180	1,146	1,033	2	1910
80	489	382	623	605	197	1,389	1,265	2	1911
80	526	430	447	424	218	1,271	1,152	2	1912
81	556	460	426	404	234	1,297	1,179	2	1913
76	542	430	443	428	210	1,271	1,143	1	1914
89	488	379	371	359	228	1,176	1,055	2	1915
82	578	496	356	350	235	1,252	1,163	2	1916
85	881	800	407	396	225	1,598	1,505	1	1917
80	1,257	1,166	462	448	240	2,038	1,933	1	1918
83	1,414	1,251	561	439	225	2,283	2,098	1	1919
69	1,490	1,255	684	663	226	2,471	2,214	3	1920
82	1,661	961	669	651	238	2,649	1,931	4	1921
77	1,310	767	735	722	261	2,381	1,826	4	1922
90	924	595	626	617	243	1,883	1,545	3	1923
82	868	636	840	834	262	2,052	1,814	4	1924
90	938	626	932	927	265	2,225	1,908	4	1925

Table A39 (continued)

	Government sector					
	Producers' durable equipment		Structures other than residential buildings		Total	
	Including military	Excluding military	Including military	Excluding military	Including military	Excluding military
1926	527	278	480	473	1,008	752
1927	530	287	508	495	1,037	782
1928	530	272	548	535	1,078	807
1929	523	280	557	545	1,080	826
1930	518	282	505	500	1,024	782
1931	546	290	503	489	1,049	779
1932	746	313	550	537	1,296	850
1933	738	295	580	560	1,317	855
1934	719	276	562	531	1,281	807
1935	739	292	628	599	1,366	891
1936	777	313	633	596	1,410	909
1937	1,361	272	517	477	1,878	749
1938	2,252	272	439	388	2,691	660
1939	2,528	308	402	335	2,930	643
1940	2,679	325	564	382	3,242	707

Source: Reprinted from LTES 1:218–21, which was compiled from LTES 4:230–33 (table 3) for nonagriculture and LTES 1:223–24 (table 22) for private agriculture.

All sectors

Livestock and perennial plants	Producers' durable equipment		Structures other than residential buildings		Resi-dential build-ings	Grand total		Less: dupli-cation between (3) and (19)	
	Includ-ing military	Exclud-ing military	Includ-ing military	Exclud-ing military		Includ-ing military	Exclud-ing military		
86	930	681	1,057	1,050	264	2,338	2,082	7	1926
93	968	725	1,116	1,103	220	2,395	2,140	8	1927
95	1,016	758	1,018	1,005	238	2,368	2,097	12	1928
94	1,073	830	1,075	1,063	263	2,504	2,251	11	1929
98	1,073	837	1,024	1,019	234	2,430	2,189	16	1930
94	879	623	979	965	244	2,197	1,927	15	1931
80	1,075	642	895	882	253	2,302	1,856	34	1932
89	1,254	811	970	950	253	2,565	2,102	37	1933
84	1,559	1,116	1,050	1,019	261	2,955	2,481	29	1934
87	1,764	1,317	1,229	1,200	277	3,355	2,880	14	1935
94	1,941	1,477	1,242	1,205	284	3,559	3,059	14	1936
70	2,588	1,499	1,281	1,241	297	4,327	3,107	13	1937
97	4,039	2,059	1,042	991	208	5,386	3,355	11	1938
109	5,072	2,852	1,510	1,443	215	6,907	4,619	12	1939
100	5,623	3,269	1,120	938	228	7,070	4,535	21	1940

Table A40. Gross Domestic Capital Formation in Current Prices, 1930–71
(1930–44, in millions of yen; 1946–71, in billions of yen)

	Gross domestic capital formation	Gross domestic fixed-capital formation								Increase in stocks		
			Private			Government						
		Total	Total private	Dwellings	Others	Total government	Dwellings	Machinery and equipment	General government	Total	Private enterprises	Government enterprises
1930	1,455	1,177	694	159	535	483	—	—	—	278	269	9
1931	1,294	888	515	155	360	373	—	—	—	406	429	−23
1932	1,363	1,379	921	170	751	458	—	—	—	−16	−20	4
1933	1,804	1,797	1,428	203	1,225	369	—	—	—	7	−38	45
1934	2,828	2,246	1,731	213	1,518	515	—	—	—	582	553	29
1935	3,109	2,374	1,860	228	1,632	514	—	—	—	735	739	−4
1936	3,590	2,616	2,055	250	1,805	561	—	—	—	974	987	−13
1937	5,794	3,949	3,300	363	2,937	649	—	—	—	1,845	1,739	106
1938	6,352	5,303	4,573	270	4,303	730	—	—	—	1,049	878	171
1939	8,934	7,453	6,513	330	6,183	940	—	—	—	1,481	1,254	227
1940	10,546	8,299	7,085	458	6,627	1,214	—	—	—	2,247	1,989	258
1941	11,722	8,984	7,697	611	7,086	1,287	—	—	—	2,738	2,414	324
1942	14,603	9,363	8,105	690	7,415	1,258	—	—	—	5,240	4,416	824
1943	15,874	13,454	11,529	777	10,752	1,925	—	—	—	2,420	1,716	704
1944	20,655	16,245	13,766	650	13,116	2,479	—	—	—	4,410	3,265	1,145
1946	105	74	48	11	37	26	—	—	—	32	28	4
1947	345	219	117	22	95	103	—	—	—	126	83	43
1948	752	443	258	47	212	185	—	—	—	309	236	73
1949	831	557	324	36	289	233	—	—	—	274	208	66
1950	1,007	694	450	60	390	244	—	—	—	314	368	−54
1951	1,664	1,034	681	72	610	353	—	—	—	629	571	58

Table A40 (continued)

	Gross domestic capital formation	Total	Private			Government				Increase in stocks		
			Total private	Dwellings	Others	Total government	Dwellings	Machinery and equipment	General government	Total	Private enterprises	Government enterprises
					Gross domestic fixed-capital formation							
1952	1,664	1,278	886	165	721	392	16	117	259	386	313	73
1953	1,691	1,549	1,066	204	862	484	25	161	298	142	205	−64
1954	1,837	1,698	1,155	244	911	542	28	169	346	140	53	86
1955	2,126	1,705	1,144	256	888	561	29	198	334	421	303	118
1956	2,797	2,290	1,682	309	1,373	608	37	234	337	507	445	62
1957	3,685	2,946	2,223	367	1,856	723	40	289	393	740	751	−11
1958	3,192	2,941	2,122	403	1,718	819	48	320	451	252	216	35
1959	3,853	3,435	2,477	458	2,019	958	49	372	537	418	381	37
1960	5,234	4,682	3,526	617	2,909	1,156	49	431	676	551	502	50
1961	7,752	6,370	4,890	788	4,102	1,481	62	606	813	1,382	1,391	−9
1962	7,595	7,136	5,171	933	4,238	1,965	86	784	1,095	459	438	21
1963	8,759	7,875	5,601	1,148	4,453	2,275	92	941	1,242	884	913	−29
1964	10,486	9,404	6,893	1,506	5,388	2,511	103	975	1,432	1,082	1,046	36
1965	10,542	9,767	6,898	1,811	5,086	2,869	131	1,146	1,594	776	641	135
1966	12,382	11,344	7,911	2,076	5,834	3,434	156	1,356	1,923	1,038	850	188
1967	16,261	13,965	10,193	2,617	7,575	3,772	181	1,574	2,018	2,296	1,930	366
1968	19,694	17,328	12,944	3,254	9,689	4,384	225	1,739	2,420	2,366	2,015	351
1969	23,168	20,939	15,957	3,963	11,994	4,981	272	1,843	2,866	2,229	2,065	164
1970	28,055	24,922	19,148	4,722	14,426	5,774	366	2,095	3,313	3,133	3,173	−40
1971	28,803	27,179	19,832	5,061	14,771	7,347	470	2,603	4,275	1,624	1,844	−220

Source: Reprinted from LTES 1:187 (table 4A). Compiled from ARNIS 1962 for 1930–51, ARNIS 1969 revised for 1952–62, and ARNIS 1973 for 1963–71.

Notes: Figures for 1945 are not available; 1946–51 data are for fiscal years.

Table A41. Gross Domestic Capital Formation in Constant Prices, 1930–71
(1930–51:1931–36 prices, in millions of yen; 1952–71:1965 prices, in billions of yen)

	Gross domestic capital formation	Gross domestic fixed-capital formation							Increase in stocks		
		Total	Private			Government					
			Total private	Dwellings	Others		Dwellings	Others	Total	Private enterprises	Government enterprises
1930	1,500	1,213	715	—	—	498	—	—	287	278	9
1931	1,572	1,083	628	—	—	455	—	—	489	517	−28
1932	1,586	1,604	1,071	—	—	533	—	—	−18	−23	5
1933	1,822	1,815	1,442	—	—	373	—	—	7	−40	47
1934	2,970	2,364	1,822	—	—	542	—	—	606	576	30
1935	3,133	2,398	1,879	—	—	519	—	—	735	739	−4
1936	3,396	2,468	1,939	—	—	529	—	—	928	940	−12
1937	4,659	3,109	2,598	—	—	511	—	—	1,550	1,461	89
1938	4,778	3,958	3,413	—	—	545	—	—	820	686	134
1939	5,983	5,002	4,371	—	—	631	—	—	981	830	151
1940	5,799	4,610	3,936	—	—	674	—	—	1,189	1,052	137
1941	5,923	4,607	3,947	—	—	660	—	—	1,316	1,160	156
1942	5,972	3,901	3,377	—	—	524	—	—	2,071	1,745	326
1943	5,591	4,771	4,088	—	—	683	—	—	820	582	238
1944	5,941	4,723	4,002	—	—	721	—	—	1,218	902	316
1946	3,375	2,545	1,645	—	—	900	—	—	812	717	95
1947	4,238	2,965	1,576	—	—	1,389	—	—	1,273	835	438
1948	4,707	2,973	1,734	—	—	1,239	—	—	1,734	1,323	411
1949	3,986	2,756	1,605	—	—	1,151	—	—	1,230	933	297
1950	4,018	2,741	1,777	—	—	964	—	—	1,277	1,500	−223
1951	4,938	2,929	1,929	—	—	1,000	—	—	2,009	1,822	187

Table A41 (continued)

Year	Gross domestic capital formation	Gross domestic fixed-capital formation — Total	Private — Total private	Private — Dwellings	Private — Others	Government — Total	Government — Dwellings	Government — Others	Increase in stocks — Total	Increase in stocks — Private enterprises	Increase in stocks — Government enterprises
1952	2,180	1,817	1,269	315	954	548	27	521	363	297	66
1953	2,137	2,091	1,438	334	1,104	653	38	615	45	160	−115
1954	2,407	2,255	1,528	376	1,152	727	42	685	153	68	85
1955	2,790	2,291	1,528	414	1,114	763	45	718	499	345	154
1956	3,272	2,798	2,030	481	1,549	767	52	715	474	416	58
1957	3,981	3,323	2,469	529	1,939	854	53	801	658	674	−16
1958	3,735	3,462	2,437	590	1,847	1,025	67	958	273	229	44
1959	4,411	3,968	2,791	633	2,158	1,177	66	1,111	443	394	49
1960	5,783	5,225	3,853	811	3,042	1,372	63	1,309	559	506	53
1961	8,059	6,700	5,059	899	4,161	1,641	70	1,570	1,359	1,367	−8
1962	7,802	7,422	5,320	1,020	4,301	2,102	92	2,010	380	411	−31
1963	9,015	8,159	5,744	1,215	4,529	2,414	97	2,317	856	896	−40
1964	10,614	9,551	6,973	1,539	5,434	2,578	105	2,473	1,062	1,023	39
1965	10,471	9,766	6,895	1,810	5,085	2,870	131	2,739	705	623	82
1966	11,869	10,920	7,624	1,959	5,665	3,295	147	3,148	949	813	136
1967	14,985	12,895	9,460	2,269	7,191	3,435	159	3,276	2,090	1,847	243
1968	17,931	15,751	11,812	2,662	9,150	3,938	190	3,748	2,181	1,944	237
1969	20,548	18,437	14,111	3,052	11,059	4,326	218	4,108	2,110	1,953	157
1970	23,808	20,966	16,233	3,388	12,845	4,732	274	4,458	2,842	2,879	−37
1971	23,892	22,512	16,597	3,465	13,132	5,915	337	5,578	1,379	1,690	−311

Source: Reprinted from LTES 1 : 222, which was compiled from the same ARNIS issues as table A40.

Notes: Figures for 1945 are not available; 1946–51 data are for fiscal years.

Table A42. Total Gross Capital Stock in 1934–36 Prices, 1885–1940

(In millions of yen)

	Livestock and plants	Producers' durable equipment	Structures other than buildings	Nonresidential buildings	Subtotal	Residential buildings	Total
1885	1,583	541	1,043	4,003	7,170	7,411	14,581
1886	1,602	559	1,107	4,177	7,445	9,396	16,841
1887	1,602	588	1,136	4,206	7,532	9,423	16,955
1888	1,602	632	1,317	4,234	7,785	9,495	17,280
1889	1,621	669	1,382	4,250	7,922	9,610	17,532
1890	1,649	708	1,414	4,270	8,041	9,727	17,768
1891	1,668	740	1,420	4,298	8,126	9,798	17,924
1892	1,700	765	1,532	4,317	8,314	9,842	18,156
1893	1,717	801	1,568	4,334	8,420	9,934	18,354
1894	1,718	881	1,637	4,401	8,637	10,009	18,646
1895	1,755	950	1,735	4,447	8,887	10,105	18,992
1896	1,789	1,028	1,922	4,513	9,252	10,176	19,428
1897	1,809	1,155	2,148	4,547	9,659	10,286	19,945
1898	1,826	1,295	2,201	4,602	9,924	10,406	20,330
1899	1,819	1,380	2,262	4,674	10,135	10,500	20,635
1900	1,816	1,488	2,356	4,741	10,401	10,561	20,962
1901	1,842	1,599	2,385	4,832	10,658	10,677	21,335
1902	1,869	1,685	2,444	4,923	10,921	10,777	21,698
1903	1,896	1,817	2,492	4,993	11,198	10,885	22,083
1904	1,885	1,991	2,553	5,029	11,458	10,899	22,357
1905	1,927	2,210	2,659	5,089	11,885	10,972	22,857
1906	2,000	2,403	2,840	5,146	12,389	11,040	23,429
1907	2,048	2,615	3,062	5,254	12,979	11,105	24,084
1908	2,095	2,873	3,236	5,372	13,576	11,199	24,775
1909	2,149	3,093	3,427	5,529	14,198	11,282	25,480
1910	2,196	3,333	3,645	5,662	14,836	11,385	26,221

Table A42 (continued)

	Livestock and plants	Producers' durable equipment	Structures other than buildings	Nonresidential buildings	Subtotal	Residential buildings	Total
1911	2,236	3,644	3,929	5,793	15,602	11,504	27,106
1912	2,274	3,969	4,228	5,934	16,405	11,660	28,065
1913	2,313	4,332	4,447	6,078	17,170	11,822	28,992
1914	2,341	4,645	4,636	6,213	17,835	11,916	29,751
1915	2,393	4,857	4,798	6,336	18,384	12,083	30,467
1916	2,451	5,210	4,957	6,502	19,120	12,248	31,368
1917	2,512	5,925	5,176	6,643	20,256	12,397	32,653
1918	2,564	6,956	5,346	6,797	21,663	12,569	34,232
1919	2,624	8,050	5,568	6,991	23,233	12,735	35,968
1920	2,657	9,141	5,963	7,198	24,959	12,849	37,808
1921	2,730	9,932	6,258	7,433	26,353	12,982	39,335
1922	2,793	10,469	6,639	7,708	27,609	13,140	40,749
1923	2,907	10,812	6,928	7,992	28,639	13,266	41,905
1924	2,941	11,197	7,229	8,269	29,636	13,426	43,062
1925	3,021	11,534	7,673	8,582	30,810	13,543	44,353
1926	3,103	11,930	8,184	9,038	32,249	13,680	45,935
1927	3,200	12,361	8,714	9,482	33,757	13,810	47,567
1928	3,293	12,819	9,148	9,964	35,224	13,957	49,181
1929	3,384	13,240	9,486	10,462	36,572	14,117	50,689
1930	3,483	13,645	9,800	10,791	37,719	14,263	51,982

Table A42 (continued)

	Livestock and plants	Producers' durable equipment	Structures other than buildings	Nonresidential buildings	Subtotal	Residential buildings	Total
1931	3,573	13,867	10,247	11,127	38,814	14,429	53,243
1932	3,647	14,115	10,720	11,510	39,992	14,583	54,575
1933	3,720	14,579	11,178	11,995	41,472	14,805	56,277
1934	3,783	15,269	11,654	12,400	43,106	15,013	58,119
1935	3,852	16,138	12,095	12,833	44,918	15,213	60,131
1936	3,935	17,189	12,649	13,317	47,090	15,336	62,426
1937	3,987	18,077	13,236	14,033	49,333	15,459	64,792
1938	4,068	19,207	13,737	14,380	51,392	15,643	67,035
1939	4,181	20,734	14,289	15,127	54,331	15,826	70,157
1940	4,276	22,623	14,814	15,390	57,103	16,013	73,116

Source: This is a REVISION of LTES 3:148–51 (table 1).

Notes: The estimates here are lower than those in LTES for producers' durable equipment. For structures and for nonresidential buildings these estimates are higher, especially for the latter after the mid 1920s. See ch. 9 for the reasons for revisions. As in LTES, estimates are for year end.

Table A43. Total Gross Capital Stock in 1965 Prices, 1954–70

(In billions of yen)

		Government sector				Nonresidential total	Primary sector	Nonprimary sector	Residential			Total including residential
	Private enter-prises	Enterprises	Public works	General	Total				Private	Government	Total	
1954	18,282	4,204	2,991	3,946	11,141	29,423	5,980	23,443	—	—	—	—
1955	19,131	4,328	3,125	4,049	11,502	30,633	6,202	24,431	17,232	285	17,517	48,150
1956	20,105	4,538	3,285	4,167	11,990	32,095	6,467	25,628	17,799	319	18,118	50,213
1957	21,516	4,763	3,444	4,356	12,563	34,079	6,684	27,395	18,406	365	18,771	52,850
1958	23,026	4,996	3,650	4,643	13,289	36,315	6,988	29,327	19,037	417	19,454	55,769
1959	24,690	5,260	3,870	4,972	14,102	38,792	7,305	31,487	19,736	491	20,227	59,019
1960	26,949	5,567	4,125	5,362	15,054	42,003	7,650	34,353	20,538	542	21,080	63,083
1961	29,957	5,961	4,435	5,872	16,268	46,225	8,066	38,159	21,296	605	21,901	68,126
1962	33,587	6,442	4,833	6,679	17,954	51,541	8,530	43,011	22,090	693	22,783	74,324
1963	37,258	7,037	5,312	7,579	19,928	57,186	9,051	48,135	23,033	780	23,813	80,999
1964	41,868	7,627	5,858	8,531	22,016	63,884	9,616	54,268	23,814	881	24,695	88,579
1965	46,059	8,385	6,533	9,533	24,451	70,510	10,242	60,268	24,021	1,011	25,032	95,542
1966	50,464	9,194	7,273	10,676	27,143	77,607	10,948	66,659	25,456	1,154	26,610	104,217
1967	55,851	10,065	8,113	11,950	30,128	85,979	11,865	74,114	26,319	1,311	27,630	113,609
1968	62,666	11,097	9,070	13,362	33,529	96,195	12,984	83,211	27,212	1,501	28,713	124,908
1969	70,811	12,189	10,075	14,943	37,205	108,016	14,174	93,842	28,134	1,721	29,855	137,871
1970	80,957	13,398	11,247	16,847	41,492	122,449	15,390	107,059	—	—	—	—

Sources: Private sector: Keizai Kikakucho: *Minkan Kigyo Soshihon Sutokku no Suikei 1954–72* (1974). Others: Keizai Kikakucho: unpublished worksheets.

Table A44. Government Expenditures

Fiscal year	Consumption expenditures	Current transfers to households and private nonprofit institutions	Current subsidies	Transfers to the rest of the world	Capital expenditures[b]	Total
1868[a]	8.0	1.9	—	—	1.9	11.8
1869[a]	8.0	3.5	—	—	2.3	13.8
1870[a]	6.4	6.4	—	—	3.8	16.6
1871[a]	7.7	5.5	—	—	2.9	16.1
1872[a]	26.9	16.8	—	—	6.8	50.5
1873[a]	32.6	19.4	—	—	6.9	58.9
1874[a]	37.2	34.4	—	—	9.3	80.9
1875[a]	26.6	33.7	—	—	3.0	63.3
1875	33.9	27.9	—	—	6.6	68.4
1876	40.3	19.7	0.4	—	7.4	67.8
1877	49.3	16.0	0.3	—	7.1	72.7
1878	30.9	14.8	1.1	—	6.7	52.7
1879	43.1	14.9	1.1	—	9.4	68.5
1880	48.1	14.8	0.8	—	10.4	74.1
1881	51.1	14.3	0.9	—	10.0	76.3
1882	62.7	14.1	1.6	—	12.7	91.1
1883	67.2	13.7	1.5	—	12.5	94.9
1884	66.3	14.2	2.1	—	12.5	95.1
1885	51.3	7.3	1.8	—	12.5	72.9
1886	67.7	15.6	2.8	—	12.3	98.4
1887	67.1	14.1	2.6	—	13.6	97.4
1888	68.1	14.5	2.6	—	14.2	99.4
1889	66.3	13.4	4.6	—	16.3	100.6
1890	76.9	16.1	3.2	—	18.3	114.5
1891	69.6	15.2	7.1	—	28.5	120.4
1892	78.8	14.5	3.0	—	20.7	117.0
1893	70.3	13.6	11.5	—	23.4	118.8
1894	175.3	17.8	2.5	—	25.9	221.5
1895	170.5	21.5	2.9	—	25.6	220.5
1896	129.4	33.0	10.7	—	46.3	219.4
1897	175.5	27.0	28.2	—	63.3	294.0
1898	199.7	25.4	6.1	—	61.4	292.6
1899	218.8	23.8	14.1	—	73.0	329.7
1900	250.7	24.0	10.6	—	86.3	371.6
1901	243.3	25.8	11.1	—	91.2	366.4
1902	228.3	26.4	4.7	—	85.7	345.1
1903	290.1	36.3	11.7	—	92.6	430.7
1904	709.2	104.0	7.1	—	61.0	881.3
1905	702.4	127.9	5.8	—	79.3	915.4

Table A44 (continued)

Fiscal year	Consumption expenditures	Current transfers to households and private nonprofit institutions	Current subsidies	Transfers to the rest of the world	Capital expenditures[b]	Total
1906	497.8	119.5	21.1	—	85.2	723.6
1907	378.6	97.4	23.9	—	150.0	649.9
1908	389.7	86.3	24.5	—	183.5	684.0
1909	383.4	88.1	18.7	—	157.8	648.0
1910	408.9	84.4	19.7	—	187.5	700.5
1911	509.4	81.0	24.4	—	231.2	846.0
1912	430.2	70.3	11	—	207.3	718.8
1913	416.3	68.6	11	—	213.6	709.5
1914	447.7	68.3	18	—	195.1	729.1
1915	437.4	69.2	8	—	174.1	688.7
1916	436.1	75.8	10	—	171.3	693.2
1917	604.3	75.2	11	—	240.7	931.2
1918	878.8	95.0	7	—	306.3	1,287.1
1919	1,267.9	111.6	5	—	464.8	1,849.3
1920	1,527.1	132.1	6	—	722.5	2,387.7
1921	1,555.8	160.9	6	—	742.4	2,465.1
1922	1,553.0	172.3	6	—	848.4	2,579.7
1923	1,355.7	196.5	31	—	840.6	2,423.8
1924	1,387.3	229.4	31	—	886.0	2,533.7
1925	1,292.2	262.6	43	—	868.9	2,466.7
1926	1,344.7	266.8	19	—	996.0	2,626.5
1927	1,675.4	280.7	3	—	1,016.2	2,975.3
1928	1,984.9	294.6	3	—	1,015.4	3,297.9
1929	1,736.8	299.6	4	—	1,025.7	3,066.1
1930	1,624	204	2	—	774	2,604
1931	1,939	206	0	—	710	2,855
1932	2,217	224	4	—	808	3,253
1933	2,464	236	5	—	851	3,556
1934	2,421	252	4	—	796	3,473
1935	2,637	266	0	—	917	3,820
1936	2,723	272	2	—	907	3,904
1937	4,714	317	2	—	865	5,898
1938	6,699	401	6	—	894	8,000
1939	7,126	468	17	—	956	8,567
1940	9,646	516	77	—	1,246	11,485
1941	13,495	675	150	—	1,611	15,931
1942	17,118	867	545	—	2,082	20,612
1943	22,855	956	775	—	2,629	27,215
1944	27,672	1,238	1,833	—	3,624	34,367

Table A44 (continued)

Fiscal year	Consumption expenditures	Current transfers to households and private nonprofit institutions	Current subsidies	Transfers to the rest of the world	Capital expenditures[b]	Total
1946	54.8	5.9	26.4	−13.7	29.7	103.1
1947	102.2	7.6	36.7	−60.7	146.1	231.9
1948	282.3	22.5	109.8	−130.5	258.0	542.1
1949	393.8	58.2	211.1	−184.9	298.6	776.8
1950	437.3	86.9	68.0	−41.4	189.2	740.0
1951	555.2	112.2	37.6	0.2	398.5	1,103.7
1952	699.5	172.3	64.9	0.2	447.3	1,384.2
1953	801.5	210.2	76.3	0.6	551.1	1,639.7
1954	870.7	339.0	33.1	1.8	546.9	1,791.5
1955	900.6	353.5	24.6	9.4	683.7	1,971.8
1956	944.0	359.1	21.8	14.6	653.8	1,993.3
1957	1,029.7	391.6	45.8	30.1	764.8	2,262.0
1958	1,124.7	445.3	16.2	91.2	890.2	2,567.6
1959	1,235.0	511.6	22.0	27.4	1,073.5	2,869.5
1960	1,421.1	590.6	52.6	36.7	1,252.9	3,353.9
1961	1,666.6	702.0	90.9	31.7	1,623.1	4,114.3
1962	1,942.5	829.4	101.5	31.8	2,110.7	5,015.9
1963	2,274.1	1,013.0	124.6	28.6	2,325.0	5,765.3
1964	2,656.9	1,213.9	165.0	32.4	2,671.1	6,739.3
1965	3,037.8	1,446.2	209.8	36.6	3,139.5	7,869.9
1966	3,413.5	1,686.5	327.8	53.0	3,653.5	9,134.3
1967	3,862.3	1,953.7	415.3	57.2	4,326.2	10,614.7
1968	4,394.3	2,274.7	467.2	53.7	4,897.4	12,087.3
1969	5,080.4	2,604.5	633.3	60.0	5,284.4	13,662.6
1970	6,028.6	3,168.9	822.6	68.7	6,188.3	16,277.1

Source: REVISION of LTES 7:172–73 (table 7a). The revisions are in the prewar capital expenditure series, and in the postwar official data. Data for 1951–70 are from ARNIS, 1975 edition.

Notes: Classification is by ARNIS titles, but there are differences in actual coverage between the pre- and postwar series.

The government expenditure data in tables A1, A4, and LTES 1 are on a calendar-year basis, and thus are not directly comparable to these. In particular, LTES 1:182 (table 3) on general government consumption expenditure excludes military investment from consumption, while here it is included in current purchases. The LTES table total is disposal of current revenue, with a series of government savings as a residual. This table gives total expenditure, including that financed by debt issue. Government savings in the LTES table plus debt issue (table A46) approximately equal nonmilitary capital expenditure in this table, with fiscal versus calendar year timing accounting for the differences. For additional notes on the data, see LTES 7:278–79.

[a] Accounting periods irregular.

[b] Increase in stocks is not estimated for the prewar period. Capital expenditures since 1941 are EPA estimates which include them.

Table A45. Military Expenditures, 1868–1940
(In millions of yen)

	Military expenditures	Current account	Government current expenditure (including military investment)	Government revenue (excluding national and local bond revenues)	Ratios (in percent)		
					To government current expenditures	To government revenue	To GNE
1868	5.6	5.6	8.0	—	70.0	—	—
1869	4.7	4.5	9.6	—	49.0	—	—
1870	2.9	2.8	6.7	—	43.3	—	—
1871	3.9	3.8	9.6	—	40.6	—	—
1872	8.2	7.9	23.0	—	35.7	—	—
1873	9.8	9.8	32.6	—	30.1	—	—
1874	13.6	13.6	37.2	—	36.6	—	—
1875	18.4	14.2	43.6	—	42.2	—	—
1876	22.4	19.0	37.1	—	60.4	—	—
1877	30.4	25.9	44.8	—	67.9	—	—
1878	19.0	15.2	40.1	—	47.4	—	—
1879	10.7	9.0	37.0	—	28.9	—	—
1880	12.0	10.1	45.6	86	26.3	13.8	—
1881	12.4	10.8	49.6	95	25.0	13.0	—
1882	12.6	10.9	56.9	105	22.1	12.0	—
1883	16.3	12.2	65.0	108	25.1	15.0	—
1884	20.1	13.6	66.8	108	30.1	18.6	—
1885	22.3	14.9	67.4	114	33.1	19.5	2.8
1886	21.7	16.6	68.1	111	31.9	19.5	2.7
1887	22.2	17.0	67.2	110	33.0	20.1	2.7
1888	22.8	17.1	67.7	112	33.7	20.3	2.6
1889	23.7	17.3	65.4	115	36.2	20.6	2.5
1890	21.8	14.7	73.1	113	29.8	19.2	2.1
1891	23.6	16.1	70.5	112	33.5	21.0	2.1
1892	24.5	17.0	77.5	120	31.6	20.4	2.2
1893	25.6	18.8	72.8	128	35.2	20.0	2.1
1894	103.5	78.4	149.1	134	69.4	77.2	7.7
1895	121	98	171	143	70.6	84.5	7.8
1896	87	65	140	157	61.8	55.1	5.2
1897	104	51	164	175	63.5	59.4	5.3
1898	115	52	194	207	59.3	55.5	5.2
1899	117	52	214	252	54.5	46.3	5.0
1900	132	73	242	282	54.5	46.7	5.5

Table A45 (continued)

	Military expen- ditures	Current account	Govern- ment current expen- diture (including military invest- ment)	Govern- ment revenue (excluding national and local bond revenues)	Ratios (in percent)		
					To govern- ment current expen- ditures	To govern- ment revenue	To GNE
1901	117	73	245	307	47.7	38.0	4.7
1902	95	65	232	330	40.9	28.7	3.7
1903	139	106	274	338	50.7	41.0	5.2
1904	547.1	487.8	605	376	90.4	145.5	18.1
1905	725.5	648.2	703	465	103.2	156.0	23.5
1906	492.0	428.2	549	547	89.7	89.9	15.0
1907	283.6	213.7	408	634	69.5	44.8	7.6
1908	239.5	160.0	387	676	62.0	35.5	6.4
1909	211.6	146.3	385	679	55.0	31.2	5.6
1910	208.7	145.4	401	713	52.0	29.3	5.3
1911	226.7	149.3	484	782	46.8	29.0	5.1
1912	228.6	148.4	450	802	50.8	28.6	4.8
1913	221.6	140.7	420	811	52.8	27.4	4.4
1914	243	157	440	790	55.2	30.6	5.1
1915	264	189	441	771	59.9	34.2	5.3
1916	294	219	436	862	67.5	34.1	4.8
1917	391	252	563	1,062	69.5	36.8	4.6
1918	610	383	809	1,298	75.4	46.9	5.2
1919	930	639	1,171	1,737	79.4	53.5	6.0
1920	994	617	1,462	1,892	68.0	52.5	6.3
1921	924	496	1,548	2,098	59.7	44.0	6.2
1922	791	436	1,553	2,408	50.9	32.8	5.1
1923	618	377	1,405	2,315	44.0	26.6	4.1
1924	579	387	1,379	2,413	42.0	23.9	3.7
1925	552	309	1,316	2,517	41.9	21.9	3.4
1926	535	336	1,332	2,528	40.2	21.1	3.4
1927	581	378	1,594	2,593	36.5	22.9	3.6
1928	615	396	1,907	2,719	32.2	22.6	3.7
1929	605	418	1,799	2,729	33.6	22.1	3.7
1930	561	388	1,625	2,271	34.5	24.7	3.8
1931	563	387	1,861	2,064	30.2	27.2	4.2
1932	751	442	2,148	2,069	35.0	36.3	5.5
1933	950	595	2,401	2,176	39.6	43.6	6.2
1934	1,047	620	2,433	2,460	43.1	42.5	6.2
1935	1,134	668	2,584	2,672	43.9	42.4	6.2

Table A45 (continued)

	Military expenditures	Current account	Government current expenditure (including military investment)	Government revenue (excluding national and local bond revenues)	Ratios (in percent)		
					To government current expenditures	To government revenue	To GNE
1936	1,197	680	2,700	2,912	44.4	41.1	6.2
1937	2,606	1,000	4,215	3,959	61.8	65.8	11.4
1938	4,180	1,023	6,203	4,152	67.4	100.6	15.8
1939	5,290	1,674	7,019	4,616	75.4	114.6	16.9
1940	6,634	2,440	9,016	6,097	73.6	109.1	18.0

Sources: Military expenditures: LTES 7:186–89 (table 10); military investment: LTES 4:224–25 (table 1); military expenditures in the current account is the difference between these two.

Government nonmilitary current expenditures are derived from LTES 7:172 (table 7), and LTES 1:182 (table 3). Nonmilitary capital formation is from LTES 4:224–25 (table 6).

Prior to 1879, local government revenues are unavailable; for 1880–84, data are from LTES 7:174–75 (table 7), and for 1885–1940, from LTES 1:182 (table 3).

All figures here are recomputed in terms of calendar year.

Notes: Military expenditures in this table include (a) regular defense expenses (army and navy expenses included in the General Account) plus expenses for conscription; (b) war expenses in the Extraordinary Military Special Account and in ministries other than army and navy; and (c) war-related expenses (military allowances to surviving families plus annuities and pensions). For 1937–40, the war expenses in the Extraordinary Military Special Account had a breakdown into "forces in homeland" and "others," so in our estimate the forces in homeland figures are used. This is important because the same account included military expenses in China and other foreign countries.

Table A46. Government Revenues, 1868–1970
  (1868–1945 in millions of yen; 1946–70 in billions of yen)

Fiscal year	Total revenue	New debt issue	Current revenue					
				Taxes			Govt. ent. surplus	Non-tax revenue
			Total	Total	National	Local		
1868	—	—	—	—	3.2	—	—	—
1869	—	—	—	—	4.4	—	—	—
1870	—	—	—	—	9.3	—	0.1	—
1871	15.5	0	15.5	12.8	12.8	—	0.7	2.0
1872	47.2	23.2	24.0	21.8	21.8	—	1.1	1.1
1873	80.6	12.6	68.0	65.0	65.0	—	2.5	0.5
1874	76.3	6.3	70.0	65.3	65.3	—	3.9	0.8
1875	73.2	8.9	64.3	59.4	59.4	—	4.0	0.9
1876	55.5	−1.9	57.4	52.0	52.0	—	3.9	1.5
1877	235.8	184.3	51.5	48.2	48.2	—	2.0	1.3
1878	68.7	14.2	54.5	51.8	51.8	—	1.9	0.8
1879	82.3	−2.2	84.5	79.9	55.9	24.0	2.1	2.5
1880	87.3	−0.9	88.2	82.6	55.6	27.0	2.4	3.2
1881	98.2	−3.2	101.4	95.1	62.0	33.1	2.3	4.0
1882	102.8	−5.6	108.4	103.3	68.0	35.3	2.0	3.1
1883	93.7	−12.8	106.5	103.8	69.8	34.0	1.8	0.9
1884	122.9	14.2	108.7	101.2	68.5	32.7	2.4	5.1
1885	93.6	4.8	88.8	81.5	53.5	28.0	2.5	4.8
1886	111.3	3.2	108.1	97.1	65.6	31.5	1.7	9.3
1887	117.0	6.1	110.9	97.6	67.8	29.8	2.2	11.1
1888	111.0	1.1	109.9	96.1	66.6	29.5	2.9	10.9
1889	119.4	3.0	116.4	102.6	73.3	29.4	3.3	10.5
1890	127.1	15.2	111.9	100.2	69.6	30.6	5.6	6.1
1891	113.4	0.8	112.6	98.3	68.1	30.2	5.3	9.0
1892	127.7	5.5	122.2	103.5	71.4	32.1	5.5	13.2
1893	124.4	−5.3	130.0	108.6	75.1	33.5	7.7	13.7
1894	194.4	59.3	135.1	111.7	76.4	35.3	10.2	13.2
1895	229.2	83.7	145.5	122.8	84.0	38.8	12.0	10.7
1896	161.0	0.9	162.1	135.8	89.4	46.4	11.9	12.4
1897	196.4	16.7	179.7	165.2	111.5	53.7	11.6	2.9
1898	214.8	−0.9	215.7	175.2	109.2	66.0	15.8	24.7
1899	314.7	101.3	263.4	222.1	145.5	76.6	16.3	25.0
1900	312.1	23.5	288.6	243.3	153.5	89.8	17.8	27.5
1901	372.0	58.3	313.7	264.4	112.7	101.7	22.6	26.7
1902	361.1	26.0	335.1	286.1	177.3	108.8	23.5	25.5
1903	376.7	38.7	338.3	286.3	175.2	111.1	28.0	24.0
1904	847.9	459.4	388.5	327.2	239.1	88.2	38.4	22.9
1905	1,522.5	1,032.4	490.1	408.5	315.1	93.4	44.1	37.5

Table A46 (continued)

			Current revenue					
Fiscal year	Total revenue	New debt issue	Total	Taxes			Govt. ent. surplus	Non-tax revenue
				Total	National	Local		
1906	794.8	228.5	566.3	457.9	350.3	107.6	48.5	59.9
1907	641.1	− 10.3	656.4	509.5	376.7	132.8	79.3	67.6
1908	680.7	− 1.6	682.3	557.3	406.9	150.4	73.5	51.5
1909	1,099.3	421.5	177.8	576.7	412.6	164.1	52.7	48.4
1910	859.2	134.6	724.6	576.9	406.6	170.3	88.4	59.3
1911	890.2	88.8	801.4	604.4	421.5	182.9	65.3	131.7
1912	822.3	19.5	802.8	650.3	655.9	194.4	64.6	87.9
1913	759.5	− 54.2	813.7	659.5	469.6	189.9	74.3	79.9
1914	755.2	− 26.8	782.0	617.2	427.1	190.1	83.9	80.9
1915	785.2	18.0	767.2	601.2	413.6	187.6	84.6	81.4
1916	902.9	8.0	893.9	652.1	454.5	197.6	141.5	100.3
1917	1,365.8	247.9	1,117.9	787.1	561.0	226.1	202.1	128.7
1918	1,752.8	394.6	1,358.2	956.1	674.1	282.0	223.4	178.7
1919	2,133.2	269.5	1,863.7	1,249.7	845.8	404.0	254.8	359.2
1920	2,653.0	666.7	1,901.3	1,477.7	903.8	573.9	169.9	253.7
1921	2,572.8	409.3	2,163.5	1,633.8	996.5	637.4	227.3	302.4
1922	2,895.0	405.2	2,489.8	1,817.3	1,112.9	704.3	276.4	599.6
1923	2,840.1	583.9	2,856.2	1,013.8	1,003.7	610.1	247.3	395.1
1924	2,773.2	308.4	2,464.8	1,756.4	1,128.2	628.2	283.5	424.9
1925	2,947.9	418.6	2,534.3	1,763.7	1,139.4	644.3	301.8	448.8
1926	2,970.7	444.7	2,526.0	1,801.1	1,136.7	604.4	266.6	458.3
1927	3,304.5	689.2	2,615.3	1,790.2	1,153.4	636.8	309.4	515.7
1928	3,421.4	117.9	2,753.5	1,848.3	1,179.7	668.6	334.2	571.0
1929	3,020.5	299.7	2,720.8	1,827.7	1,150.6	677.1	302.3	590.8
1930	2,540.6	419.6	2,121.0	1,715.1	1,103.1	612.0	165.0	240.9
1931	2,416.5	371.5	2,045.0	1,521.7	991.4	530.3	181	340.3
1932	3,127.7	1,050.7	2,077.0	1,402.1	940.4	521.7	231	383.9
1933	3,443.6	1,234.6	2,309.0	1,559.9	1,001.6	558.3	281	368.1
1934	3,581.2	1,038.2	2,543.0	1,709.7	1,113.8	596.0	399	434.3
1935	3,700.3	985.3	2,715.0	1,836.7	1,202.3	634.4	419	459.3
1936	4,021.3	1,043.3	2,979.0	2,032.8	1,360.8	672.0	438	507.2
1937	6,505.9	2,219.9	4,286.0	2,441.3	1,782.8	658.6	1,259	585.7
1938	8,818.2	4,711.2	4,107.0	3,040.5	2,336.8	703.7	450	616.5
1939	10,521.3	5,736.3	4,785.0	3,691.2	2,908.0	763.2	434	659.8
1940	14,026.0	7,516.0	6,510.0	4,924.7	4,140.8	783.9	464	1,121.3
1941	18,111.6	10,834.6	7,277.0	5,697.1	4,818.9	879.2	130	1,448.9
1942	25,655.7	15,529.7	10,126.0	8,284.3	7,350.5	933.8	231	1,600.7
1943	41,323.9	28,146.9	13,183.0	10,923.1	9,731.2	991.9	915	1,544.9
1944	87,586.6	67,293.6	15,293.0	13,577.6	12,715.1	862.4	− 608	2,323.4
1945	—	50,168.8	—	12,526.5	11,541.4	985.2	—	—

Table A46 (continued)

				Current revenue				
					Taxes		Govt.	
Fiscal	Total	New debt					ent.	Non-tax
year	revenue	issue	Total	Total	National	Local	surplus	revenue
1946	116.6	65.8	50.8	41.2	39.4	3.7	−2.2	11.8
1947	342.7	108.9	233.8	209.8	189.6	20.2	−15.4	39.4
1948	782.9	181.4	601.5	525.5	447.7	77.7	−41.3	117.3
1949	1,176.2	146.5	1,029.7	778.8	636.4	142.4	63.9	187.0
1950	858.2	−43.9	902.1	759.1	570.8	188.3	23.3	119.7
1951	1,368.2	149.4	1,218.8	995.4	723.1	272.3	17.8	205.6
1952	1,630.2	266.7	1,363.5	1,150.8	843.0	307.8	44.3	168.4
1953	1,668.8	152.9	1,515.9	1,278.7	942.5	336.2	47.1	190.1
1954	1,860.2	199.2	1,606.1	1,291.6	924.1	367.5	65.1	249.4
1955	1,887.0	241.4	1,645.6	1,292.1	910.2	381.9	53.5	300.0
1956	1,987.4	67.1	1,920.3	1,514.9	1,065.0	449.9	75.1	330.3
1957	2,301.8	45.8	2,256.0	1,699.5	1,172.4	527.2	164.1	392.4
1958	2,482.3	178.3	2,304.0	1,702.1	1,158.2	543.9	160.4	441.5
1959	2,901.5	262.8	2,638.7	1,950.4	1,339.5	610.9	167.8	520.5
1960	3,557.7	208.2	3,349.5	2,509.5	1,765.2	744.2	213.1	626.9
1961	4,269.2	81.1	4,188.1	3,088.9	2,182.5	906.5	299.8	799.4
1962	5,017.9	343.3	4,674.6	3,416.6	2,360.0	1,056.7	300.6	957.4
1963	5,566.7	196.9	5,369.8	3,909.4	2,696.6	1,212.9	345.1	1,115.3
1964	6,641.9	574.6	6,067.3	4,514.5	3,114.9	1,399.6	256.6	1,296.2
1965	7,653.8	966.5	6,687.3	4,779.4	3,230.0	1,549.4	198.2	1,709.7
1966	9,168.8	1,548.0	7,620.8	5,372.5	3,603.9	1,768.6	297.1	1,951.2
1967	10,842.9	1,735.3	9,107.6	6,422.3	4,272.8	2,149.5	362.1	2,323.2
1968	12,418.3	1,578.7	10,830.6	7,755.9	5,175.8	2,580.1	396.9	2,677.8
1969	14,475.7	1,366.2	13,109.5	9,372.5	6,282.3	3,090.2	611.9	3,125.1
1970	17,639.2	1,751.0	15,888.2	11,320.9	7,570.2	3,750.7	750.7	3,816.6

Source: Compiled by Hiromitsu Ishi from the various Ninon Ginko and Okurasho sources listed in ch. 10.

Note: Non-tax revenue is a residual.

Table A47. Factor Incomes in Nonagriculture, 1906–40 and 1953–70
(In millions of yen for prewar, in billions of yen for postwar years)

	Corporate sector			Noncorporate sector			Total	
	Income of corporate sector Y1 = A1 + W1	Corporate income and interest A1	Compensation of employees W1	Income of unincorporated sector Y2	Imputed wages of self-employed workers W2	Income distributed Y = Y1 + Y2	Wage income W = W1 + W2
1906	956	218	738	974	466	1,930	1,204
1907	1,091	214	877	990	542	2,081	1,419
1908	1,179	230	949	1,130	587	2,309	1,536
1909	1,212	242	970	1,115	595	2,327	1,565
1910	1,298	293	1,005	1,182	594	2,480	1,599
1911	1,452	355	1,097	1,187	600	2,639	1,697
1912	1,592	404	1,188	1,239	627	2,831	1,815
1913	1,774	493	1,281	1,243	645	3,017	1,926
1914	1,887	599	1,288	1,191	656	3,078	1,944
1915	2,208	824	1,384	1,324	665	3,532	2,049
1916	2,671	1,159	1,512	1,574	730	4,245	2,242
1917	3,294	1,273	2,021	2,251	892	5,545	2,913
1918	4,297	1,351	2,946	2,704	1,246	7,001	4,192
1919	6,159	1,521	4,638	3,816	1,970	9,975	6,608
1920	7,083	1,682	5,401	4,007	2,210	11,090	7,611
1921	6,823	1,357	5,466	4,237	2,452	11,060	7,918
1922	7,045	1,391	5,654	4,536	2,370	11,581	8,074
1923	7,044	1,238	5,806	4,488	2,285	11,532	8,091
1924	7,460	1,674	5,786	4,749	2,315	12,209	8,101
1925	7,969	1,968	6,001	4,733	2,384	12,702	8,385

Table A47 (continued)

	Corporate sector			Noncorporate sector		Total	
	Income of corporate sector Y1 = A1 + W1	Corporate income and interest A1	Compensation of employees W1	Income of unincorporated sector Y2	Imputed wages of self-employed workers W2	Income distributed Y = Y1 + Y2	Wage income W = W1 + W2
1926	8,161	1,924	6,232	4,566	2,470	12,727	8,702
1927	7,931	2,005	5,926	4,275	2,494	12,206	8,420
1928	8,352	2,281	6,071	4,292	2,594	12,644	8,665
1929	8,008	2,435	5,573	4,312	2,335	12,320	7,908
1930	7,082	2,184	4,878	4,011	1,985	11,093	6,883
1931	6,423	1,959	4,464	3,570	1,883	9,993	6,347
1932	6,520	2,095	4,425	3,287	1,781	9,807	6,206
1933	7,363	2,363	5,000	3,556	1,981	10,919	6,981
1934	8,055	2,666	5,389	3,912	2,005	11,967	7,394
1935	8,603	2,859	5,744	4,216	2,058	12,819	7,802
1936	9,054	2,978	6,076	4,282	2,062	13,336	8,138
1937	10,632	3,672	6,960	4,506	2,114	15,138	9,074
1938	12,472	4,463	8,009	5,340	2,275	17,812	10,284
1939	15,848	5,295	10,573	6,547	2,713	22,395	13,286
1940	18,856	6,718	12,638	7,802	2,796	26,658	15,434
1953	3,524.6	767.5	2,757.1	1,035.8	692.1	4,560.4	3,449.2
1954	3,993.2	954.9	3,038.3	1,080.8	774.3	5,074.0	3,812.6
1955	4,272.8	951.9	3,320.9	1,180.2	832.5	5,453.0	4,153.4
1956	4,944.8	1,153.5	3,791.3	1,323.3	893.2	6,268.1	4,684.5
1957	6,095.9	1,744.9	4,351.0	1,383.9	974.7	7,479.8	5,325.7
1958	6,488.9	1,743.1	4,745.8	1,370.6	1,013.9	7,859.5	5,759.7
1959	7,355.2	2,050.3	5,304.9	1,469.2	1,103.3	8,824.4	6,408.2
1960	9,158.1	2,973.3	6,184.8	1,768.0	1,265.1	10,926.1	7,449.9

Table A47 (continued)

	Corporate sector			Noncorporate sector		Total	
	Income of corporate sector Y1 = A1 + W1	Corporate income and interest A1	Compensation of employees W1	Income of unincorporated sector Y2	Imputed wages of self-employed workers W2	Income distributed Y = Y1 + Y2	Wage income W = W1 + W2
1961	10,953.1	3,610.9	7,342.2	2,117.6	1,436.0	13,070.7	8,778.2
1962	12,749.2	3,975.2	8,774.0	2,371.2	1,632.4	15,120.4	10,406.4
1963	14,672.0	4,318.9	10,353.1	2,857.2	1,968.5	17,529.2	12,321.6
1964	17,011.4	5,029.6	11,981.8	3,324.1	2,279.9	20,335.5	14,261.7
1965	19,171.3	5,271.3	13,900.0	3,584.4	2,615.3	22,755.7	16,515.3
1966	22,590.8	6,607.9	15,982.9	3,904.5	2,976.7	26,495.3	18,959.6
1967	26,407.6	7,941.9	18,465.7	4,619.2	3,459.3	31,026.8	21,925.0
1968	31,627.2	10,018.6	21,608.6	5,826.5	4,140.6	37,453.7	25,749.2
1969	37,106.3	11,855.3	25,251.0	6,814.0	4,895.9	43,920.3	30,146.9
1970	45,097.9	14,645.1	30,452.8	7,785.0	5,788.9	52,882.9	36,241.7

Sources: Prewar estimates are those of Minami and Ono (see ch. 11). Postwar data are from ARNIS.

Notes: Prewar figures EXCLUDE land and house rents and imputed interest.

Estimating procedures for A1, W1, and Y2 are explained in ch. 11. W2 is calculated by imputing the average wage in the noncorporate sector to labor supplied by self-employed workers.

Table A48. Factor Incomes in Industry, 1906–40 and 1953–70
(In millions of yen for prewar, in billions of yen for postwar years)

	Corporate sector			Noncorporate sector		Total	
	Income of corporate sector Y1 = A1 + W1	Corporate income and interest A1	Compensation of employees W1	Income of unincorporated sector Y2	Imputed wages of self-employed workers W2	Income distributed Y = Y1 + Y2	Wage income W = W1 + W2
1906	500	106	394	428	262	928	656
1907	565	112	453	410	290	975	743
1908	609	117	492	537	316	1,146	808
1909	631	121	510	526	324	1,157	834
1910	683	152	531	577	315	1,260	846
1911	770	176	594	543	305	1,313	899
1912	841	191	650	552	312	1,393	962
1913	925	204	721	533	318	1,458	1,039
1914	984	276	708	518	319	1,502	1,027
1915	1,213	435	778	602	314	1,815	1,092
1916	1,465	602	863	687	356	2,152	1,219
1917	1,920	709	1,211	879	425	2,799	1,636
1918	2,605	782	1,823	1,324	602	3,929	2,425
1919	3,540	785	2,755	1,746	892	5,286	3,647
1920	4,245	747	3,498	1,832	1,126	6,077	4,624
1921	3,894	743	3,151	2,145	1,136	6,039	4,287
1922	4,125	740	3,385	2,314	1,084	6,439	4,469
1923	4,160	642	3,518	2,428	993	6,588	4,511
1924	4,364	939	3,425	2,354	985	6,718	4,410
1925	4,670	1,176	3,494	2,328	977	6,998	4,471

Table A48 (continued)

	Corporate sector			Noncorporate sector		Total	
	Income of corporate sector Y1 = A1 + W1	Corporate income and interest A1	Compensation of employees W1	Income of unincorporated sector Y2	Imputed wages of self-employed workers W2	Income distributed Y = Y1 + Y2	Wage income W = W1 + W2
1926	4,902	1,239	3,663	2,183	1,033	7,085	4,696
1927	4,643	1,324	3,319	2,137	1,040	6,780	4,359
1928	4,973	1,544	3,429	2,150	1,125	7,123	4,554
1929	4,998	1,577	3,421	2,206	1,143	7,204	4,564
1930	4,578	1,352	3,226	1,984	1,065	6,562	4,891
1931	4,098	1,276	2,822	1,706	998	5,804	3,820
1932	4,096	1,299	2,797	1,513	922	5,609	3,719
1933	4,528	1,495	3,033	1,641	966	6,169	3,999
1934	5,070	1,729	3,341	1,879	970	6,949	4,311
1935	5,593	1,973	3,620	2,102	1,008	7,695	4,628
1936	5,993	2,065	3,928	2,110	1,023	8,103	4,951
1937	7,229	2,545	4,684	2,262	1,037	9,491	5,721
1938	8,792	3,154	5,638	2,930	1,177	11,722	6,815
1939	11,686	3,684	8,002	3,829	1,548	15,515	9,550
1940	14,109	4,232	9,877	4,655	1,572	18,764	11,449
1953	2,001.4	455.7	1,545.7	255.8	155.0	2,257.2	1,700.7
1954	2,258.3	570.0	1,688.3	296.6	178.9	2,554.9	1,867.2
1955	2,340.1	517.9	1,822.2	320.2	195.0	2,660.3	2,017.2
1956	2,769.4	653.8	2,115.6	365.4	206.3	3,134.8	2,321.9
1957	3,465.6	1,041.5	2,424.1	403.5	216.8	3,869.1	2,640.9
1958	3,605.2	956.3	2,648.9	425.6	243.6	4,030.8	2,892.5
1959	4,142.5	1,110.0	3,032.5	477.8	265.2	4,620.3	3,297.7
1960	5,245.7	1,684.6	3,561.1	591.9	315.6	5,837.6	3,876.7

Table A48 (continued)

	Corporate sector			Noncorporate sector		Total	
	Income of corporate sector Y1 = A1 + W1	Corporate income and interest A1	Compensation of employees W1	Income of unincorporated sector Y2	Imputed wages of self-employed workers W2	Income distributed Y = Y1 + Y2	Wage income W = W1 + W2
1961	6,384.7	2,073.2	4,311.5	731.4	373.7	7,116.1	4,685.2
1962	7,287.7	2,136.3	5,151.4	807.2	452.6	8,094.9	5,604.0
1963	8,248.6	2,347.2	5,901.4	982.2	535.5	9,230.8	6,436.9
1964	9,459.4	2,571.7	6,887.7	1,159.9	640.9	10,619.3	7,528.6
1965	10,141.2	2,376.6	7,764.6	1,224.6	728.7	11,365.8	8,493.3
1966	11,788.7	2,897.4	8,891.3	1,329.6	875.0	13,118.3	9,766.3
1967	14,020.1	3,759.4	10,260.7	1,644.5	1,090.3	15,664.6	11,351.0
1968	16,752.1	4,830.6	11,921.5	2,058.4	1,371.5	18,810.5	13,293.0
1969	19,658.0	5,712.7	13,945.3	2,406.1	1,703.0	22,064.1	15,648.3
1970	23,650.5	6,906.7	16,743.8	2,728.9	2,075.0	26,379.4	18,818.8

Source and Notes: Same as table A47.

(In millions of yen for prewar, in billions of yen for postwar years)

	Corporate sector			Noncorporate sector		Total	
	Income of corporate sector Y1 = A1 + W1	Corporate income and interest A1	Compensation of employees W1	Income of unincorporated sector Y2	Imputed wages of self-employed workers W2	Income distributed Y = Y1 + Y2	Wage income W = W1 + W2
1906	456	112	344	546	204	1,002	548
1907	526	102	424	580	252	1,106	676
1908	570	113	457	593	271	1,163	728
1909	581	121	460	589	271	1,170	731
1910	615	141	474	605	279	1,220	753
1911	682	179	503	644	295	1,326	798
1912	751	213	538	687	315	1,438	853
1913	849	289	560	710	327	1,559	887
1914	903	323	580	673	337	1,576	917
1915	995	389	606	722	351	1,717	957
1916	1,206	557	649	887	374	2,093	1,023
1917	1,374	564	810	1,372	467	2,746	1,277
1918	1,692	569	1,123	1,380	644	3,072	1,767
1919	2,619	736	1,883	2,070	1,078	4,689	2,961
1920	2,838	935	1,903	2,175	1,084	5,013	2,987
1921	2,929	614	2,315	2,092	1,316	5,021	3,631
1922	2,920	651	2,269	2,222	1,286	5,142	3,555
1923	2,884	596	2,288	2,060	1,292	4,944	3,580
1924	3,096	735	2,361	2,395	1,330	5,491	3,691
1925	3,299	792	2,507	2,405	1,407	5,704	3,914
1926	3,259	690	2,569	2,383	1,437	5,642	4,006
1927	3,288	681	2,607	2,138	1,454	5,426	4,061
1928	3,379	737	2,642	2,142	1,469	5,521	4,111
1929	3,010	858	2,152	2,106	1,192	5,116	3,344
1930	2,504	832	1,672	2,027	920	4,531	2,592

Table A49 (continued)

	Corporate sector			Noncorporate sector		Total	
	Income of corporate sector Y1 = A1 + W1	Corporate income and interest A1	Compensation of employees W1	Income of unincorporated sector Y2	Imputed wages of self-employed workers W2	Income distributed Y = Y1 + Y2	Wage income W = W1 + W2
1931	2,325	683	1,642	1,864	885	4,189	2,527
1932	2,424	796	1,628	1,774	859	4,198	2,457
1933	2,835	868	1,967	1,915	1,015	4,750	2,982
1934	2,985	937	2,048	2,033	1,035	5,018	3,083
1935	3,010	886	2,124	2,114	1,050	5,124	3,174
1936	3,061	913	2,148	2,172	1,039	5,233	3,187
1937	3,403	1,127	2,276	2,244	1,077	5,647	3,353
1938	3,680	1,309	2,371	2,410	1,098	6,090	3,469
1939	4,162	1,591	2,571	2,718	1,165	6,880	3,736
1940	4,747	1,986	2,761	3,147	1,224	7,894	3,985
1953	1,523.2	311.8	1,211.4	780.0	537.1	2,303.2	1,748.5
1954	1,734.9	384.9	1,350.0	784.2	595.4	2,519.1	1,945.4
1955	1,932.7	434.0	1,498.7	860.0	637.5	2,792.7	2,136.2
1956	2,175.4	499.7	1,675.7	957.9	686.9	3,133.3	2,362.6
1957	2,630.3	703.4	1,926.9	980.4	757.9	3,610.7	2,684.8
1958	2,883.7	786.8	2,096.9	945.0	770.3	3,828.7	2,867.2
1959	3,212.7	940.3	2,272.4	991.4	838.1	4,204.1	3,110.5
1960	3,912.4	1,288.7	2,623.7	1,176.1	949.5	5,088.5	3,573.2
1961	4,568.4	1,537.7	3,030.7	1,386.2	1,062.3	5,954.6	4,093.0
1962	5,461.5	1,838.9	3,622.6	1,564.0	1,179.8	7,025.5	4,802.4
1963	6,423.4	1,971.7	4,451.7	1,875.0	1,433.0	8,298.4	5,884.7
1964	7,552.0	2,457.9	5,094.1	2,164.2	1,639.0	9,716.2	6,733.1
1965	9,030.1	2,894.7	6,135.4	2,359.8	1,886.6	11,389.9	8,022.0
1966	10,802.1	3,710.5	7,091.6	2,574.9	2,101.7	13,377.0	9,193.3
1967	12,387.5	4,182.5	8,205.0	2,974.7	2,369.0	15,362.2	10,574.0
1968	14,875.1	5,188.0	9,687.1	3,768.1	2,769.1	18,643.2	12,456.2

Table A50. Major Price Indexes, 1885–1940
(1934–36 = 100)

	GNE deflator	Consumers' goods	Investment goods	Agricultural products	Manufactured goods	Commerce–service sector
1885	20.7	22.3	31.2	25.9	34.4	16.8
1886	19.3	20.3	31.4	23.7	33.3	15.5
1887	18.6	19.9	32.7	22.0	35.3	14.7
1888	19.1	20.0	35.7	21.1	35.4	15.7
1889	20.0	20.9	35.9	24.5	36.6	14.3
1890	22.8	24.3	35.1	32.9	38.0	16.0
1891	22.3	23.2	33.6	28.7	35.7	17.0
1892	22.4	23.2	35.0	29.4	37.1	16.2
1893	22.5	23.5	35.1	30.1	38.3	16.2
1894	24.1	24.9	37.5	34.3	40.2	16.5
1895	26.3	27.1	42.4	34.4	43.3	18.3
1896	28.3	29.6	45.0	37.0	45.8	20.1
1897	34.0	34.7	51.0	44.7	52.4	23.9
1898	36.4	38.2	51.7	52.7	56.3	24.1
1899	36.2	36.9	52.9	45.3	58.7	24.0
1900	38.5	40.7	55.6	47.4	61.9	27.6
1901	38.2	39.7	54.5	44.8	59.9	27.2
1902	39.5	41.2	51.6	48.8	59.3	28.6
1903	41.6	43.4	52.4	55.4	62.3	31.6
1904	42.4	44.0	53.3	53.6	65.9	34.6
1905	45.9	47.2	56.7	54.4	72.4	36.7
1906	48.5	49.5	59.3	57.7	74.8	34.6
1907	52.2	52.4	65.0	63.8	81.0	36.2
1908	51.6	53.7	61.2	60.9	77.3	38.3
1909	50.1	52.2	57.0	54.3	74.7	39.8
1910	49.3	51.6	57.4	55.3	75.0	38.4
1911	54.6	57.9	58.3	68.0	78.1	41.1
1912	60.4	62.2	63.7	79.3	81.4	41.2
1913	61.8	64.6	63.5	78.8	79.8	43.7
1914	57.7	56.7	60.8	56.5	76.3	51.3
1915	57.1	53.8	64.9	53.3	80.6	44.5
1916	65.5	58.5	80.2	60.5	100.5	43.7
1917	85.0	72.8	107.2	85.5	129.4	52.6
1918	108.5	98.5	133.9	132.7	160.8	60.0
1919	134.7	131.0	139.4	182.0	186.0	78.0
1920	138.2	133.6	177.1	145.6	195.2	99.5

Table A50 (continued)

	GNE deflator	Consumers' goods	Investment goods	Agricultural products	Manufactured goods	Commerce– service sector
1921	126.2	123.6	146.4	143.3	150.3	85.9
1922	130.2	120.8	144.9	127.8	151.2	99.1
1923	129.7	121.1	148.3	138.5	154.6	95.1
1924	131.6	121.9	146.7	148.5	155.3	97.1
1925	129.9	125.1	130.0	148.8	147.7	103.8
1926	126.6	119.8	121.5	134.1	130.9	106.9
1927	122.5	114.4	118.5	117.3	122.6	104.8
1928	119.3	111.9	115.5	115.6	123.7	99.1
1929	117.1	108.6	116.1	114.3	119.6	97.2
1930	103.8	99.6	96.6	75.3	96.8	116.6
1931	93.8	87.6	82.3	69.3	79.7	95.5
1932	93.0	88.7	90.7	77.8	87.8	84.5
1933	96.1	91.8	100.8	85.6	102.4	86.8
1934	97.8	96.2	99.1	92.2	100.0	94.4
1935	99.5	100.7	99.1	101.0	98.7	104.4
1936	102.4	102.9	101.8	106.8	101.2	102.5
1937	116.4	111.2	131.0	118.0	131.6	105.0
1938	127.3	122.9	141.4	126.8	140.1	113.8
1939	140.2	131.8	152.1	171.8	151.8	105.2
1940	159.0	149.7	175.7	190.2	167.0	122.0

Sources: GNP deflator: A REVISION of the index given in LTES 1:232 to reflect changes in the foreign trade price indexes (see table A30); consumers' goods, LTES 6:106; investment goods, LTES 8:134; agricultural products, LTES 8:165; manufactured goods, LTES 8:192–93; and commerce–services, LTES 1:232.

Table A51. Major Price Indexes, 1952–72
$$(1934–36 = 1)^a$$

	GNP deflator	Personal consumption	Fixed investment
1952	285.7	280.8	339.9
1953	304.8	301.0	358.2
1954	318.7	317.5	364.0
1955	321.6	315.2	359.7
1956	335.5	317.5	396.0
1957	354.2	328.0	428.8
1958	349.4	327.1	410.5
1959	359.0	331.7	418.7
1960	377.2	344.0	433.2
1961	402.6	362.8	459.8
1962	419.4	385.3	464.6
1963	437.6	411.0	466.5
1964	455.3	428.4	476.2
1965	479.3	458.1	483.5
1966	502.3	481.0	502.3
1967	523.9	499.8	523.6
1968	543.5	526.9	531.8
1969	566.0	552.5	549.2
1970	603.9	595.1	574.8
1971	631.7	631.3	583.5
1972	663.3	662.0	612.0

Sources: ARNIS.
[a]Original ARNIS figures have 1965 = 100.

Table A52. Nominal Daily Wages for Production Workers by Sector, 1880–1940 and 1952–70
(In yen per day)

	Agriculture			Industry	Services[a]	Manufacturing		
	Both sexes	Male	Female	Both sexes	Both sexes	Both sexes	Male	Female
1880	0.189	0.231	0.146	—	—	0.14	0.20	0.11
1881	0.189	0.231	0.146	—	—	0.15	0.22	0.12
1882	0.189	0.231	0.146	—	—	0.15	0.23	0.13
1883	0.163	0.200	0.125	—	—	0.14	0.21	0.11
1884	0.136	0.168	0.104	—	—	0.11	0.17	0.09
1885	0.131	0.158	0.104	—	—	0.11	0.19	0.08
1886	0.121	0.147	0.094	—	—	0.11	0.17	0.08
1887	0.120	0.146	0.094	—	—	0.11	0.18	0.08
1888	0.119	0.144	0.094	—	—	0.11	0.18	0.08
1889	0.136	0.162	0.110	—	—	0.11	0.17	0.08
1890	0.143	0.170	0.115	—	—	0.11	0.16	0.09

Table A52 (continued)

	Agriculture			Industry	Services[a]	Manufacturing		
	Both sexes	Male	Female	Both sexes	Both sexes	Both sexes	Male	Female
1891	0.161	0.190	0.131	—	—	0.11	0.19	0.09
1892	0.168	0.199	0.137	—	—	0.13	0.20	0.10
1893	0.191	0.229	0.153	—	—	0.13	0.20	0.10
1894	0.207	0.245	0.168	—	—	0.13	0.20	0.10
1895	0.217	0.254	0.179	—	—	0.14	0.21	0.10
1896	0.241	0.282	0.200	—	—	0.15	0.24	0.11
1897	0.290	0.338	0.242	—	—	0.18	0.28	0.14
1898	0.352	0.399	0.304	—	—	0.20	0.31	0.16
1899	0.303	0.341	0.264	—	—	0.22	0.34	0.17
1900	0.319	0.365	0.273	—	—	0.24	0.38	0.17
1901	0.319	0.356	0.282	—	—	0.24	0.37	0.17
1902	0.342	0.395	0.288	—	—	0.23	0.36	0.17
1903	0.369	0.415	0.323	—	—	0.24	0.37	0.18
1904	0.340	0.377	0.303	—	—	0.25	0.41	0.18
1905	0.340	0.379	0.300	0.34	0.27	0.26	0.41	0.18
1906	0.361	0.406	0.316	0.36	0.28	0.27	0.41	0.19
1907	0.397	0.438	0.356	0.40	0.31	0.30	0.48	0.21
1908	0.403	0.445	0.361	0.43	0.33	0.32	0.50	0.23
1909	0.376	0.413	0.339	0.43	0.33	0.33	0.48	0.24
1910	0.382	0.420	0.343	0.43	0.33	0.32	0.48	0.24
1911	0.442	0.504	0.380	0.46	0.35	0.35	0.52	0.24
1912	0.495	0.564	0.426	0.47	0.37	0.36	0.54	0.26
1913	0.525	0.589	0.461	0.49	0.38	0.39	0.55	0.27
1914	0.437	0.507	0.367	0.49	0.38	0.38	0.54	0.27
1915	0.417	0.486	0.347	0.48	0.38	0.38	0.55	0.26
1916	0.457	0.522	0.392	0.51	0.40	0.41	0.58	0.28
1917	0.577	0.646	0.507	0.63	0.50	0.55	0.77	0.34
1918	0.877	1.009	0.745	0.88	0.70	0.75	1.02	0.49
1919	1.381	1.634	1.128	1.29	1.19	1.26	1.74	0.84
1920	1.398	1.637	1.159	1.53	1.22	1.30	1.81	0.85
1921	1.370	1.570	1.170	1.71	1.41	1.53	2.12	0.97
1922	1.350	1.510	1.180	1.71	1.38	1.51	2.13	0.93
1923	1.320	1.470	1.160	1.64	1.32	1.43	2.05	0.95
1924	1.280	1.420	1.130	1.68	1.34	1.44	2.10	0.89
1925	1.300	1.440	1.150	1.66	1.39	1.42	2.07	0.89
1926	1.220	1.360	1.070	1.67	1.37	1.44	2.12	0.91
1927	1.320	1.430	1.200	1.69	1.35	1.44	2.15	0.87
1928	1.230	1.390	1.070	1.73	1.35	1.47	2.19	0.85
1929	1.180	1.310	1.050	1.70	1.09	1.45	2.18	0.82
1930	0.980	1.120	0.840	1.59	0.83	1.35	2.05	0.71

Table A52 (continued)

	Agriculture			Industry	Services[a]	Manufacturing		
	Both sexes	Male	Female	Both sexes	Both sexes	Both sexes	Male	Female
1931	0.780	0.890	0.660	1.47	0.78	1.26	1.91	0.64
1932	0.670	0.780	0.560	1.46	0.75	1.25	1.94	0.61
1933	0.710	0.810	0.600	1.48	0.86	1.29	1.99	0.61
1934	0.720	0.810	0.630	1.51	0.87	1.34	2.02	0.61
1935	0.760	0.860	0.650	1.50	0.87	1.33	1.98	0.62
1936	0.790	0.900	0.680	1.52	0.86	1.35	1.95	0.63
1937	0.920	1.010	0.820	1.62	0.92	1.45	2.04	0.68
1938	1.100	1.210	0.990	1.75	0.96	1.60	2.17	0.71
1939	1.450	1.600	1.290	1.94	1.05	1.77	2.32	0.78
1940	1.710	1.900	1.510	—	—	—	—	—
1952	272	301	243	543	707	502	628	278
1953	300	330	270	629	815	569	716	305
1954	332	366	298	681	860	606	757	328
1955	340	374	305	712	859	609	769	331
1956	349	384	314	765	884	660	840	348
1957	366	404	328	822	945	697	887	363
1958	386	419	340	808	945	685	869	357
1959	393	428	358	854	1005	743	943	387
1960	424	460	387	916	1061	807	1017	429
1961	509	554	464	1019	1117	896	1124	496
1962	617	671	563	1134	1247	992	1225	577
1963	724	787	661	1251	1371	1102	1362	649
1964	829	913	744	1397	1497	1229	1216	720
1965	902	991	812	1547	1653	1349	1652	809
1966	944	1037	851	1735	1853	1523	1866	908
1967	1054	1151	956	1930	2034	1718	2122	1004
1968	1271	1378	1163	2198	2300	2007	2404	1185
1969	1405	1523	1286	2587	2720	2395	2927	1428
1970	1605	1788	1422	3034	3083	2797	3449	1669
1971	1801	2007	1596	3468	3569	3188	3901	1922
1972	1957	2180	1734	4033	4240	3724	4521	2254

Source: Calculated by Minami and Ono (see ch. 13).

Notes: Agricultural wages are daily contract worker wages in agriculture, including meals provided by employers (*makanai*). Industrial and service sector wages include irregular payments such as bonuses, except for construction workers in the prewar period.

[a] Prewar data are weighted averages of wages for commerce, home servants, and miscellaneous occupations. Postwar data are for two subindustry groups: finance–insurance and wholesale–retail trade. There is thus a discontinuity in coverage.

Table A53. Population and Gainful Workers by Major Sector, 1872–1970
(In thousands)

Year	Population	Gainful workers		
		Total	Agriculture and forestry	Nonagriculture
		Series A		
1872	34,269	21,371	15,711	5,660
1873	34,451	21,399	15,741	5,658
1874	34,625	21,421	15,761	5,660
1875	34,792	21,466	15,768	5,698
1876	35,037	21,554	15,792	5,762
1877	35,359	21,661	15,811	5,850
1878	35,663	21,754	15,828	5,926
1879	35,969	21,806	15,846	5,960
1880	36,165	21,875	15,863	6,012
1881	36,490	21,946	15,869	6,077
1882	36,793	21,971	15,868	6,103
1883	37,112	22,083	15,870	6,213
1884	37,521	22,237	15,883	6,354
1885	37,878	22,339	15,868	6,471
1886	38,116	22,401	15,862	6,539
1887	38,289	22,477	15,867	6,610
1888	38,627	22,643	15,868	6,775
1889	39,082	22,853	15,874	6,979
1890	39,516	23,042	15,898	7,144
1891	39,869	23,182	15,917	7,265
1892	40,135	23,329	15,927	7,402
1893	40,500	23,466	15,913	7,553
1894	40,792	23,589	15,914	7,675
1895	41,212	23,724	15,944	7,780
1896	41,650	23,843	16,001	7,842
1897	42,067	23,998	16,000	7,998
1898	42,560	24,132	16,048	8,084
1899	43,076	24,246	16,100	8,146
1900	43,521	24,378	16,116	8,262
1901	44,056	24,495	16,105	8,390
1902	44,663	24,619	16,138	8,481
1903	45,246	24,764	16,122	8,642
1904	45,856	24,900	16,127	8,773
1905	46,343	24,982	16,103	8,879
1906	46,747	25,061	16,358	8,703
1907	47,131	25,190	16,298	8,892
1908	47,654	25,317	16,250	9,067
1909	48,225	25,397	16,109	9,288
1910	48,851	25,475	16,055	9,420
1911	49,489	25,602	16,168	9,434
1912	50,178	25,764	16,159	9,605
1913	50,925	25,951	16,137	9,814
1914	51,672	26,129	16,118	10,011
1915	52,389	26,305	15,321	10,984
1916	53,110	26,525	15,122	11,403
1917	53,768	26,760	15,195	11,565
1918	54,366	26,906	14,276	12,630
1919	54,711	26,986	14,339	12,647
1920	55,033	27,125	14,139	12,986
		Series B		
1920	55,963	27,260	14,181	13,080
1921	56,666	27,405	14,262	13,143
1922	57,390	27,635	14,169	13,466
1923	58,119	27,872	13,678	14,194
1924	58,876	27,873	13,876	13,997
1925	59,737	28,105	13,735	14,370
1926	60,741	28,434	13,681	14,753
1927	61,659	28,484	13,753	14,731
1928	62,595	28,826	13,896	14,930
1929	63,461	29,169	14,087	15,082
1930	64,450	29,619	14,131	15,488

Table A53 (continued)

Series B (continued)

Gainful workers

Year	Population	Total	Agriculture and forestry	Nonagriculture
1931	65,457	29,936	14,251	15,685
1932	66,434	30,223	14,495	15,728
1933	67,432	30,544	14,345	16,199
1934	68,309	30,827	14,182	16,645
1935	69,254	31,211	13,932	17,279
1936	70,114	31,607	13,965	17,642
1937	70,630	31,695	13,746	17,949
1938	71,013	31,858	13,567	18,291
1939	71,380	32,198	13,454	18,744
1940	71,933	34,177	13,841	20,335

Series C

Gainful workers

Year	Population	Total	Agriculture and forestry	Nonagriculture
1950	83,200	36,160	17,410	18,310
1951	84,541	36,600	16,170	20,050
1952	85,808	37,750	16,370	20,920
1953	86,981	39,890	16,070	23,290
1954	88,239	40,550	15,670	24,210
1955	89,276	41,940	16,040	25,140
1956	90,172	42,680	15,610	26,370
1957	90,928	43,630	15,210	27,830
1958	91,767	43,870	14,710	28,540
1959	92,641	44,330	14,070	29,610
1960	93,419	45,110	13,910	30,670

Gainful workers

Year	Population	Total	Agriculture and forestry	Nonagriculture
1961	94,287	45,620	13,530	31,610
1962	95,181	46,140	13,110	32,600
1963	96,156	46,520	12,400	33,690
1964	97,182	47,100	11,970	34,710
1965	98,275	47,870	11,540	35,900
1966	99,036	48,910	11,140	37,300
1967	100,196	49,830	9,700	39,510
1968	101,331	50,610	9,340	40,680
1969	102,536	50,980	8,990	41,410
1970	103,720	51,530	8,420	42,510

Sources and Notes: Series A are Umemura's estimates from SIL 3 (pp. 132–39) for Japanese only (that is, excluding foreigners resident in general such as Koreans and Taiwanese) at the beginning of each year.

Series B and C are based on census figures for census years (every fifth year beginning with 1920, except 1945). The data are as of Oct. 1 for all persons living in Japan, so there is a discontinuity with series A.

Gainful workers in series A and B are Umemura's estimates (SIL 3: 132–39) using the Uniform Industrial Classification. Series C uses the Standard Industrial Classification.

Okinawa is included before the war, and excluded since.

Table A54. Gainful Workers by Industry, 1906–40 and 1950–70
(In thousands)

	Fishing	Mining	Construction	Manufacturing	Commerce	Support and utilities[a]	Service
				Series A			
1906	551	199	558	2,709	2,313	658	1,715
1907	595	204	552	2,745	2,393	743	1,660
1908	553	197	623	2,828	2,439	735	1,692
1909	556	232	625	2,931	2,523	724	1,697
1910	556	211	631	2,941	2,602	731	1,748
1911	566	210	651	2,942	2,590	715	1,760
1912	562	231	686	2,971	2,652	740	1,763
1913	555	232	704	3,100	2,683	703	1,837
1914	577	326	689	3,000	2,758	745	1,916
1915	542	314	749	3,480	3,063	812	2,024
1916	603	290	762	3,668	3,126	907	2,047
1917	566	321	752	3,887	3,103	873	2,063
1918	550	453	771	4,249	3,165	1,039	2,403
1919	502	421	758	4,295	3,204	1,057	2,410
1920	534	422	775	4,577	3,360	1,156	2,162
				Series B			
1920	536	429	787	4,604	3,380	1,170	2,174
1921	519	317	792	4,499	3,710	1,135	2,171
1922	529	273	827	4,770	3,726	1,128	2,213
1923	509	282	843	5,059	4,043	1,220	2,238
1924	520	325	882	4,649	4,155	1,210	2,256
1925	520	303	918	4,813	4,267	1,235	2,314
1926	523	313	957	4,906	4,535	1,218	2,301
1927	531	337	948	4,633	4,620	1,215	2,447
1928	544	323	982	4,620	4,697	1,248	2,516
1929	557	338	998	4,651	4,693	1,272	2,573
1930	569	316	995	4,754	4,930	1,294	2,630
1931	563	255	986	4,767	5,117	1,288	2,707
1932	555	225	988	4,671	5,326	1,296	2,667
1933	597	242	1,025	4,851	5,413	1,251	2,820
1934	557	261	998	5,131	5,444	1,301	2,953
1935	585	306	1,016	5,380	5,520	1,353	3,119
1936	572	327	1,023	5,588	5,569	1,392	3,171
1937	551	385	988	5,811	5,321	1,390	3,503
1938	533	443	956	6,052	5,082	1,392	3,833
1939	516	505	935	6,313	4,880	1,408	4,187
1940	543	598	990	6,955	4,898	1,523	4,818

Table A54 (continued)

	Fishing	Mining	Construction	Manufacturing	Commerce	Support and utilities[a]	Service
				Series C			
1950	690	490	1,200	6,230	3,740	1,710	4,050
1951	520	510	1,360	6,300	5,150	1,840	4,370
1952	520	610	1,460	6,530	5,410	1,900	4,480
1953	620	600	1,630	7,190	6,240	1,920	5,110
1954	520	570	1,700	7,440	6,810	1,870	5,290
1955	500	490	1,810	7,560	7,150	1,920	5,690
1956	540	430	1,830	8,050	7,440	2,040	6,030
1957	590	550	2,000	8,530	7,740	2,140	6,260
1958	490	500	2,060	9,000	8,000	2,210	6,260
1959	550	580	2,260	9,010	8,250	2,350	6,620
1960	580	510	2,360	9,510	8,490	2,450	6,800
1961	560	460	2,550	10,160	8,420	2,540	6,940
1962	580	480	2,700	10,720	8,470	2,660	6,990
1963	560	400	2,730	11,120	8,950	2,770	7,170
1964	540	360	2,890	11,370	9,270	2,940	7,360
1965	580	360	3,080	11,570	9,560	3,040	7,720
1966	590	330	3,290	11,870	10,000	3,210	8,020
1967	660	260	3,590	12,520	10,850	3,160	8,460
1968	540	270	3,700	13,050	11,110	3,290	8,670
1969	470	240	3,710	13,450	11,330	3,380	8,780
1970	440	200	3,940	13,770	11,440	3,530	9,120

Sources and Notes: See table A53.
[a]Includes workers in the transportation, communication, and electric, gas, and water utility industries.

Index

Economic Growth Center Book Publications

Werner Baer, *Industrialization and Economic Development in Brazil* (1965).

Werner Baer and Isaac Kerstenetzky, eds., *Inflation and Growth in Latin America* (1964).

Bela A. Balassa, *Trade Prospects for Developing Countries* (1964). Out of print.

Albert Berry and Miguel Urrutia, *Income Distribution in Colombia* (1976).

Thomas B. Birnberg and Stephen A. Resnick, *Colonial Development: An Econometric Study* (1975).

Benjamin I. Cohen, *Multinational Firms and Asian Exports* (1975).

Carlos F. Díaz Alejandro, *Essays on the Economic History of the Argentine Republic* (1970).

Robert Evenson and Yoav Kislev, *Agricultural Research and Productivity* (1975).

John C. H. Fei and Gustav Ranis, *Development of Labor Surplus Economy: Theory and Policy* (1964).

Gerald K. Helleiner, *Peasant Agriculture, Government, and Economic Growth in Nigeria* (1966).

Samuel P. S. Ho, *Economic Development of Taiwan, 1860–1970* (1978).

Lawrence R. Klein and Kazushi Ohkawa, eds., *Economic Growth: The Japanese Experience since the Meiji Era* (1968).

Paul W. Kuznets, *Economic Growth and Structure in the Republic of Korea* (1977).

A. Lamfalussy, *The United Kingdom and the Six* (1963). Out of print.

Markos J. Mamalakis, *The Growth and Structure of the Chilean Economy: From Independence to Allende* (1976).

Markos J. Mamalakis and Clark W. Reynolds, *Essays on the Chilean Economy* (1965).

Donald C. Mead, *Growth and Structural Change in the Egyptian Economy* (1967).

Richard Moorsteen and Raymond P. Powell, *The Soviet Capital Stock* (1966).

Kazushi Ohkawa and Miyohei Shinohara, eds. (with Larry Meissner), *Patterns of Japanese Economic Development: A Quantitative Appraisal* (1979).

Douglas S. Paauw and John C. H. Fei, *The Transition in Open Dualistic Economies: Theory and Southeast Asian Experience* (1973).

Howard Pack, *Structural Change and Economic Policy in Israel* (1971).

Frederick L. Pryor, *Public Expenditures in Communist and Capitalist Nations* (1968).

Gustav Ranis, ed., *Government and Economic Development* (1971).

Clark W. Reynolds, *The Mexican Economy: Twentieth-Century Structure and Growth* (1970).

Lloyd G. Reynolds, *Image and Reality in Economic Development* (1977).

Lloyd G. Reynolds, ed., *Agriculture in Development Theory* (1975).

Lloyd G. Reynolds and Peter Gregory, *Wages, Productivity, and Industrialization in Puerto Rico* (1965).

Donald R. Snodgrass, *Ceylon: An Export Economy in Transition* (1966).